the **designer's**
LEXICON

the designer's
LEXICON

The Illustrated Dictionary of Design, Printing, and Computer Terms

by Alastair Campbell

CHRONICLE BOOKS

SAN FRANCISCO

To my mother, Margot

First Published in the United States in 2000 by Chronicle Books
Copyright © 2000 by the Ivy Press Limited and Alastair Campbell.
All rights reserved. No part of this book may be reproduced in any
form without prior written permission from the publisher.

Library of Congress Cataloging-in-Publication Data available.
ISBN 0-8118-2625-2

This book was conceived, designed, and produced by Alastair Campbell
and the Ivy Press Limited

Editorial Director: Sophie Collins
Art Director: Peter Bridgewater
Editor: Andrew Kirk
Illustrations: Alastair Campbell, Alex Charles, John Woodcock
Additional material by Graham Davis, Marilyn Tolhurst, David Broad,
Simon Phillips, Joe Bernard

Cover design: Jeremy G. Stout

Printed in China

Distributed in Canada by Raincoast Books
8680 Cambie Street
Vancouver, BC V6P 6M9

10 9 8 7 6 5 4 3 2 1

Chronicle Books
85 Second Street
San Francisco, CA 94105

www.chroniclebooks.com

Way back, it seemed straightforward enough: apart from imagination and talent, pretty much the only piece of equipment a graphic designer needed was a layout pad and colored markers. True, we would sometimes be required to display a little technical prowess with scissors and paste — essential tools for the exacting task of sticking small pieces of paper on to larger pieces of paper. Also true that we needed a sound understanding of the vernacular of the "graphic arts": typesetting, color reproduction, printing, and binding. But we were also secure in the cozy knowledge that each of these trades was staffed by very capable and learned people — if there was something we didn't know, then we knew a man who did.

How things have changed. "Way back" may sound like the dark ages, but the "new technology" has been with us a mere 12 years or so, and in that time the once-separate process of "typesetting" has all but disappeared and color reproduction is being brought ever nearer the designer's desktop. "The man who does" is becoming increasingly elusive. And as if our heads aren't crammed full enough with the nomenclature of our profession (and several others), completely new "things" are being thrown at us at every turn (HTML, WEFT, Java, etc.).

This book, then, was born out of my own frustration with the contemporary phenomenon of "knowledge fade" — a condition (identified by a high street bank) in which it is recognized that we are increasingly losing our capacity to assimilate the mass of acronyms, abbreviations, and jargon to which we are relentlessly subjected. Thus I compiled this book to provide somewhat of an alter ego for "the man who does."

Conventional glossaries are arranged alphabetically, meaning that unless you have a very clear idea of the word you are looking for — or at least its first few letters — you face a daunting struggle to find it without having to scour the entire book from end to end. However, with words being added to our vocabulary at such a rate it's quite likely that you, like me, find that knowledge fade kicks in alarmingly prematurely and a term someone may have mentioned last week — or even yesterday — has indeed faded from memory. Consequently, I have organized this book in two parts, rather like a thesaurus. The first is the "Word Finder," where you can look up specific words if you know them. Here, terms are arranged in alphabetical order, each with a reference number that indicates the location of the definition of the term given in the "Lexicon," which forms the second part of the book. The Lexicon itself is subdivided into nine broad categories and within each category terms are arranged — not alphabetically — into loose groups of like terms. The purpose of this is so that, should you be familiar with, say, a process or technique but not know its "correct" label, you will be able to find it without having to trawl through pages and pages of disparate information.

Many people have helped me while I worked on this book, and for their patience and understanding I am most grateful, particularly to Peter Bridgewater and to Andrew Kirk. But my special thanks go to Heather, Rebecca, and Rosie who patiently endured my prolonged but reluctant absence from family life.

Alastair Campbell, *Cambridge, England, Y2K*

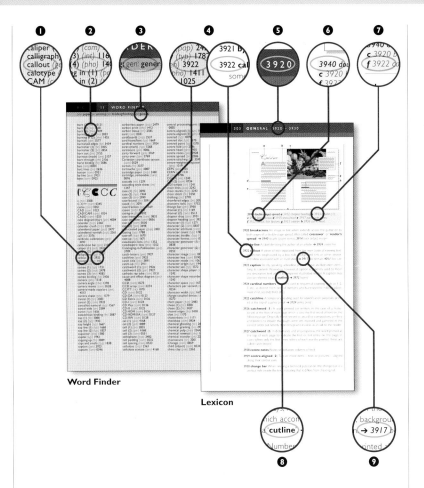

Word Finder

Lexicon

❶ Word Finder
To look up the meaning of a term first refer to the Word Finder, where all 5,000 terms in the Lexicon are listed in alphabetical order.

❷ Category
Alongside each term listed in the Word Finder is a category abbreviation.

❸ Key to categories.

❹ Entry number
This follows each entry in the Word Finder and gives the location in the Lexicon of the explanation of the term.

❺ Entry numbers run consecutively throughout the Lexicon. *Terms are not arranged alphabetically within each category, but are (loosely) grouped among similar terms.*

❻ Illustration captions These are linked by entry numbers to their explanations in the Lexicon.

❼ Some illustration captions may refer to more than one term.

❽ Alternative terms Many names listed in the Word Finder are alternatives for other listed terms. These may be grouped under a single definition in the Lexicon, where they are identified in bold.

❾ Cross-references Similar or relevant terms are cross-referred to the appropriate location in the Lexicon.

Key: *gen:* general; *com:* computing; *int:* internet; *pho:* photography; *typ:* typography;

© *(gen)* 3568
@ *(int)* 1109
® *(gen)* 3569
4-bit *(com)* 0753
8-bit *(com)* 0750
12mo *(pap)* 2458
16-bit color *(com)* 0725
16mo *(gen)* 3892
18mo *(gen)* 3946
24-bit color *(com)* 0779
24mo *(gen)* 3905
32mo *(pap)* 2457
64mo *(gen)* 3893

AᴄᴬᴬAAA

AA *(gen)* 3702
AAAA *(gen)* 3645
ABA *(gen)* 3777
aberration *(pho)* 1349
ablation plate *(pri)* 2894
abort *(com)* 0923
abrasion *(pap)* 2323
abrasion resistance *(pri)* 2895
absolute leading *(typ)* 1826
absolute page number *(gen)* 3911
absolute path *(com)* 0332
absolute URL *(int)* 1162
absolute value *(gen)* 3570
absorbency *(pri)* 2555
absorption *(pri)* 2555
AC *(gen)* 3702
accelerator board *(com)* 0040
accent *(typ)* 1553
accent characters *(typ)* 1554
access path *(com)* 0894
access provider *(int)* 1143
access time *(com)* 0073
accordion fold *(fin)* 3237
acetate *(gen)* 4168
achromatic *(gen)* 3490
achromatic color removal *(pre)* 1993
acid *(pri)* 2847
acid fixer *(pho)* 1435
acid resist *(pri)* 2896
ACR *(pre)* 1993
Acrobat *(com)* 0511
acronym *(gen)* 3571
active *(com)* 0895
active desktop *(int)* 1163
active hyperlink *(int)* 1164
active icon *(com)* 0896
active matrix display *(com)* 0148
active window *(com)* 0897
ActiveMovie *(int)* 0940
ActiveX Controls *(int)* 1229
acutance *(pho)* 1373
acute *(typ)* 1553
adaptive smoothing *(com)* 0510
ADB *(com)* 0185
addendum/addenda *(gen)* 3778
additive colors *(gen)* 3491
additivity failure *(pri)* 2756
add-on board *(com)* 0043
address (1) *(com)* 0046

address (2) *(int)* 1106
adhesive binding *(fin)* 3073
adhesive decal *(pri)* 2594
adhesive stitch binding *(fin)* 3074
Adobe Acrobat *(com)* 0511
Adobe Font Metrics *(com)* 0828
Adobe Type Manager *(com)* 0829
ADSL *(int)* 1065
advance copies *(fin)* 3238
advances *(fin)* 3238
advance sheets *(pri)* 3283
advert(isement) *(gen)* 3646
aerate *(pri)* 2556
AFK *(gen)* 3572
AFM *(com)* 0828
after-tack *(pri)* 2757
Afterburner *(int)* 1230
against the grain *(fin)* 3366
agate *(typ)* 1649
agate line *(gen)* 3647
AI *(com)* 0267
AIFF *(com)* 0898
AIGA *(gen)* 3682
air bar *(pri)* 2897
air bells *(pap)* 2234
airbrush tool *(com)* 0512
airbrush(ing) *(gen)* 4076
air-knife coater *(pap)* 2351
air pull *(pri)* 3037
Alaska seal *(fin)* 3367
album binding *(fin)* 3075
albumen plate *(pri)* 2898
album paper *(pap)* 2459
alert *(com)* 0899
alert box *(com)* 0900
alfa grass *(pap)* 2352
algorithm *(com)* 0333
algorithmically defined *(com)* 0334
alias *(com)* 0901
aliasing *(com)* 0726
aligned left/right/center *(typ)* 1903
aligning numerals *(typ)* 1966
alignment *(typ)* 4006
alley *(gen)* 4007
all in hand *(pre)* 2144
allocation block *(com)* 0074
all up *(pre)* 2145
alphabet length *(typ)* 1650
alpha channel *(com)* 0513
alphanumeric set *(typ)* 1555
alpha test *(com)* 0335
alpha version *(com)* 0336
Alt key *(com)* 0221
aluminum ink *(pri)* 2758
AM screening *(pre)* 1994
ambient *(com)* 0514
American book sizes *(pap)* 3243
ampersand *(typ)* 1556
amplitude *(com)* 1022
amplitude modulated screening *(pre)* 1994
analog computer *(com)* 0001
analog/analogue *(gen)* 3573
anamorphic scan *(pre)* 2092
anastigmatic lens *(pre)* 2093
anchor (1) *(com)* 0515

anchor (2) *(int)* 1231
angle bar *(pri)* 2848
angle of view (1) *(gen)* 4077
angle of view (2) *(pho)* 1374
aniline *(pri)* 2759
aniline printing *(pri)* 2982
anilox system *(pri)* 2965
animal-sized *(pap)* 2353
animated GIF *(int)* 1232
animation *(gen)* 4078
Animation *(com)* 0781
animation value *(com)* 0782
annex *(fin)* 3076
annotation (1) *(gen)* 3912
annotation (2) *(gen)* 3913
anodized plate *(pri)* 2899
anonymous FTP *(int)* 1066
ANSI *(gen)* 3574
antisetoff sprayer *(pri)* 2557
antialias(ing) *(com)* 0727
antihalation backing *(pre)* 2146
antiqua *(typ)* 1724
antiquarian *(pap)* 2414
antique gold edges *(fin)* 3423
antique laid *(pap)* 2460
antique paper *(pap)* 2460
antique wove *(pap)* 2460
antisetoff spray *(pri)* 3071
antisetoff *(pri)* 2557
AOL *(int)* 1126
APA *(gen)* 3779
"A" paper sizes *(pap)* 2432
aperture *(pho)* 1314
aperture priority *(pho)* 1315
API *(com)* 1020
apochromatic lens *(pre)* 2094
append *(com)* 0516
appendix *(gen)* 3780
Apple Desktop Bus *(com)* 0185
Apple event *(com)* 0902
Apple Graphics *(com)* 0793
Apple menu *(com)* 0903
Apple Remote Access *(com)* 0904
AppleScript *(com)* 0905
AppleShare *(com)* 0906
applet *(int)* 1233
AppleTalk *(com)* 0907
Apple Video *(com)* 0816
application *(com)* 0518
application memory (heap) *(com)* 0047
application memory size/partition *(com)* 0048
application menu *(com)* 0908
application programming interface (API) *(com)* 1020
application (support) file *(com)* 0517
APR *(pre)* 2096
apron *(pri)* 2558
Aqua-trol *(pri)* 2760
aquatint *(pri)* 2849
ARA *(com)* 0904
arabesque *(typ)* 1725
arabic numerals *(typ)* 1557
archetype *(gen)* 3701
Archie *(int)* 1127
archival backup *(com)* 0716
archival paper *(pap)* 2461
archival printing *(pri)* 2966

pap: paper; *pre:* prepress; *pri:* printing; *fin:* finishing/binding;

archive *(com)* 0713
argument *(int)* 1234
arrow pointer *(com)* 0442
art canvas *(fin)* 3368
art gilt edges *(fin)* 3424
artifact/artefact *(com)* 0728
artificial intelligence *(com)* 0337
artificial parchment *(pap)* 2540
art-lined envelope *(pap)* 2235
art paper *(pap)* 2462
art vellum *(pap)* 2463
art(work) *(gen)* 4079
ASA *(pho)* 1406
ascender *(typ)* 1934
ascent *(typ)* 1651
ASCII *(com)* 0338
aspect ratio *(gen)* 4080
ASPIC *(pre)* 2095
assembled negative *(pre)* 2147
assembly *(pre)* 2148
associative linking *(int)* 1235
as to press *(pri)* 2850
asterisk *(typ)* 1558
astigmatism *(pho)* 1316
Asymmetrical Digital Subscriber Line *(int)* 1065
asynchronous *(com)* 0282
asynchronous communication *(com)* 0283
asynchronous execution *(com)* 0339
asynchronous transfer mode *(com)* 0284
atlas folio *(pap)* 2415
ATM (1) *(com)* 0829
ATM (2) *(com)* 0284
attaching *(fin)* 3077
attachment *(int)* 1107
attribute (1) *(int)* 1236
attribute (2) *(com)* 0519
audiovideo interleaved *(com)* 0909
audiovisual aids *(gen)* 3575
authentication *(int)* 1128
author's alteration *(gen)* 3702
author's proof *(gen)* 3703
authoring *(com)* 0520
authoring tool *(com)* 0521
authoring application *(com)* 0521
autoflow *(com)* 0831
auto-key event *(com)* 0186
auto-key rate *(com)* 0187
auto-key threshold *(com)* 0188
auto leading *(com)* 0830
automated publication *(gen)* 3781
automatic font downloading *(com)* 0850
automatic hyphenation *(com)* 0832
automatic picture replacement *(pre)* 2096
automatic text box *(com)* 0833
automatic text chain *(com)* 0833
automatic transfer press *(pri)* 2900
auto page insertion *(com)* 0522

autopaster *(pri)* 2610
autoplate machine *(pri)* 2991
autopositive *(pho)* 1407
auto-reversing film *(pre)* 2149
autoscreen *(pre)* 1995
autotrace *(com)* 0523
A/UX *(com)* 0893
auxiliary dictionary *(com)* 0524
auxiliary file *(com)* 0517
auxiliary roll stand *(pri)* 2901
AVA *(com)* 3575
Avatar *(int)* 1129
AVI *(com)* 0909
a/w *(gen)* 4079
axial lighting *(pho)* 1477
axis *(gen)* 4081
azure *(pap)* 2464
azured tooling *(fin)* 3425

B ℬ **B** B *B*

back *(fin)* 3078
backbone (1) *(fin)* 3203
backbone (2) *(com)* 0285
back cornering *(fin)* 3079
back cylinder *(pri)* 2628
backed (1) *(pri)* 2564
backed (2) *(fin)* 3082
back edge curl *(pri)* 2902
back (edge) margin *(gen)* 3914
back end *(com)* 0189
background (1) *(com)* 0340
background (2) *(gen)* 4082
background color *(com)* 0729
background printing/processing *(com)* 0340
backing (away) *(pri)* 2761
backing strip *(fin)* 3080
back(ing) up (1) *(com)* 0714
back(ing) up (2) *(pri)* 2562
back (jacket) flap *(fin)* 3854
back lining *(fin)* 3080
back mark *(pri)* 2561
back matter *(gen)* 3806
back printing *(pri)* 2559
back projection *(pho)* 1478
backs (1) *(fin)* 3914
backs (2) *(pri)* 2565
back scatter *(pho)* 1479
backside cache *(com)* 0049
backslanted type *(typ)* 1948
backslash *(typ)* 1634
back step collation *(pri)* 2560
back(step) mark *(pri)* 2561
back-to-back *(pri)* 2563
backup *(com)* 0715
backup, archival *(com)* 0716
backup, baseline *(com)* 0717
backup, global *(com)* 0717
backup, incremental *(com)* 0718
backup, mirror-image *(com)* 0719
backup registration *(pri)* 2566
backup, same disk *(com)* 0720
backup set *(com)* 0721
bad break *(typ)* 1827
bad color *(pri)* 2762

bad copy *(gen)* 3705
bagged *(gen)* 3648
ballooning *(com)* 0149
band *(fin)* 3129
banding *(pre)* 1996
bandwidth *(int)* 1067
bank paper *(pap)* 2465
banker envelope *(pap)* 2236
banner (1) *(gen)* 3649
banner (2) *(int)* 1165
bar code *(gen)* 3576
barn doors *(pho)* 1480
baryta paper *(pap)* 2466
bas relief *(gen)* 4083
base alignment *(typ)* 1828
base artwork *(pre)* 2097
base film *(pre)* 2150
base lighting *(pho)* 1481
base line *(typ)* 1829
baseline *(typ)* 1935
baseline backup *(com)* 0717
baseline grid *(typ)* 1830
baseline shift *(typ)* 1831
base stock *(pap)* 2354
Basic Input/Output System *(com)* 0003
basic size *(pap)* 2416
basic weight *(pap)* 2417
basil *(fin)* 3369
basis weight *(pap)* 2417
bastard (1) *(pri)* 2567
bastard (2) *(pap)* 2418
bastard (3) *(typ)* 1559
bastard title *(gen)* 3832
batch mode *(com)* 0002
batch processing *(com)* 0002
baud *(int)* 1068
baud rate *(int)* 1069
Baumé scale *(pri)* 2763
BBS *(int)* 1130
BCP *(com)* 0343
beard *(typ)* 1936
bearers *(pri)* 2903
bearoff *(typ)* 1832
beating *(pap)* 2355
bed (1) *(pri)* 2992
bed (2) *(fin)* 2239
begin even *(typ)* 1833
bellows *(pho)* 1317
belly *(typ)* 1937
below the line *(gen)* 3650
belt press *(pri)* 2967
bender *(pap)* 2237
benday/Ben Day tints *(pre)* 1997
bender *(pap)* 2237
bestiary *(gen)* 4122
beta test *(com)* 0341
beta version *(com)* 0342
bevel (1) *(typ)* 1938
bevel (2) *(typ)* 2568
beveled boards *(pap)* 2467
Bézier curve *(com)* 0343
Bézier handle *(com)* 0343
Bézier point *(com)* 0343
b/f (1) *(gen)* 3704
b/f (2) *(typ)* 1726
bible paper *(pap)* 2468
bibliography *(gen)* 3782
bicycling *(pri)* 2569
bimetal(lic) plate *(pri)* 2904
bimetal varnish *(pri)* 3052
binary *(com)* 0910

binary code *(com)* 0911
binary digit *(com)* 0914
binary file *(com)* 0912
binary system *(com)* 0913
binder's board *(fin)* 3370
binder's brass *(fin)* 3426
binder's cloth *(fin)* 3374
binder's creep *(fin)* 3240
binder's die *(fin)* 3426
binding *(fin)* 3082
binding edge *(fin)* 3203
binding margin *(pri)* 3914
binding varnish *(pri)* 3052
BinHex *(int)* 1108
BIOS *(com)* 0003
bit *(com)* 0914
bit density *(com)* 0915
bit depth *(fin)* 0730
bit map/bitmap *(com)* 0916
bitmapped font *(com)* 0834
bitmapped graphic *(com)* 0731
bit rate *(com)* 0286
black art *(pre)* 2097
black box *(pre)* 2098
black letter *(typ)* 1727
black out *(pre)* 2099
black patch *(pre)* 2099
black printer (1) *(pri)* 2570
black printer (2) *(pre)* 2151
blad *(gen)* 3783
blade coater *(pap)* 2356
blanc fixe *(pap)* 2357
blank (1) *(pap)* 2469
blank (2) *(pri)* 2571
blank dummy *(gen)* 3788
blanker *(com)* 0468
blanket (1) *(pri)* 2905
blanket (2) *(pri)* 2993
blanket cylinder *(pri)* 2906
blanket piling *(pri)* 2907
blanket smash *(pri)* 2908
blanket-to-blanket press *(pri)* 2909
blanking interval *(com)* 0150
blank line *(typ)* 1930
bleach(ed)-out *(pho)* 1375
bled-off *(pri)* 2572
bleed (1) *(pri)* 2573
bleed (2) *(pri)* 2764
bleedoffs *(pri)* 2572
blend(ing) *(com)* 0732
blessed folder *(com)* 1003
blind blocking *(pri)* 3053
blind emboss *(pri)* 3053
blind folio *(pri)* 2574
blind image *(pri)* 2575
blinding *(pri)* 2910
blind P *(typ)* 1560
blind stamp *(pri)* 3053
blind stamping *(pri)* 3053
blind tooling *(fin)* 3427
blister card/pack *(gen)* 4167
block (1) *(pri)* 2994
block (2) *(fin)* 3428
block (3) *(com)* 0075
block book *(pri)* 2995
blocking *(fin)* 3429
blocking foils *(fin)* 3430
blocking press *(fin)* 3431
block letter *(typ)* 1728
block printing *(pri)* 2996
block stitching *(fin)* 3362

blooming letters *(typ)* 1729
Blue Book *(com)* 0120
blueline (1) *(pre)* 2152
blueline (2) *(gen)* 4008
blueline (3) *(pre)* 2100
blueline (4) *(pre)* 2153
blueline flat *(pre)* 2153
blueprint *(pre)* 2152
blues *(pre)* 2152
blurb *(gen)* 3651
board (1) *(pap)* 2470
board (2) *(com)* 0041
board covers *(fin)* 3371
boarded leather *(fin)* 3372
board glazed *(pap)* 2358
board paper *(fin)* 3105
boards *(pap)* 2471
bocasin *(fin)* 3373
body (1) (type) *(typ)* 1939
body (2) (book) *(gen)* 3784
body (3) (HTML) *(int)* 1237
body (4) *(pri)* 2765
body copy *(gen)* 3915
body matter *(gen)* 3915
body paper *(pap)* 2359
body size *(typ)* 1652
body stock *(pap)* 2359
body type *(typ)* 1786
bogus *(gen)* 3652
bold (face) *(typ)* 1940
bolts *(fin)* 3241
bomb *(com)* 0931
bond paper *(pap)* 2472
bonding strength (1) *(pri)* 2766
bonding strength (2) *(pap)* 2238
book *(gen)* 3785
bookbinding *(fin)* 3083
book block *(fin)* 3242
book cloth *(fin)* 3374
book face *(typ)* 1730
book jacket *(gen)* 3801
booklet *(gen)* 3786
book makeup *(pre)* 2197
Bookmark *(int)* 1166
book paper *(pap)* 2473
bookplates *(gen)* 3787
book proof *(pri)* 2576
book sizes *(fin)* 3243
Boolean *(com)* 0344
boom *(pho)* 1482
boot blocks *(com)* 0917
boot disk *(com)* 0110
boot(ing) up *(com)* 0918
border *(gen)* 4009
bosses *(fin)* 3432
'bot (robot) *(int)* 1211
bottomband *(fin)* 3084
bottoming *(pri)* 2997
bottom out *(gen)* 3916
bottom printing *(pri)* 2577
bounce lighting *(pho)* 1483
bound book *(fin)* 3085
bounding box *(com)* 0525
bourgeois *(typ)* 1653
bowl *(typ)* 1941
box (1) *(gen)* 4010
box (2) *(com)* 0526
box feature *(gen)* 3917
boxhead *(gen)* 3918
box rule *(gen)* 4011
box story *(gen)* 3917

"B" paper sizes *(pap)* 2432
bpi *(com)* 0915
BPOP *(pri)* 3054
bps *(com)* 0286
brace *(typ)* 1561
brace end *(typ)* 1562
bracket(s) *(typ)* 1563
bracketed type *(typ)* 1942
bracketing *(pho)* 1376
brass *(fin)* 3433
break (1) *(gen)* 3919
break (2) *(pap)* 2239
break-line *(typ)* 1834
breakacross *(gen)* 3920
breaking length *(pap)* 2240
breakthrough *(pri)* 2767
breve *(typ)* 1564
brevier *(typ)* 1654
bridge *(com)* 0287
bright enamel *(pap)* 2474
brightness range *(pho)* 1377
brilliant *(typ)* 1655
bring up *(pri)* 2578
bristol board *(pap)* 2475
British book sizes *(fin)* 3243
broad fold *(fin)* 3244
broadsheet *(pri)* 2580
broadside page *(pri)* 2579
broadside *(pri)* 2580
brochure *(fin)* 3245
broken images *(pri)* 2581
bromide *(pho)* 1408
bronzing (1) *(pri)* 2768
bronzing (2) *(pri)* 2769
brownline *(pre)* 2152
brownprint *(pre)* 2152
browser (1) *(int)* 1167
browser (2) *(com)* 0527
bruising *(pap)* 2241
brush graining *(pre)* 2933
brush-coated paper *(pap)* 2476
bubblejet printer *(com)* 0251
buckle folder *(fin)* 3246
buckram *(fin)* 3375
buckskin *(fin)* 3380
buffer *(com)* 0050
buffing *(pri)* 2851
bug *(com)* 0919
built fraction *(typ)* 1565
bulk (1) *(pap)* 3247
bulk (2) *(pap)* 2419
bulk factor *(pap)* 2420
bulking dummy *(gen)* 3788
bulldog *(pri)* 2582
bullet *(typ)* 1566
bulleted list *(int)* 1238
bulletin board service (BBS) *(int)* 1103
bull's eye *(pri)* 2622
bumped out (1) *(typ)* 1835
bumped out (2) *(typ)* 1836
bumping up *(pri)* 2998
bump map *(com)* 0733
bump up (1) *(pri)* 2998
bump up (2) *(gen)* 4012
bundle (1) *(com)* 0920
bundle (2) *(pap)* 2421
bundling *(fin)* 3248
bureau *(pri)* 2225
burin *(pri)* 2852
burn (1) *(pre)* 2154

burn (2) *(com)* 0121
burn (3) *(int)* 1168
burn (4) *(pho)* 1409
burning in (1) *(pri)* 2853
burning in (2) *(pho)* 1455
burnish *(gen)* 3577
burnished edges *(fin)* 3434
burnisher (1) *(fin)* 3435
burnisher (2) *(pri)* 2854
burn out *(pre)* 2155
burnout (mask) *(pre)* 2157
burn through *(pre)* 2156
burst binding *(fin)* 3086
bus *(com)* 0004
butt lines *(pri)* 2636
button *(com)* 0921
by-line *(gen)* 3921
byte *(com)* 0922

c *(pre)* 3508
C, C++ *(com)* 0345
cache *(com)* 0051
CAD *(com)* 1023
CAD/CAM *(com)* 1024
CADD *(com)* 1023
cake diagram/chart *(gen)* 4084
calender *(pap)* 2360
calender crush *(pap)* 2241
calendered paper *(pap)* 2477
calendered varnish *(pap)* 2361
calf *(fin)* 3376
calibrate, calibration *(gen)* 3492
calibration bar *(pre)* 2102
caliper (1) *(pap)* 2422
caliper (2) *(pap)* 2423
calligraphy *(typ)* 1787
callout *(gen)* 3922
calotype *(pho)* 1411
CAM *(com)* 1025
cameo (1) *(typ)* 1731
cameo (2) *(pap)* 2478
cameo (3) *(gen)* 4085
cameo binding *(fin)* 3436
camera *(pho)* 1318
camera angle *(pho)* 1378
camera moves *(com)* 0528
camera-ready copy/art *(gen)* 4013
camera shake *(pho)* 1379
cancel (1) *(pri)* 2583
cancel (2) *(com)* 0923
canceled numeral *(typ)* 1567
cancel-title *(pri)* 2584
canon *(typ)* 1656
caoutchouc binding *(fin)* 3087
cap (1) *(fin)* 3088
cap (2) *(typ)* 1943
cap height *(typ)* 1667
cap line (1) *(typ)* 1668
cap line (2) *(typ)* 1837
capacitor *(pho)* 1380
capital *(typ)* 1943
capping up *(fin)* 3089
caps and smalls *(typ)* 1838
caption *(gen)* 3923
capture *(com)* 0346

carbonless paper *(pap)* 2479
carbon print *(pho)* 1412
carbon tissue *(pri)* 2585
card *(com)* 0041
card(board) *(pap)* 2537
card fount/font *(typ)* 1669
cardinal numbers *(gen)* 3924
caret (mark) *(typ)* 1568
caricature *(gen)* 4086
carry forward *(gen)* 3769
carry over *(gen)* 3769
Cartesian coordinate system *(com)* 0529
carton *(fin)* 3377
cartouche *(gen)* 4087
cartridge paper *(pap)* 2480
cartridge, removable *(com)* 0076
cascade *(int)* 1239
cascading style sheet *(int)* 1247
case (1) *(fin)* 3090
case (2) *(typ)* 1944
case (3) *(pri)* 2999
case bound *(fin)* 3091
cased *(fin)* 3091
case fraction *(typ)* 1569
casein *(pap)* 2362
casing-in *(fin)* 3092
case insensitive *(com)* 0835
case sensitive *(com)* 0836
cast (1) *(com)* 0530
cast (2) *(pri)* 3498
cast-coated paper *(pap)* 2481
casting *(typ)* 1788
cast-off *(typ)* 1670
cast-up *(typ)* 1671
catadioptic lens *(pho)* 1352
catadioptric lens *(pho)* 1352
Cataloging-in-Publication *(gen)* 3789
catch-letters *(gen)* 3927
catchline *(gen)* 3925
catch title *(gen)* 3891
catch-up *(pri)* 2911
catchword (1) *(gen)* 3926
catchword (2) *(gen)* 3927
cathode ray tube *(pho)* 1351
cause-and-effect diagram *(gen)* 4088
CCD *(com)* 0273
CCD array *(com)* 0274
CCITT *(int)* 1070
CD *(com)* 0122
CD-DA *(com)* 0123
CD Extra *(com)* 0136
CD-I *(com)* 0124
CD Plus *(com)* 0136
CD-R *(com)* 0125
CD-ROM *(com)* 0126
CD-ROM/XA *(com)* 0127
CD-RW *(com)* 0128
cel (1) *(gen)* 4168
cel (2) *(gen)* 4089
cell (1) *(pri)* 2855
cell (2) *(gen)* 4168
cell (3) *(com)* 0531
cellophane *(pap)* 2482
cell padding *(com)* 0532
cell spacing *(com)* 0533
cellulose *(pap)* 2363
cellulose acetate *(gen)* 4168

central processing unit *(com)* 0005
center-aligned (1) *(typ)* 1839
center-aligned (2) *(gen)* 3929
centered *(typ)* 1839
centered dot *(typ)* 1570
centered point *(typ)* 1570
center fold *(pri)* 2586
center head *(gen)* 3935
center notes *(gen)* 3928
center spread *(pri)* 2586
center-stitching *(fin)* 3249
center-weighted exposure *(pho)* 1319
CEPS *(pre)* 2101
CERN *(int)* 1131
cf *(gen)* 3706
CGI (1) *(int)* 1240
CGI (2) *(com)* 0734
CGI scripts *(int)* 1241
chain lines *(pap)* 2242
chain marks *(pap)* 2242
chain stitch *(fin)* 3250
chalking *(pri)* 2770
chamfered edges *(fin)* 3093
chancery italic *(typ)* 1732
change bar *(gen)* 3930
channel (1) *(int)* 1169
channel (2) *(com)* 0513
chapter drop *(gen)* 3931
chapter heading *(gen)* 3932
character (1) *(typ)* 1571
character (2) *(com)* 0837
character attribute *(com)* 0519
character count *(typ)* 1789
character, double *(typ)* 1591
character format *(com)* 0856
character generator (1) *(com)* 0838
character generator (2) *(com)* 0252
character image *(com)* 0839
character key *(com)* 0190
character mode *(int)* 1063
character origin *(typ)* 1945
character set *(typ)* 1572
character shape player *(int)* 1242
character shape recorder *(int)* 1243
character space *(typ)* 1672
characters per second *(com)* 0254
character width *(typ)* 1673
charge-coupled device *(com)* 0273
chart paper *(pap)* 2483
chase (1) *(pri)* 3000
chase (2) *(fin)* 3437
chased edges *(fin)* 3438
chat *(int)* 1170
chatterbots *(int)* 1171
checkbox *(com)* 0924
chemical ghosting *(pri)* 2616
chemical graining *(pri)* 2933
chemical pulp *(pap)* 2364
chemical reversal *(pho)* 1413
chemical transfer *(pri)* 2209
chiaroscuro *(pri)* 3001
Chicago *(com)* 0859
child (object) *(com)* 0534
china clay *(pap)* 2365

chip *(com)* 0006
chipboard *(pap)* 2484
choke *(pre)* 1998
chopper fold *(fin)* 3333
chroma *(gen)* 3493
chrome coated paper *(pap)* 2485
chromolithography *(pri)* 2912
chromo paper *(pap)* 2485
chuck *(pri)* 2856
chute delivery *(pri)* 3055
Cibachrome *(pho)* 1414
cicero *(typ)* 1674
CIE *(gen)* 3494
CIE L*a*b* color space *(com)* 0735
c.i.f. *(gen)* 3578
Cinepak *(com)* 0783
CIP *(gen)* 3789
circuit board *(com)* 0041
circuit edges *(fin)* 3094
circular *(gen)* 3653
circular screen *(pre)* 1999
circumflex *(typ)* 1573
CISC *(com)* 0032
cissing *(pri)* 2771
CIX *(int)* 1132
clamshell press *(pri)* 2968
clarity *(typ)* 1902
classified ad(vertisement) *(gen)* 3654
clay-coated paper *(pap)* 2462
clean install *(com)* 0925
clean proof *(gen)* 3707
ClearType *(com)* 0840
cliché *(pri)* 3002
clickable map/image *(int)* 1244
client *(com)* 0288
client pull *(int)* 1172
client/server *(com)* 0290
client-side *(com)* 0289
client-side image map *(int)* 1245
clinometer *(pho)* 1484
clip art *(com)* 0535
clipboard *(com)* 0926
clip media *(com)* 0535
clipping *(gen)* 4090
clipping path *(com)* 0347
clipping plane *(com)* 0536
clip test *(pho)* 1415
clock rate *(com)* 0007
clock speed *(com)* 0007
clogged *(pri)* 2792
clone *(com)* 0736
close (1) *(fin)* 3241
close (2) *(typ)* 1574
close up *(typ)* 1840
closed file *(com)* 0348
closed h *(typ)* 1946
closed section *(fin)* 3251
closed signature *(fin)* 3251
cloth boards *(fin)* 3095
cloth faced *(pap)* 2294
cloth joints *(fin)* 3096
cloth lined *(pap)* 2294
cloverleaf symbol *(com)* 1026
club line *(gen)* 3979
CLUT *(com)* 0737
CMC7 *(typ)* 1733
CMM *(com)* 0740
CMS *(com)* 0741

CMY *(gen)* 3495
CMYK *(gen)* 3496
co-edition *(gen)* 3790
coated lens *(pho)* 1320
coated paper *(pap)* 2486
coating slip *(pap)* 2366
cock (end) *(typ)* 1575
cock-up figure *(typ)* 1643
cock-up initial *(typ)* 1900
cock-up letter *(typ)* 1643
cockle *(pap)* 2243
cockled *(pap)* 2244
cockling *(pap)* 2244
cockroach *(typ)* 1841
code *(com)* 0349
codec *(com)* 0784
codet *(pre)* 2102
cold boot *(com)* 0918
cold composition *(typ)* 1790
cold type *(typ)* 1791
cold-set ink *(pri)* 2772
colinear *(com)* 0350
collate *(fin)* 3252
collating mark *(pri)* 2561
collotype *(pri)* 2913
colophon (1) *(gen)* 3791
colophon (2) *(gen)* 3792
Color-Key™ *(pre)* 2158
color (1) *(gen)* 3497
color (2) *(typ)* 1842
color bar *(pre)* 2102
color-blind emulsion *(pre)* 2162
color-blind film *(pre)* 1418
color break *(pre)* 2000
color burnout *(pri)* 2773
color calibrate *(gen)* 3492
color cast *(gen)* 3498
color chart *(pre)* 2103
color coder *(pre)* 2008
color correction *(pre)* 2159
color depth *(com)* 0730
colored edges *(fin)* 3439
colored link *(int)* 1164
colored printings *(pap)* 2487
colored tops *(fin)* 3439
colorfast *(pho)* 3527
color filters *(pho)* 1381
color gamut *(com)* 0738
color library *(com)* 0739
color management module *(com)* 0740
color management system *(com)* 0741
color model *(gen)* 3499
color negative film *(pho)* 1416
color picker (1) *(com)* 0742
color picker (2) *(gen)* 3500
color positives *(pre)* 2160
color printing *(pri)* 2774
color reversal film *(pho)* 1417
color rotation *(pri)* 2775
color scanner *(pre)* 0281
color separation *(pre)* 2104
color separations *(pre)* 2161
color sequence *(pri)* 2775
color space *(com)* 0738
color swatch *(gen)* 3501
color table *(com)* 0743
color temperature *(gen)* 3502
color transparency (film) *(pho)* 1417

color value *(gen)* 3503
color wheel *(gen)* 3504
column (1) *(gen)* 3933
column (2) *(typ)* 1843
column centimeter *(gen)* 3655
column-face rule *(gen)* 4014
column inch *(gen)* 3655
column rule *(gen)* 4014
come-and-go *(pri)* 2587
coma *(pho)* 1321
comb binding *(fin)* 3175
combination folder *(fin)* 3253
combination line and halftone *(pre)* 2001
combination plate *(pri)* 2914
coming and going *(pri)* 2587
comma *(typ)* 1576
comma-delimit *(com)* 0351
command *(com)* 0927
command-line interface *(com)* 0928
comment *(int)* 1246
commercial a *(int)* 1109
commercial art *(gen)* 4015
commercial color *(pre)* 2002
commercial register *(pri)* 2588
Common Gateway Interface (1) *(int)* 1240
Common Gateway Interface (2) *(com)* 0734
Common Ground *(int)* 1173
comp (1) *(pre)* 4018
comp (2) *(typ)* 1792
compact disc *(com)* 0122
compact disc digital audio (CD-DA) *(com)* 0123
compact disc interactive (CD-I) *(com)* 0124
compact disc recordable (CD-R) *(com)* 0125
compact disc read-only memory (CD-ROM) *(com)* 0126
compact disc read-only memory/extended architecture (CD-ROM/XA) *(com)* 0127
compact disc rewritable (CD-RW) *(com)* 0128
compiler *(com)* 0352
comping *(gen)* 4016
complementary colors *(gen)* 3505
complex instruction set computing *(com)* 0032
complex object *(com)* 0537
Component Video *(com)* 0785
compose *(typ)* 1792
composing *(typ)* 1792
composing room *(typ)* 1793
composite art(work) *(gen)* 4017
composite book *(gen)* 3793
composite color file *(com)* 0744
composite film *(pre)* 2184
composite video *(com)* 0152
composing machine *(typ)* 1802
compositing machine *(typ)* 1802
composition *(typ)* 1794
composition size(s) *(typ)* 1675

daemon *(int)* 1073
dagger *(typ)* 1578
daguerrotype *(pho)* 1385
Dahlgren *(pri)* 2918
daisy wheel *(typ)* 1796
daisy-chain *(com)* 0193
dampening *(pri)* 2919
dampening fountain *(pri)* 2920
dandy roll *(pap)* 2369
dark field illumination *(pre)* 2006
dark reaction *(pre)* 2165
darkfield lighting *(pho)* 1486
darkslide *(pho)* 1325
dash *(typ)* 1579
DAT *(com)* 0196
data *(com)* 0358
data bank *(com)* 0194
database *(com)* 0545
database engine *(com)* 0546
database management system *(com)* 0546
database manager *(com)* 0546
data bits *(com)* 0359
data blocks *(com)* 0075
data bus *(com)* 0010
data compression *(com)* 0786
data encryption *(com)* 0376
data file *(com)* 0372
data fork *(com)* 0935
Data Interchange Format *(com)* 0360
data processing *(com)* 0361
data transfer rate *(com)* 0011
dateline *(gen)* 3938
datum *(com)* 0358
daughterboard *(com)* 0042
daylight film *(pho)* 1420
dazzle *(typ)* 1951
DBMS *(com)* 0546
DCA *(com)* 0304
DCS *(com)* 0747
DDCP *(pre)* 2169
DDES *(com)* 0291
dead *(pap)* 2258
dead matter *(pre)* 2166
deadline *(gen)* 3584
debug(ging) *(com)* 0362
decal *(pri)* 2594
decimal point *(typ)* 1580
decimal tab *(typ)* 1844
deckle (1) *(pap)* 2370
deckle (2) *(pap)* 2371
deckle edge *(pap)* 2259
deckle strap *(pap)* 2370
decompressor *(com)* 0784
decryption *(com)* 0363
dedicated *(gen)* 3585
dedicated flash *(pho)* 1487
deep-etch halftone *(pre)* 2007
deep-etch(ing) *(pri)* 2921
deep-etched plate *(pri)* 2921
deeply-etched halftone *(pri)* 2922
deep gold *(fin)* 3441
deep line cut *(pri)* 3040
deerskin *(fin)* 3380

default *(com)* 1027
definition *(gen)* 4101
deflection *(pri)* 2972
defragment(ing) *(com)* 0077
degauss(ing) *(com)* 0154
degradability *(int)* 1248
degradation *(gen)* 4102
degrade *(gen)* 4102
degradé/degradee *(gen)* 3509
de-inking *(pap)* 2260
delamination (1) *(pri)* 2781
dele *(gen)* 3710
delete *(gen)* 3710
delimit *(com)* 0364
delimited *(com)* 0364
delimiter *(com)* 0364
delineate *(gen)* 4103
delivery *(gen)* 3586
delta frame *(com)* 0796
DEM *(com)* 0368
demand printing *(pri)* 2973
demographic edition *(gen)* 3796
dendritic growths *(pap)* 2261
denominator *(typ)* 1581
dense *(gen)* 3510
densitometer *(pre)* 2008
density (1) *(typ)* 1845
density (2) *(gen)* 3511
density (3) *(pap)* 2425
density range *(gen)* 3512
deprecated *(int)* 1064
depth *(pri)* 2595
depth of field *(pho)* 1386
depth of focus *(pho)* 1387
depth of strike *(typ)* 1952
desaturate *(gen)* 3513
desaturated color *(gen)* 3514
descender *(typ)* 1953
descreen(ing) *(com)* 0745
deselect *(com)* 0365
desensitize *(pri)* 2923
design motif *(gen)* 4140
designation marks *(pre)* 2596
desk copy *(gen)* 3797
desktop *(com)* 0936
desktop color *(com)* 0746
desktop color separation *(com)* 0747
desktop computer *(com)* 0012
desktop publishing *(gen)* 3684
desktop (publishing) system *(com)* 0255
desktop scanner *(com)* 0275
destination *(com)* 0496
detail *(gen)* 3515
detail enhancement *(pre)* 2088
detail paper *(pap)* 2491
Deutsche Industrie-Norm *(gen)* 3587
develop *(pho)* 1421
developer *(pho)* 1422
developing agent *(pho)* 1422
developing ink *(pre)* 2167
developing tank *(pho)* 1423
development *(pri)* 2924
device (1) *(com)* 0195
device (2) *(gen)* 3798
device driver *(com)* 1033
device independent *(com)* 0366
DHTML *(int)* 1253

di litho *(pri)* 2925
diacritical mark *(typ)* 1582
diaeresis/dieresis *(typ)* 1583
dial-up *(int)* 1074
dialog box *(com)* 0937
diamond *(typ)* 1680
diaphragm *(pho)* 1326
diapositive *(pho)* 1424
diarylide yellow *(pri)* 2782
diazo process *(pre)* 2168
diazo(type) *(pre)* 2168
diazoprint *(pre)* 2168
DIC Color Guide *(pri)* 2783
dichroic filter *(pho)* 1388
dichroic fog *(pho)* 1425
dictionary *(com)* 0547
Didone *(typ)* 1783
Didot point *(typ)* 1681
die (1) *(pri)* 3007
die (2) *(fin)* 3266
diecutting *(fin)* 3267
dielectric printing *(pri)* 2974
die press *(pri)* 3008
diesis *(typ)* 1592
die stamping *(pri)* 3009
DIF *(com)* 0360
difference frame *(com)* 0796
differential letterspacing *(typ)* 1682
diffraction *(pho)* 1488
diffuse *(pho)* 1489
diffuse highlight *(pre)* 2009
diffuser *(pho)* 1490
diffusion *(pho)* 1489
diffusion transfer *(pre)* 2209
digit (1) *(typ)* 1584
digit (2) *(typ)* 1585
digital *(com)* 1028
digital audio tape *(com)* 0196
digital camera *(pho)* 1327
digital data *(com)* 0367
Digital Data Exchange Standard *(com)* 0291
digital device *(com)* 0013
digital dot *(com)* 0748
digital elevation model *(com)* 0368
digital photography *(pho)* 1389
Digital Subscriber Line *(int)* 1065
digital versatile disk *(com)* 0130
digital video interactive *(com)* 0155
digitalize *(com)* 1029
digitize *(com)* 1029
digitizer *(com)* 0276
digitizing pad *(com)* 0277
digitizing tablet *(com)* 0277
digraph *(gen)* 3711
dimensional stability *(pap)* 2262
dimensions *(gen)* 4104
DIMM *(com)* 0055
dimmed command *(com)* 0938
dimmed icon *(com)* 0939
DIN *(gen)* 3587
dingbat *(typ)* 1586
dinky *(pap)* 2263
dinky dash *(gen)* 4038
diopter *(pho)* 1328
diorama *(gen)* 3588

DIP *(com)* 0015
DIP SIMM *(com)* 0053
DIP switch *(com)* 0014
diphthong *(typ)* 1587
diploma paper *(pap)* 2492
direct access *(com)* 0292
direct cost *(gen)* 3589
direct digital color proof *(pre)* 2169
direct entry *(com)* 0197
direct halftone *(pre)* 2010
directional *(gen)* 3939
direct litho(graphy) *(pri)* 2925
direct mail *(gen)* 3658
directory *(com)* 0369
directory structure *(com)* 0370
direct positive *(pre)* 2124
direct-positive *(pre)* 2168
direct reading *(pho)* 1491
direct screen color separation *(pre)* 2011
direct screening *(pre)* 2011
DirectShow *(com)* 0940
direct to plate *(pri)* 2590
dirty proof *(gen)* 3712
dis, diss *(typ)* 1797
disabled *(com)* 0938
disc *(com)* 0129
disc drive *(com)* 0081
discrete value *(gen)* 3590
discretionary hyphen *(com)* 0841
Disc Operating System *(com)* 0975
disk *(com)* 0078
disk buffer *(com)* 0050
disk crash *(com)* 0079
disk drive head *(com)* 0103
diskette *(com)* 0087
disk image *(com)* 0080
disk optimizing *(com)* 0099
disk partition *(com)* 0101
disk track *(com)* 0113
disk drive *(com)* 0081
display advertisement *(gen)* 3659
display board *(pap)* 2493
display (device) *(com)* 0165
display matter *(typ)* 1683
display size(s) *(typ)* 1684
display type *(typ)* 1683
dissonance *(gen)* 4020
distortion copy *(pre)* 2012
distribute *(typ)* 1797
distributed rendering *(com)* 0371
distribution roller *(pri)* 2597
dither(ing) *(com)* 0749
ditto marks *(typ)* 1588
diurnal *(gen)* 3799
divergent lens *(pho)* 1329
diverging lens *(pho)* 1329
D-max *(pho)* 1383
D-min *(pho)* 1384
DNS *(int)* 1178
D.O. *(gen)* 4058
dock *(com)* 0198
doctor blade (1) *(pri)* 2598
doctor blade (2) *(pap)* 2372
doctor(ing) *(pri)* 2784
document (1) *(com)* 0372

document (2) *(int)* 1249
document-based queries *(int)* 1177
document content architecture *(com)* 0373
Document Exchange Format *(com)* 0374
document heading *(int)* 1250
document root *(int)* 1251
document transfer rate *(int)* 1176
Document Type Definition *(int)* 1252
documentary (photography) *(pho)* 1390
dodge/dodging *(pho)* 1426
dog's cock *(typ)* 1589
dog-ear(ed) *(pap)* 2264
dogleg *(gen)* 4021
dolly (shot) *(pho)* 1492
Domain Name System *(int)* 1178
dongle *(com)* 0199
DOS *(com)* 0975
dot *(com)* 1030
dot and tickle *(gen)* 4105
dot area *(pre)* 2013
dot, elliptical *(pre)* 2031
dot etching *(pre)* 2014
dot-for-dot (1) *(pri)* 2600
dot-for-dot (2) *(pre)* 2022
dot formation *(pre)* 2015
dot fringe *(pre)* 2037
dot gain *(pre)* 2016
dot, hard *(pre)* 2047
dot leader *(typ)* 1590
dot loss *(pre)* 2017
dot-matrix printer *(com)* 0256
dot pattern *(pre)* 2018
dot pitch *(com)* 0156
dot range *(pre)* 2019
dot, round *(pre)* 2020
dot shape *(pre)* 2020
dot slur(ring) *(pri)* 2599
dot, soft *(pre)* 2078
dot spread *(pri)* 2016
dot, square *(pre)* 2081
dot value *(pre)* 2021
dots per inch (dpi) *(com)* 1131
double-black duotone *(pre)* 2029
double burn down *(pre)* 2170
double character *(typ)* 1591
double-click *(com)* 0200
double coated paper *(pap)* 2494
double column *(typ)* 1860
double dagger *(typ)* 1592
double density *(com)* 0087
double digest fold *(fin)* 3268
double-dot halftone *(pre)* 2023
double etch *(pre)* 2171
double image *(pri)* 2601
double-page spread *(gen)* 3940
double pica *(typ)* 1685
double print down *(pre)* 2170
double prime *(typ)* 1588
double rule *(typ)* 1588
double rule *(gen)* 4022
double spread *(gen)* 3940
double sided *(com)* 0087
double sized *(pap)* 2287
double-thick cover stock

(pap) 2495
double title page *(gen)* 3800
double tone ink *(pri)* 2785
double truck *(gen)* 3940
doubling *(pri)* 2602
doublures *(fin)* 3381
Dow etch *(pri)* 2858
down stroke *(typ)* 1954
down time *(gen)* 3591
down tree *(com)* 0548
download *(int)* 1075
downloadable font *(com)* 0842
downsample *(com)* 0771
DP format *(int)* 1173
dpi *(com)* 1031
dpsi/dpi2 *(gen)* 3592
draft *(gen)* 3713
drag *(com)* 1032
drag-and-drop *(com)* 0941
DRAM *(com)* 0054
draw (1) *(pre)* 2603
draw (2) *(fin)* 3269
drawdown *(pri)* 2786
draw(ing) application *(com)* 0549
drawn on (cover) *(fin)* 3102
dressing *(pri)* 2926
driers *(pri)* 3057
drill *(fin)* 3382
drill(ing) *(fin)* 3270
drive *(com)* 0081
drive head *(com)* 0082
driver *(com)* 1033
driving out *(typ)* 1846
drop (1) *(gen)* 3941
drop (2) *(gen)* 3942
drop cap(ital) *(typ)* 1847
drop down *(pri)* 3943
drop-down menu *(com)* 0942
drop folios *(gen)* 3944
droplet *(com)* 0943
drop letter *(typ)* 1847
dropout (1) *(pre)* 2024
dropout (2) *(gen)* 4058
dropout blue *(pre)* 2025
dropout color *(pre)* 2025
drop-out halftone *(pre)* 2007
dropout ink *(pre)* 2026
dropout (mask) *(pre)* 2027
dropped head *(gen)* 3945
dropped initial *(typ)* 1847
dropped-out halftone *(pre)* 2007
dropped-out type *(typ)* 1848
dropping out *(pre)* 2028
drop shadow *(gen)* 4106
drop tone *(pre)* 2122
drum (1) *(pri)* 2604
drum (2) *(pri)* 2787
drum (3) *(pri)* 2110
drum scanner *(pre)* 2111
dry-back *(pri)* 2789
dry finish *(pap)* 2265
drying in *(pri)* 3041
dry litho *(pri)* 2927
dry mounting *(gen)* 4169
dry offset *(pri)* 2927
dry printing *(pri)* 2605
dry proof *(pre)* 2172
dry stripping *(pre)* 2173
dry transfer lettering *(gen)* 4170

dry trapping *(pri)* 2788
dry-up *(pri)* 2911
DSL *(int)* 1065
DTD *(int)* 1252
DTP *(gen)* 3684
dual-inline memory module *(com)* 0055
dual in-line package *(com)* 0015
dual roll stand *(pri)* 2859
duck foot quotes *(typ)* 1593
duct *(pri)* 2606
ductor roller *(pri)* 2928
dull finish *(pap)* 2266
dull seal *(pap)* 2496
dumb quotes *(typ)* 1594
dumb terminal *(com)* 0201
dummy (1) *(gen)* 3788
dummy (2) *(gen)* 4023
dumpbin *(gen)* 3660
duodecimo *(pap)* 3243
duotone *(pre)* 2029
dupe *(gen)* 3593
dupe film *(pre)* 2174
duplex *(gen)* 3594
duplex board *(pap)* 2497
duplex decal *(pri)* 2594
duplex halftone *(pre)* 2030
duplex paper *(pap)* 2497
duplex stock *(pap)* 2497
duplicate *(gen)* 3593
duplicate film *(pre)* 2174
duplo *(pre)* 2112
dusting *(pri)* 2929
dust jacket *(gen)* 3801
dust wrapper *(gen)* 3801
dutch paper *(pap)* 2498
DVD *(com)* 0130
DVD-Audio *(com)* 0131
DVD-R *(com)* 0132
DVD-RAM *(com)* 0133
DVD-ROM *(com)* 0134
DVD-Video *(com)* 0135
DVI *(com)* 0155
Dvorak keyboard *(com)* 0202
dwell *(pri)* 2607
DXF *(com)* 0374
dye-based ink *(pri)* 2790
dye cloud *(pho)* 1427
dye diffusion *(pre)* 2975
dyeline *(pre)* 2168
dye pastes *(pri)* 2790
dye sub(limation) (printing) *(pri)* 2975
dye-sensitization *(pho)* 1428
Dylux *(pre)* 2175
Dynamic HTML *(int)* 1253
dynamic RAM *(com)* 0054

E13B *(typ)* 1736
ear *(gen)* 3661
easel-binder *(fin)* 3103
easing *(com)* 0550
e-commerce *(int)* 1111
e-design *(gen)* 3685
edge acuity *(pri)* 2791
edge gilding *(fin)* 3442

edges *(fin)* 3271
edge staining *(fin)* 3443
edit *(gen)* 3715
Edit menu *(com)* 0944
edition *(gen)* 3802
edition binding *(fin)* 3104
EDO *(com)* 0056
e.g. *(gen)* 3714
eggshell finish *(pap)* 2499
egyptian *(typ)* 1737
eight-bit/8-bit *(com)* 0750
eighteenmo/18mo *(gen)* 3946
eight sheet *(gen)* 3662
electric etching *(pri)* 2860
electrographic printing *(pri)* 2974
electro/electrotype *(pri)* 3011
electronic commerce *(int)* 1111
electronic design *(gen)* 3685
electronic engraving machine *(pri)* 2861
electronic flash *(pho)* 1501
electronic imaging *(pre)* 2113
electronic mail *(int)* 1112
electronic publishing *(gen)* 3684
electroplating *(pri)* 2862
electrostatic copying *(pri)* 2976
electrostatic printing *(pri)* 2977
electro(type) *(pri)* 3010
element (1) *(com)* 0551
element (2) *(int)* 1254
elephant face *(typ)* 1738
elephant folio *(pap)* 2426
elephant hide *(fin)* 3383
elevation *(gen)* 4107
elevation model *(com)* 0368
ELF *(com)* 0157
elhi books *(gen)* 3803
ellipse *(gen)* 4108
ellipse tool *(com)* 0552
ellipsis (1) *(typ)* 1595
ellipsis (2) *(com)* 0945
elliptical dot (screen) *(pre)* 2031
em *(typ)* 1686
e-mail *(int)* 1112
embedded program *(int)* 1179
embedded style sheet *(int)* 1255
emblem book *(gen)* 3804
emboss(ing) *(fin)* 3444
embossed binding *(fin)* 3445
embossed finish *(pap)* 2267
embossing cylinder *(pap)* 2373
embossing plate *(pap)* 2374
embroidered binding *(fin)* 3446
em dash/rule *(typ)* 1596
emerald *(typ)* 1689
em quad *(typ)* 1687
em space *(typ)* 1688
emulation *(com)* 1034
emulsion *(pho)* 1429
emulsion down *(pre)* 2221
emulsion side *(pre)* 2176
emulsion speed *(pho)* 1430
emulsion up *(pre)* 2221
en *(typ)* 1690

enamel *(pap)* 2268
encapsulated PostScript *(com)* 0375
encode *(com)* 1035
encryption *(com)* 0376
encyclopedia *(gen)* 3805
end a break *(typ)* 1849
en dash/rule *(typ)* 1597
end cap *(typ)* 0553
end even *(typ)* 1850
end time *(com)* 0554
end-leaf *(fin)* 3105
end-of-line character *(com)* 0868
end-of-line decisions *(typ)* 1798
end matter *(gen)* 3806
endlims *(gen)* 3806
endoscope *(pho)* 1330
endpapers *(fin)* 3105
engine-sized *(pap)* 2375
English finish *(pap)* 2500
english/English *(typ)* 1693
engraved face *(typ)* 1739
engraving (1) *(pri)* 2863
engraving (2) *(pri)* 2864
Enhanced Music CD *(com)* 0136
Enhanced Screen Quality font *(com)* 0843
enlarged edition *(gen)* 3884
enlargement *(gen)* 4109
enlarger *(pho)* 1331
en quad *(typ)* 1691
en space *(typ)* 1692
Enter key *(com)* 0203
entrelac *(fin)* 3447
entrelac initial *(typ)* 1740
environment map *(com)* 0555
Envoy *(int)* 1134
EO *(com)* 0128
EP *(gen)* 3684
ephemeris (1) *(gen)* 3807
ephemeris (2) *(gen)* 3808
ephemeris (3) *(gen)* 3809
epigraph *(gen)* 3810
epitome *(gen)* 3811
EPS *(com)* 0375
equalize *(com)* 0751
equivalent weight *(pap)* 2427
erasable optical (media) *(com)* 0137
erase *(com)* 0083
erased characters *(typ)* 1642
ergonomics *(gen)* 3595
errata *(gen)* 3812
erratum (slip) *(gen)* 3812
error-checking *(com)* 0947
error code *(com)* 0948
error correction *(com)* 0293
error diffusion *(com)* 0752
error message *(com)* 0946
ES *(pap)* 2375
Esc(ape) key *(com)* 0204
esparto *(pap)* 2501
ESQ *(com)* 0843
establishing shot *(com)* 0556
et al *(gen)* 3716
et seq *(gen)* 3717
etch *(pre)* 2177
etchant *(pri)* 2847
etching (1) *(pre)* 2177

etching (2) *(pri)* 2865
E-text *(int)* 1113
ethernet *(com)* 0294
Etruscan binding *(fin)* 3106
eucalyptus fibre *(pap)* 2376
even folios *(gen)* 3813
even pages *(gen)* 3814
even s. caps *(typ)* 1851
even smalls *(typ)* 1851
even working *(pri)* 2608
event *(com)* 0949
event-driven *(com)* 0950
event-handling mechanism *(com)* 0951
ex libris *(gen)* 3718
excelsior *(typ)* 1657
exception dictionary *(com)* 0557
excerpt *(gen)* 3815
exotic *(typ)* 1741
expandable cloth *(fin)* 3384
expanded type *(typ)* 1955
expansion board *(com)* 0043
expansion card *(com)* 0043
expansion slot *(com)* 0044
expediting changes *(gen)* 3761
expert set *(typ)* 1956
expert system *(com)* 0337
expertosis *(gen)* 3596
explicit *(gen)* 3719
exploded view *(gen)* 4110
Explorer *(int)* 1180
export *(com)* 0558
export filter *(com)* 0395
exposure *(pho)* 1493
exposure latitude *(pho)* 1494
exposure meter *(pho)* 1495
exposure setting *(pho)* 1496
expressed folio *(pri)* 2574
expurgated edition *(gen)* 3816
extended character set *(typ)* 1598
extended data output *(com)* 0056
extended type *(typ)* 1955
Extensible Markup Language *(int)* 1256
Extensible Style Language *(int)* 1257
extension (1) *(com)* 0818
extension (2) *(pho)* 1332
extension cover *(fin)* 3107
extension conflict *(com)* 0819
extension manager *(com)* 0820
external command *(com)* 0821
external device *(com)* 0205
external (disk) drive *(com)* 0084
external function *(com)* 0822
external reference *(com)* 0823
extra bound *(fin)* 3108
extra calf *(fin)* 3385
extra cloth *(fin)* 3386
extracts *(gen)* 3947
extranet *(int)* 1076
extremely low frequency *(com)* 0157
extrude *(com)* 0559
extruders *(typ)* 1957
eye point *(com)* 0560
eyedropper tool *(com)* 0561

F ℱ **F** F *F*

Fabriano *(pap)* 2502
face *(typ)* 1742
face margin *(gen)* 3958
face material *(gen)* 2269
face out blue *(pre)* 2025
facet edge *(pri)* 2866
facsimile *(gen)* 3598
facsimile edition *(gen)* 3817
facsimile halftone *(pre)* 2032
factory settings *(com)* 1027
factotum *(typ)* 1599
fade out blue *(pre)* 2025
fadeback *(pri)* 4117
fall off *(com)* 0562
false bands *(fin)* 3109
false double *(gen)* 3940
false duotone *(pre)* 2029
family *(typ)* 1743
fan binding *(fin)* 3110
F and C's, F/Cs *(fin)* 3283
F and G's, F/Gs *(fin)* 3283
fan fold *(fin)* 3237
fanfare *(fin)* 3111
FAQs *(com)* 1036
fart box *(typ)* 1820
fascicule *(gen)* 3818
fashion board *(pap)* 2503
fast emulsion/film *(pho)* 1430
FAT *(com)* 0085
fat face *(typ)* 1744
fat matter *(typ)* 1852
fatty *(pre)* 2080
Favorite *(int)* 1181
fax *(gen)* 3598
FDHD *(com)* 0087
feather(ing) *(gen)* 4111
featherweight paper *(pap)* 2504
fecit *(gen)* 3720
feeding edge *(pri)* 2617
feet *(typ)* 1958
feet margin *(gen)* 3948
feint ruling *(pri)* 2978
felt finish *(pap)* 2270
felt side *(pap)* 2271
felting *(pap)* 2377
felts *(pap)* 2378
ferrotype *(pho)* 1431
festoon *(pap)* 2272
fiber *(pap)* 2379
fiber cut *(pap)* 2380
fiber optic cable *(com)* 0295
fiber puffing *(pap)* 2381
field *(com)* 0377
field camera *(pho)* 1334
field curvature *(pho)* 1335
figure (1) *(typ)* 1600
figure (2) *(gen)* 3949
figure number *(gen)* 3950
figure space *(com)* 0844
file *(com)* 0378
file allocation table *(com)* 0085
file compression *(com)* 0787
file corruption *(com)* 0381
file creator *(com)* 0932
file dependency *(com)* 0379
file directory *(com)* 0369

file extension *(com)* 0824
file format *(com)* 0380
file fragmentation *(com)* 0090
File menu *(com)* 0952
filename *(com)* 0383
file partition *(com)* 0101
file recovery *(com)* 0381
file server *(com)* 0296
file tag *(com)* 0086
file transfer *(com)* 0297
File Transfer Protocol *(int)* 1077
file type *(com)* 0382
fill *(com)* 0563
fill character *(com)* 0845
filler *(pap)* 2382
fillet *(fin)* 3448
filling in/up *(pri)* 2792
filling up *(pri)* 2792
film (1) *(gen)* 4171
film (2) *(pho)* 1432
film assembly *(pre)* 2148
film base *(pho)* 1433
film coating *(pap)* 2273
film format *(pho)* 1391
film lamination *(fin)* 3272
film makeup *(pre)* 2148
film negative *(pho)* 1434
film plane *(pho)* 1339
film positive *(pre)* 2178
filmsetting *(pre)* 2179
film speed *(pho)* 1430
Filmstrip *(com)* 0564
filter (1) *(com)* 0565
filter (2) *(com)* 0395
filter (3) *(pho)* 1497
filter (4) *(pre)* 2033
filter factor *(pho)* 1498
final draft *(gen)* 3713
final film *(pre)* 2180
final render(ing) *(com)* 0566
final size *(fin)* 4112
finder *(com)* 0953
fine etch *(pre)* 2181
fine rule *(gen)* 4024
fine whites *(pap)* 2274
fine-line copy *(pre)* 2114
finger(ed)/fingering *(int)* 1114
finial letter *(typ)* 1745
finish *(pap)* 2275
finished art(work) *(gen)* 4025
finished page area *(gen)* 3951
finished rough *(gen)* 4018
finishing *(fin)* 3273
firewall *(int)* 1182
firmware *(com)* 1037
first edition *(gen)* 3819
first generation copy *(gen)* 4026
first impression *(gen)* 3819
fish-eye lens *(pho)* 1336
fishbone diagram *(gen)* 4088
fist *(typ)* 1585
fit (1) *(typ)* 1700
fit (2) *(pre)* 2182
fix *(pho)* 1435
fixative *(pho)* 1436
fixed-focus lens *(pho)* 1337
fixed-size font *(com)* 0846
fixed-width (font) *(typ)* 1765
fixed word spacing *(typ)* 1853
Fkey *(com)* 0206

french joints *(fin)* 3119
french morocco *(fin)* 3387
french rule *(gen)* 4033
french sewing *(fin)* 3290
french shell *(pap)* 2506
french stitch *(fin)* 3290
frequency modulated
  screening *(pre)* 2036
frequently asked questions
  (com) 1036
fresnel factor *(com)* 0577
Fresnel lens *(pho)* 1343
fringe *(pre)* 2037
frisket *(gen)* 4172
front end (1) *(com)* 0299
front end (system) (2) *(com)*
  0209
front-facing polygons *(com)*
  0578
frontispiece *(gen)* 3827
front (jacket) flap *(gen)* 3854
front lay edge *(pri)* 2637
front matter *(gen)* 3874
front projection *(pho)* 1503
frothing *(pap)* 2282
FSI *(gen)* 3826
f-stop *(pho)* 1333
FTP *(int)* 1077
fugitive color *(pri)* 2795
full bleed *(pri)* 2611
full bound *(fin)* 3120
full color *(gen)* 3518
full edition *(gen)* 3828
full face *(typ)* 1959
full gilt *(fin)* 3452
full on the body *(typ)* 1694
full out *(typ)* 1855
full point *(typ)* 1604
full-scale black *(pre)* 2038
full shadow *(typ)* 1752
full space *(typ)* 1856
full stop *(typ)* 1605
full-text indexing *(com)* 0858
full word wrap *(typ)* 1857
fuming ghosting *(pri)* 2616
function keys *(com)* 0210
furnish *(pap)* 2384
fuzz *(pap)* 2277
f-value *(pho)* 1333
FYI *(gen)* 3599

G, GB, gig *(com)* 0387
Gall projection *(gen)* 4100
galley *(typ)* 3724
galley proof *(gen)* 3724
gamma *(com)* 0754
gamma correction *(com)* 0755
gamut *(com)* 0738
GAN *(com)* 0300
gang shooting *(pre)* 2117
gang up (1) *(pri)* 2612
gang up (2) *(pre)* 2118
Garalde *(typ)* 1783
gas plasma monitor *(com)*
  0160
gatefold *(fin)* 3291
gateway *(com)* 1038

gathering (1) *(fin)* 3292
gathering (2) *(fin)* 3293
GB, G, gig *(com)* 0387
GCR *(pre)* 2039
gear marks *(pri)* 2613
gear streaks *(pri)* 2614
gel *(pri)* 2796
gelatin filter *(pho)* 1504
gelatin process *(pri)* 2867
gem *(typ)* 1658
generation *(gen)* 3600
generic *(com)* 0211
Geneva *(com)* 0859
get in (1) *(typ)* 1858
get in (2) *(typ)* 1859
getup *(gen)* 3829
ghost *(pri)* 2615
ghosted icon *(com)* 0939
ghosting (1) *(gen)* 4117
ghosting (2) *(gen)* 4118
GIF *(int)* 1261
GIF89a *(int)* 1261
gig(abyte) *(com)* 0387
giggering *(fin)* 3453
gigo *(com)* 0388
gild *(fin)* 3454
gilding rolls *(fin)* 3455
gilt after rounding *(fin)* 3457
gilt edges *(fin)* 3456
gilt solid *(fin)* 3457
gilt top *(fin)* 3458
gimbel lock *(com)* 0579
glassine *(pap)* 2507
glazed *(pap)* 2283
glazed morocco *(fin)* 3388
global area network *(com)*
  0300
global backup *(com)* 0717
global renaming *(int)* 1185
global system for mobile
  communications *(com)* 0301
gloss (1) *(pap)* 2284
gloss (2) *(gen)* 3959
glossary (1) *(gen)* 3830
glossary (2) *(com)* 0580
gloss finishing *(fin)* 3294
gloss ghosting *(pri)* 2616
gloss ink *(pri)* 2797
glued back only *(fin)* 3121
glued down to ends *(fin)* 3122
glue lap *(fin)* 3295
gluing up *(fin)* 3123
glyph *(gen)* 3686
glyphic *(typ)* 1753
g/m² *(pap)* 2429
goffered edges *(fin)* 3438
gold *(fin)* 3459
gold blocking *(fin)* 3460
golden section *(gen)* 3687
goldenrod *(pre)* 2187
gold leaf *(fin)* 3461
gold tooling *(fin)* 3460
golf ball *(typ)* 1800
gopher *(int)* 1136
gothic *(typ)* 1727
gouache *(com)* 4119
Gouraud shading *(com)* 0581
grabber hand/tool *(com)* 0582
gradation *(gen)* 3519
grade *(pho)* 1438
gradient *(gen)* 3519
graduation *(gen)* 3519

grain (1) *(pap)* 2285
grain (2) *(pho)* 1439
grain (3) *(pri)* 2932
grain direction *(pap)* 2286
grained leather *(fin)* 3389
graininess *(pho)* 1440
graining *(pap)* 2933
graining boards *(fin)* 3390
grain-long *(pap)* 2286
grain-short *(pap)* 2286
grammage *(pap)* 2429
grammes per square meter
  (pap) 2429
granite finish *(pap)* 2508
graphic (1) *(typ)* 1754
graphic (2) *(gen)* 4120
graphical user interface *(com)*
  0956
graphic arts *(gen)* 3688
graphic design *(gen)* 3689
graphic interchange format
  (int) 1261
Graphics *(com)* 0793
graphics tablet/pad *(com)* 0277
graticule *(gen)* 4121
gravure *(pri)* 2868
gravure screen *(pri)* 2869
gray *(gen)* 3521
gray balance *(pri)* 2798
gray component replacement
  (pre) 2039
gray level *(com)* 0756
grayed command *(com)* 0938
grayed icon *(com)* 0939
grayness *(pri)* 2799
grayscale (1) *(pho)* 1505
grayscale (2) *(com)* 0756
great primer *(typ)* 1659
Greek alphabet *(typ)* 1606
greek, greeking *(gen)* 4034
greeking sheet *(gen)* 4173
green *(gen)* 3520
Green Book *(com)* 0139
grid (1) *(gen)* 4035
grid (2) *(com)* 0583
gripper edge *(pri)* 2617
gripper margin *(pri)* 2618
gripper(s) *(pri)* 2619
groove *(typ)* 1960
grooved boards *(fin)* 3124
grooved joints *(fin)* 3119
grotesque (1) *(gen)* 4122
grotesque (2) *(typ)* 1755
grots *(typ)* 1755
ground *(pri)* 2177
ground light *(pho)* 1506
ground lighting *(pho)* 1481
ground plane *(com)* 0584
groundwood *(pap)* 2393
groundwood free *(pap)* 2553
group *(com)* 0585
GSM (1) *(com)* 0301
gsm (2) *(pap)* 2429
g.t. *(fin)* 3458
g.t.e. *(fin)* 3458
guarding *(fin)* 3125
guarding-in *(fin)* 3125
guards *(fin)* 3125
GUI *(com)* 0956
guides *(com)* 0586
guillemets *(typ)* 1593
guillotine *(fin)* 3296

Key: *gen:* general; *com:* computing; *int:* internet; *pho:* photography; *typ:* typography;

gum (1) *(pri)* 2935
gum (2) *(gen)* 4123
gum blinding *(pri)* 2935
gusseting *(fin)* 3297
gutter *(gen)* 3960
gutter bleed *(gen)* 3961
gutter margin *(gen)* 3914
gutting *(gen)* 3666
gyro stabilizer *(pho)* 1344
Gzip *(com)* 0389

H H H *H*

H&J, H/J *(typ)* 0861
hairline register *(typ)* 2620
hairline rule *(gen)* 4036
hairlines *(typ)* 1961
hairspace *(typ)* 1695
halation *(pho)* 1507
half-bound/binding *(fin)* 3126
half cloth *(fin)* 3127
half-diamond indentation *(typ)* 1868
half duplex *(int)* 1078
half-leather *(fin)* 3128
half-measure *(typ)* 1860
half sheet *(pri)* 2621
half title (1) *(gen)* 3831
half title (2) *(gen)* 3832
half-scale black *(pri)* 2831
half sheet work *(pri)* 2751
half-stuff *(pap)* 2385
halftone (1) *(pre)* 2040
halftone (2) *(pre)* 2041
halftone blowup *(pre)* 2042
halftone cell *(pre)* 2043
halftone dot *(pre)* 2044
halftone gravure *(pri)* 2870
halftone mottle *(pri)* 2650
halftone process *(pre)* 2040
halftone screen *(pre)* 2045
halftone step scale *(pho)* 1505
halftone tint *(pre)* 2046
half-uncial *(typ)* 1756
half-up *(gen)* 4124
halo *(pre)* 2037
hand *(typ)* 1585
hand composition *(typ)* 1801
handles (1) *(com)* 0587
handles (2) *(com)* 0343
handmade paper *(pap)* 2509
handshake *(com)* 0302
hang *(com)* 0931
hanging cap(ital) *(typ)* 1861
hanging figures *(typ)* 1973
hanging indent *(typ)* 1862
hanging paragraph *(typ)* 1862
hanging punctuation *(typ)* 1863
hardback *(fin)* 3091
hardbound *(fin)* 3091
hardbound edition *(gen)* 3833
hard copy *(gen)* 3725
hard cover edition *(gen)* 3833
hard disk crash *(com)* 0079
hard (disk) drive *(com)* 0078
hard dot *(pre)* 2047
hard-grain morocco *(fin)* 3391
hard hyphen *(typ)* 1607
hard sized *(pap)* 2287

hard space *(com)* 0869
hardware *(com)* 0212
HDTV *(com)* 0178
head (1) *(gen)* 3966
head (2) *(int)* 1237
head (3) *(com)* 0103
head band *(fin)* 3129
head bolt *(fin)* 3241
headcap *(fin)* 3130
head crash *(com)* 0092
header *(com)* 0390
header card *(gen)* 3667
header file *(int)* 1262
heading (1) *(gen)* 3964
heading (2) *(int)* 1263
headless paragraph *(gen)* 3965
headline (1) *(gen)* 3966
headline (2) *(gen)* 3967
head margin *(gen)* 3962
head-piece *(gen)* 3963
head to foot *(pre)* 2188
head to head *(pre)* 2188
head to tail *(pre)* 2188
head trim *(gen)* 3298
heap *(com)* 0057
heat-release decal *(pri)* 2594
heat sealing *(fin)* 3299
heat-set ink *(pri)* 2800
heavy (face) *(typ)* 1962
Helio-Klischograph *(pri)* 2871
help *(com)* 0957
helper application *(int)* 1264
hemp *(pap)* 2386
heraldic colors *(gen)* 4125
hertz (Hz) *(com)* 0161
hex(adecimal) *(gen)* 3601
HFS *(com)* 0958
hickie/hickey *(pri)* 2622
hierarchical file system *(com)* 0958
hierarchical menu *(com)* 0959
hierarchical structure *(com)* 0960
high contrast *(gen)* 3506
high density *(com)* 0093
high gloss ink *(pri)* 2797
high key *(pho)* 1508
high-level domain *(int)* 1178
high-level language *(com)* 0391
highlight (1) *(gen)* 4126
highlight (2) *(com)* 0961
highlight dots *(pre)* 2048
highlight halftone *(pre)* 2049
high mill finish *(pap)* 2510
high-profile *(gen)* 3602
hinged *(fin)* 3300
hinges *(fin)* 3131
hints/hinting *(com)* 0860
histogram *(com)* 0392
historiated letters *(typ)* 1757
history (list) *(int)* 1186
hither plane *(com)* 0536
HLS *(gen)* 3523
HLV *(gen)* 3523
holding line *(pre)* 2119
holdout *(pap)* 2288
holiday *(fin)* 3132
holing out *(fin)* 3462
holland *(fin)* 3392
hollow *(fin)* 3133
hollow back *(fin)* 3134
hologram *(gen)* 3690

holograph *(gen)* 3726
holster book *(gen)* 3834
home page *(int)* 1187
honing *(pri)* 2623
hooked *(fin)* 3135
hook in *(typ)* 1864
hooking *(fin)* 3135
hooks *(typ)* 1608
horizontal blanking interval *(com)* 0150
horizontal format *(gen)* 4040
horizontal justification *(typ)* 1874
horizontal scaling *(typ)* 1865
host *(int)* 1079
hostname *(int)* 1188
hot metal (type) *(typ)* 1802
hot-melt adhesive *(fin)* 3136
hot-press lettering *(typ)* 1803
hot-pressed (H.P.) *(pap)* 2511
hot-rolled *(pap)* 2512
HotJava *(int)* 1265
hotlist *(int)* 1266
hotspot, hot spot *(com)* 0962
hourglass *(com)* 1018
house corrections *(gen)* 3727
house organ *(gen)* 3835
house style *(gen)* 3683
H.P. *(pap)* 2511
HSB *(gen)* 3523
HSL *(gen)* 3523
HSV *(gen)* 3523
H/T *(pre)* 2040
HTML *(int)* 1267
http *(int)* 1189
httpd *(int)* 1190
https *(int)* 1191
hue *(gen)* 3522
hue, lightness, saturation *(gen)* 3523
hue, saturation, brightness *(gen)* 3523
hue, saturation, lightness *(gen)* 3523
hue, saturation, value *(gen)* 3523
Humane *(typ)* 1783
human engineering *(gen)* 3595
human interface *(com)* 0965
humidified *(pap)* 2289
hygrometer *(pap)* 2290
hygroscope *(pap)* 2290
hyperfocal distance *(pho)* 1345
hyperlink *(int)* 1268
hypermedia *(int)* 1269
hypertext *(int)* 1270
hypertext link *(int)* 1268
hypertext markup language *(int)* 1267
hypertext transfer protocol *(int)* 1189
hyphen *(typ)* 1609
hyphenate *(typ)* 1866
hyphenation and justification *(com)* 0861
hyphenation exceptions *(com)* 0862
hyphenation zone *(com)* 0863
hyphenless justification *(typ)* 1867
hypo *(pho)* 1441
Hz *(com)* 0161

pap: paper; *pre:* prepress; *pri:* printing; *fin:* finishing/binding;

I ♪ I I

Alphabet *(gen)* 3627
International Standard Book Number *(gen)* 3849
Internaut *(int)* 1194
interneg(ative) *(pho)* 1443
Internet *(int)* 1139
Internet access provider *(int)* 1143
Internet Engineering Task Force *(int)* 1138
Internet Protocol *(int)* 1140
Internet Protocol address *(int)* 1141
Internet Relay Chat *(int)* 1195
Internet Service Provider *(int)* 1143
interpolate, interpolation *(com)* 0760
interpreter *(com)* 1042
interrupt button *(com)* 1043
intersect(ion) *(com)* 0590
intranet *(int)* 1144
intrinsic mapping *(com)* 0591
introduction *(gen)* 3850
invert (1) *(com)* 0592
invert (2) *(com)* 0593
inverted commas *(typ)* 1611
invisible character *(com)* 0865
invisible file *(com)* 0405
invisibles *(com)* 0865
I/O *(com)* 0213
IP *(int)* 1140
IP address *(int)* 1141
IPA *(gen)* 3627
iph *(pri)* 2631
IPnG *(int)* 1142
IRC *(int)* 1195
iris diaphragm *(pho)* 1326
ISBN *(gen)* 3849
ISDN *(int)* 1080
ISO *(gen)* 3607
ISO/Adobe character set *(com)* 0866
ISO A-series sizes *(pap)* 2432
ISO B-series sizes *(pap)* 2432
ISO C-series sizes *(pap)* 2432
ISOC *(int)* 1145
isotype *(gen)* 3693
ISP *(int)* 1143
ISSN *(gen)* 3851
issue (1) *(gen)* 3852
issue (2) *(gen)* 3853
IT *(com)* 1044
italic *(typ)* 1963
item *(com)* 0406
item tool *(com)* 0594
ivory board *(pap)* 2518

jacket *(gen)* 3801
jacket flaps *(gen)* 3854
jacketing machine *(fin)* 3139
jaconet *(fin)* 3393
jaggies *(com)* 0726
Japanese vellum *(pap)* 2519
Java *(int)* 1277
Java-based Extendable Typography *(int)* 1281

Java class library *(int)* 1278
Java virtual machine *(int)* 1279
JavaScript *(int)* 1280
jaw folder *(fin)* 3304
JET *(int)* 1281
jim-dash *(gen)* 4038
job bag *(gen)* 3694
job inks *(pri)* 2810
job jacket *(gen)* 3694
jobbing *(pri)* 2632
jog(ging) *(fin)* 3305
jogger *(fin)* 3305
joint *(fin)* 3140
Joint Photographic Experts Group *(com)* 0761
joule *(pho)* 1510
JPEG, JPG *(com)* 0761
JScript *(int)* 1280
jump *(gen)* 3969
jump line *(gen)* 3970
justification/justified *(typ)* 1874
justified left/right *(typ)* 1874
jute board *(pap)* 2520

K (1), k *(gen)* 3524
K (2) KB *(com)* 0408
k (3), kb, kbit *(com)* 0407
K (4) *(gen)* 3525
kaolin *(pap)* 2365
kb, kbit *(com)* 0407
kbps *(com)* 0304
Kbyte *(com)* 0408
keep down/up *(typ)* 1875
keep in/out *(typ)* 1876
keep standing *(pri)* 2633
Kelvin temperature scale (K) *(gen)* 3525
kenaf *(pap)* 2387
kermit *(int)* 1081
kern *(typ)* 1964
kerned letters *(typ)* 1696
kerning *(typ)* 1696
kerning pair *(typ)* 1697
kerning table *(typ)* 1698
kerning value *(typ)* 1699
key (1) *(pri)* 2634
key (2) *(com)* 0214
keyboard *(com)* 0216
keyboard character *(com)* 0217
key(board) combination *(com)* 1045
keyboard command *(com)* 0970
keyboard equivalent *(com)* 1045
keyboard event *(com)* 1046
keyboarding *(com)* 0219
keyboard map *(com)* 0218
keyboard shortcut *(com)* 1045
keyboard special character *(com)* 1045
key frame *(com)* 0796
keying *(com)* 0214
key letters *(gen)* 3971
key light *(pho)* 1511
keyline (1) *(pre)* 2119

keyline (2) *(gen)* 4039
keyline (3) *(pre)* 2120
keyline (4) *(com)* 0595
keyline view *(com)* 0595
key numbers *(gen)* 3971
keypad *(com)* 0225
key plate *(pri)* 2634
key reading *(pho)* 1512
key repeat rate *(com)* 0215
keystroke *(com)* 0220
key tone *(pho)* 1513
kicker *(gen)* 3855
kill *(typ)* 1805
kilo *(gen)* 3608
kilobit *(com)* 0407
kilobits per second *(com)* 0304
kilobyte *(com)* 0408
kipskin *(fin)* 3394
Kirlian photography *(pho)* 1514
kiss impression *(pri)* 2635
Klischograph *(pri)* 2873
knife folder *(fin)* 3306
knockout *(pre)* 2051
knocked-out type *(typ)* 1848
knocking up *(fin)* 3305
knowledge fade *(gen)* 3609
K.O. *(pre)* 2051
Kodalith MP System *(pre)* 2192
kraft (paper) *(pap)* 2521

L*a*b* color *(com)* 0735
laced on *(fin)* 3141
lacing in *(fin)* 3142
lacquer *(fin)* 3307
lacuna *(typ)* 1877
laid paper *(pap)* 2522
lamination/laminate *(fin)* 3308
lampblack *(pri)* 2811
LAN *(com)* 0305
lands (1) *(pri)* 2874
lands (2) *(com)* 0129
landscape format *(gen)* 4040
lap *(pre)* 2193
lap lines *(pri)* 2636
lapis lazuli *(gen)* 4135
laptop (computer) *(com)* 0019
large-screen emulation *(com)* 1047
laser *(com)* 0140
laser font *(com)* 0872
laser printer *(com)* 0258
lasso *(com)* 0596
latency time *(com)* 0073
latent image *(pho)* 1444
lateral reverse *(gen)* 4041
lathe, lathing *(com)* 0597
latin (1) *(typ)* 1612
latin (2) *(typ)* 1759
latin text *(typ)* 4034
latitude *(pho)* 1515
launch *(com)* 0598
lay edges *(pri)* 2637
layer *(com)* 0599
laying on *(fin)* 3465
layout *(gen)* 4042
layout element *(int)* 1282

M *M* **M** *M*

recognition *(com)* 0261
magnetic ink characters *(typ)* 1761
magnetic media *(com)* 0096
magnetic storage *(com)* 0096
magneto-optical disc *(com)* 0141
magnifier *(gen)* 3614
magnify tool *(com)* 0605
magnifying glass *(gen)* 3614
mailto: *(int)* 1118
main board *(com)* 0041
main exposure *(pre)* 2054
mainframe *(com)* 0021
main memory *(com)* 0058
majordomo *(int)* 1119
majuscule *(typ)* 1943
make even *(typ)* 1884
makeover (1) *(pre)* 2055
makeover (2) *(pre)* 2198
make-ready *(pri)* 2645
makeup (1) *(pre)* 2197
makeup (2) *(fin)* 3311
making *(pap)* 2392
making ready *(pri)* 2645
manila *(pap)* 2528
Manuaire *(typ)* 1783
manuscript *(gen)* 3737
map file *(int)* 1272
mapping (1) *(com)* 0414
mapping (2) *(com)* 0762
mapping resource *(gen)* 4137
maquette binding *(fin)* 3153
marbled calf *(fin)* 3395
marbling *(pap)* 2529
marching ants *(com)* 0416
marginal notes *(gen)* 3975
margin guides *(com)* 0606
margin(s) *(typ)* 3974
maril *(fin)* 3396
marked proof *(gen)* 3738
markup (1) *(gen)* 4046
markup (2) *(int)* 1286
markup language *(com)* 0415
marquee *(com)* 0416
mask (1) *(gen)* 3530
mask (2) *(pho)* 1395
masking (1) *(pre)* 2056
masking (2) *(gen)* 4174
masking film (1) *(pre)* 2223
masking film (2) *(gen)* 4174
master *(gen)* 3739
master cylinder *(pri)* 2646
master directory block *(com)* 0417
master page *(com)* 0607
master plate *(pri)* 2938
master proof *(gen)* 3740
masthead (1) *(gen)* 3861
masthead (2) *(gen)* 3862
mat(rix) *(typ)* 1807
MatchPrint *(pre)* 2199
math coprocessor *(com)* 0009
mathematical setting *(typ)* 1617
mathematical signs *(typ)* 1618
matrix *(pri)* 2983
matt art *(pap)* 2530
matt/matte *(gen)* 4175
matt(e) finish *(pap)* 2299
matter *(gen)* 3741
Mb *(com)* 0419

MB *(com)* 0420
Mbit *(com)* 0419
Mbps *(com)* 0307
Mbyte *(com)* 0420
mean-line *(typ)* 1723
mean noon sunlight *(pho)* 1520
measure *(typ)* 1703
Mécane *(typ)* 1783
mechanical *(gen)* 4013
mechanical binding *(fin)* 3154
mechanical ghosting *(pri)* 2647
mechanical tint *(pre)* 2057
mechanical (wood) pulp *(pap)* 2393
medallion *(fin)* 3466
media (1) *(gen)* 3697
media (2) *(com)* 0047
median (filter) *(com)* 0608
medical symbols *(typ)* 1619
medical lens *(pho)* 1351
medium (1) *(com)* 4138
medium (2) *(pap)* 2436
medium (3) *(typ)* 1969
medium (4) *(pre)* 2058
meeting guards *(fin)* 3155
mega *(com)* 0418
megabit *(com)* 0419
megabits per second *(com)* 0307
meg(abyte) *(com)* 0420
megahertz (MHz) *(com)* 0022
membrane *(fin)* 3397
memory *(com)* 0059
memory allocation *(com)* 0967
memory-management coprocessor *(com)* 0062
menu *(com)* 0968
menu bar *(com)* 0969
menu command *(com)* 0970
menu-driven *(com)* 0973
menu indicator *(com)* 0971
menu title *(com)* 0972
Mercator projection *(gen)* 4100
merge *(com)* 0609
MESECAM *(com)* 0177
mesh *(pri)* 3042
mesh marks *(pri)* 3043
mesh warp *(com)* 0610
message box *(com)* 0900
meta-information *(int)* 1287
metacharacter *(int)* 1288
metallic ink *(pri)* 2815
metallography *(pri)* 2939
metameric *(gen)* 3531
meteorological symbols *(gen)* 4047
metrication *(gen)* 3615
metrics *(com)* 0867
metzograph *(pre)* 2059
mezzograph *(pre)* 2059
mezzotint *(pri)* 2877
MF *(pap)* 2525
mf *(gen)* 3742
MG *(pap)* 2526
MHz (megahertz) *(com)* 0022
MICR *(com)* 0261
microchip *(com)* 0006
microfiche *(gen)* 3863
microform publishing *(gen)* 3863

micrometer *(gen)* 3616
microprocessor *(com)* 0031
microwave drying *(pri)* 3062
mid(dle) space *(typ)* 1704
middletones *(gen)* 3532
MIDI *(com)* 1051
midtone dot *(pre)* 2060
midtones *(gen)* 3523
milking machine *(typ)* 1820
millboards *(fin)* 3398
mill brand *(pap)* 2300
mille *(gen)* 3617
mill-finished *(pap)* 2525
millisecond *(gen)* 3618
mill ream *(pap)* 2437
MIME *(int)* 1120
minikin *(typ)* 1661
minion *(typ)* 1662
minionette *(typ)* 1689
minuscule *(typ)* 1970
minus leading *(typ)* 1887
minus linespacing *(typ)* 1887
mips *(com)* 0023
mirror-image backup *(com)* 0719
mirror lens *(pho)* 1352
misregister *(pri)* 2696
missal caps *(typ)* 1762
misting *(pri)* 2816
miter(ed) (1) *(fin)* 3156
miter(ed) (2) *(com)* 0611
mixed composition *(typ)* 1885
mnemonic *(com)* 0421
MO/MOD disc *(com)* 0141
mock-up *(gen)* 4018
modal dialog box *(com)* 0974
model *(gen)* 3533
modeling lamp *(pho)* 1521
modem *(int)* 1083
modern face *(typ)* 1763
modern numerals *(typ)* 1966
modifier key *(com)* 0221
modular system *(gen)* 3620
module *(com)* 0612
moiré *(pre)* 2061
mold *(pap)* 2394
mold-made paper *(pap)* 2301
monetary symbol *(typ)* 1620
monitor *(com)* 0165
monk *(pri)* 2648
mono(chrome) (1) *(gen)* 3534
mono(chrome) (2) *(com)* 0166
monogram *(typ)* 1764
monograph *(gen)* 3864
monorail *(pho)* 1353
monospaced (font) *(typ)* 1765
monotone *(gen)* 3535
Monotype *(typ)* 1808
montage *(gen)* 4139
mordant (1) *(fin)* 3467
mordant (2) *(pri)* 2649
morocco *(fin)* 3399
morph *(com)* 0800
mortise (1) *(pre)* 2200
mortise (2) *(pri)* 1705
mosaic binding *(fin)* 3468
mosaic gold *(fin)* 3469
MOTD *(int)* 1146
motherboard *(com)* 0041
mother set *(pri)* 3019
motif *(gen)* 4140

Motion Picture Experts Group *(com)* 0801
motor-drive *(pho)* 1354
mottle *(pri)* 2650
mottled calf *(fin)* 3400
mottling *(pri)* 2650
mould *(pap)* 2394
mould-made paper *(pap)* 2301
mounting and flapping *(gen)* 4048
mounting board *(pap)* 2531
mouse *(com)* 0222
mouse-down *(com)* 0223
mouse event *(com)* 0223
mouse mat *(com)* 0224
mouse pad *(com)* 0224
mouse-up *(com)* 0223
movable type *(typ)* 1809
moving banner *(int)* 1198
MPEG *(com)* 0801
MPPP *(int)* 1084
ms *(gen)* 3618
MS(S) *(gen)* 3737
MS-DOS *(com)* 0975
mtf *(gen)* 3742
mull *(fin)* 3401
Mullen tester *(pap)* 2302
Multilink Point-to-Point Protocol *(int)* 1084
multimedia *(com)* 0423
multipattern metering *(pho)* 1522
multiple exposure *(pho)* 1523
multiple flash *(pho)* 1524
multiple flats *(pre)* 2201
multiple screens *(com)* 0167
multiple-selected items *(com)* 0424
multiplex(ing) *(int)* 1085
multipurpose Internet mail extensions (MIME) *(int)* 1120
multi-ring binder *(fin)* 3157
multiscreen *(com)* 0167
multitasking *(com)* 1050
multithreaded *(com)* 0976
multi-user *(com)* 0422
mump *(typ)* 1810
murex *(gen)* 4141
musical instrument digital interface *(com)* 1051
music printing *(pri)* 2984
music program *(com)* 0613
mutt(on) *(typ)* 1687
M weight *(pap)* 2435

nailhead *(fin)* 3158
nameplate *(gen)* 3861
nanosecond (ns) *(com)* 0024
nap roller *(pri)* 2940
narrowcasting *(int)* 1147
narrow copy *(fin)* 3159
National Center for Supercomputing Applications *(int)* 1148
National Television Standards Committee *(com)* *0168
native file format *(com)* 0425

natural *(pri)* 2586
natural tint *(pap)* 2303
navigate *(com)* 0614
navigation bar *(com)* 0615
navigation button *(com)* 0616
Navigator *(int)* 1199
NCR paper *(pap)* 2479
NCSA *(int)* 1148
near-print *(pri)* 2941
neck *(typ)* 1971
neck line *(typ)* 1886
neg(ative) (1) *(pho)* 1445
negative (2) *(com)* 0592
negative element *(pho)* 1329
negative leading *(typ)* 1887
negative light *(com)* 0617
negative line spacing *(typ)* 1887
negative-working plate *(pre)* 2202
nested folder *(com)* 0977
nesting *(com)* 0978
netiquette *(int)* 1200
NetShow *(int)* 1289
netTV *(int)* 1201
netTV viewers *(int)* 1202
network *(com)* 0308
network link *(com)* 0309
Network News Transfer Protocol *(int)* 1149
neutral density filter *(pho)* 1525
new edition *(gen)* 3884
new line character *(com)* 0868
news server *(int)* 1149
newsgroup *(int)* 1150
newsprint *(pap)* 2532
Newton's rings *(pho)* 1396
next reading matter *(gen)* 3669
next text matter *(gen)* 3669
NFNT *(typ)* 0852
nib/nibbed *(fin)* 3312
nibble *(com)* 0426
nick *(typ)* 1972
nickname *(int)* 1121
night lens *(pho)* 1355
nip (1) *(fin)* 3313
nip (2) *(pri)* 2651
nippers *(fin)* 3160
nipping *(fin)* 3161
nipping up *(fin)* 3162
NLQ *(pri)* 2941
NNTP *(int)* 1149
no-carbon-required paper *(pap)* 2479
node (1) *(int)* 1203
node (2) *(com)* 0310
nodename *(int)* 1086
noise (1) *(int)* 1087
noise (2) *(com)* 0763
noise function *(com)* 0618
nom-de-plume *(gen)* 3865
nonactinic (light) *(pho)* 1526
nonbreaking space *(com)* 0869
noncontact printing *(com)* 0262
noncontiguous *(com)* 0098
noncontiguous selection *(com)* 0427
noncontiguous space *(com)* 0098

nondiscrete value *(gen)* 3590
None *(com)* 0802
nongear streaks *(pri)* 2652
nonimage area *(pri)* 2942
nonimpact printing *(com)* 0262
nonlining figures *(typ)* 1973
nonlining numerals *(typ)* 1973
nonpareil *(typ)* 1663
nonprinting characters *(com)* 0865
nonread color *(pre)* 2025
nonread ink *(pre)* 2026
nonreflective ink *(pri)* 2817
nonrepro blue *(pre)* 2025
normal(s) *(com)* 0619
northlight *(pho)* 1527
not *(pap)* 2533
notch binding *(fin)* 3163
np *(gen)* 3743
ns *(com)* 0024
NTSC *(com)* 0168
NuBus *(com)* 0025
NuBus slot *(com)* 0025
nudge *(com)* 0620
null modem cable *(com)* 0311
numbered copy *(gen)* 3866
numbered list *(int)* 1290
numbering format *(typ)* 1621
numerals *(typ)* 1974
numerator *(typ)* 1622
numeric coprocessor *(com)* 0009
numeric keypad *(com)* 0225
nybble *(com)* 0358

oasis goat *(fin)* 3402
o.b.a. *(pap)* 2395
obelisk *(typ)* 1578
obelus *(typ)* 1578
object *(com)* 0621
object, child *(com)* 0534
object linking and embedding *(com)* 0622
object-oriented *(com)* 0428
object, parent *(com)* 0633
oblique *(com)* 0870
oblique stroke *(typ)* 1634
oblong *(gen)* 3976
OBR *(com)* 3576
obsolete (element) *(int)* 1204
OCR *(com)* 1052
OCR-A *(typ)* 1767
OCR-B *(typ)* 1767
octavo *(pap)* 2438
octodecimo *(gen)* 3946
odd *(pap)* 2439
OEM *(com)* 0226
off-cut *(fin)* 3314
off-line/offline *(com)* 0312
offline converting *(fin)* 3315
offline finishing *(fin)* 3315
off-press proofing *(pre)* 2203
off-print *(pri)* 2653
offset (1) *(pri)* 2943
offset (2) *(pri)* 2654
offset blanket *(pri)* 2944
offset cartridge *(pap)* 2534

offset gravure *(pri)* 2878
offset ink *(pri)* 2945
offset letterpress *(pri)* 3016
offset litho(graphy) *(pri)* 2946
offside *(fin)* 3164
OK press/sheet *(pri)* 2655
Old English *(typ)* 1727
old face *(typ)* 1766
old style *(typ)* 1766
old-tech *(gen)* 3621
OLE *(com)* 0622
olivined edges *(fin)* 3470
omni light *(com)* 0623
omnibus book *(gen)* 3867
OMR *(gen)* 3576
on-demand *(gen)* 3622
on-demand printing *(pri)* 2973
one on and two off *(fin)* 3165
one-and-a-half-up *(gen)* 4124
one-piece film *(pre)* 2184
one-up *(pri)* 2656
one-way halftone *(pre)* 2077
onionskin *(pap)* 2535
onlaying *(fin)* 3471
online/on-line *(com)* 0313
on-line help *(com)* 0624
on-line service provider *(int)* 1151
ooze leather *(fin)* 3403
o.p. *(gen)* 3868
op. cit. *(gen)* 3744
opacity (1) *(gen)* 4176
opacity (2) *(com)* 0625
opaline *(pap)* 2536
opaque *(gen)* 4177
opaquing *(pre)* 2204
open (1) *(com)* 0979
open (2) *(gen)* 4049
open architecture *(com)* 0026
open back *(fin)* 3134
OpenDoc *(com)* 0980
open flash *(pho)* 1528
opening *(gen)* 3977
open letters *(typ)* 1768
open matter *(typ)* 1888
open prepress interface *(pre)* 2123
open time *(gen)* 3623
OpenType *(com)* 0871
open up *(pre)* 2062
operating system *(com)* 0981
OPI *(pre)* 2123
optical alignment *(gen)* 4051
optical bar recognition *(gen)* 3576
optical bleaching agents *(pap)* 2395
optical center *(gen)* 4051
optical character recognition *(com)* 1052
optical disc *(com)* 0142
optically even spacing *(typ)* 1889
optical mark recognition *(gen)* 3576
optical media *(com)* 0142
optical (type) font *(typ)* 1767
optimize *(com)* 0099
option *(com)* 1053
Option key *(com)* 0221
Orange Book *(com)* 0143
orange peel *(fin)* 3316

ordinal numbers *(gen)* 3745
oriental leaf *(fin)* 3472
oriental type *(typ)* 3472
orientation *(gen)* 3978
origin *(com)* 0626
original *(gen)* 3708
original equipment manufacturer *(com)* 0226
origination *(pre)* 2125
ornament *(typ)* 1602
orphan *(gen)* 3979
orphan file *(int)* 1205
orthochromatic *(pre)* 2205
ortho film *(pre)* 2205
orthogonal line tool *(com)* 0601
orthographic (1) *(gen)* 4142
orthographic (2) *(pho)* 1446
OS *(com)* 0981
OTF metering *(pho)* 1356
out *(typ)* 1890
outer margin *(gen)* 3958
outline font *(com)* 0872
outline halftone *(gen)* 4099
outline letter *(typ)* 1768
outliner *(com)* 0627
out of print *(gen)* 3868
out-of-register *(pri)* 2696
out of series *(pri)* 2699
out-of-memory *(com)* 0060
output *(com)* 0227
output device *(com)* 0263
output resolution *(pre)* 2206
outrig frame *(pho)* 1529
outsert/outset *(fin)* 3848
outside margin *(gen)* 3958
outsides *(pap)* 2304
oval tool *(com)* 0552
overcasting *(fin)* 3317
overdevelop *(pho)* 1447
overexpose (1) *(pho)* 1530
overexpose (2) *(pri)* 2657
overflow *(typ)* 1891
overhang cover *(fin)* 3166
overhead *(com)* 0429
overhead cost *(gen)* 3624
overhead projector *(gen)* 3625
overlay *(gen)* 4068
overlaying *(pri)* 2658
overmatter *(typ)* 1891
overprint (1) *(pri)* 2659
overprint (2) *(pri)* 2660
overprint (3) *(pri)* 2653
overprint color *(pri)* 2828
overrun *(typ)* 1892
overs *(pri)* 2661
overset (1) *(typ)* 1893
overset (2) *(typ)* 1891
oversewing *(fin)* 3317
oversize (1) *(gen)* 4143
oversize (2) *(com)* 0628
oversize (3) *(pap)* 2440
oversize (4) *(fin)* 3318
own ends *(fin)* 3895
Oxford corners *(gen)* 4052
Oxford rule *(gen)* 4053
Ozalid *(pre)* 2207

P & P P *P*

p, pp *(gen)* 3980
packet *(int)* 1088
packing *(pri)* 2947
page (1) *(int)* 1206
page (2) *(gen)* 3869
page (3) *(com)* 0061
page break *(gen)* 3981
page description language *(com)* 1054
paged memory-management unit *(com)* 0062
page flex *(fin)* 3167
page flipping *(int)* 1207
page guides *(com)* 0629
page head *(gen)* 3966
page layout *(gen)* 4042
page layout application *(com)* 0630
page makeup *(pre)* 2197
page makeup application *(com)* 0630
page preview *(com)* 0631
page proofs *(gen)* 3746
page reader *(com)* 1052
Page Setup *(com)* 0430
pages to view *(pri)* 2662
pagination *(gen)* 3982
paint application *(com)* 0632
paint program *(com)* 0589
painted edges *(fin)* 3450
PAL *(com)* 0169
pale gold *(fin)* 3441
palette *(com)* 0431
palette, floating *(com)* 0569
pallet *(fin)* 3473
pamphlet *(gen)* 3870
pan film *(pho)* 1448
pan(ning) *(pho)* 1531
panchromatic *(pho)* 1448
panel *(pri)* 2663
panel back *(fin)* 3474
panel printing *(pri)* 2664
panel stamp *(fin)* 3475
pantograph *(pho)* 1532
PANTONE® *(gen)* 3536
paper absorbency *(pap)* 2306
paperback *(fin)* 3169
paperback edition *(gen)* 3895
paper basis weight *(pap)* 2441
paperboard *(pap)* 2537
paper boards *(fin)* 3404
paper covers *(fin)* 3405
paper grade *(pho)* 1438
paper permanence *(pap)* 2306
paper sizes *(pap)* 2442
paper substance *(pap)* 2443
paper to paper *(fin)* 3280
paper weight *(pap)* 2444
paper wrappered *(fin)* 3168
papeterie *(pap)* 2538
papier-mâché *(pri)* 3020
papyrus *(pap)* 2539
paragon *(typ)* 1664
paragraph *(int)* 1291
paragraph format *(com)* 0857
paragraph mark *(typ)* 1560
parallax *(gen)* 4144

parallel fold *(fin)* 3319
parallel interface *(com)* 0314
parallel mark *(typ)* 1623
parallel rule *(gen)* 4054
parameter *(com)* 0432
parameter RAM *(com)* 0063
parchment *(pap)* 2540
parenthesis *(typ)* 1624
parent object *(com)* 0633
parent relative *(com)* 0634
paring *(fin)* 3476
parity bit *(com)* 0315
parked *(com)* 0100
partition(ing) *(com)* 0101
partwork *(gen)* 3871
Pascal *(com)* 0433
pass *(pri)* 2665
pass for press *(pri)* 2666
passive matrix display *(com)* 0170
pass sheet *(pri)* 2667
paste *(com)* 0434
pasteboard (1) *(com)* 0636
pasteboard (2) *(pap)* 2307
pasted down to ends *(fin)* 3122
paste-downs *(fin)* 3170
paste-grain *(fin)* 3406
paste in *(fin)* 3072
pastel shades *(gen)* 3537
paste on *(fin)* 3320
paster (1) *(fin)* 3321
paster (2) *(pri)* 2879
paste-replace *(com)* 0635
paste-up/pasteup *(gen)* 4055
pasting *(fin)* 3171
pasting down *(fin)* 3172
patch *(com)* 0435
patent *(gen)* 3626
path (1) *(com)* 0436
path (2) *(com)* 0637
path (3) *(com)* 0027
pathname *(com)* 0437
PC *(com)* 0028
PC board *(com)* 0041
PC lens *(pho)* 1357
PCI *(com)* 0229
PCMCIA *(com)* 0230
PD *(gen)* 3630
PDF *(com)* 0443
PDL *(com)* 1054
PDS *(com)* 0045
PE *(typ)* 1811
peaking *(com)* 0764
pearl *(typ)* 1665
peasant binding *(fin)* 3173
pebbling *(fin)* 3322
peculiars *(typ)* 1638
peer-to-peer *(com)* 0316
PEL *(typ)* 0438
perfect *(pri)* 3063
perfect binding *(fin)* 3073
perfect copy *(fin)* 3323
perfecting *(pri)* 2562
perfecting press *(pri)* 2909
perfector *(pri)* 2909
perforate/perf *(pap)* 2308
perf strip *(fin)* 3174
period *(typ)* 1625
peripheral cable *(com)* 0228
peripheral component
  interconnect *(com)* 0229

peripheral device *(com)* 0205
Perl *(int)* 1089
permanence *(pap)* 2306
permanent font *(com)* 0873
personal computer *(com)* 0028
Personal Computer Memory
  Card International
  Association *(com)* 0230
personal Java *(int)* 1292
perspective *(gen)* 4145
perspective correction lens
  (pho) 1357
PFR *(int)* 1259
pharmaceutical symbols *(typ)*
  1619
phase alternation by line *(com)*
  0169
Phong shading *(com)* 0638
phonogram *(gen)* 3627
phosphor *(com)* 0171
Photo CD *(com)* 0439
photocell *(com)* 0279
photocomposition *(typ)* 2179
photodirect *(pre)* 2124
photoelectric cell *(com)* 0279
photoengraving *(pri)* 2880
photoflood *(pho)* 1533
photogelatin printing *(pri)*
  2913
photogram *(pho)* 1397
photographic film *(pho)* 1432
photography *(pho)* 1398
photogravure *(pri)* 2881
Photo JPEG *(com)* 0803
photolithography *(pri)* 2946
photomacrography *(pho)* 1399
photomechanical (1) *(pri)* 2668
photomechanical (2) *(gen)*
  4013
photomechanical
  reproduction *(pri)* 2880
photomechanical transfer
  (pre) 2209
photomicrography *(pho)* 1400
photomontage *(gen)* 4139
photo-opaque *(pre)* 2208
photopolymer (printing)
  plates *(pri)* 2985
photoresist *(pri)* 2669
photosensitive *(pho)* 1449
photosite *(com)* 0279
phototypesetting *(typ)* 2179
physical dot gain *(pri)* 2670
pi character *(typ)* 1638
pi font *(typ)* 1975
pica *(typ)* 1706
pica, double *(typ)* 1685
picking *(pri)* 2672
pick resistance *(pap)* 2309
pick-up *(pri)* 2671
PICS animation *(com)* 0804
PICT *(com)* 0440
pictogram *(gen)* 4146
pictograph *(gen)* 4146
picture box *(com)* 0639
picture element *(com)* 0370
picture library *(gen)* 4130
picture skew *(com)* 0640
piece fraction *(typ)* 1565
pierced *(pri)* 3021
pie diagram *(gen)* 4084
pie (type) *(typ)* 1894

PIG chart *(pri)* 2818
pigment *(gen)* 4147
piling *(pri)* 2948
pincushion *(com)* 0172
pinholes *(pho)* 1450
pin register *(pre)* 2210
pin seal *(fin)* 3407
pin seal morocco *(fin)* 3408
pinxit *(gen)* 3747
pipe *(int)* 1090
pit *(com)* 0144
pitch (1) *(typ)* 1707
pitch (2) *(com)* 0641
pitch (3) *(com)* 0264
pixel *(com)* 0982
pixel depth *(com)* 0765
pixelation *(com)* 0766
pixellization *(com)* 0766
place *(com)* 0642
plagiarism *(gen)* 3748
planographic *(pri)* 2949
plastic coil binding *(fin)* 3175
plastic comb binding *(fin)* 3175
plastic plates *(pri)* 2950
plate (1) *(pri)* 2951
plate (3) *(pri)* 2673
plate (3) *(pho)* 1451
plate-boring machine *(pri)*
  3022
plate cylinder *(pri)* 2674
plated paper *(pap)* 2311
plate finish *(pap)* 2310
plate folder *(fin)* 3246
plate glazed *(pap)* 2310
platemaking *(pri)* 2675
plate mark *(pri)* 2866
platen press *(pri)* 3023
plating *(pri)* 3024
platter *(com)* 0102
playback *(com)* 0505
plotter *(com)* 0265
plucking *(pri)* 2672
plug and play *(com)* 0231
plug-in *(com)* 0643
plugging *(pri)* 2676
ply *(pap)* 2445
ply thickness *(pap)* 2446
PMMU *(com)* 0062
PMS *(com)* 3536
PMT *(pre)* 2209
PNG *(int)* 1293
pocket edition *(gen)* 3872
pocket envelope *(pap)* 2312
point (1) *(typ)* 1708
point (2) *(com)* 0441
pointer *(com)* 0442
point holes *(pho)* 1450
pointing interface *(com)* 0956
point of presence *(int)* 1092
point of sale *(gen)* 3670
Point-to-Point Protocol *(int)*
  1091
poise *(pri)* 2840
polarization *(pho)* 1534
polarize *(pho)* 1534
polarizing filter *(pho)* 1534
Polaroid *(pho)* 1358
polished calf *(fin)* 3409
polygon *(com)* 0644
polygon resolution *(com)* 0645
polygon tool *(com)* 0646
polyline *(com)* 0647

Key: *gen:* general; *com:* computing; *int:* internet; *pho:* photography; *typ:* typography;

polymesh *(com)* 0648
POP (1) *(int)* 1092
POP (2) *(int)* 1093
POP account *(int)* 1093
pop-down menu *(com)* 0942
pop-up menu *(com)* 0983
pop-ups *(fin)* 3324
pope roll *(pap)* 2396
porosity *(pap)* 2313
port *(com)* 0029
portable document format *(com)* 0443
Portable Font Resource *(int)* 1259
portable network graphics *(int)* 1293
port address *(com)* 1055
portrait format *(com)* 4056
portrait monitor *(com)* 0173
position marks *(pre)* 2132
position proof *(pre)* 2211
positive *(pho)* 1452
positive reversal process *(pre)* 2921
positive-working plate *(pre)* 2212
post binder *(fin)* 3176
poster board *(pap)* 2541
posterize *(pho)* 1453
Post Office Protocol *(int)* 1093
postlims *(gen)* 3806
post-production *(gen)* 3628
PostScript *(com)* 1056
PostScript font *(com)* 0887
PostScript interpreter *(com)* 1057
PostScript printer *(com)* 0266
PostScript Printer Description file *(com)* 1058
pothook *(typ)* 1976
POTS *(int)* 1094
pouncing *(pap)* 2314
powdered *(fin)* 3477
powdering *(pri)* 2929
powderless etching *(pri)* 2882
power filter *(com)* 0246
PPD *(com)* 1058
ppi *(com)* 0444
PPP *(int)* 1091
PRAM *(com)* 0063
PRAM chip *(com)* 0064
prebinding *(fin)* 3177
pre-coated plates *(pri)* 2952
preface *(gen)* 3873
preferences *(com)* 0445
preflighting *(com)* 0767
prefs file *(com)* 0446
pregather *(fin)* 3325
preliminary pages *(gen)* 3874
prelims *(gen)* 3874
premake ready *(pri)* 2677
premask *(pre)* 2213
prepress *(pre)* 2125
prepress proofing *(pre)* 2203
preprint *(pri)* 2678
preproofing *(pre)* 2203
prescreen *(pre)* 2063
prescreened film *(pre)* 2064
pre-sensitized plates *(pri)* 2953
presentation visual *(gen)* 4018
presets *(com)* 1027
press *(pri)* 2679

pressboards *(pap)* 3398
press gain *(pri)* 2680
pressing unit *(fin)* 3326
press mark *(pap)* 2292
press proof *(pri)* 2642
press revise *(pri)* 2681
press run *(pri)* 2682
presswork *(pri)* 2683
pretzel symbol *(com)* 1026
preview *(com)* 0649
prima *(pri)* 2684
primary binding *(fin)* 3178
primary colors *(gen)* 3538
primary letter *(typ)* 1977
prime marks *(typ)* 1588
primes *(typ)* 1588
primitive *(com)* 0650
print (1) *(pho)* 1454
print (2) *(pri)* 2685
print (3) *(pri)* 2686
print buffer *(com)* 0267
print convertors *(fin)* 3327
Printed circuit board *(com)* 0041
printed edges *(fin)* 3478
printer *(pre)* 2214
printer description file *(com)* 0447
printer driver *(com)* 1033
printer font *(com)* 0872
printer port *(com)* 0030
printer's flower *(typ)* 1602
printer's imprint *(gen)* 3838
printer's mark *(gen)* 3798
printer's ornament *(typ)* 1586
printer's reader *(pri)* 2129
printer's ream *(pap)* 2447
printing down *(pri)* 2954
printing down frame *(pri)* 2229
printing plate *(pri)* 2951
printing press *(pri)* 2679
printing pressure *(pri)* 2688
printing processes *(pri)* 2689
printing unit *(pri)* 2690
printing-in *(pri)* 1455
printmaking *(pri)* 2691
PrintMonitor *(com)* 0448
print origination *(pre)* 2125
print-out *(com)* 0268
print run *(pri)* 2682
print spooler *(com)* 0483
print to paper *(pri)* 2687
prism *(pho)* 1535
process block *(pri)* 2883
process blue *(gen)* 3508
process camera *(pre)* 2126
process color *(gen)* 3496
process color printing *(pri)* 3517
process color separation *(pre)* 2161
process engraving *(pri)* 2880
process ink *(gen)* 3496
process ink gamut chart *(pri)* 2818
processor (chip) *(com)* 0031
processor direct slot *(com)* 0045
process photography *(pre)* 2127
process red *(gen)* 3529
process white *(gen)* 3539

process work *(pri)* 2692
process yellow *(gen)* 3567
production press *(pri)* 2693
program *(com)* 0480
program defaults *(com)* 0504
programmer *(com)* 0449
programming *(com)* 0450
programming language *(com)* 0451
progressive JPEG *(int)* 1294
progressive proofs/progs *(pre)* 2215
projection mapping *(com)* 0651
proJPEG *(int)* 1294
promotion *(gen)* 3671
promotional books/edition *(gen)* 3876
promotion copies *(gen)* 3875
prompt *(com)* 0452
proof *(gen)* 3749
proof correction marks *(gen)* 3750
proof corrections *(gen)* 3751
proof(ing) press *(pre)* 2216
proofing *(gen)* 3752
proofing chromo *(pap)* 2542
proofreader *(gen)* 3753
proofreader's marks *(gen)* 3754
propeller symbol *(com)* 1026
property *(com)* 0453
proportional (letter) spacing *(typ)* 1895
proportionality failure *(pri)* 2694
proprietary *(gen)* 3629
proprietary system *(gen)* 3585
protocol *(com)* 0984
prove *(pre)* 2217
provider *(int)* 1143
pseudoclass *(int)* 1295
pseudonymous *(gen)* 3877
public domain *(gen)* 3630
publicity face *(typ)* 1769
publisher *(gen)* 3878
publisher's binding *(fin)* 3179
publisher's cloth *(fin)* 3410
publisher's imprint *(gen)* 3838
publisher's ream *(pap)* 2447
puck *(com)* 0232
puff *(gen)* 3672
pull *(gen)* 3749
pull-down menu *(com)* 0942
pulling *(pri)* 2672
pull out *(fin)* 3279
pull-out section *(gen)* 3879
pull-processing *(pho)* 1456
pull quote *(gen)* 3983
pull (sheet) *(pri)* 2695
pull (technology) *(int)* 1208
pull test *(fin)* 3328
pulp *(pap)* 2397
pulp board *(pap)* 2543
pulpwood *(pap)* 2398
punch register *(pre)* 2210
punctuation mark *(typ)* 1626
punctuation space *(typ)* 1709
pure *(pap)* 2553
purity *(gen)* 3540
push button *(com)* 0985
pushout *(fin)* 3240

push-processing *(pho)* 1457
Push (technology) *(int)* 1208
put down/up *(typ)* 1896
put to bed *(pri)* 2992

QA *(gen)* 3756
qq.v. *(gen)* 3755
quad (1) *(pap)* 2448
quad (2) *(typ)* 1710
quad center *(typ)* 1897
quadding *(typ)* 1710
quad folder *(fin)* 3329
quad left *(typ)* 1898
quad middle *(typ)* 1897
quadracolor *(pre)* 2128
quadrata *(typ)* 1775
quad right *(typ)* 1899
quality control *(gen)* 3631
quarter binding *(fin)* 3180
quarter-bound *(fin)* 3180
quarternion *(gen)* 3880
quartertone *(pri)* 2065
quarto/4to *(pap)* 2449
query *(gen)* 3757
quick printing *(pri)* 2632
quick-set inks *(pri)* 2819
QuickDraw *(com)* 0986
QuickTime *(com)* 0806
QuickTimeVR *(com)* 0807
quire (1) *(pap)* 2450
quire (2) *(fin)* 3330
quires/quire stock *(fin)* 3331
quirewise *(fin)* 3332
Quit *(com)* 0987
quotation marks *(typ)* 1627
quotations *(gen)* 3984
quotes (1) *(typ)* 1627
quotes (2) *(gen)* 3984
q.v. *(gen)* 3755
qwerty *(com)* 0233

R & D *(gen)* 3623
rack-jobbing distribution *(gen)* 3668
radial fill *(com)* 0652
radiation shield *(com)* 0174
radio button *(com)* 0924
rag content *(pap)* 2315
ragged *(typ)* 1903
rag paper/pulp *(pap)* 2316
RAID *(com)* 0104
raised bands *(fin)* 3181
raised cap(ital) *(typ)* 1900
raised dot *(typ)* 1628
raised initial *(typ)* 1901
raised period *(typ)* 1628
raised point *(typ)* 1628
RAM *(com)* 0068
RAM cache *(com)* 0065
RAM chip *(com)* 0070
RAM disk *(com)* 0066
random access *(com)* 0067

random access memory *(com)* 0068
random proof *(pre)* 2224
ranged left/right *(typ)* 1903
ranged/ranging figures *(typ)* 1966
RA paper sizes *(pap)* 2451
raster image file format *(com)* 0461
raster image *(com)* 0768
raster image processor *(pre)* 2218
raster(ization) *(com)* 0175
rate determining factor *(gen)* 3633
Raw *(com)* 0454
raytracing *(com)* 0653
RDF *(gen)* 3633
readability *(typ)* 1902
reader *(pre)* 2129
reader's spread *(gen)* 3920
reading gravity *(gen)* 4057
read only *(com)* 1059
read-only memory *(com)* 0069
read/write head *(com)* 0103
real-time *(com)* 0455
RealAudio *(int)* 1296
Réale *(typ)* 1783
RealMedia *(int)* 1296
RealVideo *(int)* 1296
ream *(pap)* 2452
reboot *(com)* 0988
rebuild desktop *(com)* 0989
receptivity *(pri)* 2293
recessed cords *(fin)* 3182
recess printing *(pri)* 2884
reciprocity failure *(pho)* 1536
reciprocity law *(pho)* 1537
record *(com)* 0456
recorder element *(com)* 0260
rectangle tool *(com)* 0654
recto *(gen)* 3881
recycled paper *(pap)* 2317
red *(gen)* 3541
Red Book *(com)* 0145
red lake C *(pri)* 2820
red under gilt edges *(fin)* 3479
redraw rate *(com)* 0769
reduced instruction set computing *(com)* 0032
reducer (1) *(pri)* 2821
reducer (2) *(pho)* 1458
reduction glass *(com)* 0605
reduction tool *(com)* 0605
redundant array of independent disks *(com)* 0104
reel-fed *(pri)* 2747
reel gold *(fin)* 3480
reference colors *(gen)* 3542
reference mark *(typ)* 1629
references *(gen)* 3758
refining *(pap)* 2318
reflectance *(gen)* 3543
reflected light reading *(pho)* 1538
reflection copy *(pre)* 2130
reflection tool *(com)* 0655
reflective artwork *(pre)* 2130
reflex copy *(pre)* 2131
reflow *(gen)* 3985
refraction *(gen)* 3544

refractive index *(gen)* 3545
refresh rate *(com)* 0176
registered design *(gen)* 3634
register marks *(pre)* 2132
register, registration *(pri)* 2696
register ribbon *(pri)* 3183
register sheet *(pri)* 2697
register table *(pre)* 2219
registration color *(com)* 0770
registration marks *(pre)* 2132
registration table *(pre)* 2219
reinforced binding *(fin)* 3184
reinforced signatures *(fin)* 3185
relational database *(com)* 0656
relative humidity *(gen)* 3635
relative URL *(int)* 1209
release version *(com)* 0457
relief block *(pri)* 3025
relief map *(gen)* 4148
relief offset *(pri)* 3016
relief plate *(pri)* 3026
relief printing *(pri)* 3027
relief stamping *(fin)* 3009
remainders *(gen)* 3876
removable media *(com)* 0105
removes *(gen)* 3986
render(ing) *(com)* 0657
replenisher *(pho)* 1459
reportage *(pho)* 1401
repped *(pap)* 2400
reprint *(gen)* 3882
repro (1) *(pri)* 2133
repro (2) *(pre)* 2134
repro camera *(pre)* 2126
reproduction camera *(pre)* 2126
reproduction copy *(pre)* 2134
reproduction proof *(pre)* 2134
reproduction pull *(pre)* 2134
reproduction ratio *(gen)* 4149
reproduction size *(gen)* 4149
reprographic printing *(pre)* 2135
reprography *(gen)* 3636
repro proof *(pre)* 2134
repro pull *(pre)* 2134
request *(int)* 1210
resample *(com)* 0771
rescale *(com)* 0772
rescreened halftone *(pre)* 2066
ResEdit *(com)* 0458
resident font *(com)* 0874
resin *(pri)* 2822
resin-coated paper *(pho)* 1460
resist *(pri)* 2698
resolution *(com)* 0773
resolving power *(pho)* 1461
resource (1) *(com)* 0990
resource (2) *(com)* 0588
resource (3) *(com)* 0991
resource fork *(com)* 0992
response *(com)* 0317
rest in pro(portion) *(gen)* 4150
restart *(com)* 0988
restore (1) *(com)* 0722
restore (2) *(com)* 0459
result code *(com)* 0948
reticulation *(pho)* 1462
retouching *(gen)* 4151
retransfer *(pri)* 2955

retree *(pap)* 2319
retree copy *(pri)* 2699
retroussage *(pri)* 2885
retting *(pap)* 2399
Return key *(com)* 0234
returns *(gen)* 3883
reversal developing *(pho)* 1463
reversal film *(pho)* 1464
reversal processing *(pho)* 1463
reverse b to w *(typ)* 1904
reversed calf *(fin)* 3412
reversed type *(gen)* 4058
reverse image *(gen)* 3546
reverse indent *(typ)* 1862
reverse l to r *(typ)* 4041
reverse out type *(gen)* 4058
reverse P *(typ)* 1560
reverse printing *(pri)* 2559
reverse reading *(pre)* 2232
reverse type *(gen)* 4058
reversing *(pri)* 2886
revise *(pre)* 2220
revised edition *(gen)* 3884
RGB *(gen)* 3547
RH *(gen)* 3635
rhodamine *(pri)* 2823
ribbed paper *(pap)* 2400
rich black *(pri)* 2824
rich text format *(com)* 0460
rider roller *(pri)* 2700
RIFF *(com)* 0461
rifle stock *(pho)* 1359
right-aligned *(typ)* 1903
right-angle fold *(fin)* 3333
right justified *(typ)* 1903
right indent *(typ)* 1905
right reading *(pre)* 2221
right side *(pap)* 2271
ringflash *(pho)* 1539
RIP (1) *(pre)* 2218
RIP (2) *(gen)* 4150
RISC *(com)* 0032
river *(typ)* 1906
roan *(fin)* 3411
robot *(int)* 1211
roll (1) *(gen)* 3885
roll (2) *(com)* 0658
roll (3) *(fin)* 3481
roller *(pri)* 2704
roller stripping *(pri)* 2825
roller train *(pri)* 2823
roll-fed *(pri)* 2747
roll film *(pho)* 1465
rollover *(int)* 1297
roll set curl *(pap)* 2320
roll stand *(pap)* 2321
roll-to-roll printing *(pri)* 2701
roll-to-sheet *(pri)* 2702
roll-up *(pri)* 2703
ROM *(com)* 0069
roman notation *(gen)* 3759
roman numerals *(gen)* 3760
roman (type) *(typ)* 1978
root directory *(com)* 0462
root level *(com)* 0462
ROP (1) *(pri)* 2687
ROP (2) *(pri)* 2707
rosette(s) *(pre)* 2018
rosin *(pap)* 2322
rotary press *(pri)* 2705
rotation tool *(com)* 0659
rotogravure *(pri)* 2887

rough *(gen)* 4059
rough calf *(fin)* 3412
rough draft *(gen)* 3713
rough etch *(pri)* 2706
rough gilt *(fin)* 3482
roughness map *(com)* 0660
rough proof/pull *(pre)* 2222
round dot *(pre)* 2020
rounded and backed *(fin)* 3186
routine *(com)* 0463
royalty-free *(gen)* 3582
RRED *(pre)* 2221
RREU *(pre)* 2221
RTF *(com)* 0460
rubber sheeting *(com)* 0610
rubber stereo *(pri)* 3028
rub-down lettering *(gen)* 4170
rub-off *(pri)* 2827
rub-off lettering *(gen)* 4170
rub-ons *(gen)* 4170
rubric *(gen)* 3886
ruby *(typ)* 1666
Rubylith *(pre)* 2223
rule *(gen)* 4060
rule, double *(gen)* 4022
rule, parallel *(gen)* 4054
ruler *(com)* 0661
ruler guide *(com)* 0662
ruler origin *(com)* 0626
ruling machine *(pri)* 2986
run *(pri)* 2682
runaround *(typ)* 1912
run back *(typ)* 1907
run chart *(gen)* 4161
run down *(typ)* 1908
run-in heading *(gen)* 3987
run-in sheets *(pri)* 2709
runners *(typ)* 1913
running feet *(gen)* 3966
running foot *(gen)* 3954
running head(line) *(gen)* 3966
running text *(typ)* 1914
running title *(gen)* 3966
run of paper (1) *(pri)* 2687
run-of-paper (2) *(gen)* 3673
run of press *(pri)* 2707
run on (1) *(pri)* 3064
run on (2) *(typ)* 1909
run on chapters *(typ)* 1910
run out and indented *(typ)* 1911
run ragged *(typ)* 1903
run round *(typ)* 1912
run-through work *(pri)* 2987
run up *(pri)* 2708
run-up spine *(fin)* 3483
rush changes *(gen)* 3761
russia cowhide *(fin)* 3413
russia leather *(fin)* 3414

sabattier effect *(pho)* 1466
sad Mac icon *(com)* 0993
saddle-sewn *(fin)* 3334
saddle-stitched *(fin)* 3335
saddleback book *(fin)* 3187
safelight *(pho)* 1526
safety paper *(pap)* 2544

sale or return *(gen)* 3883
same disk backup *(com)* 0720
same size *(gen)* 4152
sample *(com)* 0774
sample size *(com)* 0464
sampler (1) *(com)* 0235
sampler (2) *(pri)* 3674
sampling *(com)* 0774
sans serif *(typ)* 1770
sarsanet *(fin)* 3415
satin finish *(pap)* 2545
satin white *(pap)* 2546
saturation *(gen)* 3548
save *(com)* 0465
save as *(com)* 0466
Save dialog box *(com)* 0994
save out *(gen)* 4058
sawtooth *(com)* 3044
SC *(typ)* 1983
sc. *(gen)* 3762
scalable font *(com)* 0872
scalar processor architecture
    (com) 0033
scale *(gen)* 4152
scale an animation *(com)* 0808
scale drawing *(gen)* 4153
scaling text *(typ)* 1865
scamp *(gen)* 4059
scan dot *(com)* 0280
scan(ning) *(pre)* 2136
scanned image *(pre)* 2137
scanner *(com)* 0281
scanner, desktop *(com)* 0275
scanner, drum *(pre)* 2111
scanner, flatbed *(pre)* 2115
scan plates *(pri)* 2888
s caps *(typ)* 1983
scatter diagram *(gen)* 4155
scatter proof *(pre)* 2224
school edition *(gen)* 3887
scoop *(pho)* 1540
scorcher *(pri)* 3029
score (2) *(com)* 0663
score (1)/scoring *(fin)* 3336
scraperboard *(gen)* 4156
scratch comma *(typ)* 1630
scratch pad *(gen)* 4157
scratch (space) *(com)* 0106
screamer *(gen)* 3763
screen (1) *(com)* 0165
screen (2) *(pre)* 2045
screen (3) *(pri)* 3045
screen angle *(pre)* 2067
screen blanker *(com)* 0468
screen capture *(com)* 0467
screen clash *(pre)* 2061
screen distance *(pre)* 2068
screen dump *(com)* 0467
screened print *(pre)* 2075
screen filter *(com)* 0174
screen font *(com)* 0834
screen frequency *(pre)* 2069
screen grab *(com)* 0467
screening *(pre)* 2076
screenless printing *(pre)* 2083
screen, linear *(pre)* 2020
screen marks *(pri)* 3043
screen negative *(pre)* 2070
screen positive *(pre)* 2071
screen printing *(pri)* 3046
screen process work *(pre)* 2072

screen resolution *(pre)* 2073
screen ruling *(pre)* 2073
screen saver *(com)* 0468
screen shot *(com)* 0467
screen size *(com)* 0165
screen tester *(com)* 2074
screen tint/tone *(pre)* 2046
screen type *(pre)* 2020
scribing *(pri)* 2710
scrim (1) *(fin)* 3401
scrim (2) *(pho)* 1541
script(ing) (1) *(com)* 0469
script (2) *(typ)* 1771
Scripte *(typ)* 1783
scroll (1) *(gen)* 3888
scroll(ing) (2) *(com)* 0995
scroll arrow *(com)* 0996
scroll bar *(com)* 0997
scroll box *(com)* 0998
SCSI *(com)* 0236
SCSI bus *(com)* 0237
SCSI chain *(com)* 0238
SCSI device *(com)* 0239
SCSI ID (number) *(com)* 0240
SCSI partition *(com)* 0101
SCSI port *(com)* 0241
SCSI terminator *(com)* 0242
scuffing *(pap)* 2323
scum(ming) *(pri)* 2956
SDK *(com)* 0481
SEA *(com)* 0724
seal *(fin)* 3416
search and replace *(com)* 0664
search engine *(com)* 0665
search path *(com)* 0470
search tool *(int)* 1212
SECAM *(com)* 0177
secondary binding *(fin)* 3188
secondary color *(pri)* 2828
second cover *(pri)* 3065
section (1) *(com)* 0666
section (2) *(fin)* 3337
section (3) *(typ)* 1631
section-sewn book *(fin)* 3338
sector *(com)* 0107
sector interleave factor *(com)* 0094
secure area *(int)* 1213
see copy *(gen)* 3764
see-through *(pap)* 2297
seek time *(com)* 0108
segment *(com)* 0471
select(ing) *(com)* 0472
selectasine *(pri)* 3047
selection marquee *(com)* 0473
selection rectangle *(com)* 0473
selector *(com)* 0474
self ends *(fin)* 3189
self-extracting archive *(com)* 0724
self wrapper/cover *(fin)* 3190
semiconcealed cover *(fin)* 3191
semi-uncial *(typ)* 1756
semi-yapp *(fin)* 3192
sensitize *(pho)* 3549
separate *(gen)* 3889
separation *(pre)* 2161
separation artwork *(pre)* 2138
separation filters *(pre)* 2139
separation guide *(pho)* 1542
separator *(typ)* 1632

sepia *(gen)* 3550
sepia toning *(pho)* 1467
serial (1) *(com)* 0034
serial (2) *(gen)* 3890
serial flash *(pho)* 1524
serial interface *(com)* 0243
serial line Internet protocol *(int)* 1095
serial port *(com)* 0244
series *(typ)* 1750
serif *(typ)* 1979
serigraphy *(pri)* 3048
server *(com)* 0318
server-side *(com)* 0319
server-side image map *(int)* 1214
service bureau *(pre)* 2225
service provider *(int)* 1151
set (1) *(typ)* 1711
set (2) *(typ)* 1812
set and hold *(pri)* 2711
setback *(pri)* 2712
set close *(typ)* 1915
set flush *(typ)* 1916
setoff *(pri)* 3066
setoff reel *(pri)* 3067
set size *(typ)* 1712
set solid *(typ)* 1917
set-top *(int)* 1096
set width *(typ)* 1712
sewing *(fin)* 3339
sewn book *(fin)* 3340
sexto-decimo *(gen)* 3892
sexto/6to *(pap)* 2453
SGML *(int)* 1305
sgraffito *(pri)* 3030
shade *(pri)* 2829
shaded letter (1) *(typ)* 1773
shaded letter (2) *(typ)* 1772
shading *(com)* 0667
shadow (area) *(gen)* 3551
shadow font *(typ)* 1773
shared disk *(com)* 0109
shareware *(com)* 0475
sharpen edges *(com)* 0764
sharpen(ing) *(com)* 0775
sharpness *(pho)* 1402
sheet *(pap)* 2324
sheeter *(pap)* 2401
sheet-fed (press) *(pri)* 2714
sheet proof *(pri)* 2626
sheet stock *(fin)* 3331
sheetwise *(pri)* 2715
sheet work *(pri)* 2713
shelf back *(fin)* 3193
shift-click(ing) *(com)* 1060
Shift key *(com)* 0245
shift lens *(pho)* 1357
shiners *(pap)* 2425
shingle *(fin)* 3259
shingling *(fin)* 3259
shining *(fin)* 3341
shining-up table *(pre)* 2219
Shocked *(int)* 1298
Shockwave *(int)* 1299
shoes *(pri)* 3194
shopping cart *(int)* 1223
short and *(typ)* 1556
short-focus lens *(pho)* 1360
short grain *(pap)* 2391
short ink *(pri)* 2830
short page *(gen)* 3988

short ream *(pap)* 2454
shoulder (1) *(typ)* 1980
shoulder (2) *(fin)* 3195
shoulder-heads *(gen)* 3989
shoulder-notes *(gen)* 3990
show side *(pri)* 3417
show-through *(pap)* 2297
shrink wrap(ping) *(gen)* 4178
shuffling *(com)* 0668
shut down *(com)* 0035
shutter *(pho)* 1361
shutter priority *(pho)* 1362
shutter speed *(pho)* 1363
sic *(gen)* 3765
sidebar *(pho)* 3917
sidebearing *(typ)* 1713
side gluing *(fin)* 3196
side-heads *(gen)* 3992
side notes *(gen)* 3991
side-sewing *(fin)* 3342
side sorts *(typ)* 1633
side-stitch/stab *(fin)* 3343
sides *(fin)* 3197
sidewiring *(fin)* 3343
siding *(fin)* 3198
signature (1) *(pri)* 2716
signature (2) *(int)* 1122
signature rotary *(pri)* 3031
signature title *(gen)* 3891
signet *(fin)* 3199
silhouette *(gen)* 4099
silkscreen printing *(pri)* 3049
silurian *(pap)* 2547
silver nitrate *(pho)* 1468
silverprint *(pho)* 1469
SIMM *(com)* 0070
Simple Mail Transfer Protocol *(int)* 1097
simplex *(pri)* 2717
simplex decal *(pri)* 2594
simplified geometry *(com)* 0669
single-color press *(pri)* 2719
Single in-line memory module *(com)* 0070
single lens reflex (camera) *(pho)* 1364
single-line halftone *(pre)* 2077
single printing *(pri)* 2718
single quotes *(gen)* 3766
single-sided floppy disk *(com)* 0087
singleton *(int)* 1300
sinkage *(gen)* 3993
sit *(com)* 0723
sitemap *(int)* 1301
sixteen sheet *(gen)* 3675
sixteenmo/16mo *(gen)* 3892
sixty-fourmo/64mo *(gen)* 3893
size *(pap)* 2402
sizing (1) *(pap)* 2326
sizing (2) *(gen)* 4158
skeleton black *(pri)* 2831
skew(ing) *(com)* 0670
skewings *(fin)* 3484
skin *(com)* 0671
skinny *(pre)* 1998
skylight *(pho)* 1543
slab serif *(typ)* 1774
slash *(typ)* 1634
slave unit *(pho)* 1544
slice *(pap)* 2403

slide *(pho)* 1417
SLIP *(int)* 1095
slipcase *(gen)* 3894
slip page *(gen)* 3274
slip proof *(gen)* 3274
slips *(fin)* 3200
slip-sheeting *(pri)* 3061
slipsheeting *(pri)* 3068
slit *(pri)* 3069
slitter *(fin)* 3344
sloped roman/type *(typ)* 1981
slot *(com)* 0044
slug (1) *(typ)* 1982
slug (2) *(gen)* 3994
slur *(pri)* 2720
slurry *(pap)* 2405
slushing *(pap)* 2404
small ad *(gen)* 3654
small capitals/caps *(typ)* 1983
small computer system
  interface *(com)* 0236
small pica *(typ)* 1714
smart quotes *(typ)* 1635
smash(ing) *(fin)* 3201
smoothing *(com)* 0776
smoothness *(pap)* 2327
smooth point *(com)* 0476
smooth washed *(fin)* 3418
SMPTE *(com)* 0178
SMTP *(int)* 1097
Smyth sewn *(fin)* 3202
snail mail *(gen)* 3637
snap to *(com)* 0672
snoot *(pho)* 1545
snowflaking *(pri)* 2957
socialware *(com)* 0477
Society of Motion Picture and
  Television Engineers *(com)*
  0178
socket *(int)* 1215
soft *(pho)* 1403
softback edition *(gen)* 3895
softback *(fin)* 3169
soft copy (1) *(com)* 0478
soft copy (2) *(com)* 0479
soft copy (3) *(typ)* 1813
soft cover *(fin)* 3169
soft dot *(pre)* 2078
soft focus *(pho)* 1546
soft-sized *(pap)* 2328
software *(com)* 0480
Software Developers Kit
  (com) 0481
solarize *(gen)* 3552
solid *(pri)* 2832
solid matter *(typ)* 1917
solidus *(typ)* 1634
solus position *(gen)* 3676
SONET *(com)* 1098
sophisticated *(fin)* 3345
sort (1) *(com)* 0673
sort (2) *(typ)* 1636
sorts *(typ)* 1571
source (1) *(com)* 0482
source (2) *(com)* 1061
source code *(int)* 1302
source document (1) *(com)*
  0482
source document (2) *(pre)*
  2140
source volume *(com)* 0482
space *(typ)* 1715

spacer *(int)* 1303
spam(ming) *(int)* 1123
SPARC *(com)* 0033
special character *(typ)* 1637
special sorts *(typ)* 1638
spec(ification) *(gen)* 4061
Specifications for Web Offset
  Publications *(pre)* 2226
specimen book *(gen)* 3698
specimen page *(gen)* 3699
specimen sheet *(typ)* 1814
spectral response *(pho)* 1470
spectral sensitivity *(pho)* 1470
spectrum *(gen)* 3553
specular highlight *(pre)* 2079
specular map *(com)* 0674
specular reflectance *(gen)*
  3554
spell(ing) checker *(com)* 0675
SPH *(pri)* 2721
spherical aberration *(pho)*
  1365
spherical map(ping) *(com)*
  0676
spider *(int)* 1216
spike suppressor *(com)* 0246
spine *(fin)* 3203
spinner *(gen)* 3677
spiral binding *(fin)* 3204
spirex binding *(fin)* 3204
splayed M *(typ)* 1984
spline *(com)* 0677
split boards *(fin)* 3205
split dash *(gen)* 4062
split-duct printing *(pri)* 2722
split fountain *(pri)* 2722
split fraction *(typ)* 1639
split rule *(gen)* 4062
spoils *(pap)* 2329
spool/spooler *(com)* 0483
spooling *(com)* 0483
spot color *(pri)* 2723
spot glue *(fin)* 3206
spotlight (1) *(com)* 0678
spotlight (2) *(pho)* 1547
spotting *(pho)* 1471
spot varnishing *(pri)* 3070
spray powder *(pri)* 3071
spread (1) *(gen)* 3940
spread (2) *(pre)* 2080
spreadsheet *(com)* 0679
sprinkled calf *(fin)* 3419
sprinkled edges *(fin)* 3485
square back (book) *(fin)* 3112
square capitals *(typ)* 1775
square corner tool *(com)* 0680
square dot *(com)* 2081
squared(-up) halftone *(pre)*
  2082
square folding *(fin)* 3346
squares *(fin)* 3207
square serif *(typ)* 1774
squash *(pri)* 2806
squeegee *(pri)* 3050
SRA paper sizes *(pap)* 2455
S/S *(gen)* 4152
SSL *(int)* 1304
stabbing (1) *(fin)* 3347
stabbing (2) *(fin)* 3348
stabilization paper *(pho)* 1472
stacking order *(com)* 0681
staging out *(pri)* 2726

stained edges *(fin)* 3439
staircasing *(com)* 0726
stairstepping *(com)* 0726
stamp (1) *(typ)* 1640
stamp (2) *(fin)* 3486
stamping *(typ)* 1815
stamping die *(fin)* 3486
standalone (system) *(com)*
  0036
standard character set *(com)*
  1572
Standard Generalized Markup
  Language *(int)* 1305
standing matter *(pre)* 2227
standing time *(gen)* 3623
standing type *(pre)* 2227
stapling *(fin)* 3349
star *(typ)* 1641
starburst filter (1) *(pho)* 1548
starburst (2) *(com)* 0682
star network *(com)* 0320
star signature *(fin)* 3350
start *(fin)* 3208
start bit *(com)* 0321
start time *(com)* 0683
start-of-print line *(pri)* 2724
startup *(com)* 0999
startup disk *(com)* 0110
startup document *(com)* 0825
state of the art *(gen)* 3583
static RAM *(com)* 0054
stationery *(com)* 0484
stationery binding *(fin)* 3143
status bar *(com)* 1000
steel engraving *(pri)* 2889
stem *(typ)* 1985
stencil *(pri)* 3051
step and repeat *(com)* 0684
step index *(fin)* 3220
step tablet *(pho)* 1505
step wedge *(pho)* 1505
stereo(type) *(pri)* 3032
stereography *(pho)* 1404
stet *(gen)* 3767
sticking *(pri)* 2725
stickup initial *(typ)* 1901
stiff leaves *(fin)* 3209
stiffened and cut flush *(fin)*
  3262
stigmatypy *(typ)* 1918
stilted covers *(fin)* 3210
stipple engraving *(pri)* 2890
stitch(ing) *(fin)* 3211
stochastic screening *(pre)*
  2083
stock (1) *(pap)* 2330
stock (2) *(pap)* 2405
stock sizes *(pap)* 2456
stop *(pho)* 1366
stop bit *(com)* 0322
stop(ping) out *(pri)* 2726
storage *(com)* 0111
storage media *(com)* 0097
storage set *(com)* 0721
straight matter *(typ)* 1919
strap *(gen)* 3995
strawboards *(pap)* 2548
streak photography *(pho)*
  1405
streamer *(gen)* 3678
stress *(typ)* 1986
strike-on *(typ)* 1790

strike-on composition *(typ)* 1816
strike through (1) *(pri)* 2833
strike through (2) *(typ)* 1642
striking *(typ)* 1776
string *(com)* 0485
stripe pitch *(com)* 0156
stripping (1) *(pre)* 2148
stripping (2) *(pre)* 2141
stripping up as one *(pre)* 2228
strobe *(pho)* 1549
strobe effect *(com)* 0159
stroke (1) *(typ)* 1987
stroke (2) *(typ)* 1988
strongfold paper *(pap)* 2549
stub (1) *(typ)* 1920
stub (2) *(fin)* 3212
stuff *(pap)* 2405
stuffer *(gen)* 3679
style (1) *(com)* 0890
style (2) *(int)* 1306
style sheet *(com)* 0685
stylus *(com)* 0247
subhead(ing) *(gen)* 3996
subdirectory *(com)* 0486
subdomain *(int)* 1178
subject *(gen)* 4063
submenu *(com)* 0959
subscript *(typ)* 1610
subsidiaries *(gen)* 3806
subsidy publishing *(gen)* 3907
substance *(pap)* 2443
substrate *(pap)* 2331
subtitle *(gen)* 3997
subtractive colors *(gen)* 3555
suction feed *(pri)* 2727
suitcase file *(com)* 0875
sunk joints *(fin)* 3119
sunken cords *(fin)* 3213
sunken flexible *(fin)* 3214
super *(fin)* 3401
super-calender *(pap)* 2406
super-calendered paper *(pap)* 2407
superior character *(typ)* 1643
superior figure *(typ)* 1643
superior letter *(typ)* 1643
superscript *(typ)* 1644
SuperVGA *(com)* 0179
supplement *(gen)* 3897
support *(gen)* 3638
supra *(gen)* 3773
surf *(int)* 1194
surface *(com)* 0686
surface geometry *(com)* 0687
surface mapping *(com)* 0689
surface paper *(pap)* 2486
surface sizing *(pap)* 2408
surge suppressor *(com)* 0246
surge protector *(com)* 0246
surprinting *(pri)* 2659
SVGA *(com)* 0179
swash characters *(typ)* 1989
swatch *(gen)* 3556
swelled dash/rule *(gen)* 4064
SWF *(int)* 1307
SWOP *(pre)* 2226
SYLK *(com)* 0487
symbol *(gen)* 3700
symmetrical point *(com)* 0488
synchronous communication/ transmission *(com)* 0323

synchronous optical network *(int)* 1098
synopsis *(gen)* 3898
syntax *(com)* 0489
syntax checker *(com)* 0490
synthesized small caps *(typ)* 1983
sysop *(int)* 1152
system *(com)* 1001
system disk *(com)* 1002
system error *(com)* 0931
system extension *(com)* 0818
System Folder *(com)* 1003
system heap *(com)* 0057
system operator *(int)* 1152
system software *(com)* 0981

tab-delimit *(com)* 0492
tab index *(fin)* 3215
table (1) *(fin)* 3239
table (2) *(int)* 1217
tablet *(com)* 0277
tabloid *(gen)* 3998
tab stop *(com)* 0491
tabular work *(typ)* 1921
tabulate *(typ)* 1922
tack *(pri)* 2834
tag *(com)* 0493
tagged image file format *(com)* 0494
tail *(gen)* 3999
tail band *(fin)* 3129
tail-end hook *(pri)* 2902
tail margin *(gen)* 3999
tail-piece *(gen)* 4000
take *(typ)* 1817
take back *(typ)* 1923
take down *(fin)* 3216
take forward *(gen)* 3769
take in *(gen)* 3768
take over *(gen)* 3769
tall copy *(pri)* 2728
tangent line *(com)* 0688
tanned leather *(fin)* 3420
tape drive *(com)* 0112
taper *(com)* 0777
taper angle *(com)* 0778
Targa *(com)* 0495
target *(com)* 0496
target document *(com)* 0496
target printer *(com)* 0269
TCP, TCP/IP *(int)* 1101
TDMA *(com)* 0327
tear sheet *(gen)* 3639
tear-off menu *(com)* 1004
technical camera *(pho)* 1367
t.e.g. *(fin)* 3458
telecommunications *(com)* 0324
telephoto lens *(pho)* 1368
television service provider *(int)* 1153
Telnet *(int)* 1154
temp file *(com)* 0497
tempera *(gen)* 4159
template (1) *(gen)* 4160
template (2) *(com)* 0498

tenant *(int)* 1155
tensile strength *(pap)* 2332
terabyte *(com)* 0499
terminal *(com)* 0325
terminal emulation *(int)* 1100
terminator, terminating resistor *(com)* 0242
tertiary *(gen)* 3557
text (1) *(typ)* 1818
text (2) *(gen)* 4001
textbook *(gen)* 3899
text box *(com)* 0876
text chain *(com)* 0877
text editor *(com)* 0878
text field *(com)* 0879
text file *(com)* 0500
textile bindings *(fin)* 3421
text insertion bar *(com)* 0398
text inset *(com)* 0880
text letter *(typ)* 1777
text marker *(typ)* 1819
text matter *(typ)* 1716
text mode *(int)* 1063
text path *(com)* 0881
text reflow *(com)* 3985
text retrieval terminal *(typ)* 1820
text string *(com)* 0882
text tool *(com)* 0963
text type *(typ)* 1716
texture mapping *(com)* 0689
text wrap *(typ)* 1912
thermal ink jet *(com)* 0251
thermal printer *(com)* 0270
thermal transfer *(com)* 0271
thermography *(pri)* 2988
thermoplastic binder *(fin)* 3217
thesaurus *(gen)* 3900
thick space *(typ)* 1717
thickening *(pri)* 2835
thickness copy *(gen)* 3788
thin *(pho)* 1552
thin space *(typ)* 1718
third-party *(com)* 0226
thirty-two sheet *(gen)* 3680
thirty-twomo/32mo *(pap)* 2457
thread (1) *(int)* 1124
thread (2) *(fin)* 3339
threadless binding *(fin)* 3218
three-color black *(pri)* 2836
three-color (process) reproduction *(pri)* 2837
three-part binding *(fin)* 3180
three-quarter bound *(fin)* 3219
throughput (1) *(com)* 0326
throughput (2) *(pri)* 2729
through-the-lens meter *(pho)* 1369
throw in *(fin)* 3303
thrown clear *(fin)* 3351
thrown out *(fin)* 3352
thrust *(fin)* 3240
thumb edge *(gen)* 4002
thumb index *(fin)* 3220
thumbnail (1) *(gen)* 4065
thumbnail (2) *(com)* 0690
T1 *(int)* 1099
tied letters *(typ)* 1613
ties *(fin)* 3221
TIFF, TIF *(com)* 0494

pap: paper; *pre:* prepress; *pri:* printing; *fin:* finishing/binding;

UNIX *(com)* 1010
unjustified *(typ)* 1903
unmount *(com)* 0037
unopened *(fin)* 3228
unsewn binding *(fin)* 3218
unsharp masking *(pre)* 2088
untouched edges *(fin)* 3228
unwanted colors *(pre)* 2089
up vector *(com)* 0702
upgrade *(com)* 1011
upload *(com)* 0503
upper case *(typ)* 1990
upright format *(gen)* 4056
upstroke *(typ)* 1991
URI *(int)* 1219
URL *(int)* 1220
URL-encoded text *(int)* 1221
URN *(int)* 1222
USB *(com)* 0250
UseNet *(int)* 1156
user *(com)* 1012
user group *(com)* 1013
user interface *(com)* 0965
user-specified defaults *(com)* 0504
USM *(pre)* 2088
utility (program) *(com)* 0505
uudecode *(com)* 1014
u-v coordinates *(com)* 0699
UV light *(gen)* 3563

vacuum frame *(pre)* 2229
value *(gen)* 3503
Vandyke print *(pre)* 2230
vanity publishing *(gen)* 3907
vantage *(pri)* 2740
variable printing *(pri)* 2989
varnish *(fin)* 3358
varnishing *(fin)* 3359
vat machine *(pap)* 2368
vat paper *(pap)* 2409
VDT *(com)* 0165
VDU *(com)* 0165
vector *(com)* 0428
vegetable ink *(pri)* 2839
vegetable parchment *(pap)* 2550
vehicle *(gen)* 4138
vellum *(pap)* 2551
velocity *(com)* 0703
velox *(pre)* 2209
venetian types *(typ)* 1782
verbatim et literatim *(gen)* 3772
verification, verify *(com)* 0114
verso *(gen)* 4004
vertex *(com)* 0704
vertex animation *(com)* 0815
vertical alignment *(gen)* 4069
vertical bar pointer *(com)* 0442
vertical blanking interval *(com)* 0150
vertical camera *(pre)* 2143
vertical centring *(gen)* 4070
vertical justification *(gen)* 4070
vertical page *(gen)* 4071

very low frequency *(com)* 0157
VGA *(com)* 0182
vide *(gen)* 3773
Video (1) *(com)* 0816
video (2) *(gen)* 3774
video card *(com)* 0183
videoconferencing *(int)* 1102
video display terminal *(com)* 0165
video display unit *(com)* 0165
video fades *(com)* 0817
Video Graphic Array *(com)* 0182
video RAM *(com)* 0184
view angle *(gen)* 4077
view camera *(pho)* 1370
view distance *(com)* 0705
viewing conditions *(gen)* 3643
ViewMovie *(int)* 1309
viewpoint *(gen)* 4163
vignette *(gen)* 4164
vignetted dots *(pre)* 2090
virtual *(com)* 0506
virtual machine *(int)* 1279
virtual memory *(com)* 0071
Virtual Reality Modeling Language *(int)* 1310
virtual reality *(com)* 0506
virtual server *(int)* 1157
virtual shopping cart *(int)* 1223
virtual world *(com)* 1310
virus *(com)* 0507
virus protection utility *(com)* 0508
viscosity *(pri)* 2840
visible spectrum *(gen)* 3553
visual *(gen)* 4059
visual interface *(com)* 0956
visualize, visualizer *(gen)* 4072
viz. *(gen)* 3775
VLF *(com)* 0157
volume (1) *(com)* 0115
volume (2) *(gen)* 3908
volume bitmap *(com)* 0116
volume directory *(com)* 0369
volume rights *(gen)* 3909
voucher body *(gen)* 3910
Vox classification *(typ)* 1783
VRAM *(com)* 0184
VRML *(int)* 1310

W3 *(int)* 1227
W3C *(int)* 1161
waffling *(fin)* 3444
WAIS *(int)* 1158
walk off *(pri)* 2741
wall *(pri)* 2891
wallet edged *(fin)* 3229
wallet envelope *(pap)* 2341
wallet fold *(pri)* 3291
WAN *(com)* 0329
wanderer *(int)* 1211
wanted colors *(pre)* 2091
warehouse work *(pri)* 2742
warm boot *(com)* 0918
warm colors *(gen)* 3564

warping *(fin)* 3230
wash coating *(pap)* 2273
wash drawing *(pre)* 4165
washing up *(pri)* 2744
wash marks *(pri)* 2960
wash-out process *(pri)* 2743
water-based inks *(pri)* 2841
watercolor inks *(pri)* 2841
watercolor printing *(pri)* 2842
watered silk *(fin)* 3422
water finish *(pap)* 2410
waterleaf *(pap)* 2411
waterless lithography *(pri)* 2961
water lines *(pap)* 2342
watermark (1) *(pap)* 2343
watermark (2) *(int)* 1311
watermark (3) *(com)* 0780
water pan *(pri)* 2920
water streaks *(pri)* 2960
web (1) *(pap)* 2344
Web (2) *(int)* 1227
Web authoring *(int)* 1312
web break *(pri)* 2745
Web browser *(int)* 1167
Web Embedding Font Tool *(int)* 1313
web-fed *(pri)* 2747
Webmaster *(int)* 1160
web offset *(pri)* 2962
Web page *(int)* 1224
web (printing) press *(pri)* 2746
Web server *(int)* 1159
Web site *(int)* 1225
Web spider *(int)* 1216
wedding paper *(pap)* 2552
weft (1) *(pri)* 2963
WEFT (2) *(int)* 1313
weight (1) *(typ)* 1992
weight (2) *(pap)* 2444
well *(pri)* 2892
wet-on-wet printing *(pri)* 2844
wet pick *(pri)* 2748
wet plate *(pho)* 1475
wet printing process inks *(pri)* 2843
wet rub *(pap)* 2345
wet strength *(pap)* 2346
wet stripping *(pre)* 2231
wetting *(pri)* 2845
wetting agent *(pho)* 1476
wet trapping *(pri)* 2085
w.f. *(typ)* 1929
what you see is what you get *(com)* 1019
whipstitching *(fin)* 3360
white letter *(typ)* 1784
white light *(gen)* 3565
white line *(typ)* 1930
white-lined black letter *(typ)* 1758
white out (1) *(gen)* 4073
white out (2) *(typ)* 1931
whiteprint *(pre)* 2168
white space *(gen)* 4074
whole bound *(fin)* 3120
wide area Information Service *(int)* 1158
wide area network *(com)* 0259
wide-angle lens *(pho)* 1371
widget *(gen)* 3644
widow (line) *(gen)* 4005

X&**X**X*X*

Y*Y***Y**Y*Y*

Z*Z***Z**Z*Z*

0001 **analog computer** A computer that uses a physical variable such as voltage to process information or make calculations. → *3573 analog*

0002 **batch mode/processing** The processing of data in automated batches, as distinct from data that is processed as it is input (interactive mode, or "real-time"). For example, a spellchecker runs in batch mode when applied to a block of text, but not when applied to an individual word. An example of batch processing is when you apply a Photoshop "Action" to two or more files. → *0455 realtime; 0402 interactive mode*

0003 **BIOS** *abb.:* **basic input/output system** The code, usually residing on a chip placed on the motherboard of a computer, which handles basic hardware input and output operations, such as interactions with a keyboard or hard disk drive. → *0213 I/O*

0004 **bus** A path along which information or data is passed in a computer, or between one device and another.

0005 **CPU** *abb.:* **central processing unit** Referring to either the main microchip that performs a computer's core calculating functions (in other words, its brain), or, just as frequently, the box (which also holds all the other bits) in which the chip resides.

0006 **chip/microchip** The most essential computer component, consisting of a small piece of silicon impregnated with miniature electronic circuits. Chips provide the basis of computer processing functions as performed, for example, by CPUs and memory (RAM). → *0005 CPU; 0068 RAM*

0007 **clock speed/rate** The speed at which a computer's central processing unit (CPU) can process instructions. This is regulated by the pulses of a quartz crystal, the frequency of which is measured in megahertz (millions of cycles per second) — the more there are, the faster the computer. Clock speed determines the speed of such operations as screen redraw or RAM access. → *0005 CPU*

0008 **computer** An electronic device that can process data (usually binary) according to a predetermined set of variable instructions — a "program." → *0910 binary; 0911 binary code; 0518 application program*

0009 **coprocessor** A microprocessor chip that sits alongside your computer's main processing unit (CPU), and that carries out specific specialized functions, such as speeding up graphics display or handling data-intensive tasks such as math calculations. A coprocessor may sometimes be described by its specific function, for example, a "floating point unit" (FPU) or "math coprocessor," both of which carry out math calculations. The functions of some coprocessors may be integrated into the CPU. → *0005 CPU*

0010 **data bus** The path, or circuitry, along which data is transmitted by a processor, as distinct from the circuitry used by the processor to handle memory. → *0004 bus; 0059 memory*

0011 **data transfer rate** Strictly speaking, the speed at which data is transferred from one device to another, but generally referring to the transfer of data from a disk drive into computer memory (RAM) and measured, usually, in megabytes per second. → *0059 memory; 0420 megabyte; 0094 interleave ratio*

0012 **desktop computer** Those personal computers that not only perform all the necessary functions of desktop publishing, but will also fit on a real desktop. → *3684 desktop publishing*

0013 digital device Any piece of equipment that operates by means of instructions or signals represented by binary digits, such as a computer. → *1028 digital; 0914 bit*

0014 DIP switch Small switches on some hardware devices that are used to select an operating mode, such as giving the device a unique identity number when connected to others. → *0240 SCSI ID*

0015 DIP *abb.:* **dual in-line package** The particular way in which some chips are mounted — with two parallel rows of pins — so they can be plugged into a computer circuit board.

0016 IBM *abb.:* **International Business Machines** A major manufacturer of computing hardware. → *0017 IBM PC*

0017 IBM PC *abb.:* **IBM personal computer** Used to describe a PC made by IBM, but also often used as a generic term for any PC that is "IBM compatible" (usually meaning one that runs either Microsoft's "DOS" or "Windows" operating systems), thus distinguishing them from other computers, such as Apple Computer's "Macintosh" series. → *0016 IBM; 0020 Macintosh; 0975 MS-DOS; 1017 Windows*

0018 integrated circuit The electronic circuit embedded in a microchip.

0019 laptop (computer) A small, portable computer, as distinct from the larger "desktop" variety.

0020 Macintosh The brand name of Apple Computer, Inc's, line of personal computers (named after the variety of the apple fruit). The Macintosh was the first commercially available computer successfully to utilize the "graphical user interface" (GUI) pioneered by Xerox Corporation's Palo Alto Research Center (PARC), although the concept was first seen in Apple's unsuccessful "Lisa" computer. The Macintosh heralded the concept of "plug and play" computing, while the use of a GUI provided the platform for the software applications that gave rise to the phenomenon of "desktop publishing" (DTP), thus revolutionizing not only the graphic design profession, but the entire graphic arts industry — all in the space of 10 years. → *0966 Mac OS; 0956 GUI; 3684 desktop publishing*

0021 mainframe (computer) A large computer system used mainly to manage vast databases where simultaneous processing of transactions is required, such as in banks or insurance companies.

0022 megahertz (MHz) One million hertz (or cycles, occurrences, or instructions per second), often used as an indication (not necessarily accurate) of the speed of a computer's central processing unit (CPU), and thus sometimes referred to as "clock speed."

0023 mips *abb.:* **million instructions per second** Usually used in the context of processor speeds. → *0161 hertz; 0031 processor*

0024 nanosecond (ns) One billionth of a second, usually used in the context of measuring the speed of memory chips. The fewer ns, the faster.

0025 NuBus The "bus architecture" found mainly in older Macintosh computers, which provides "slots" for adding circuit boards such as video cards and accelerator cards. → *0004 bus; 0041 circuit board*

0026 open architecture The facility, in the design of a computer system, for unrestricted modification and improvement of the computer and its system. Macintosh computers are not "open" in as much as the ROM

0031 Processor showing a RAM chip

chip used as the basis of the operating system can only be used in non-Apple manufactured machines ("clones") under license.

0027 **path** (**3**) The route ("bus") taken by data as it travels along circuits from chip to chip or device to device.

0028 **PC** *abb.:* **personal computer** The name originally used to describe IBM PCs, but now used to describe any personal computer that is IBM compatible or that runs the Windows operating system. Distinct from computers running the Mac OS, although, strictly speaking, they are also personal computers.

0029 **port** A socket or sensor on a computer or device by which other devices are connected.

0030 **printer port** The socket via which a computer is connected to a printer or, on Macintosh computers, a network or modem.

0031 **processor** (**chip**) A silicon "chip," containing millions of micro "switches," which respond to binary electrical pulses, which performs specific functions in a computer, such as the "central processor" (CPU) and memory (RAM). Also known as a "microprocessor" or "microchip." → *0005 CPU; 0009 coprocessor; 0006 chip*

0032 **RISC** *abb.:* **reduced instruction set computing** A microprocessor that provides high-speed processing while requiring only a limited number of instructions. Distinct from "complex instruction set computing" (CISK), which requires more instructions and is thus slower.

0033 **SPARC** *abb.:* **scalar processor architecture** A powerful microprocessor developed by Sun Microsystems. Forms the basis of the UNIX operating system.

0034 **serial** (**1**) The process of transmitting data sequentially, or consecutively in a sequence, as opposed to simultaneously.

0035 **shut down** To switch off your computer in a safe manner, i.e., having first saved and closed any open files, ejected any disks, etc.

0036 **standalone** (**system**) The ability of a computer or system to operate independently of others, usually referring to one that is not networked or dependent on other devices.

0037 **unmount** To remove a volume (disk) from the desktop either by disconnecting or ejecting it. → *0078 disk*

0038 **workstation** (**1**) Any single computer, which may or may not be on a network, dedicated to one person's use. → *0039 workstation (2)*

0039 **workstation** (**2**) A powerful computer — often UNIX-based — that is typically used for CAD/CAM and 3D applications. → *1024 CAD/CAM*

0040 **accelerator board/card** A circuit board added to a computer, generally as an optional extra, to speed up various computer operations, either generally such as with the central processing unit (CPU), or specifically such as in some graphics tasks. → *0005 CPU; 0043 expansion board/card; 0041 circuit board*

0041 **circuit board** The support — made of fiberglass or pressboard — upon which chips and other electronic components are mounted. Components are usually linked to one another by connections that are stamped onto the board with metallic ink, which are called "printed circuit boards" (PC boards). The main board in your computer — bearing the CPU, ROM,

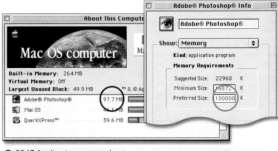

O *0047 Application memory heap*
O *0048 Application memory size*

and RAM chips — is called the **motherboard** or **logic board**. A board that plugs into an expansion slot is called an "add-on board" (or card). A board that plugs into another board is called a "daughterboard." ➔ *0042 daughterboard*; *0006 chip*

0042 **daughterboard** A circuit board that plugs into another board, such as the "motherboard" (the board containing the main circuitry and processors of a computer). ➔ *0041 circuit board*

0043 **expansion card/board** A circuit board added to a computer that allows you to extend its capabilities — an accelerator card, for example. ➔ *0041 circuit board*

0044 **expansion slot** The place in a computer where additional circuit boards can be plugged in. ➔ *0041 circuit board*; *0043 expansion card*

0045 **processor direct slot** (**PDS**) An expansion slot that connects to the CPU directly rather than indirectly through a "bus." ➔ *0004 bus*

0046 **address** (**I**) The number or code identifying the location of data in a computer's memory. An address can be "logical" — used when an instruction is executed — or "physical" — when the computer translates the logical address into a physical location on a disk drive, for example.

0047 **application memory** (**heap**) The portion of the computer's memory (RAM) occupied for use by an application when it is launched or opened. The application heap is reserved for use only by that application, and separates it from the memory reserved for other applications or the computer's operating system. ➔ *0981 operating system*; *0048 application memory size/partition*; *0068 RAM*

0048 **application memory size/partition** The amount of memory (RAM), measured in megabytes, reserved by an application when it is being used. ➔ *0047 application memory (heap)*; *0068 RAM*

0049 **backside cache** A dedicated chip for temporary storage of frequently accessed data. "Backside" means that the chip is connected directly to the main CPU of a computer, thus bypassing the speed limitations of the data transfer "bus" (the path along which data travels). ➔ *0051 cache*

0050 **buffer** An area of computer memory set aside for the storage or processing of data while it is in transit. The buffer can either be in RAM or on a hard disk — within your computer the buffer is called the "cache." Buffers are commonly used by output devices such as modems and printers, which are then able to process data more quickly, while at the same time freeing up your computer so you can keep on working. ➔ *0051 cache; 0068 RAM; 0483 spool*

0051 cache (pron.: kash) A small area of memory (RAM) set aside for the temporary storage of frequently accessed data. This has the effect of speeding up some computer operations — accessing font information, for example — since data accessed from RAM is processed much faster than that from disk. Cache can also be stored in a separate hardware chip that comes soldered to the motherboard of some computers and add-on circuit boards. ➔ *0068 RAM; 0050 buffer; 0049 backside cache*

0052 contiguous Adjacent, or next to; contiguous "space" is particularly important in the context of memory (RAM) as, in order to run, an application requires the amount of memory allocated to it to be joined together in one chunk — that is, while your computer may indicate that the amount of available memory is adequate to open a large application, you may find that, if you have opened and closed several applications during a session, the application will not run. This is because the memory has been gradually split into smaller chunks, so, in order to create enough "contiguous" memory, you will probably need to restart ("reboot") your computer. Contiguous space is also important for storing files on disk, for while data files can be split up into many pieces ("fragments") and still be usable, the more fragments there are, the longer it takes the disk drive "head" to find them. Therefore, files stored contiguously on disk will be accessed faster and will thus open more quickly. There are many commercial utilities for cleaning up the files on your hard disk and rearranging them (called optimizing or defragmenting). ➔ *0068 RAM; 0077 defragment; 0988 reboot*

0053 DIP SIMM A "high profile" (taller) SIMM chip. ➔ *0070 SIMM*

0054 DRAM Acronym for dynamic RAM (random access memory), pronounced "dee-ram." Memory that is only active while supplied by an electric current, and is thus lost when power is turned off. Generally referred to simply as RAM. The more expensive static RAM (SRAM) does not lose its memory in the absence of power. DRAM comes in the form of chips that plug into the motherboard of your computer. ➔ *0068 RAM*

0055 dual-inline memory module (**DIMM**) A standard type of computer memory (RAM) chip. ➔ *0068 RAM; 0059 memory; 0070 SIMM*

0056 EDO *abb.:* **extended data output** A RAM chip with fast access time.

0057 heap A part of RAM set aside exclusively for use on demand by a computer operating system (called **system heap**) or applications. ➔ *0047 application memory; 0068 RAM*

0058 main memory A term used to describe installed memory (RAM) to distinguish it from "virtual memory." ➔ *0068 RAM; 0071 virtual memory*

0059 memory The recall of digital data on a computer. Typically, this refers to either "dynamic RAM," the volatile "random access" memory that is emptied when a computer is switched off (data needs to be stored on media such as a hard disk for future retrieval), or ROM, the stable "read only" memory that contains unchanging data, for example, the basic start-up and initialization functions of some computers, such as Macintosh. As an analogy, think of your own memory — when you die, everything in your head is lost unless you write it down, thus "saving" it for posterity. "Memory" is often erroneously used to describe "storage," probably because both are measured in megabytes. ➔ *0068 RAM; 0069 ROM*

0060 out-of-memory message A message that tells you there is not enough memory (RAM) available to perform the task that you require. Typical out-of-memory messages relate to reasons such as the system heap being too small; having too many system files open (such as fonts); application heaps that may be set too small, or a particularly memory-intensive task (particularly those involving bitmapped images) exceeding available RAM. → *0047 application memory; 0057 heap*

0061 page (**3**) A contiguous segment of memory. → *0059 memory*

0062 PMMU *abb.:* **paged memory–management unit** A microchip on older Macintosh computers that enhances memory capabilities, such as enabling the use of virtual memory. The PMMU is integrated into the CPU of more modern computers. → *0005 CPU*

0063 PRAM (pron.: pee-ram) *abb.:* **parameter RAM** An area of memory — stored in a chip — in Macintosh computers that maintains basic settings such as time and date, even when it is switched off (unlike the memory provided by RAM, which is lost when the computer is switched off). The PRAM chip is provided with a continuous power supply from its own lithium battery.

0064 PRAM chip The hardware chip that stores parameter RAM. → *0063 PRAM; 0072 zapping the PRAM*

0065 RAM cache (pron.: ram-kash) A piece of RAM that stores the most recent actions you have carried out, so if you need them again they do not need to be retrieved from disk. → *0051 cache*

0066 RAM disk A feature provided by some operating systems or utility software whereby a part of memory (RAM) can be temporarily "tricked" into thinking that that particular part is a disk drive. Because the process of retrieving data from RAM is so much faster than from disk, operations performed by items — such as applications or documents — stored in a RAM "disk" will speed up. This "disk" is erased when you switch your computer off. → *0068 RAM*

0067 random access Digital data that can be retrieved at random, such as from a disk or from memory, as distinct from data that can only be retrieved sequentially, as from a tape.

0068 RAM *abb.:* **random access memory** The "working space" made available by the computer, into which some or all of an application's code is loaded and remembered while you work with it. However, an item is memorized in RAM only for as long as your computer is switched on, or until you save it to disk. The amount of memory is important, since not only do some graphics applications require substantial memory to operate, some specific tasks may demand even more. Operating system and application extensions also add to the demand on memory.

0069 ROM *abb.:* **read-only memory** Memory that can be read from, but not written to. As distinct from RAM, in which data can be written to memory but is lost when power to the computer is switched off.

0070 SIMM *abb.:* **Single in-line memory module** A computer chip that provides RAM (memory). → *0053 DIP SIMM; 0055 dual-inline memory module; 0068 RAM*

0071 virtual memory A technique of making memory (RAM) seem larger than it really is by using other means of storing data such as on a hard disk. This means that you can work with as much memory as you have disk space, but the trade-off for this luxury is speed — virtual memory is only as fast as the data transfer speed of the disk. Also called **scratch space** in some applications. ➔ *0506 virtual*

0072 zapping the PRAM The resetting of the parameter RAM (PRAM) on a Macintosh computer to its "factory" setting. You do this by holding down the Option-Command-P-R keys while restarting your computer. Date and time settings are not be affected. ➔ *0063 PRAM*

0073 access time The time taken by a disk drive to access data. This is measured as an average of the seek time (the time the drive head takes to find the data), and latency time (the time the data sector takes to rotate under the head). Also known as **average access time**. ➔ *0107 sector*

0074 allocation block The predefined, or "formatted," space on a hard disk where data files are stored. Only one file is permitted per allocation block, so if the file is small but the allocation block is large, space is wasted. Allocation blocks grow larger as disk capacity increases, therefore less storage is wasted if high capacity disks are divided into smaller "partitions." ➔ *0101 partition; 0089 formatting*

0075 block (**3**) A place, or area, regarded as a single unit, where data is stored either temporarily in memory or on a storage medium such as a hard disk. ➔ *0074 allocation block*

0076 cartridge, removable Storage media protected by a plastic casing so it can be transported from one drive to another. Strictly speaking, the term can apply to any removable media, whether magnetic or optical, but it generally excludes floppy disks. ➔ *0087 floppy disk*

0077 defragment(ing) The technique of joining together pieces of "fragmented" files — those that, due to a shortage of contiguous storage space on the disk, have been split into smaller pieces — so that they are easier for the drive heads to access, thus speeding up disk operations. The process is also known as optimizing. ➔ *0052 contiguous; 0099 optimize*

0078 disk A circular platter with a magnetic surface on which computer data is stored. Data is written to and read from the disk by a mechanism called a disk drive. Disks may be rigid (**hard disk**) or flexible (floppy disk), and may reside on a disk drive installed inside your computer (internal disk drive), in a device connected to your computer (external disk drive), or in a cartridge that can be transported between disk drives (removable disk). A disk drive may contain several "platters," but is referred to in the singular — "disk." Not to be confused with "disc," which is much the same thing, but uses optical rather than magnetic techniques to store data. There is also a third type of disk that combines both techniques and is called a magneto-optical disk (MO). ➔ *0129 disc; 0141 magneto-optical disk*

0079 disk crash A colloquialism describing the operating failure of a hard disk drive, preventing you from accessing data. This may be brought about by corruption of the disk's format (the way information is arranged on the disk), dirt or dust on the disk's surface, or failure of a mechanical part in the drive. If the former, repairs can sometimes be made with a disk maintenance utility, but in the latter case repair is unlikely and may result in complete loss of all your data. You should always regard a disk crash as being inevitable — not a question of "if" but "when" — and back up your data regularly. ➔ *0931 crash (1); 0078 disk; 0089 formatting*

0080 disk image A single file that represents an entire volume such as a floppy disk, hard disk, or CD-ROM, and which, when opened ("mounted"), can be used as though it were a separate disk. Disk images are typically used for making copies of "installer" disks, and also for creating partitions for recording data to CD-R discs (also called **software partitions** or **file partitions**). Not to be confused with an "image file," which is a picture file stored on disk. ➜ *0758* image file; *0101* partition

0081 disk/disc drive Often referred to simply as a drive, this is a hardware device that "writes" data to, or "reads" it from, a disk (or disc). A disk drive may contain several "platters" housed in a sealed unit (sometimes called a hard drive to distinguish it from other kinds), or it may be a device that reads disks (or discs) that are inserted into it. It may be installed inside your computer (internal disk drive) or it may be a remote device connected to your computer (external disk drive). ➜ *0129* disc; *0078* disk

0082 drive head The part of any kind of disk drive that extracts (reads) data from, and deposits (writes) data to, a disk or tape, for example. In hard drives, one read/write head is positioned above each side of every disk platter (a hard drive may consist of several platters). These move on rails over the surface of the platter, which rotates at high speed. ➜ *0081* disk drive

0083 erase An option in some dialog boxes to erase the selected disk, thus deleting everything on it.

0084 external (disk) drive Any disk drive connected to a computer that does not reside inside the computer's case. ➜ *0205* external device; *0081* disk/disc drive

0085 file allocation table (FAT) A method used by computer operating systems to keep track of files stored on a hard disk. ➜ *0086* file tag

0086 file tag Information relating to data stored on a disk, which, with the appropriate software, allows you to recover deleted files. "File tag" should not be confused with the term "tag," which is the formal name for a markup language formatting command, such as that used for HTML.

0087 floppy disk A flexible circular platter coated with a magnetic medium and housed in a plastic case, on which computer data is stored. Floppy disks are typically 3.5in diameter and may be single-sided (400K capacity, now more or less obsolete), double-sided (800K, also obsolete), or high density ('FDHD' — floppy disk, high density, 1.4MB). Also called diskettes, floppy disks are becoming less viable as a storage medium and will eventually disappear as modern computers are increasingly being built without floppy disk drives. ➜ *0081* disk drive

0088 floppy (disk) drive A hardware device for reading and writing data to and from floppy disks. Although internal floppy disk drives are standard on most computers built to date, the low storage capacity of floppy disks makes them less viable as a storage medium, and they will eventually disappear as computers are increasingly being built without floppy disk drives. ➜ *0087* floppy disk

0089 formatting The process of preparing a new disk so it can be used with a computer for organizing and storing data. When a disk is formatted, sectors, tracks, and empty directories are created. ➜ *0397* initialize; *0079* disk crash

0090 fragment(ed) The state of files stored on a hard disk when, over time, they become split into noncontiguous chunks, leaving only small areas of free space into which new data can be written. The consequence of this is

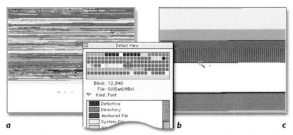

a   b   c

*0099 Optimize; 0090 Fragment; 0077 Defragment; Fragmented files on a disk (**a**), with detail (**b**) before being defragmented by optimizing (**c**).*

that new files are divided into smaller pieces so they will fit onto the disk; thus both the disk and the files on it are said to be fragmented. The result can be a dramatic increase in the time it takes to access data, since any files being accessed may be spread over several areas of the disk. Many applications are available that "defragment" disks by rearranging the files contiguously. → *0099 optimize; 0077 defragment*

0091 free space A memory block that is available for allocation — in other words, space on a disk that is free and ready for writing data to. → *0059 memory; 0075 block (3)*

0092 head crash The failure of a disk drive, sometimes caused by one of its read/write heads coming into contact with, and damaging, the surface of a platter. → *0103 read/write head; 0102 platter*

0093 high density A term that, particularly in relation to all things digital, invariably means more, thus better.

0094 interleave ratio The ratio between the numbers and the order of track sectors on a disk. Sectors that are numbered consecutively have a ratio of 1:1, while a ratio of 3:1 means the numbers run consecutively only in every third sector. This indicates how many times a disk needs to rotate so that all data in a single track is read; a computer with a slow data transfer rate requires a disk to spin more often so it has time to absorb all of the data in a track, thus a 3:1 interleave ratio requires a disk to rotate three times because it only reads every third sector. The fastest ratio is 1:1 because all the data in a track will be read in a single revolution of the disk. Also called **sector interleave factor**. → *0011 data transfer rate; 0107 sector*

0095 locked disk A removable or floppy disk that is write-protected and thus can only be read from.

0096 magnetic media/storage Any computer data storage system that uses a magnetic medium, such as disk, tape, or card, to store information. → *0078 disk*

0097 media (2) A plural term now accepted as a singular to describe the item itself on which digital data is stored, such as a floppy, hard, CD-ROM, etc., as distinct from the devices in which they are used. → *0078 disk*

0098 noncontiguous space Free space on a computer disk, which is broken up into small chunks, as distinct from being arranged contiguously. → *0052 contiguous*

0099 optimize/optimizing The technique of speeding up disk operations by using special "utility" software to shuffle files around and join together

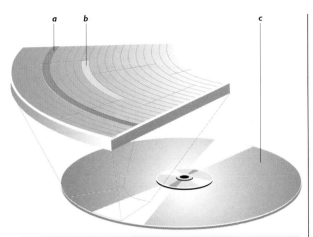

*0113 Track (**a**); 0107 Sector (**b**); 0102 Platter (**c**);*

those that, due to a shortage of contiguous storage space on the disk, have become fragmented (split into smaller pieces). This also creates contiguous areas of unused storage space on your drive, thus allowing files to be written to disk faster when you save them. ➜ *0052 contiguous; 0077 defragment*

0100 **parked** The state of a disk drive's read/write heads when they are at rest, important if the drive or cartridge is to be moved without damage to the disk.

0101 **partition(ing)** The division of a hard disk into smaller volumes, each of which behaves as if it were a separate disk. There are two kinds of partitions: real partitions (sometimes called **SCSI partitions**) in which you divide the disk up during formatting, and file partitions (also called **disk images**), which are large files created on an existing disk drive. ➜ *0080 disk image*

0102 **platter** A single, circular, magnetically coated metal disk that, usually with others, forms the storage medium of a hard disk drive.

0103 **read/write head** The part of a disk drive that "reads" data from, and "writes" data to, a disk. One read/write head is positioned above each side of every disk platter in a disk drive, which may consist of several platters. These move, on rails, over the surface of the platter, which rotates at speed. ➜ *0078 disk*

0104 **RAID** *abb.:* **redundant array of independent disks** A collection of hard disks that function as one system. They are often used for backing up data as well as processing vast amounts of data.

0105 **removable media** Hard disks or optical discs that can be ejected from their media, thus making it easier to transport large amounts of data between computers that are not networked, and to back up data.

0106 **scratch (space/disk)** Disk space that, not needed for normal data storage, has been set aside as "virtual memory" for temporary data storage by an application. ➜ *0071 virtual memory*

0107 **sector** A segment of a track on a disk, and the smallest contiguous space in which data can be stored, allowing space for, usually, 512 consecutive bytes. ➜ *0075 block (3)*

0108 **seek time** The time it takes for a disk head to move from whatever track it is on to whatever track you tell it to read next. ➜ *0073* *access time*

0109 **shared disk** Any hard disk attached to a networked computer that other computers on the network can access. ➜ *0308* *network*

0110 **startup disk** Any hard drive, floppy disk, zip disk, or CD disk containing an operating system and used to start up a computer. Also called a "boot disk." ➜ *0999* *startup*

0111 **storage** The preservation of data (on disk, tape, etc.) so that it can be accessed at a future date, as distinct from "memory" where data is in transit. ➜ *0059* *memory*

0112 **tape drive** A device used for copying data from a primary storage device, such as a hard disk, for backup archiving purposes. A tape drive uses magnetic tape housed in removable cartridges. Tape drives are not used for primary storage because the data is stored on them "sequentially" (in a linear form, from end to end), and cannot be accessed at random, as it can on disks. ➜ *0196* *DAT*

0113 **track** (**1**) The concentric "rings" circumscribing a "platter" in a hard disk drive, on which data is stored. Each track is divided into "sectors." ➜ *0102* *platter*; *0107* *sector*

0114 **verification/verify** The process of testing the integrity of data or the data blocks on a disk drive by repeatedly writing and reading data to the disk. ➜ *0358* *data*

0115 **volume** (**1**) A device or partition where data is stored — in other words, a disk tape or part of either.

0116 **volume bitmap** A record of the used blocks (represented by an "on" bit) and unused blocks ("off" bit) of a volume.

0117 **write-enable** To enable a computer drive or disk to receive ("write") data by "unlocking" it either by means of software or by a tab on the case of the disk. The opposite of write-protect. ➜ *0118* *write-protect*

0118 **write-protect** To protect a computer disk from being erased, accidentally or otherwise, or from contamination by viruses, by preventing any data from being written to it or deleted from it, although the contents can still be read. Some removable media is equipped with a small tab that, when moved to reveal a hole, write-protects the disk. Sliding it back again to fill the hole "write-enables" the disk so data can be added or deleted. ➜ *0117* *write-enable*

0119 **write/writing head** The part of a disk drive that retrieves (reads) data from, and deposits (writes) data to, a disk. One read/write head is positioned above each side of every disk platter (a hard drive may consist of several platters). These move, on rails, across the surface of the platter while the platter rotates at speed. ➜ *0081* *disk drive*

0120 **Blue Book** The document that specifies all parameters for Enhanced Music CD (CD Extra) interactive technology, a multisession CD that contains audio tracks in one session and a data track in the other. ➜ *0136* *Enhanced Music CD*

0121 **burn** (**2**) The process of writing data to optical media such as a CD-R disc. So called because the process involves literally burning small pits — the size of which determines a 0 or a 1 — into the surface of a platter. ➜ *0142* *optical media*; *0125* *CD-R*

0122 CD *abb.:* **compact disc** A digital storage technology developed by Philips and Sony Corp. on which data is stored by means of tiny pits burned into the disk's surface, the size of which determines a 0 or a 1.

0123 CD-DA *abb.:* **compact disc digital audio** A storage technology that uses the CD format for storing high-quality digital audio. ➔ *0122 CD; 0145 Red Book*

0124 CD-I *abb.:* **compact disc interactive** A compact disk technology similar to CD-ROM and originally intended for the consumer electronics market. Developed by Philips, CD-I disks require a special player but can be viewed on a regular television set. CD-I technology has been supplanted by the widespread acceptance of CD-ROM technology in both the consumer and business markets, and also by the introduction of the highly capacious DVD (digital versatile disc). ➔ *0126 CD-ROM; 0130 DVD; 0139 Green Book*

0125 CD-R *abb.:* **compact disc recordable** Specially made CDs that can record data by means of a laser that burns microscopic holes ("pits") into a thin recording layer. CD-Rs can be read by standard CD-ROM players, but are rather more fragile than mass-replicated CDs. ➔ *0126 CD-ROM; 0146 WORM; 0143 Orange Book; 0122 CD; 0121 burn (2)*

0126 CD-ROM Acronym for compact disc read-only memory. A CD technology developed for the storage and distribution of digital data for use on computers. Data is stored by means of tiny pits — the size of which determine a 0 or a 1 — burned into an encapsulated layer and read by a laser that distinguishes the pits from "lands" (the spaces between the pits). Based on audio CD technology, CD-ROMs are 5-inch diameter and come in two capacities: 74 minutes in duration (CD capacity is calibrated by the time it takes to record a whole disk), giving a data capacity of around 650Mb, or 63-minute discs giving a data capacity of 550Mb. Exact capacity can vary from one manufacturer to another. ➔ *0122 CD; 0124 CD-I; 0125 CD-R; 0147 Yellow Book; 0121 burn (2)*

0127 CD-ROM/XA *abb.:* **compact disc read-only memory/extended architecture** An extended version of the original CD-ROM standard that enhances the real-time playback capability of time-based data. CD-ROM/XA is similar to CD-I technology, but is intended for use with computer CD-ROM drives rather than with special players. A CD-ROM/XA drive will also read CD-ROM and CD-I discs. ➔ *0126 CD-ROM; 0124 CD-I*

0128 CD-RW *abb.:* **compact disc rewritable** A recordable CD to which data can be written over and over again, much like magnetic media. Also called an EO (erasable optical) disc. ➔ *0125 CD-R; 0146 WORM; 0122 CD*

0129 disc A circular platter on which digital data is stored in the form of minute pits (the size of which represents a 0 or a 1), which are "burned" by a laser into a shiny metallic layer encapsulated in the disc. The data is optically "read" by reflecting a laser beam, which distinguishes the pits from "**lands**" (the spaces between the pits), off the disc. Usually referred to as CDs and DVDs (both of which have many variants), optical discs are widely used for audio and video recording as well as for data storage. Optical discs, particularly DVDs, are capable of holding large amounts of data and are more resilient to damage than magnetic media. Not to be confused with a disk, which is much the same thing, but uses magnetic rather than optical techniques to store data. There is a third type of disk that combines both techniques and is called a magneto-optical disc (MO). ➔ *0078 disk; 0141 magneto-optical disk; 0122 CD; 0130 DVD*

0130 **DVD** *abb.:* **digital versatile disc** A high-capacity (up to 17.08 giga-bytes of data) storage disc similar to a CD-ROM, onto which data is "writ-ten" by means of tiny pits burned into the disc's surface by a laser, but which uses a shorter wavelength laser so the pits can be closer together. There are four capacities of DVD, some of which are double-sided, others with two layers of information on each side: DVD5 (which holds 4.7Gb of data), DVD9 (8.5Gb), DVD10 (9.4Gb), and DVD18 (17.08Gb), as well as several different types: DVD-Video, DVD-ROM, DVD-Audio, DVD-R (recordable), and DVD-RAM (rewritable). All DVD drives can generally read all four capacities, although not necessarily all types, of DVD, as well as "old-fashioned" CD-ROMs. → *0126 CD-ROM; 0134 DVD-ROM; 0135 DVD-Video; 0132 DVD-R; 0133 DVD-RAM; 0131 DVD-Audio*

0131 **DVD-Audio** *abb.:* **digital versatile disc-audio** Similar to an audio CD, but with a capacity of 17Gb — enough for around 32 hours of music! → *0130 DVD; 0134 DVD-ROM; 0135 DVD-Video; 0132 DVD-R*

0132 **DVD-R** *abb.:* **digital versatile disc-recordable** A high-capacity stor-age media that, in much the same way as a CD-R, allows you to write your own DVDs. → *0125 CD-R; 0134 DVD-ROM; 0130 DVD; 0135 DVD-Video; 0133 DVD-RAM; 0131 DVD-Audio*

0133 **DVD-RAM** A DVD (digital versatile disc) that is rewritable in much the same way as a CD-RW but more capacious. → *0128 CD-RW; 0130 DVD; 0134 DVD-ROM; 0135 DVD-Video; 0132 DVD-R; 0131 DVD-Audio*

0134 **DVD-ROM** *abb.:* **digital versatile disc-read only memory** A highly capacious version of a CD-ROM, holding up to 17 gigabytes of data. → *0126 CD-ROM; 0130 DVD; 0135 DVD-Video; 0132 DVD-R; 0133 DVD-RAM; 0131 DVD-Audio*

0135 **DVD-Video** *abb.:* **digital versatile disc-video** A high-capacity DVD used for storing feature-length movies for playing back via set-top boxes plugged into a TV. The DVD players contain an MPEG decoder, which allows many playback features — a choice of camera angles, for example — in a variety of formats such as wide-screen or HDTV (high-definition TV). → *0130 DVD; 0134 DVD-ROM; 0132 DVD-R; 0133 DVD-RAM; 0131 DVD-Audio; 0801 MPEG*

0136 **Enhanced Music CD** Also known as CD Extra (formerly CD Plus), this is the standard for interactive CDs defined in the "Blue Book," which specifies that the discs consist of two parts ("sessions"), the first containing pure audio tracks, the second containing data. Although the audio tracks of Enhanced Music CDs can be played on audio CD players, the data session will not be played. → *0123 CD-DA; 0120 Blue Book*

0137 **erasable optical** (**media**) Optical storage media that can be written to repeatedly, commonly referred to as CD-RW (compact disc rewritable) media. → *0128 CD-RW; 0125 CD-R; 0146 WORM; 0143 Orange Book*

0138 **floptical** A contraction of "floppy" and "optical." A floptical is a "magneto-optical" (MO) disc of the same size as a common 3½-inch "floppy" disk, but containing much more data — up to 230MB compared with 1.4MB of a floppy. → *0141 magneto-optical disc*

0139 **Green Book** The document that specifies all parameters for CD-I technology. → *0124 CD-I*

0140 **laser** Acronym for light amplification by stimulated emission of radia-tion. The process of generating an intense, fine beam of light, sometimes with considerable energy (the term also describes the device used to generate the light). It is used extensively in computer hardware such as optical discs, printers, and scanners, and for various commercial printing activities such as platemaking and engraving.

0141 **magneto-optical disc** (**MO/MOD**) A rewritable storage medium that combines the technologies of a laser and an electromagnet for writing and reading data, the result being that data cannot be corrupted by stray magnetic fields. ➔ *0129 disc; 0078 disk; 0138 floptical*

0142 **optical disc/media** A medium for storing digitized data by means of minute pits embedded into the surface of the disk. The binary digits of 1 and 0 are determined by the size of the pits, and these are "read" by an optical pick-up using a laser reflected off a shiny metallic layer on the disk's surface. Optical discs are widely used for audio and video recording and for computer data storage, and are capable of holding huge amounts of data. Commonly called CDs (compact disks) or DVDs (digital versatile disks), optical discs are more resilient than magnetic media and thus provide more secure data storage.

0143 **Orange Book** The document that specifies all parameters for recordable CD (CD-R) technology, developed by Sony and Philips. ➔ *0125 CD-R*

0144 **pit** A tiny cavity burned by a laser in the surface of an optical disc. It equates to one bit of digital information. ➔ *0129 disc*

0145 **Red Book** The document that specifies all parameters for the original Compact Disk Digital Audio (CD-DA) technology developed by Sony and Philips. In addition to defining the format in which an audio CD must be recorded so it is playable in every CD player, it also specifies what the CD player must do to play CDs correctly. ➔ *0123 CD-DA*

0146 **WORM** *abb.:* **write once read many** Large-capacity optical storage media such as CD-recordable (CD-R) disks that can be written to only once and cannot be erased. ➔ *0125 CD-R; 0129 disc; 0141 magneto-optical disc; 0143 Orange Book*

0147 **Yellow Book** The document that specifies all parameters for CD-ROM technology, guaranteeing that disks can be read by all CD-ROM drives. ➔ *0126 CD-ROM*

0148 **active matrix display** An LCD (liquid crystal display) monitor technology that uses tiny transistors to generate the display. ➔ *0163 LCD; 0170 passive matrix display*

0149 **ballooning** An aberration in cheaper monitors when voltage fluctuations that occur during the switch from light images to dark cause the image to spread out. ➔ *0165 monitor; 0172 pincushion*

0150 **blanking interval** The split second when the beam of electrons in a video monitor switches off. This occurs each time the beam moves from the end of one horizontal line to the beginning of the next (the "horizontal blanking interval"), and also when it moves from the last line at the bottom of the screen to the first line at the top (the "vertical blanking interval"). ➔ *0165 monitor*

0151 **cathode ray tube** (**CRT**) The standard video display device consisting of a glass vacuum tube containing a cathode that projects a beam of electrons onto a sensitized flat surface at the far end of the tube. ➔ *0158 flat screen/panel (display)*

0152 **composite video** A video "bus," or signal, in which all the color information is combined, such as in the "video out" port on older VCRs (video cassette recorders). This results in loss of quality. On computer monitors quality is maintained by keeping each of the RGB color signals separate. ➔ *0004 bus; 3547 RGB*

0153 **convergence** In color monitors, the adjustment of the three RGB beams so they come together in the right place on the screen. ➔ *3547 RGB; 0165 monitor*

0154 **degauss**(**ing**) The technique of removing, or neutralizing, any magnetic field that may have built up over time in a color monitor. Magnetism can distort the fidelity of color display. Since most modern monitors perform a degauss automatically, this process is usually only necessary on older monitors.

0155 **digital video interactive** (**DVI**) A computer chip developed by Intel that compresses and decompresses video images.

0156 **dot/stripe pitch** The distance between the dots or pixels (actually, holes or slits in a screen mesh) on your monitor — the closer the dots, the finer the display of image (although dot pitch has nothing to do with the resolution of the image itself). ➔ *0982 pixel; 0773 resolution*

0157 **extremely low frequency** (**ELF**) The electromagnetic radiation generated by certain types of electrical current that some research has shown to be potentially carcinogenic (cancer-causing) in the event of sustained exposure. Computer monitors emit ELF radiation in various quantities depending on factors such as size, although modern monitors filter out the radiation. The sides and back of a monitor emit greater amounts of radiation than the screen. VLF (very low frequency) radiation is also emitted, but is easier to filter and considered to be less harmful than ELF.

0158 **flat screen/panel** (**display**) A flat panel computer display that uses technologies such as liquid crystal or gas plasma to generate the image, rather than a bulky cathode ray tube (CRT). ➔ *0151 cathode ray tube*

0159 **flicker** A vibrating image on a computer monitor, usually caused by a slow refresh rate. Also known as a strobe effect. ➔ *0176 refresh rate*

0160 **gas plasma monitor** A computer display panel comprising a large matrix of tiny glass cells, each filled with a combination of gases. The simple structure means that gas plasma displays can be made in large sizes, typically ranging from 30 to 50 inches. ➔ *0165 monitor*

0161 **hertz** (**Hz**) A measurement of frequency. One hertz is one cycle, or occurrence, per second.

0162 **LED** *abb.:* **light emitting diode** An electronic component providing miniature light sources that are used to display alphanumeric characters on some hardware devices.

0163 **LCD** *abb.:* **liquid crystal display** A digital display technology commonly seen on calculators, clocks, and computer displays, particularly on portables and laptops.

0164 **luminance** The strength of a grayscale video signal.

0165 **monitor** The unit containing your computer screen. Monitors display images in color, grayscale, or monochrome, and are available in a variety of sizes from 9in. (229mm) (measured diagonally) to 21in. (534mm) or more. Although most monitors use cathode ray tubes, some contain liquid crystal displays (LCDs), particularly portables and laptops and, more recently, gas plasma (large matrices of tiny, gas-filled glass cells). Monitors are variously called screens, displays, VDUs, and VDTs. → *0153 convergence; 0151 cathode ray tube; 0160 gas plasma monitor; 0163 LCD*

0166 **mono(chrome)/monochromatic (2)** A computer monitor that displays pixels as either black or white, rather than in shades of gray as "grayscale" monitors. → *0165 monitor*

0167 **multiple screens/multiscreen** Two or more monitors attached to a single computer, used for presentations or to increase the workspace.

0168 **NTSC** *abb.:* **National Television Standards Committee** A television and video standard used mainly in the United States and Japan, which uses 525 lines and displays images at 30 frames per second.

0169 **PAL** *abb.:* **phase alternation by line** A Western European (except France) color television standard that uses 625 lines and displays images at 25 frames per second. → *0168 NTSC; 0177 SECAM*

0170 **passive matrix display** An LCD (liquid crystal display) monitor technology, usually found on cheaper laptop computers, which uses fewer transistors to generate the display, thus giving an inferior image quality to "active" matrix displays. → *0148 active matrix display*

0171 **phosphor** The coating on the inside surface of cathode ray tubes that glows momentarily when struck by a bombardment of electrons, creating a brief image. → *0151 cathode ray tube*

0172 **pincushion** The tendency of a monitor image to either bulge out or curve in along its vertical sides. → *0149 ballooning*

0173 **portrait monitor** A monitor in which the screen is in an upright format, as distinct from the more usual landscape format. → *0165 monitor*

0174 **radiation shield/screen** A wire mesh or glass filter that fits over a monitor to reduce the level of radiation being emitted. → *0157 ELF*

0175 **raster(ization)** Deriving from the Latin word *rastrum*, meaning rake, the method of display (and of creating images) employed by video screens, and thus computer monitors, in which the screen image is made up of a pattern of several hundred parallel lines created by an electron beam "raking" the screen from top to bottom at a speed of about one-sixtieth of a second. An image is created by the varying intensity of brightness of the beam at successive points along the raster. The speed at which a complete screen image, or frame, is created is called the "frame" or "refresh" rate. → *2218 raster image processor*

0176 **refresh rate** The frequency at which a screen image, or "frame" (a single pass of an electron beam that "rakes" the screen from top to bottom) is redrawn. Measured in hertz (Hz), a refresh rate of 72Hz means that the image is "refreshed" 72 times every second. A screen with a slow refresh rate may produce undesirable flicker. The refresh rate is often confused (erroneously) with the "redraw rate." → *0769 redraw rate*

0177 **SECAM** *abb.:* **Système Electronique pour Couleur avec Mémoire** A color television standard used in France, Eastern Europe, Russia, and the Middle East (where it is known as MESECAM), which uses 625 lines and displays images at 25 frames per second. → *0168 NTSC; 0169 PAL*

0178 **SMPTE** *abb.:* **Society of Motion Picture and Television Engineers** An American organization that defines broadcast standards such as **HDTV** (high definition television).

0179 **SuperVGA** (**SVGA**) A video display standard that supports 256 colors or more in a variety of resolutions. ➔ *0165 monitor*

0180 **twitter** A colloquial term for the visible vibrations on a video display caused by 1-pixel-high images.

0181 **two-page display** (**TPD**) Sometimes used to describe a 21-in. monitor.

0182 **VGA** *abb.:* **video graphic array** A basic video display standard. ➔ *0165 monitor; 0179 SuperVGA*

0183 **video card** A plug-in board that controls an external monitor.

0184 **VRAM** *abb.:* **video RAM** (read-only memory), pronounced vee-ram. Special RAM reserved for monitor display. ➔ *0068 RAM*

0185 **Apple Desktop Bus** (**ADB**) The standard connection bus on Macintosh computers for connecting input devices such as the mouse, keyboard, digitizing tablets, etc. ➔ *0004 bus*

0186 **auto-key event** A command, called an "event," generated repeatedly when a character key is held down on the keyboard. ➔ *0949 event; 0187 auto-key rate; 0188 auto-key threshold; 1046 keyboard event*

0187 **auto-key rate** The rate at which a character key repeats when it is held down. ➔ *0186 auto-key event; 0188 auto-key threshold*

0188 **auto-key threshold** The length of time a character key must be held down before it begins repeating. ➔ *0187 auto-key rate; 0186 auto-key event*

0189 **back end** A general term describing the part of the computing process when heavy-duty data processing is carried out, by servers or imagesetters, for example, as distinct from the "front end," where data is input by the user. ➔ *0299 front end (1); 0318 server*

0190 **character key** Any keyboard key that, when pressed, generates an image (keyboard event) on-screen, as distinct from a "modifier" key, such as the shift or control keys, which does nothing until a character key is pressed. ➔ *0221 modifier key*

0191 **console** The part of a mechanical system — computer-driven or otherwise — where instructions are given, either via switches or a keyboard.

0192 **control character** A nonprinting character generated by the "control key" (a modifier key — one that is used in conjunction with another) that is used by some applications to perform a particular function. ➔ *0221 modifier key*

0193 **daisy-chain** The linking together, in a line, of computer hardware devices. Typically, networked devices such as printers and disk drives are daisy-chained to a computer. ➔ *0308 network*

0194 **data bank** Any place or hardware device where large amounts of data are stored for ready access.

0195 **device** (**1**) An alternative term for any piece of hardware, but usually used to describe a piece of equipment that is peripheral to the computer itself (a "peripheral device"). ➔ *0205 external device*

0196 **DAT** *abb.:* **digital audio tape** A magnetic medium used to store large amounts of data. Used for either backing up or archiving data, DAT tapes are "linear" — that is, they run from beginning to end — and thus cannot be used for "primary" storage like a hard disk, because the data cannot be accessed at random.

0197 **direct entry** Any matter that is entered into a computer directly, such as via a keyboard, rather than input by some other means, such as via a scanner.

0198 **dock** To connect one device — usually a computer — to another, such as when you connect a laptop to a desktop computer.

0199 **dongle** A hardware "key" that plugs into a computer port to enable its associated software to run. Once a common method of copy-protecting software, dongles now generally accompany only very expensive, high-end applications.

0200 **double-click** The action of clicking the mouse button twice in rapid succession. Double-clicking while the pointer is positioned in an appropriate place is a shortcut to performing functions such as opening documents or highlighting words in text. ➜ *0222 mouse*

0201 **dumb terminal** A display device and keyboard that does not possess any computing power on its own, but which is networked to a server on which it relies for intelligent processing. ➜ *0325 terminal; 1154 Telnet*

0202 **Dvorak keyboard** A keyboard layout on which the more frequently typed keys are positioned most comfortably in relationship to your dominant typing fingers. An alternative layout to the familiar and widely used QWERTY arrangement found on typewriters and computer keyboards. ➜ *0233 qwerty*

0203 **Enter key** On keyboards, the key that confirms an entry or command or may force a carriage return. On some computer systems the Enter key duplicates much of the function of the Return key. In some applications, it may also have a specific function. ➜ *0234 Return key*

0204 **Esc(ape) key** A keyboard key, the function of which depends on the operating system or application you are using, but generally used to cancel something you are doing.

0205 **external device** Any item of hardware that is connected to a computer but resides externally — a disk drive, for example, may reside internally or externally Also called a **peripheral device**. ➜ *0195 device (1)*

0206 **Fkey** A contraction of "function keys." Fkeys have nothing to do with the special function keys on some keyboards (F1, F2, etc.); they are the keyboard equivalents for basic functions such as copying and pasting. ➜ *1045 keyboard equivalent; 0210 function key*

0207 **footprint** The exact space on a surface occupied by an object or piece of hardware.

0208 **forward delete key** A key found on some keyboards that deletes characters to the right of the text insertion point rather than the left, as with the standard delete key.

0209 **front end** (**system**) (**2**) The collection of hardware devices such as keyboards and scanners on which data is input. So called to distinguish it from the collection of devices on which data is output, such as imagesetters and printers.

0210 **function keys** A set of keys on some keyboards that can be assigned specific functions to carry out a sequence of mouse and keyboard actions, such as those defined by a "macro" program. Not to be confused with Fkeys, which execute default commands. ➜ *0206 Fkey*

0211 **generic** Hardware devices, such as disk drives and printers, whose mechanisms are common to other brands.

0222 Mouse

0216 keyboard
- 0190 character keys
- 0221 modifier keys
- 0206 FKeys
- 0225 numeric keypad

0212 **hardware** Any physical piece of equipment, generally in a computer environment, thus distinguishing it from firmware (programs built into hardware) and software (programs). ➔ *0480 software; 1037 firmware*

0213 **I/O** *abb.:* **input/output** The hardware interactions between a computer and other devices, such as the keyboard and disk drives. ➔ *0003 BIOS*

0214 **key** (**2**) To enter matter (input) into a computer via a keyboard.

0215 **key repeat rate** The speed at which a character may be duplicated if you hold down a key on the keyboard.

0216 **keyboard** A device for entering data into a computer.

0217 **keyboard character** Any character generated by typing a key on the keyboard. ➔ *0216 keyboard; 1045 keyboard equivalent/shortcut*

0218 **keyboard map** Characters as displayed on a monitor, which correspond with the arrangement on a keyboard.

0219 **keyboarding** A term used, traditionally, to describe the typesetting procedure of inputting copy, but now referring to the action of computer input via a keyboard. ➔ *0214 key (2)*

0220 **keystroke** A single press of any key on a keyboard, whether or not it generates a character (a space, for example). The traditional means of assessing the cost of typesetting.

0221 **modifier key** A nonprinting key (on a keyboard) that, when used in conjuction with a character key, enables the selection of a character not normally visible on the keyboard, such as accented letters or other symbols (©, ®, Ω, etc.). The most commonly used modifier keys are Shift, Command, Option/Alt, and Control, or a combination of these. Modifier keys can also be used as keyboard shortcuts. ➔ *0190 character key; 1045 keyboard equivalent/shortcut*

0222 **mouse** The small, handheld, mechanical device that you manipulate to position the pointer on your monitor.

0223 **mouse event** The action (event) initiated by pressing the button on your mouse. This can happen at the moment you press the button down (mouse-down), or when you release it (mouse-up). ➔ *0222 mouse*

0224 **mouse mat/pad** A small, easy-to-clean pad with a surface designed to facilitate the smooth and accurate motion of a mouse. ➔ *0222 mouse*

0225 **numeric keypad** A cluster of number keys situated to the right on most keyboards.

0226 **OEM** *abb.:* **original equipment manufacturer** The manufacturer of an item that may be marketed under a different name, a common practice with disk drives. Sometimes called a third-party supplier.

0227 **output** Any data or matter extracted from a computer, by whatever means, but typically via a monitor, printer, or storage device.

0228 **peripheral cable** A cable that connects a peripheral device to a computer.

0229 **PCI** *abb.:* **peripheral component interconnect** A high-performance, 32-bit or 64-bit "bus" for connecting external devices to a computer.

0230 **PCMCIA** *abb.:* **Personal Computer Memory Card International Association** A standard format for a type of expansion card used mainly in portable computers for adding features such as external devices, modems, and memory.

0231 **plug and play** The marketing description of computer or hardware devices that do not require complicated setting up — in other words, you just plug them in and start using them. ➔ *0020 Macintosh*

0232 **puck** The rather more complex "mouse" used in CAD systems. ➔ *0247 stylus; 0277 digitizing tablet; 1023 CAD (1)*

0233 **qwerty** The standard typewriter-based keyboard layout used by most computer keyboards. The name comes from the first six characters of the top row of letter keys.

0234 **Return key** The key on a computer keyboard that performs operations similar to a typewriter "carriage return" key, in that it moves the text insertion point to the beginning of the next line, usually creating a new paragraph as it does so. In many applications and dialog boxes, it also duplicates the actions of the Enter key, for example, confirming a command. ➔ *0203 Enter key*

0235 **sampler** (1) A device used to digitize sound so it can be manipulated by a computer. ➔ *1029 digitize*

0236 **SCSI** *abb.:* **small computer system interface** A computer industry standard for interconnecting peripheral devices such as hard disk drives and scanners.

0237 **SCSI bus** The data path that links SCSI devices to a computer. ➔ *0236 SCSI*

0238 **SCSI chain** Sequential linking of a number of SCSI devices to a computer. Also called a daisy-chain. ➔ *0193 daisy-chain; 0236 SCSI*

0239 **SCSI device** A device such as a disk drive or scanner that can be attached to a computer by means of a SCSI connection. SCSI devices may be inside the computer (internal device) or outside (external device). ➔ *0236 SCSI; 0195 device (1)*

0240 **SCSI ID** (**number**) The identifying number or "address" assigned to each SCSI device attached to a computer. Each number must be unique. ➔ *0014 DIP switch; 0288 SCSI chain; 0239 SCSI device*

0241 **SCSI port** The point at which the SCSI chain connects to the computer by means of a connecting plug. SCSI ports can be of the 25-pin or 50-pin variety. The devices themselves almost always have 50-pin ports, while some computers (Macintosh, for example) have 25-pin ports. ➔ *0236 SCSI*

0242 **SCSI terminator** A device for protecting the SCSI bus from "signal echo," which can corrupt data transfer. ➔ *0236 SCSI*

0243 **serial interface** The connection between computer hardware devices in which data is transmitted sequentially, one chunk at a time. As distinct from parallel interface. ➜ *0314 parallel interface*

0244 **serial port** The socket, or port, on a computer, used for the connection of devices that use a serial interface — modems or printers, for example. ➜ *0195 device (1); 0243 serial interface*

0245 **Shift key** The modifier key used to generate upper case, and other characters, on a keyboard.

0246 **spike suppressor** A device installed in the in-line power supply of computers that eliminates power surges and voltage fluctuations. Also called a **surge suppressor**, **surge protector**, or **power filter**.

0247 **stylus** The penlike pointing device used with digitizing tablets, replacing the mouse. ➜ *0277 digitizing tablet*

0248 **trackball** A device that replaces the mouse, actually resembling an upturned mouse — i.e., with the mouse ball on top rather than underneath. You move the pointer by manipulating the ball. The device remains stationary, thus occupying less desk space than the conventional mouse.

0249 **trackpad** A flat pad found on portable computers that replaces a mouse. The pad is sensitive to finger movements, which control the position of the cursor on screen.

0250 **USB** *abb.:* **Universal Serial Bus** A port (socket) for connecting peripheral devices, which can be daisy-chained together, to your computer. These can include devices such as scanners, printers, keyboards, and hard drives. ➜ *0244 serial port; 0029 port; 0193 daisy chain; 0205 external device*

0251 **bubblejet printer** A type of inkjet printer in which the ink is heated to boiling point, creating bubbles that eject the ink. ➜ *0257 inkjet printer*

0252 **character generator** (**2**) The VDU of a phototypesetting machine or word processor that displays characters.

0253 **corona wire** Thin wires through which an electrical charge is passed to fuse toner particles in laser printers and photocopiers. ➜ *0258 laser printer; 0140 laser*

0254 **cps** *abb.:* **characters per second** The output speed of a printing machine, such as an inkjet or dot-matrix printer, or the number of characters transmitted by a modem in each second. ➜ *0257 inkjet printer; 0256 dot-matrix printer; 1083 modem*

0255 **desktop (publishing) system** A collection of standard desktop hardware devices and off-the-shelf software applications capable of handling the entire desktop publishing process. As distinct from specialized equipment, such as drum scanners, used in high-end prepress systems. ➜ *3684 desktop publishing; 0012 desktop computer*

0256 **dot-matrix printer** A simple but cheap "impact" printer that uses a grid of metal pins to create the printed image, with hammers hitting the correct combination of pins to make the shape of a type character.

0257 **inkjet printer** A printing device that creates an image by spraying tiny jets of ink onto a paper surface at high speed. ➜ *0251 bubblejet printer; 2973 demand printing; 2169 DDCP*

0258 **laser printer** A printer that uses a laser as part of the mechanical process of printing onto paper. ➜ *0140 laser; 2973 demand printing*

0259 limitcheck error An error sometimes encountered when printing a complex document, caused either by too little RAM in the printer or by an illustration containing too many line segments for PostScript to handle. ➜ *0068 RAM*

0260 machine dot The tiny dots made by an imagesetter that form everything in the output image, including halftone dots. They are invisible at high resolutions — even with a loupe. The shape of a machine dot is consistently square and cannot be modified as a halftone dot's shape can. Changing the resolution of machine dot (printer resolution) does not affect the resolution of halftone screen ruling, although the relationship between screen ruling and printer resolution determines the tonal range that can be printed — as the screen ruling increases, the size of the halftone "cell" (the largest size of halftone dot) decreases, thus fewer machine dots are used to create the halftone dot, so fewer shades will be rendered. Machine dots are also called printer dots or recorder elements. ➜ *2044 halftone dot; 0280 scan dot*

0261 magnetic ink character recognition (**MICR**) A process in which specially designed characters are printed with magnetic ink so they can be "read" by a machine. Used widely for security printing, for example, bank checks. ➜ *2814 magnetic ink; 1052 OCR*

0262 nonimpact printing Printing processes in which the printing surface does not strike the surface of the substrate, when using plotters, laser, and ink-jet printers, for example.

0263 output device Any hardware device capable of producing or displaying computer data in a visible form, such as a monitor, printer, plotter, imagesetter, etc.

0264 pitch (**3**) An expression of the resolution of imaging devices. For example, "dot pitch" refers to the frequency of dots in, say, a monitor or imagesetter.

0265 plotter An output device that uses inked pens to produce large format prints, particularly in the CAD and CAD/CAM industries.

0266 PostScript printer Any printing device that uses the Adobe-licensed PostScript page description language (PDL). ➜ *1056 PostScript; 1054 page description language*

0267 print buffer A hardware device where items are stored ("queued") while waiting for a printer to become available, thus allowing you to continue working. As distinct from a print spooler. ➜ *0050 buffer; 0483 spool*

0268 print-out Digital data "output" from a printer as a "hard copy." ➜ *3725 hard copy*

0269 target printer The device that a document is sent to for printing. ➜ *0496 target*

0270 thermal printer A device that uses heat-sensitive paper to produce an image, sometimes found in older fax machines.

0271 thermal transfer A method of transferring an image by melting wax-based ink on a ribbon.

0272 toner The plastic powder used in laser printers and photocopiers to produce an image.

0273 CCD *abb.:* **charge-coupled device** A tiny light sensor ("photosite") — sensitized by giving it an electrical charge prior to exposure — used in flat-bed scanners and digital cameras for converting light into data. ➔ *1318 camera*

0274 CCD array A collection of CCDs arranged in a line. ➔ *0273 CCD*

0275 desktop scanner A small flatbed (usually) device for scanning images and text, which forms part of a desktop system. Although such scanners are becoming increasingly sophisticated and capable, the quality of image generated by them cannot yet match that produced by a high-end drum scanner. ➔ *0281 scanner; 2111 drum scanner*

0276 digitizer Strictly speaking, any hardware device such as a scanner or camera that converts drawn or photographed images into binary code so you can work with them on your computer. However, the term is generally used more specifically with reference to "digitizing tablets." ➔ *0277 digitizing tablet*

0277 digitizing tablet/pad A hardware device consisting of a flat, rectangular pad that allows you to input images into your computer by drawing on it with a "stylus" (a penlike instrument) as though you were working on paper. Also called a **graphics tablet/pad**. ➔ *0247 stylus*

0278 input device Any item of hardware specifically designed to, or capable of, entering data into a computer — a keyboard or scanner, for example. ➔ *0195 device (1)*

0279 photoelectric cell A device that produces an electric signal in response to the amount of light striking it. Also called a **photocell** or **photosite**. ➔ *0273 CCD*

0280 scan dot The resolution of a scanning device, measured — like machine dots — in dots per inch. However, the formula for calculating scan dot resolution does not relate to that of calculating machine dot resolution. A rough rule of thumb is that for images that will eventually be printed with a halftone screen ruling greater than 133lpi, the scan resolution should be 1.5 times the lpi screen ruling, and for screens equal to, or less than, 133lpi, the scan resolution should be 2.0 times the lpi ruling. Scanning at higher resolutions will not make any difference because the halftone dots will not be small enough to reproduce the extra detail. ➔ *2044 halftone dot; 0260 machine dot; 0982 pixel*

0281 scanner An electronic device that uses a sequentially moving light beam to convert artwork or photographs into digital form so they can be manipulated by a computer or output to separated film. A scanner can be a simple flatbed type, used on the desktop for positioning pictures only, or a sophisticated reprographic device (drum scanner) used for high-quality color separation. ➔ *2002 commercial color; 2075 desktop scanner; 2111 drum scanner*

0282 asynchronous A communications protocol in which data bits are transmitted one after the other, start-and-stop bits denoting the beginning and end of each character transmitted. ➔ *0283 asynchronous communication; 0323 synchronous communication*

0283 asynchronous communication A communications protocol in which data bits are transmitted one after another. A start/stop signal indicates the beginning and end of each character being transmitted, thus allowing data to move back and forth without being restricted to rigid timing signals. ➔ *0323 synchronous communication*

0284 asynchronous transfer mode (ATM) A very fast communications technology in which data can be transferred at rates of up to 24 gigabits per second.

0285 backbone (2) The main high-speed link between nodes linking networked devices. → *0308 network*

0286 bit rate The speed at which data is transmitted across communications channels, measured in bits per second (bps). Modem speeds typically range from 2,400bps to 56,000bps, but higher speeds are measured in kilobits (kbps) or even megabits (mbps) per second — ISDN connections, for example, are usually either 65kbps or 128kbps. Bit rate is sometimes erroneously referred to as baud rate. → *1068 baud; 0914 bit; 1069 baud rate; 0304 kbps; 1080 ISDN*

0287 bridge A link between two or more networked devices. → *0308 network; 1038 gateway*

0288 client In a client/server arrangement, such as on a network or on the Web, the client is the end-user (your computer). On the Web, your browser is a "client program," which talks to Web servers. → *0290 client/server; 0318 server; 1227 World Wide Web; 0308 network*

0289 client-side Processing done by you on your own computer rather than by a network server (server-side). → *0319 server-side*

0290 client/server An arrangement that divides computing into two separate functions, connected by a network. The client is the end-user (your computer), while the server is a centralized computer, which holds and manages information or shared activities that your computer and others can access when necessary. → *0288 client; 0318 server; 0308 network*

0291 Digital Data Exchange Standard An ANSI/ISO-approved standard that allows equipment produced by different manufacturers to communicate ("interface") with each other.

0292 direct access Access to an item by means of a single direct path. For example, your computer when connected to another by means of a continuous, dedicated telephone line rather than via modems and regular telephone lines, has direct access. → *1083 modem*

0293 error correction (protocol) A method of checking the integrity of data transmission (usually by modem). A "parity" error check is a typical method, in which seven bits of data are transmitted, followed by an eighth that indicates whether the sum of the previous seven is either odd or even. If a discrepancy occurs, the data will be retransmitted.

0294 Ethernet A hardware connection standard used on local area networks (LAN) that offers fast data transfer. → *0308 network; 0305 LAN*

0295 fiber-optic cable A conduit used for high-speed data transmission. Made of glass or plastic fibers, it carries data transmitted as pulses of light.

0296 file server A computer that serves a network of other computers and provides central storage of files and programs. → *0308 network*

0297 file transfer The transmission of a file from one computer to another either over a network or over telecommunication lines, using a modem. → *0308 network; 1083 modem*

0298 flow control A method of organizing the flow of data as it is transmitted via a modem or across a network.

0299 front end (1) In a networked system where your computer is connected to a server, the software used to gain access and interact with the server (the "back end"). A Web browser is one such front end.

0300 GAN *abb.:* **global area network** A worldwide network of computers, similar to the Internet but linking "wide area networks" (WANs).

0301 GSM *abb.:* **global system for mobile communications** A telecommunication standard used increasingly throughout the world.

0302 handshake The procedure of two networked computers or other devices introducing themselves to each other when initial contact is made, in order to establish data transmission protocols. → *0984 protocol; 0330 XON/XOFF*

0303 internal modem A modem that is installed inside a computer. → *1083 modem*

0304 kbps *abb.:* **kilobits per second** A measurement of the speed at which data is transferred across a network or through a modem connection, a kilobit being equal to 1,024 bits, or characters.

0305 LAN *abb.:* **local area network** A collection of hardware devices in a small ("local") area — one room, say — linked together via appropriate connections and software. At its simplest, a LAN may be a single computer linked to a printer.

0306 log on; log in To connect to a network.

0307 megabits per second A measure of data transfer speed.

0308 network The connection of two or more computers or peripheral devices to each other, and the hardware and software used to connect them. → *0287 bridge*

0309 network link The part of the network that forms the link between your computer and the network itself, such as a telephone line or Ethernet cable. → *0294 Ethernet*

0310 node (2) Any device connected to a network, such as a computer, printer, or server.

0311 null modem cable A communications link between two computers, usually over a short distance, without using a modem (null = nonexistent).

0312 off-line/offline Work done on a computer with access to a network or the Internet, but not actually while connected to the network. The opposite of on-line. → *0313 online*

0313 on-line/online Any activity taking place on a computer or device while it is connected to a network such as the Internet. The opposite of off-line. → *0312 offline; 0308 network; 3608 in-line*

0314 parallel interface A computer connection in which data is transmitted simultaneously in the same direction along a single cable. As distinct from serial interface. → *0243 serial interface*

0315 parity bit An extra bit of data used to verify that bits received by one communications device match those transmitted by another. → *0914 bit*

0316 peer-to-peer A network system in which files are spread around different computers, the users of which access them from each other rather than from a central server.

0317 response On a network, the server's reply to a user's request for information. → *1210 request*

0318 server A networked computer that serves client computers, providing a central location for files and services, and typically handling such things as e-mail and Web access. → *0290 client/server; 0288 client*

0319 server-side Processing done by a network server rather than by your own computer (client-side). → *0289 client-side*

0320 star network A network configuration in which every terminal (node) is wired directly to the central processor, radiating from it in a star shape. → *0308 network*

0321 start bit A single bit used in data communication to indicate the beginning of transmission. → *0914 bit; 0322 stop bit*

0322 stop bit In data communication, the bit that indicates the end of one byte. → *0321 start bit; 0283 asynchronous communication*

0323 synchronous communication/transmission High-speed data transmission whereby data is sent in chunks between rigid electronic timing signals. → *0283 asynchronous communication*

0324 telecommunications The transmission of data by any means, but primarily via telephone lines.

0325 terminal Any device used to communicate with another computer via a network. → *0308 network*

0326 throughput (1) A unit of time measured as the period elapsing between the start and finish of a particular activity. For example, the amount of data that is passed along a communications line in a given period of time.

0327 TDMA *abb.:* **time division multiple access** A communications protocol for sending multiple signals along a single line.

0328 token ring A method of linking computers in a ring network. Data can only be sent from one to another after a digital code or token is transmitted from one computer to the next. → *0305 LAN; 0329 WAN*

0329 WAN *abb.:* **wide area network** A series of local area networks (LAN) connected together by terrestrial or satellite links. → *0305 LAN; 0308 network; 0300 GAN*

0330 XON/XOFF A "handshaking" protocol used by computers when communicating via modems. → *0984 protocol; 0302 handshake*

0331 zone One part of two or more connected networks. → *0308 network*

0343 Bézier curve

0332 absolute path The path, or route, taken to locate a file by starting at the highest level (usually the "root" level) and searching through each directory (or folder) until the file is found. The path is spelled out by listing each directory en route. ➔ *0894 access path; 0462 root directory*

0333 algorithm A predetermined procedure for solving a specific problem. ➔ *0334 algorithmically defined*

0334 algorithmically defined Usually used to describe a font in which each character is drawn "on-the-wing" according to the calculations made by a software program, rather than residing on the computer as a predrawn font file.

0335 alpha test The first testing, usually by the team developing it, of a complete software program in order to discover and eliminate errors (debugging). ➔ *0336 alpha version*

0336 alpha version The first complete version of a newly developed software program, prior to testing and eventual release. ➔ *0335 alpha test; 0342 beta version; 0457 release version*

0337 artificial intelligence (AI) Software programs that learn from criteria provided by the user and are thus able to modify results.

0338 ASCII (*pron.:* asskee) Acronym for the American Standard Code for Information Interchange, a code that assigns a number to the 256 letters, numbers, and symbols (including carriage returns and tabs) that can be typed on a keyboard. ASCII is the cross-platform, computer industry-standard, text-only file format. ➔ *0933 cross-platform*

0339 asynchronous execution The freedom of a program to perform other tasks after initiating an asynchronous routine, until the routine is completed. ➔ *0283 asynchronous communication*

0340 background (I) Any software activity, such as printing, that takes place while you are working on other software in the foreground.

0341 beta test Software that is released — after alpha testing and prior to commercial release — for testing by designated members of the public for the purpose of eliminating errors (debugging). ➔ *0335 alpha test; 0342 beta version*

0342 beta version The version of a software program prior to commercial release, used for final checks for errors (beta tests). Beta versions are also frequently used for review purposes. ➔ *0341 beta test; 0336 alpha version; 0457 release version*

0343 Bézier curve In drawing applications, a curved line between two "control" points. Each point is a tiny database, or vector, which stores information about the line, such as its thickness, color, length, and direction. Complex shapes can be applied to the curve by manipulating "handles," which are dragged out from the control points. ➔ *0428 object-oriented*

0344 Boolean Named after G. Boole, a 19th-century English mathematician, Boolean is used to describe a shorthand for logical computer operations, such as those that link values — and, or, not, nor, etc., called "Boolean operators." The search of a database could be refined using Boolean operators, for example, "book and recent or new but not published." "Boolean expressions" compare two values and come up with the result ("return") of either true or false, represented by 1 and 0. In 3D applications, Boolean describes the joining or removing of one shape to/from another.

0347 Clipping path

0354 Control point

0345 C/C++ A programming language widely used for software programs, particularly for Macintosh computers. ➔ *0518 application program*

0346 capture The recording of an image by whatever means, taking a photograph or scanning a picture, for example — you "capture" the image. ➔ *0467 screen capture*

0347 clipping path A Bézier outline that defines which areas of an image should be considered transparent or "clipped." This lets you isolate the foreground object and is particularly useful when images are to be placed on top of a tint background in a page layout, for example. Clipping paths are generally created in an image-editing application such as Adobe Photoshop and are embedded into the image file when you save it in EPS format. Some page-layout applications such as QuarkXPress allow you to create clipping paths for images, but, be warned, these are only saved with the application file, so if your placed images are low-resolution FPO files that are to be replaced by the high-resolution versions, or if they are the preview files of a five-file DCS file, your clipping path will not have any effect. ➔ *0767 DCS; 0343 Bézier curve*

0348 closed file A file that does not have an access path, preventing you from reading from or writing to it. ➔ *0894 access path; 0409 locked file*

0349 code The instructions in a piece of software that tell the computer what to do. Code can take various forms, from binary code — a series of 1s and 0s, which is actually the form all code must take for the computer to understand it — to programming languages and scripts — code that is written in a sort of English so the user can understand it. HTML is a programming code written for Web browsers, while typical scripting codes include "lingo," which is written for Macromedia Director presentations, and AppleScript, which allows you to create shortcuts for common tasks on Macintosh computers. ➔ *0911 binary code; 0469 script (1); 1267 HTML; 0352 compiler; 1042 interpreter; 1167 browser (1); 0905 AppleScript*

0350 colinear Two or more objects that are in line.

0351 comma-delimit To separate elements of data, such as records or fields in a database, using a comma. ➔ *0492 tab-delimit*

0352 compiler Software that converts "high-level" programming code (source code), such as that written in C++, into low-level "machine code" (object code) — a language that hardware will understand. This is necessary because, while programming code for writing applications, for example, uses a language that the user can understand, a machine only understands binary code — on or off, 1s and 0s, etc. For example, if you were to instruct your computer to add two numbers in binary code, it would look something like: 1101 0011 0001 0011 1110, whereas a high-level language would allow you to write "add 1 to 2." ➔ *0353 computer language; 0911 binary code; 0345 C++; 1042 interpreter*

0353 computer language The language, or code, devised to make computers work. These may be high level — those used for writing application programs and written so the user (or, at least, the programmer) can understand it, or low level (usually binary), which only the computer can understand. ➔ *0518 application program; 0911 binary code*

0354 control point In "vector"-based (drawing) applications, a little knob, or point, in a path (line) that allows you to manipulate its shape or characteristics by means of "Bézier control handles." ➔ *0441 point (2); 0428 object-oriented; 0343 Bézier curve; 0354 control point; 0587 handles (1)*

0355 copy (**2**) The facility in virtually all computer software to copy a selected item, which places it on the "clipboard" so it can be "pasted" elsewhere. As distinct from "cut," which deletes the item while at the same time copying it. → *0926 clipboard; 0434 paste; 0356 cut (7); 0357 cut and paste*

0356 cut (**7**) In virtually all applications, a feature that allows you to remove an item from a location in a document, at the same time copying it to the "clipboard" so it can be "pasted" elsewhere. As distinct from "copy," which places the item on the clipboard while leaving the original where it is. → *0926 clipboard; 0357 cut and paste; 0355 copy (2)*

0357 cut and paste The process of removing an item from a document (cutting the item, which places it on the clipboard) and then placing it elsewhere (pasting it), either in the same or another document. → *0356 cut (7); 0926 clipboard; 0355 copy (2)*

0358 data Although strictly speaking the plural of "datum," meaning a piece of information, data is nowadays used as a singular noun to describe — particularly in the context of computers — more or less anything that can be stored or processed, whether it be a single bit, a chunk of text, an image, audio, and so on.

0359 data bits An expression used in data transmission to distinguish bits containing the data being transmitted from bits giving instructions on how the data is to be transmitted. → *0914 bit; 1101 transmission control protocol*

0360 DIF *abb.:* **Data Interchange Format** A file format used by database and spreadsheet applications for exporting records. DIF files preserve field names but not formatting. → *0380 file format; 0545 database; 0679 spreadsheet; 0377 field; 0089 formatting*

0361 data processing The systematic processing of information, whether it be sorting text or batch processing images.

0362 debug(**ging**) To hunt out and correct programming errors in computer software. → *0919 bug*

0363 decryption The process of removing the protection given to data or a document by encryption. Usually, the same software used to encrypt data must be used to decrypt it. → *0376 encryption*

0364 delimit To separate items of information, such as words, lines of text, or — in databases, for example — fields and records. This is done by placing a character ("delimiter") at the end ("limit") of each item. Commonly used characters are generated by the tab and comma keys (to separate fields) and the return key (to separate records). Files formatted thus are described as "delimited." → *0377 field; 0456 record; 0545 database*

0365 deselect To deactivate an active item, such as a picture box or highlighted text, usually by clicking outside or away from the item.

0366 device independent Any software that controls the preparation or output of pages or images regardless of the hardware device on which they are prepared or output. PostScript, for example, is a device-independent "page description language" (software that describes to a printer how the content of a page is to be arranged when it is output).

0367 digital data Information stored or transmitted as a series of 1s and 0s (bits). Because values are fixed (so-called discrete values), digital data is more reliable than analog, as the latter is susceptible to sometimes uncontrollable physical variations. → *3590 discrete value; 0914 bit; 0910 binary*

0368 Digital elevation model:
a grayscale bump map with mountain peaks white and valleys black
b rendered with light source at top left to show physical terrain.

0368 DEM *abb.:* **digital elevation model** A collection of regularly spaced elevation data from which 3D models of the earth's surface can be generated. DEMs are used extensively by cartographers to produce shaded relief maps using special software. ➔ *0733 bump map*

0369 directory An invisible catalog of information about all the files on a disk. The volume directory contains general information about the disk, whereas the file directory logs specific information such as their physical location on the disk. You should check your directory file regularly with a disk maintenance utility, since if the file becomes corrupted (damaged), you could lose all your data. ➔ *0370 directory structure; 0115 volume (1); 0378 file; 0954 folder (1)*

0370 directory structure The underlying hierarchical structure of all the files on a hard disk. ➔ *0369 directory*

0371 distributed rendering The process of rendering chunks of one or more files, such as a 3D movie, simultaneously on one or more computers. This saves considerable time since large renderings can take several hours — even days — to complete.

0372 document (1) Any file that is created or modified on a computer by means of application software, such as a letter written in a word-processing application or a design created in a page-layout application. A document file is generated on your hard disk the first time you save something — a dialog box will appear, asking you what you want to call the document and where you want it to reside. Thereafter, each time you save changes to your document, the original is updated rather than created anew. To create a new version of the same document, use the "Save as..." command. Also known as a **data file**.

0373 document content architecture (**DCA**) A file format used for transferring partially formatted text documents between applications.

0374 DXF *abb.:* **Document Exchange Format** A standard file format developed by Autodesk — originally for its AutoCAD application — for storing 3D and CAD files. ➔ *1023 CAD*

0375 EPS *abb.:* **encapsulated PostScript** A standard graphics file format used primarily for storing "object-orientated," or "vector," graphics files (a vector is a tiny database giving information about both magnitude and direction of a line or shape) generated by "drawing" applications such as Adobe Illustrator and Macromedia FreeHand. An EPS file usually has two parts: one containing the PostScript code, which tells the printer how to print the image; the other an on-screen preview, which can be in PICT, TIFF, or JPEG formats. Although used mainly for storing vector-based graphics, the EPS format is also widely used to store bitmapped images, particularly those used for desktop color separation (DCS), and these EPS files are encoded as either ASCII — a text-based description of an image — or binary, which uses numbers rather than text to store data. Bitmapped EPS files to be printed from a Windows-based system use ASCII encoding, whereas those to be printed on the Mac OS are usually saved with binary encoding, although not all printing software supports binary EPS files.

0376 encryption Complex algorithms that scramble data in order to protect information from unauthorized access. Encrypted files usually require a password or code to "unlock" the data. ➔ *0363 decryption*

0385 Flatness
a set to 3
b set to 100

0377 field In documents and dialog boxes, the term generally describing any self-contained area into which data is entered. In some applications such as databases and spreadsheets, a field is generally interactive with another field in the same (or another) record, or the same field in another record. **→ 0545** *database;* **0679** *spreadsheet;* **0360** *DIF*

0378 file A collection of data that is stored as an individual item on a disk. A file can be a document, a folder, an application, or a resource. **→ 0380** *file format*

0379 file dependency A file that depends upon the contents of another in order to function. **→ 0378** *file*

0380 file format The way a program arranges data so it can be stored or displayed on a computer. This can range from the file format used uniquely by a particular application, to those that are used by many different software programs. In order to help you work on a job that requires the use of several applications, or to work with other people who may be using applications different from yours, file formats tend to be standardized. Common file formats are TIFF and JPEG for bitmapped image files, EPS for object-oriented image files, and ASCII for text files. **→ 0494** *TIFF;* **0761** *JPEG;* **0375** *EPS;* **0338** *ASCII*

0381 file recovery The process of resurrecting a file after you have deleted it or when it has become corrupted. The data comprising a file remains on a disk even if it has been deleted — only its name is in fact erased (from the invisible directory that keeps track of all the files on a disk). Until the space the data occupies is used by your computer for something else, it is sometimes possible to recover it with the aid of one of the many utilities available for recovering deleted files. Recovering corrupted files is somewhat more difficult, and although some applications offer features for recovering corrupted files, there is no better safeguard than making very regular backup copies of your files as you work on them (many applications provide features for automating backup copies).

0382 file type In the Mac OS, the four-letter code assigned to every file when it is created that identifies its kind or format, such as APPL for an application, TEXT for text files, and so on. Special software such as ResEdit is generally necessary to identify the file type. **→ 0378** *file*

0383 filename The name given to a file. Macintosh filenames can be up to 31 characters long, whereas Windows filenames can be up to 255 characters, although it is usually safer (especially if the files are to be transferred between computer systems) to use the DOS naming convention of "8.3" (eight characters followed by a three-character suffix — all capitals). Windows filenames cannot contain any of the following characters: / \ | : * ? ' < >; and when naming Macintosh files, it is best to avoid: • : / \ since these can interfere with some program functions.

0384 flag (3) Certain attributes such as locked, invisible, busy, etc., of files stored on a disk.

0385 flatness In object-oriented drawing applications, the number of straight lines, or segments, that make up the curves in an image that will be printed on a PostScript printer (PostScript draws curves as a series of straight lines). The lower the number, the smoother the curve, although the difference between values of zero and three are barely discernible to the eye. Values higher than ten may result in visibly flattened curves, particularly when printed at low resolutions. **→ 0428** *object-oriented;* **1056** *PostScript*

0392 Histogram: unmodified grayscale image showing all pixels concentrated at the dark end of the histogram, with no pixels in the highlight (white) range.

0392 Histogram: modified grayscale image showing pixels redistributed across the full range of the histogram, from dark to light.

0386 **foreign file** A document created in a different application or computer system from the one you are using.

0387 **gigabyte** (**GB/G/gig**) One gigabyte is equal to 1,024 megabytes. ➔ *0408 kilobyte; 0420 megabyte; 0499 terabyte*

0388 **gigo** An acronym for "garbage in — garbage out"; the principle that input of a poor quality produces equally poor output, particularly when it comes to computer programming.

0389 **Gzip** File compression technology used mainly on UNIX computers.

0390 **header** A label that identifies a file, document, or page, occurring at its top, or "head," such as in an e-mail message or newsgroup posting, in which case it may contain such information as the route the message took to get to you, the recipient's e-mail address, the name of the newsreader or mail program, and so on.

0391 **high-level language** Any programming language that is based as closely as possible on English rather than machine code. ➔ *1048 machine code*

0392 **histogram** A graphic representation of data, usually in the form of solid vertical or horizontal bars. Some image-editing applications use histograms to graph the number of pixels at each brightness level in a digital image, thus giving a rapid idea of the tonal range of the image so you can tell if there is enough detail to make corrections.

0393 **IAC** *abb.:* **interapplication communication** A protocol used by software developers to allow data to be shared and exchanged between applications. ➔ *0984 protocol*

0394 **import** To bring text, pictures, or other data into a document. ➔ *0558 export*

0395 **import/export filter** In some applications, a feature for translating a file from the host format to that of another, and vice versa. ➔ *0558 export; 0394 import; 0565 filter (1)*

0396 **inheritance** The hierarchical relationship between objects in object-oriented programming. In other words, a characteristic inherited by one HTML element (a child) from another HTML element (its parent).

0397 **initialize** To clear the directory on a disk and create a new one so new data can be stored. When a hard disk is initialized, its directory is emptied of file information, but the data itself remains (although it is invisible) until written over by the new files. When a floppy disk is initialized, the disk is formatted at the same time; thus any files stored on it are deleted as well as the directory. ➔ *0089 formatting*

0398 **insertion point** The point in a document or dialog box at which the next character or action typed on the keyboard will appear. It is indicated by a blinking vertical line (text insertion bar) that can be positioned in the appropriate place by using the I-beam pointer and clicking. ➔ *0963 I-beam pointer*

0399 **install** To add any item of software to a computer so it can be used. This is invariably achieved by means of an "installer" program, which puts files in their appropriate places. ➔ *0400 installer*

0400 **installer** A program that enables you to load software onto your hard disk. Installer programs will also put the application support files in their appropriate places, creating folders for them and putting files into your system folder. Installers are also updating programs. ➔ *0399 install*

0401 interactive Any activity that involves an immediate and reciprocal action between a person and a machine, for example, driving a car, but more commonly describing dialog between a computer and its user. ➔ *0402 interactive mode*

0402 interactive mode The ability of an application to process data as it is input, as distinct from that which is processed in batches (batch mode), for example, spelling is checked as it is input rather than later as a batch. Also called real-time processing. ➔ *0401 interactive; 0455 real-time*

0403 interleaved, interleaving (**I**) The technique of displaying an image on-screen — using a Web browser, for example — so it is revealed as a whole in increasing layers of detail rather than bit by bit from the top down. The image appears gradually, starting with slices that are eventually filled in when all the pixels appear. ➔ *1094 progressive JPEG*

0404 intermediate code A representation of computer code that lies somewhere between code that can be read by you or me (such as HTML source code) and machine-readable binary code (1s and 0s). Java bytecode is one example of intermediate code. ➔ *1267 HTML; 1048 machine code; 1277 Java*

0405 invisible file Any file that is not visible but nonetheless exists, such as directory files and icon files. Files can, for security reasons, for example, be made invisible using a suitable utility program, although such files may still appear in directory dialog boxes. It is common practice to make the support files of multimedia applications invisible.

0406 item A term used to describe virtually any individual object created in a computer application, such as text boxes, picture boxes, and rules.

0407 kilobit (**kb/kbit**) One kilobit is equal to 1,024 bits. ➔ *0914 bit; 0408 kilobyte*

0408 kilobyte (**K/KB/Kbyte**) One kilobyte is equal to 1,024 bytes (8,192 bits). Since one byte represents a single character, a kilobyte is roughly equivalent to 170 words. ➔ *3608 kilo; 0420 megabyte; 0387 gigabyte; 0499 terabyte*

0409 locked file A data file that cannot be modified or deleted.

0410 logical volume A volume such as a partition created by software, as distinct from a "physical volume" such as a disk. ➔ *0101 partition*

0411 lookup field A field in a database file that provides the same information as a specified field in another file. ➔ *0545 database*

0412 MacBinary A file format that allows Macintosh files to be transferred via modem or shared with non-Mac computers by making sure all component parts such as the "resource" and "data" forks remain together.

0413 macro A term deriving from the Greek *makros*, meaning long or large. "Macroscopic," for example, means large units, whereas microscopic describes small things. In computer parlance, a macro is a single command containing several other commands — one large unit composed of smaller units — thus the term describes a sequence of actions or commands that have been recorded so they can be repeated at any time using a single command (usually a keystroke). ➔ *0210 function keys*

0414 mapping (**I**) Converting data between formats, particularly databases.

0416 Marquee
a rectangular
b oval

0415 markup language A defined set of rules describing the way files are displayed by any particular method. HTML is one such language, used for creating Web pages. ➔ *1267 HTML;* **1286** *markup (2)*

0416 marquee In some applications, a moving broken line drawn around an object or area in order to "select" it or, in some cases, an area defined by an application to show that the space within is active or selected. The moving lines are colloquially known as marching ants. ➔ *0472 select*

0417 master directory block The area of a computer disk that contains the disk directory (the catalog of files), which is put into RAM when you start or insert the disk. ➔ *0369 directory*

0418 mega A unit of metric measurement representing 1,000,000. Although the term is used widely as a measure of computer data (megabyte, for example), computers use a binary system (pairs of numbers) in which each number is doubled: 2; 4; 8; 16; 32; 64; 128; 256; 512; 1,024; etc., thus "mega" in a data context does not mean 1,000,000 but 1,048,576 (230). ➔ *3608 kilo*

0419 megabit (**Mb/Mbit**) 1,024 kilobits or 1, 048,576 bits of data.

0420 megabyte (**MB/Mbyte/meg**) 1,024 kilobytes or 1, 048,576 bytes of data. ➔ *0408 kilobyte;* **0387** *gigabyte;* **0499** *terabyte*

0421 mnemonic Anything that aids memory, often an abbreviation, such as a keyboard equivalent command that uses the initial letter of the command (O = Open, C = Copy).

0422 multi-user A qualification of a license agreement that allows more than one person to use a single piece of software.

0423 multimedia A generic term for any combination of various digital media, such as sound, video, animation, graphics, and text, incorporated into a software product or presentation.

0424 multiple-selected items The selection of two or more items so they can be modified or moved as if they were one — for example, move, group, or resize.

0425 native file format A file format for exclusive use by the application in which the files were created, although some applications may be able to read files created in another's native format.

0426 nibble/nybble Half a byte, or four bits. ➔ *0914 bit;* **0922** *byte*

0427 noncontiguous selection A feature of some applications that lets you select disconnected pieces of text.

0428 object-oriented A software technology that uses mathematical points, based on "vectors" (information giving both magnitude and direction), to define lines and shapes, these points being the "objects" referred to. As distinct from a graphic shape as an object (an "object" in computer programming is a database of mathematical formulae). The data for each shape is stored in these points, which in turn pass information from one to another on how the paths between them should be described — as straight lines, arcs, or Bézier curves. The quality of the line between each point is determined entirely by the resolution of the output device — a line produced by an imagesetter at 2,400dpi will be very much smoother than the same line output on a LaserWriter at 300dpi or when viewed on a monitor. The alternative technology for rendering computer images is that of "bitmapped" graphics, which are edited by modifying individual

0431 Palette

0442 Pointer:
a arrow
b wristwatch
c grabber hand
d, e crosshair
f text insertion

pixels or by turning them on or off. **→ 0441** *point;* **0343** *Bézier curve;* **0587** *handles*

0429 overhead The unseen formatting data contained within a document file that is saved along with the visible data.

0430 Page Setup A dialog box that allows you to select various options for printing, such as paper size, enlargement or reduction, paper orientation, inversion, etc. The available options will vary depending on the printer you are using.

0431 palette A window, often "floating" (movable), that contains features such as tools, measurements, or other functions.

0432 parameter A limit, boundary, or, in programming, a qualifier that defines the precise characteristics of a piece of software.

0433 Pascal A programming language. **→ 0451** *programming language*

0434 paste A command that places a copied item into a document. **→ 0355** *copy (2);* **0356** *cut (7);* **0926** *clipboard;* **0357** *cut and paste*

0435 patch A small piece of program code supplied for fixing bugs in software. **→ 0919** *bug*

0436 path (1) The hierarchical trail through disk and folders to a particular file. **→ 0437** *pathname*

0437 pathname A string of words identifying the entire path from disk to file, such as "mydisk:myfolder:myfile," indicating that the file named "myfile" is inside the folder named "myfolder," which is on the disk called "mydisk." Colons or forward slashes (/) are generally used to separate each name in the path, which is why colons or slashes should not be used in filenames to avoid confusion.

0438 PEL *abb.:* **picture element** The smallest unit of a computer display that can be assigned an individual color and intensity, usually a pixel.

0439 Photo CD A proprietary, cross-platform technology developed by Kodak for scanning and storing photographs on CD-ROM. Photo CD files can be opened and edited with most image-editing applications **→ 0589** *image-editing application*

0440 PICT Acronym for picture. A standard file format for storing bitmapped and object-oriented images on Macintosh computers. Originally, the PICT format only supported eight colors, but a newer version, PICT2, supports 32-bit color.

0441 point (2) In object-oriented drawing applications, the connections (Bézier points) that mathematically define the characteristics of line segments, such as where they start and end, how thick they are, and so on (each point is a "vector" or tiny database of information). Lines are manipulated by dragging "control handles" (sometimes called guidepoints) from the point, which act on the line like magnets. **→ 0343** *Bézier curve;* **0428** *object-oriented;* **0354** *control point*

0442 pointer A general term that refers to any of the many shapes on a monitor that indicate the location and operating mode of the mouse. Typical pointer shapes are the arrow pointer, vertical bar, I-beam, crossbar or crosshair, and wristwatch. Sometimes confused with the "cursor" (the typing location within a field or piece of text). **→ 0934** *cursor;* **0542** *crosshair pointer*

0443 PDF *abb.:* **portable document format** A cross-platform format that allows complex, multifeatured documents to be created, retaining all text and picture formatting, then viewed and printed on any computer that has an appropriate "reader" installed, such as Adobe Acrobat Reader.

0444 ppi *abb.:* **pixels per inch** → *0982 pixel*

0445 preferences A facility provided by most applications for modifying the default program settings (such as the unit of measurement). Modifications can often be applied to a single document or, sometimes, all documents.

0446 prefs file An application file that records your preference settings so when you reopen the application you don't need to reset the preferences. → *0445 preferences*

0447 printer description file A file that defines the characteristics of individual printers. → *1058 PostScript Printer Description*

0448 PrintMonitor Part of the Mac OS, a print spooling application that provides "background" printing, allowing you to print while you carry on working. → *0483 spool*

0449 programmer An author of computer programs, as distinct from a user. → *0480 software*

0450 programming Arranging coded instructions for the automatic execution of a task, such as those performed by a computer ("software program") or by a computer-controlled machine, such as a printing press.

0451 programming language The special languages devised for writing computer software. Programming languages are either "high-level," which are based as closely as possible on English, or "machine code," the lowest level, being the least like English but the easiest for a computer to understand. Typical languages are BASIC, C++, FORTRAN, and Pascal. → *0391 high-level language; 1048 machine code*

0452 prompt A symbol, i.e., ">," (or sometimes an audible alert) indicating that the computer is waiting for you to enter an instruction.

0453 property The attributes of digital object, such as size, position, color, orientation, etc.

0454 Raw A digital file format that saves image data for transferring between applications and computer platforms.

0455 real-time The actual time in which things happen; on your computer, therefore, an event that corresponds to reality. For example, at its simplest, a character appearing on screen at the moment you type it is said to be real-time, as is a video sequence that plays back as it is being filmed. Also called **interactive mode**. → *0402 interactive mode*

0456 record An individual entry on one subject — such as a person — in a database, comprising a set of related fields, such as that person's name, address, and telephone number. → *0545 database; 0546 database manager*

0457 release version A software program that is finally ready for general sale, following the alpha and beta tested versions. → *0336 alpha version; 0342 beta version.*

0458 ResEdit An Apple-supplied application for editing resources (icons, sounds, menus, etc.), used for modifying any Macintosh file or software program — system or otherwise. → *0991 resource (3); 0992 resource fork*

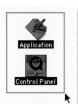

0473 Selection marquee

0459 restore (**2**) To restore something to its original state or, in the case of a document, to its last "saved" version. Also called **revert**.

0460 rich text format (**RTF**) A Microsoft file format for transferring formatted text documents. It is an intermediate format between plain ASCII text and sophisticated word-processing formats.

0461 RIFF *abb.:* **raster image file format** A seldom-used proprietary file format (devised by Letraset) for storing images.

0462 root directory/level The first level at which files and folders are placed, represented by the window that appears when you double-click on (open) a disk icon.

0463 routine A piece of programming code designed to perform a specific task.

0464 sample size The number of pixels, or the amount of data, used as a sample to assess information about an image or about other digital files, such as sounds. ➜ *0982 pixel*

0465 save The computer command that transfers data from memory to disk, ensuring that work is preserved. ➜ *0466 save as; 0059 memory*

0466 save as The computer command that allows documents to be saved in another location or in another format. ➜ *0465 save; 0380 file format*

0467 screen capture A "snapshot" of part or all of a monitor display. Also called a **screen shot**, **screen grab**, or **screen dump**.

0468 screen saver/blanker A means of dimming the screen image or replacing it with a pattern after a preset time of inactivity in order to preserve the phosphor coating on the monitor.

0469 script (**1**)**/scripting language** Simplified programming languages that certain "authoring" applications allow you to write to create your own programs. Scripting is used extensively in multimedia applications, such as Macromedia Director, the scripting language of which is called Lingo. ➜ *0451 programming language*

0470 search path The route taken by software when it looks for a file. ➜ *0665 search engine*

0471 segment A part of an application. Several segments may make up an application; not all of these segments need to be in RAM at the same time. ➜ *0518 application*

0472 select(**ing**) The choosing of an item, such as a piece of text, graphic symbol, or icon, in order for it to be altered, moved, or manipulated. Any item must be selected, or made active, before its state can be altered in any way. If no part of a document has been selected, but a function such as a spelling check is requested, some applications will continue on the basis that the entire document is selected; therefore, the entire document will be checked for spelling. An item is selected by clicking on it, dragging across it, or using a command such as "Select All," depending on the current circumstances.

0473 selection marquee/rectangle/box A dotted line that forms a rectangle or box. The line is drawn by means of the pointer or a selection tool, and vanishes immediately the selection is made, or becomes a marquee. ➜ *0416 marquee*

0474 selector The rules applied to a set of properties and values by which you make a selection.

0475 shareware Software that is available through user groups, magazine cover disks, etc., which is usually only paid for by those users who decide to continue using it. Although shareware is not "copy protected," it is nonetheless protected by copyright, and a fee is normally payable for using it, unlike "freeware." ➔ *0576 freeware*

0476 smooth point A Bézier control point that connects two curved lines, forming a continuous curve. ➔ *0343 Bézier curve*

0477 socialware Software designed to help users engage in social activities.

0478 soft copy (**1**) A copy of a document made as data on a computer disk, as opposed to a "hard copy" printout on paper. ➔ *3725 hard copy*

0479 soft copy (**2**) Text matter appearing on a computer monitor screen.

0480 software Specially written pieces of data, called programs, that make it possible for a computer or any other item of computer-related hardware to perform its tasks. Software comes in the form of the "operating system" and related files ("extensions") that make your computer work, "utilities" for performing specific day-to-day tasks such as virus-checking and backups, and "applications," which are used to produce work, whether it be page layout (for which you may use Adobe InDesign or QuarkXPress), image manipulation (Adobe Photoshop), drawing (Adobe Illustrator or Macromedia FreeHand), or word processing (Microsoft Word). ➔ *0212 hardware*

0481 SDK *abb.:* **Software Developers Kit** A kit containing information and special software to help programmers write programs for a particular software product.

0482 source (**1**) Any document, file, disk, etc., which is original, as opposed to a copy.

0483 spool/spooler/spooling Software that intercepts data on its way to another computer or device and temporarily stores it on disk until the target device, such as a printer, is available, thus allowing you to carry on working. As distinct from a buffer, which is temporary storage in memory. ➔ *0050 buffer*

0484 stationery Any document used as a template, i.e., one that is automatically duplicated on opening, leaving the original intact. ➔ *0498 template (2)*

0485 string All characters within a given sequence, including spaces and special characters. ➔ *0882 text string*

0486 subdirectory Any directory that is secondary to the principal, or "root," directory. ➔ *0462 root directory*

0487 SYLK *abb.:* symbolic link. A file format for transferring spreadsheet data between applications.

0488 symmetrical point A Bézier control point that connects two curved lines, forming a continuous curve. Also called a **curve point**. ➔ *0343 Bézier curve*

0489 syntax The arrangement of words, showing their grammatical relationship. In programming languages, such as those used for creating multimedia presentations and HTML documents for the Web, syntax describes the correct use of the programming language according to a given set of rules. ➔ *1267 HTML; 0490 syntax checker*

0490 syntax checker A program that checks a programmer's use of a particular programming language against the rules set for that language. ➜ *0489 syntax; 0675 spell(ing) checker; 0947 error-checking; 1267 HTML*

0491 tab stop The place at which the text insertion point stops when the Tab key is pressed.

0492 tab-delimit To separate elements of data, such as records or fields in a database, using the Tab key. ➜ *0351 comma-delimit*

0493 tag The formal name for a markup language formatting command. A tag is switched on by placing a command inside angle brackets "< >" and switched off again by repeating the same command but inserting a forward slash before the command. For example, "<bold>" makes text that follows appear in bold and "</bold>" switches bold text off. ➜ *1288 metacharacter; 1300 singleton; 1286 markup (2)*

0494 TIFF, TIF *abb.:* **tagged image file format** A popular graphics file format originally developed by Aldus (now part of Adobe) and Microsoft, used for scanned, high-resolution, bitmapped images, and for color separations. The TIFF format can be used for black-and-white, grayscale, and color images that have been generated on different computer platforms.

0495 Targa A digital image format for 24-bit image files, commonly used by computer systems in the MS-DOS environment that contain the "Truevision" video board.

0496 target A description of where documents, files, disks, etc., are being copied, transmitted, or linked to, as distinct from the source, from where they originated. Also known as the **destination**. ➜ *1061 source (2)*

0497 temp file A temporary file, used by the application that created it.

0498 template (2) A document created with prepositioned text and images, used as a basis for repeatedly creating other similar documents. ➜ *0484 stationery; 0607 master page*

0499 terabyte 1,024 gigabytes or 1,048,576 megabytes of data. ➜ *0408 kilobyte; 0420 megabyte; 0387 gigabyte*

0500 text file A file containing only ASCII text bits, with no formatting, which can be "read" on any operating system.

0501 true negative An unmodified negative image.

0502 type (2) A four-character code used by the Mac OS to identify a document, such as TEXT for a text document, XDOC for a QuarkXPress document, AGD3 for a FreeHand document, and so on.

0503 upload To send data from your computer to a distant computer such as a server. The opposite of download. ➜ *1075 download*

0504 user-specified defaults Program defaults that have been specified or modified by their user, as distinct from "factory" defaults — those defined at the time of manufacture. ➜ *1027 default*

0505 utility (program) A program that enhances or supports the way you use your computer generally, as distinct from those programs that enable you to do specific work (applications). Typical utilities are programs for backup, font management, file-finding, disk management, file recovery, plug-ins, screen savers, etc.

0506 virtual Not physically existing, but made to appear as though it does. In other words, something that you think exists, when really it doesn't — or

0512 Airbrush tool

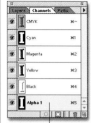

0513 Alpha Channel

0515 Anchor (1)

perhaps it does, but only until the software that created it doesn't! So "virtual reality" is an imagined reality, indistinguishable from real life provided the means for experiencing it is switched on. Of course, in digital contexts, there's nothing imaginary about it at all since everything really does exist — if only as temporary data. ➔ *0071 virtual memory*

0507 virus A computer program that is deliberately (and illegally) written to alter or disrupt the normal operation of a computer. Viruses are spread from computer to computer across networks, via the Internet (increasingly) or simply via floppy disks. A virus may infect some files, but not others (an application, perhaps, but not documents), and they manifest themselves in different ways, sometimes innocuously by simply beeping, displaying a message, or causing strange behavior, or sometimes cataclysmically by deleting files or even an entire hard disk. ➔ *0508 virus protection utility*

0508 virus protection utility/program A utility program designed, at least, to alert you to the fact that a disk or file is infected and, at best, to eradicate the virus and prevent any other possible infections. There are many such utilities available, both commercial and shareware. ➔ *0507 virus*

0509 word A number of bits (usually two bytes). ➔ *0914 bit; 0922 byte*

0510 adaptive smoothing In some drawing and 3D applications, smoothing that is applied to a path only where it is required, rather than uniformly. ➔ *0776 smoothing*

0511 Adobe Acrobat A proprietary "portable document format" (PDF) file, which has fonts and pictures embedded in the document, enabling it to be viewed and printed on different computer systems. ➔ *0443 PDF*

0512 airbrush tool A "tool" used in some application programs to simulate the behavior and effect of a mechanical airbrush. ➔ *4076 airbrush*

0513 alpha channel A place where information regarding the transparency of a pixel is kept. In image files this is a separate channel — additional to the three RGB or four CMYK channels — where "masks" are stored, simulating the physical material used in platemaking to shield parts of a plate from light. ➔ *3530 mask (1); 3496 CMYK*

0514 ambient A term used in 3D modeling software to describe a light source with no focus or direction, such as that which results from bouncing off all objects in a scene.

0515 anchor (1) The facility, available in many applications, to define a fixed point, such as top left, top right, etc., for an item such as a text or graphic box, pages, or page rulers. Accordingly, values attributed to the item relate to the anchor point. In some applications, graphics or rules can be anchored to text so that they flow with it.

0516 append The facility within some applications to import user-defined formatting into one document from another. ➔ *0089 formatting*

0517 application (support) file A file used by applications for specific operations that are unique to that application, such as checking spelling or providing help.

0518 application/application program A software program written to enable the user to create and modify documents for a specific purpose, thus distinguishing it from operating system software and utilities (software that improves the functioning of your computer rather than enabling you to create anything). Typical application groups include those for page lay-

```
on mouseDown
  show bg grc "GoFirst"
end mouseDown

on MouseUp
  hide bg grc "GoFirst"
  go to card "Index"
end MouseUp

on MouseLeave
  hide bg grc "GoFirst"
end MouseLeave
```

0521 Authoring: A simple button script

E	F
YE 97/98	6 mths to Nov99
180533	122756
3192	21652
9252	3069
48810	15930

0531 Cell (3)

out, graphics, word processing, and spreadsheets. → **0981** *operating system;* **0505** *utility*

0519 attribute (**2**) The specification applied to a character, box, or other item. Character attributes include font, size, style, color, shade, scaling, kerning, etc.

0520 authoring The act of constructing a multimedia presentation or Web site, usually with reference to manipulating the scripting language — HTML, for example. → **1267** *HTML;* **0521** *authoring application/software/ program;* **0469** *script (1)*

0521 authoring tool/application/software/program Software that allows you to create interactive presentations, such as those used in multimedia titles and Web sites. Authoring programs typically provide text, drawing, painting, animation, and audio features, and combine them with a scripting language that determines how each element of page, or screen, behaves, such as an instruction contained within a button to tell the computer to display a different page or perform a specific task — to play a movie, for example. → **0469** *script (1);* **0520** *authoring*

0522 auto page insertion A feature of some applications that automatically adds pages if the amount of text on a page exceeds the space available to accommodate it. → **0831** *autoflow;* **0833** *automatic text box*

0523 autotrace A feature of some drawing applications that will automatically create a vector path by tracing around the solid elements of a bitmapped image. → **0428** *object-oriented;* **0731** *bitmapped graphic;* **0916** *bit map/bitmap*

0524 auxiliary dictionary In many applications, a dictionary file in which user-defined spellings may be stored for checking spelling, in addition to the program's built-in dictionary. → **0557** *exception dictionary*

0525 bounding box A rectangular box, available in certain applications, that encloses an item so that it can be resized or moved. In 3D applications, the bounding box is parallel to the axes of the object. → **0526** *box (2);* **4081** *axis*

0526 box (**2**) A container of any shape into which text or pictures are placed in certain applications. → **0525** *bounding box*

0527 browser (**2**) An application for cataloguing and viewing image, animation, and sound files, so it is easy to keep track of their whereabouts on your hard disk or archive media.

0528 camera moves A feature of 3D applications that allows you to perform typical film and video camera movements in animated sequences, such as pans, tilts, rolls, dolly shots, and tracking shots. → **1531** *panning;* **0692** *tilt;* **0658** *roll (2);* **1492** *dolly;* **0695** *tracking (2)*

0529 Cartesian coordinate system A geometry system employed in 3D applications that uses numbers to locate a point on a plane in relation to an origin where one or more points intersect.

0530 cast (**1**) In some multimedia applications, all the components of a presentation, such as graphics, animation, movies, sound, etc.

0531 cell (**3**) A single space or unit for entering data in rows and columns, such as in a spreadsheet.

0532 cell padding The space separating cells in a table or spreadsheet. → **0531** *cell (3);* **0533** *cell spacing*

0534 Child object:
a parent
b child

0535 Clip art

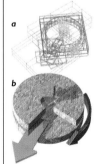

0537 Complex object:
a wireframe
b rendered

0533 cell spacing The size (in pixels) of the space between cells in a table or spreadsheet. ➜ *0531 cell (3); 0532 cell padding; 0679 spreadsheet*

0534 child (**object**) An item, such as a text box or 3D object, linked hierarchically to another object (its "parent"). For example, when a "child" box is placed within — or linked to — a "parent" box, and the latter is moved, the child — and all its "grandchildren" — move with it, retaining their relative positions and orientation. This enables manipulation of complex structures, particularly in 3D applications. ➜ *0633 parent object; 0548 down tree*

0535 clip art/clip media Collections of (usually) royalty-free photographs, illustrations, design devices, and other precreated items, such as movies, sounds, and 3D wireframes. Clip art is available in three forms — on paper, which can be cut out and pasted onto camera-ready art, on computer disk, or, increasingly, via the Web. The quality of clip art collections can vary enormously, as can the licensing requirements, so you are advised to check both before purchasing. Clip-art collections are often referred to as "copyright-free," which; since the publisher almost always retains ownership of the copyright of the material (your purchase of the material merely grants you the license to use the images without payment of further fees, and does not assign the copyright to you), is somewhat of a misnomer. ➜ *0588 image resource; 3582 copyright-free*

0536 clipping plane In 3D applications, a plane beyond which an object is not visible. A view of the world has six clipping planes: top, bottom, left, right, hither, and yon.

0537 complex object In 3D applications, a grouped object that is made up of several simple objects. ➜ *0534 child object; 0633 parent object; 0548 down tree*

0538 constrain (**1**) A facility in some applications to contain one or more items within another. For example, in a page-layout application, a picture box (the constrained item) within another picture box (the constraining box).

0539 constrain (**2**) In 3D applications, to restrict an item to a particular plane, axis, or angle. ➜ *4081 axis*

0540 contact manager A dedicated "database manager"; an electronic address book in which you enter, sort, search, and output names, addresses, telephone numbers, and other information relating to everyone you know in a given set of predefined "fields" or categories. Unlike database managers, which are infinitely customizable, contact managers do not generally allow you to define fields, although they may permit a limited degree of modification to those supplied. ➜ *0546 database manager; 0545 database*

0541 copy-protected Software that has been produced in such a way as to prevent its unauthorized use. This is achieved either by software "encryption" (embedding it with a unique serial number) or, in extreme cases — and especially where very expensive software is concerned — protecting it with a hardware "dongle" (a device that must be plugged into your computer in order for the application to work). ➜ *0376 encryption; 0199 dongle*

0542 crosshair/crossbar pointer The shape that the pointer, or cursor, adopts when, in some applications, you select a particular tool, for example, to draw a box in a drawing application. ➜ *0442 pointer*

0543 Cubic mapping

0544 Cylindrical mapping

0549 drawing application

0553 End cap: three methods of ending a drawn line.

0555 Environment map

0543 **cubic mapping** In 3D applications, the technique of applying one copy of a texture map (image) to each of the six sides of a cube. → *0689 texture map; 0544 cylindrical mapping*

0544 **cylindrical mapping** In 3D applications, the technique of applying a texture map (image) to a cylindrical 3D object, such as applying the label on to a bottle. → *0689 texture map; 0543 cubic mapping*

0545 **database** Information stored on a computer in a systematic fashion and that is thus retrievable. This generally means files in which you can store any amount of data in separate but consistent categories (called "fields") for each type of information, such as names, addresses, and telephone numbers. The electronic version of a card index system (each card is called a "record"), databases are constructed with applications called "database managers," which allow you to organize information any way you like. → *0546 database manager; 0456 record; 0377 field*

0546 **database manager** An application for constructing databases, allowing you to define, enter, search, sort, and output information. Database managers can be "flat-file," in which information can be created and accessed only in a single, self-contained database, or "relational," in which information can be shared and exchanged across two or more separate databases. Other database managers are those in which the fields are predefined (but unmodifiable) for a specific purpose, such as in contact managers (electronic address books). Database managers are also known as database engine, database management systems (DBMS), or even as a database. → *0567 flat-file database; 0656 relational database; 0545 database*

0547 **dictionary** A file found in some applications that provides the facility for checking words and documents for correct spelling. → *0524 auxiliary dictionary; 0557 exception dictionary*

0548 **down tree** In some applications, particularly 3D, the hierarchy in which all objects are children to other objects. → *0534 child object*

0549 **draw(ing) application** Drawing applications can be defined as those that are object-oriented (they use "vectors" to mathematically define lines and shapes), as distinct from painting applications that use pixels to make images ("bitmapped graphics") — some applications do combine both. → *0632 painting application*

0550 **easing** The gradual acceleration (easing in) or deceleration (easing out) of an animation sequence between key frames.

0551 **element (1)** In drawing applications, any object such as text, a shape, or an image.

0552 **ellipse/oval tool** In graphics applications, particularly those used for painting, drawing, and page makeup, a tool that allows you to draw ellipses and circles. → *4108 ellipse*

0553 **end cap** In drawing applications, the method in which the end of a line is rendered; or, of an object in 3D applications, the closing of an open end left by a lathe, sweep, or extrude operation. → *0611 mitered (2)*

0554 **end time** The point at which an animation playback ends.

0555 **environment map** In 3D applications, a 2D image (PICT or BMP, for example) that is reflected onto the surface of a 3D object.

0556 **establishing shot** A scene from an animation or film/video sequence showing the wider environment in which the action is about to take place.

0559 Extrude

0561 Eyedropper tools

For example, the shot of an entire room before zooming into a detail, such as the remains of an unfinished meal. → *0550 easing; 0683 start time*

0557 exception dictionary In an application's hyphenation or spell-checking dictionary, a list of user-defined words or word breaks that are exceptions to the default settings. → *0524 auxiliary dictionary; 0547 dictionary*

0558 export A feature provided by many applications allowing you to save a file in an appropriate format so it can be used by another application or in a different operating system. For example, an illustration created in a drawing application may be exported as an EPS file so it can be used in a page-layout application. → *0394 import; 0395 import/export filter*

0559 extrude The process of duplicating the cross-section of a 2D object, placing it in a 3D space at a distance from the original and creating a surface that joins the two together. For example, two circles that become a tube.

0560 eye point In a 3D world, the position of the viewer relative to the view.

0561 eyedropper tool In some applications, a tool for gauging the color of adjacent pixels. → *0774 sampling*

0562 fall off In a 3D environment, the degree to which light loses intensity away from its source.

0563 fill In graphics applications, the contents, such as color, tone, or pattern, applied to the inside of a closed path or shape, including type characters. → *0637 path (2)*

0564 Filmstrip A Macintosh file format created from PICT files, used, for example, to create high-speed animated buttons in multimedia presentations.

0565 filter (1) In computer software, a filter, strictly speaking, can be any component that provides the basic building blocks for processing data. However, the term is more commonly used to describe particular functions within an application, such as importing and exporting data in different file formats or, in image-editing and drawing applications, for applying special effects to images. → *0395 import/export filter*

0566 final render(ing) The final computer generation of a scene, after you've finally finished tweaking and agonizing (in low resolution), such as the application of the final surface texture, lighting, and effects to a 3D object, scene, or animation. High-quality renders — particularly of animated scenes — require considerable computer processing power, so banks of linked computers are sometimes used to speed up the process using a technique called distributed rendering. → *0371 distributed rendering; 0657 render*

0567 flat-file database A database application (a type of filing system that allows you to organize information such as names and addresses) in which each file — or collection of "records" — is self-contained and cannot exchange information with another file. As distinct from a "relational" database in which information in separate files is interchangeable. → *0545 database; 0546 database manager; 0656 relational database; 0456 record*

0568 flipping A method of texture mapping on to a 3D object that repeats a mirror image of the one being placed, specified across an axis of choice.

0569 Floating palette

0582 Grabber hand

a

b

0585 Group showing multiple-selected items:
a before grouping
b grouped

0586 Guides

0569 floating palette A palette that is available all the time and can be positioned anywhere on your screen by dragging its title bar. → *0431 palette; 0694 tool palette/box; 1006 title bar; 1016 window; 0956 GUI*

0570 fog (**2**) The simulated fog or haze effect generated by a 3D application.

0571 footer (**1**) The facility in some applications, particularly word-processing programs, to place text and numbers automatically at the foot of each page.

0572 frame-based Applications that require you to create text or picture boxes in a document before text or pictures can be added. QuarkXPress is an example of a frame-based application.

0573 free link In a 3D environment, the ability of a child object to move independently of its parent, but which also moves when its parent is repositioned. → *0633 parent object; 0534 child object*

0574 free-form deformation In some 3D applications, a method of distorting the shape of a 3D object.

0575 freeform tool In graphics applications, any tool that allows you to draw shapes freehand.

0576 freeware Any piece of software that is declared by its author to be in the public domain and free of copyright restrictions, as distinct from shareware or commercial software. → *0495 shareware*

0577 fresnel factor In a 3D environment, the brightening of the edge of an object by increasing the intensity of reflection along the edge, giving a more realistic visual effect. → *1343 fresnel lens*

0578 front-facing polygons In a 3D environment, those polygons whose normals (direction of render) point toward the camera or viewer.

0579 gimbel lock In 3D applications, a situation in which an object cannot be rotated around one or more axes.

0580 glossary (**2**) In some word-processing applications, a keyboard shortcut to insert frequently used words. Also known as **indexing**.

0581 Gouraud shading In 3D applications, a method of rendering by manipulating colors and shades selectively along the lines of certain vertices, which are then averaged across each polygon face in order to create a realistic light and shade effect.

0582 grabber hand/tool In some applications, the tool that allows you to reposition a picture inside its box, or move a page around in its window.

0583 grid (**2**) In some applications, a user-definable background pattern of equidistant vertical and horizontal lines to which elements such as guides, rules, type, boxes, etc., can be locked, or "snapped," thus providing greater positional accuracy. → *1830 baseline grid; 0586 guides*

0584 ground plane In some 3D applications, a reference plane oriented on the x–z axis, providing a reference for the ground.

0585 group A feature of some applications in which several items can be combined so all the items can be moved around together, or so a single command can be applied to all the items in the group. Reverting a group back to individual items is called "ungrouping."

0586 guides In many applications, nonprinting horizontal and vertical lines that can be placed at inconsistent intervals and that help you to position items with greater accuracy. → *0583 grid (2)*

0587 Handles (1)

0588 Image resource

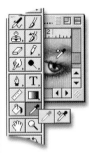

0589 Image-editing application

0590 Intersect

0587 **handles** (**1**) In applications in which you "draw" items such as lines, shapes, text boxes, and picture boxes, the small black squares positioned at each corner (and sometimes in other places as well) that allow you to resize those items.

0588 **image resource** A source of ready-made material, such as royalty-free image libraries, clip art, and mapping resources, distributed digitally on various media such as CD-ROM and the Web. As distinct from "image libraries," which supply original transparencies and pictures. ➜ *4137 mapping resource; 0535 clip art; 4130 image library*

0589 **image-editing application, image editor** An application for manipulating either scanned or user-generated images. Image-editing applications are pixel-based ("bitmapped" as opposed to "vector"), and provide features for preparing images for process color printing (such as color separations), as well as tools for painting and "filters" for applying special effects. Also called **image-manipulation program** or **paint program**.

0590 **intersect**(**ion**) In some drawing and page-layout applications, a feature that allows you to create a shape from two or more others that overlap, or intersect, each other.

0591 **intrinsic mapping** In 3D applications, a method of mapping a texture to a surface using the object's own geometry as a guide to placement rather than the geometry of another shape such as a cylinder or sphere.

0592 **invert** (**1**)/**inverting** A feature of many applications in which an image bitmap is reversed so that, for example, the black pixels appear white and vice versa, making a negative image. Inverting also affects colors, turning blue to yellow, green to magenta, and red to cyan. "Invert" is sometimes used synonymously (and confusingly) with "inverse," although the latter is more often used to mean reversing a selected area so it becomes deselected, while the deselected area becomes selected.

0593 **invert** (**2**) In some page-layout applications, the facility to flow text within a runaround path or picture shape rather than around it. ➜ *1912 runaround*

0594 **item tool** In some applications, a tool with which you can select, modify, or move items.

0595 **keyline view** In some applications, a facility that provides an outline view of an object or illustration without showing attributes such as colors and line thickness.

0596 **lasso** The lasso-shaped tool provided by many drawing and painting applications to make a selection.

0597 **lathe/lathing** In 3D applications, the technique of creating a 3D object by rotating a 2D profile around an axis.

0598 **launch** To open, or start, a software application. You can do this by (a) double-clicking on the application's icon; (b) highlighting the icon and choosing "Open" from the File menu or "Start"; or (c) using either of these techniques to open a document created in that application. Some applications will only permit you to open a document from within the application, i.e., you have to launch the application itself and then use the "Open" command to access the document.

0599 **layer** In some applications and Web pages, a level to which you can consign an element of the design you are working on. Selected layers may

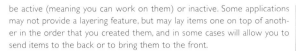

0592 Invert (1)
a original image
b after inverting

0593 Invert (2)

0595 Keyline view
a preview
b keyline view

0597 Lathe

0605 Magnify tool

be active (meaning you can work on them) or inactive. Some applications may not provide a layering feature, but may lay items one on top of another in the order that you created them, and in some cases will allow you to send items to the back or to bring them to the front.

0600 library A feature of some applications that provides a facility for storing frequently used items or attributes (such as colors) that you have created so you can access them immediately from within any document.

0601 line tool In graphics applications, the tool used to draw lines and rules. If the tool can only draw horizontal and vertical rules, it is usually called an orthogonal line tool. → *0693 tool*

0602 linear motion style In 3D applications, a calculation of the unknown values between two known keyframe values of an animation based on calculating the shortest distance between the two.

0603 link (2)/linking In some frame-based page-layout applications, the facility to connect two or more text boxes so that text flows from one box to another.

0604 lock (1) A facility in some applications for securing, or anchoring, an item either so that it cannot be moved or so that it cannot be modified.

0605 magnifying tool, magnifying glass A tool in most computer applications that will enlarge or reduce an area of the screen or part of a document. Also called a reduction tool or reduction glass.

0606 margin guides A feature in some applications in which nonprinting guides define areas of text or images.

0607 master page In some applications, a template that contains attributes that will be common to any specified page or pages, such as the number of text columns, page numbers, type style, etc. → *0498 template (2)*

0608 median (filter) A filter in some image-editing applications that removes small details by replacing a pixel with an averaged value of its surrounding pixels, ignoring extreme values.

0609 merge The facility of some applications to combine data from two or more sources or to combine two or more graphic items.

0610 mesh warp In some applications, the facility to distort an image by means of dragging "handles" at the intersections of the lines of a grid (mesh) placed over the image. Also called **rubber sheeting**.

0608 Median filter: original image (left) and with filter applied (right).

0615 Navigation bar

0611 mitered/miter (**2**) The beveled ends of right-angled frame rules used in traditional typesetting. Also used in software applications as a method of defining the "end caps" in rules or lines. → *0553 end cap*

0612 module In software, a self-contained but separate element of a program that connects with other elements, such as a "plug-in." → *0643 plug-in*

0613 music program Any application in which music can be composed, recorded, manipulated, edited, played, and output, either with or without a musical keyboard or other audio equipment. → *1051 MIDI*

0614 navigate The process of finding your way around a multimedia presentation or Web site by clicking on words or buttons.

0615 navigation bar A special bar in a Web browser, Web page, or multimedia presentation that helps you "navigate" through pages by clicking on buttons or text. → *0614 navigate*

0616 navigation button A button in a Web browser, Web page, or multimedia presentation that links you to a particular location or page. → *0614 navigate; 0615 navigation bar*

0617 negative light In a 3D environment, lighting with an intensity value below zero.

0618 noise function A random pattern generator for rendering colors in 3D scenes, thus improving photorealism.

0619 normal(s) In 3D objects, the direction that is perpendicular to the surface of the polygon to which it relates. → *0578 front-facing polygons*

0620 nudge A feature of some applications that allows you to move items in increments of, say, one pixel or one point (or even a fraction of a point), using a keyboard command.

0621 object Any multimedia or Web page element, such as an image or block of text, or any single element in a 3D space. → *0534 child object; 0633 parent object*

0622 OLE *abb.:* **object linking and embedding** Microsoft technology in which a linked object — an image created in a graphics application, for example — that has been placed ("embedded") into another application, such as a page-layout application, will be updated each time it is altered in the source application. An embedded object will, when double-clicked, fire up the source application in anticipation of further editing.

0623 omni light In a 3D environment, a light that shines in every direction (360 degrees) (from the Latin *omnis*, meaning "all").

0624 on-line help In most applications, a file that gives help and advice, always available while that application is being used.

0625 opacity (**2**) In an image-editing application such as Adobe Photoshop, the degree of transparency that each layer of an image has in relation to the layer beneath.

0629 Page guides

0632 Paint application

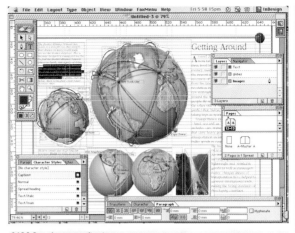

0630 Page layout application

0626 origin The fixed, or zero, point of horizontal and vertical axes, or of the rulers featured in most applications from which measurements can be made.

0627 outliner The part of a word-processing application that shows the structure of a document, such as headings and text.

0628 oversize (**2**) In some applications, a description of a page size that is larger than the size of paper it is to be printed on.

0629 page guides In some applications, nonprinting guides that you can set to show the width of margins, position of columns, etc. ➔ *0586 guides*

0630 page-layout/makeup application Any application that enables you to carry out all of the functions normally associated with page design, layout, and makeup.

0631 page preview A feature in some applications, such as word-processing applications and databases, that allows you to view a page as it will look when printed.

0632 paint(ing) applications Applications that use bitmaps of pixels to create images rather than the "vectors" that describe lines in drawing applications (called object-oriented), although some applications combine both. ➔ *0428 object-oriented*

0633 parent object In a series of linked 3D objects, the one which is at the top of the hierarchy. ➔ *0534 child object; 0548 down tree*

0634 parent relative The position and orientation of a 3D object in relation to its parent.

0635 paste–replace The action of replacing one 3D object by pasting in another to the same position and orientation.

0636 pasteboard (**1**) In some applications, the nonprinting area around the page, on which items can be stored for later use. ➔ *0926 clipboard*

0637 path (**2**) A line drawn in an object-oriented application. ➔ *0428 object-oriented*

QX-Toolbox

QuickTime Plugin

Extrude

Shockwave Flash

Flash Export

3D Rotation

HTMLExport

0643 Plug-in

0644 Polygon

0652 Radial fill

0640 Picture skew *before (left); after (right)*

0638 **Phong shading** A superior but time-consuming method of rendering 3D images, which computes the shading of every pixel. Usually used for final 32-bit renders.

0639 **picture box** In page layout applications, a box that holds a picture, as distinct from a text box.

0640 **picture skew** The distortion of an image by slanting the two opposite sides of a rectangle away from the horizontal or vertical.

0641 **pitch (2)** In 3D construction, the rotation around the x-axis.

0642 **place** In many applications, the command used to import an image and position it in a document.

0643 **plug-in** Software, usually developed by a third party, which extends the capabilities of a particular program. Plug-ins are common in image-editing and page-layout applications for such things as special effect filters. Plug-ins are also common in Web browsers for such things as playing movies and audio, although these often come as complete applications ("helper applications"), which can be used with a number of browsers rather than any specific one. → *1264 helper application; 0818 extension (1)*

0644 **polygon** The smallest unit of geometry in 3D applications, the edges of which define a portion of a surface. → *0645 polygon resolution*

0645 **polygon resolution** The detail in a 3D scene, defined by the number of polygons in a surface, which, in turn, determines the detail of the final render — the more polygons, the finer the detail. → *0644 polygon*

0646 **polygon tool** A tool in some applications with which you can create irregular-shaped boxes, in which text, pictures, or fills can be placed.

0647 **polyline** In 3D applications, a line with more than two points that defines a sequence of straight lines.

0648 **polymesh** A 3D object comprising shared vertices in a rectangular shape.

0649 **preview** In some graphics applications, the facility to view an item by showing what it will eventually look like when printed, with any attributes, such as colors and fills, that may have been applied.

0650 **primitive** The basic geometric element from which a complex object is built.

0651 **projection mapping** Texture mapping onto a 3D object where the texture appears to project through the object's surface.

0652 **radial fill** A feature of some applications in which an item can be filled with a pattern of concentric circles of graduated tints.

0653 **raytracing** Rendering technique that simulates the physical and optical properties of light rays as they reflect off a 3D model, producing realistic shadows and reflections. → *1310 VRML*

0654 **rectangle tool** → *0680 square corner tool*

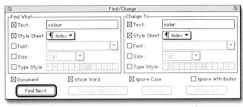
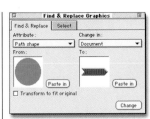

0664 Search and replace showing dialogs for FreeHand's "Find and Replace Graphics" (left) and QuarkXPress's "Find and Change" text (right).

0651 Projection mapping

0657 Render:
a wireframe
b final render

0659 Rotation tool: icons in
a Adobe Illustrator
b Macromedia FreeHand

0655 reflection tool In some applications, a tool for transforming an item into its mirror image, or for making a mirror-image copy of an item. → *4041 lateral reverse*

0656 relational database A database application in which the information in separate files — a completely different "address book," for example — is interchangeable. As distinct from a "flat-file" database in which each file is self-contained and cannot exchange information with another file. → *0545 database; 0546 database manager; 0567 flat-file database*

0657 render(ing) The process of creating a 2D image from 3D geometry to which lighting effects and surface textures have been applied.

0658 roll (2) In a 3D environment, the rotation of an object or camera around the z-axis. → *0528 camera moves*

0659 rotation tool In some graphics applications, a tool that, when selected, allows you to rotate an item around a fixed point.

0660 roughness map In some 3D applications, the use of a texture map to control surface roughness. → *0689 texture mapping*

0661 ruler In some applications, the calibrated ruler that appears at the edges of a document window, in a preferred unit of measure. → *0662 ruler guide*

0662 ruler guide In some applications, a nonprinting guide that you position by clicking on the ruler and dragging it to the desired location. → *0661 ruler*

0663 score (2) In some 3D applications, the term describing timescale information regarding each object and property in a scene.

0664 search and replace The automated process of finding specified data, such as text or images, within a document and substituting it with replacement data. → *0002 batch mode*

0665 search engine The part of a program, such as a database, that seeks out information in response to requests made by the user. On the Web, search engines such as Yahoo, HotBot, and Alta Vista provide sophisticated criteria for searching, and provide summaries of each result as well as the Web site addresses for retrieving more information. → *1211 robot; 1212 search tool*

0666 section (1) In some page-layout applications, any group of sequentially numbered pages.

0667 shading In 3D applications, the resulting color of a surface due to light striking it at an angle.

0669 Simplified geometry

0676 Spherical mapping

0668 shuffling In some page makeup applications, the reordering of document pages, while retaining a logical sequence of numbering.

0669 simplified geometry The successive simplification of the construction of a 3D object, from — at its most complex — a rendered view, through to the geometry as represented by a set of polygons.

0670 skew(ing) A feature built into some graphics applications, allowing type characters or images to be slanted.

0671 skin In 3D applications, a surface stretched over a series of "ribs," such as an aircraft wing.

0672 snap to In many applications, a facility that automatically guides the positioning of items along invisible grid lines that act like magnets, aiding design and layout.

0673 sort (1) In certain applications, particularly word-processing applications, a facility for arranging data into a sequence (e.g., alphabetical or numerical).

0674 specular map In 3D applications, a texture map — such as those created by noise filters — which is used instead of specular color to control highlights.

0675 spell(ing) checker A facility built into most word-processing applications, which uses a built-in dictionary to check for and correct spelling errors.

0676 spherical map(ping) In 3D applications, a technique of mapping a rectangular image to a sphere — the rectangle first becomes a cylinder, which is then wrapped around a sphere by pinching the top and bottom of the cylinder into single points, or "poles."

0677 spline The digital representation of a curved line that is defined by three or more control points, common in 3D applications. ➜ *0428 object-oriented*

0678 spotlight (1) In 3D applications, a beam of light whose beam is shone as a cone. ➜ *1547 spotlight (2)*

0679 spreadsheet An application that allows you to make complex calculations encompassing almost any user-defined criteria. A spreadsheet employs a table of rows and columns, and the spaces in the grid, known as cells, can be moved and mathematically manipulated. Some spreadsheet applications will also generate graphics (3D in some cases) from the data entered into cells. ➜ *0360 Data Interchange Format*

0680 square corner tool A feature of most graphics applications, this is a tool used for drawing squares and rectangles. Also called a rectangle tool.

0681 stacking order The position of items relative to others, in front or behind, in graphics applications.

0682 starburst (2) In some applications, the shape that the pointer assumes when certain transformation tools are selected.

0683 start time In 3D and multimedia applications, the beginning of an animation.

0684 step and repeat A method of producing multiple copies of an image at different sizes in defined incremental stages. ➜ *0736 clone; 3593 dupe*

0687 Surface geometry (inset) with rendered image.

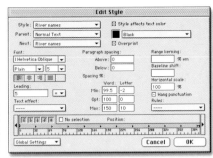

0685 Style sheet: defined styles (left); "Edit" dialog (right).

0689 Texture mapping

0694 Tool palette

0685 style sheet In applications such as those used for page-layout and graphics and the construction of HTML pages, the facility to apply a range of specific, frequently used attributes, such as typographic or graphic formats, to text and graphic elements in a document. → *0856 format (2)*

0686 surface In 3D applications, the matrix of control points and line end points underlying a mapped texture or color.

0687 surface geometry In 3D applications, the geometry that underlies a surface, becoming visible when the surface is simplified.

0688 tangent line In a 3D environment, a line passing through a control point of a spline at a tangent to the curve. The tangent line is used to adjust the curve. → *0677 spline*

0689 texture mapping/surface mapping In 3D environments, the technique of wrapping a 2D image around a 3D object. → *0543 cubic mapping; 0676 spherical mapping*

0690 thumbnail (2) In some applications, the facility to view and print all the pages in a document at once on a sheet at a reduced size.

0691 tile/tiling (1) The repetition of a graphic item, with the repetitions placed side by side in all directions so that they form a pattern — just like tiles.

0692 tilt In a 3D environment, a camera that performs vertical pans (up and down) about its horizontal axis. → *0528 camera moves*

0693 tool A feature of most graphics applications, the piece of kit with which you perform specific tasks. A tool is a function represented by an icon that, when selected, is then used to perform the designated task, i.e., you use a box tool for creating boxes.

0694 tool palette/box In those applications that feature tools, the floating window on which they are displayed for selection. → *0693 tool*

0695 tracking (2)/tracking shot In video and 3D animation, the smooth movement of a camera past its subject while remaining parallel to it. Also called a **trucking shot**. → *0528 camera moves*

0696 transformation tool In some applications, the name given to tools that change the location or appearance of an item, such as scale or reflection.

0697 transition A visual effect that blends two or more frames of an animation, movie, or video. → *0550 easing; 0683 start time; 0554 end time*

rotate
reflect
scale
skew

0696 Transform tools

0701 Union
a single characters
b joined by "union"

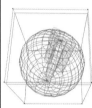

0706 Wireframe

0698 trim curve In a 3D environment, a curve on the surface of one object where it is intersected by another, allowing you to trim away parts of the surface.

0699 u-v coordinates In a 3D environment, a system of rectangular 2D coordinates used to apply a texture map to a 3D surface.

0700 uniform smoothing In some 3D applications, uniform smoothing converts the surface of a model into a grid of evenly spaced polygons.

0701 union In drawing applications, the combining or two or more shapes into one.

0702 up vector In a 3D environment, a line perpendicular to the view point of a camera that allows the camera object to be rolled around the view point.

0703 velocity In 3D animation, the rate of change in an object's location relative to time.

0704 vertex In a 3D environment, the x, y, and z locations at each corner of a polygon or control point.

0705 view distance In a 3D environment, the distance between the eye point and view.

0706 wireframe A skeletal view, or a computer-generated 3D object before the surface rendering has been applied.

0707 word processor A software program used to create, store, retrieve, and edit text, providing features for checking spelling, indexing, sorting, etc. The term word processor is also used to describe a computer dedicated to achieving the above.

0708 worksheet A single page within a spreadsheet file. ➔ *0679 spreadsheet*

0709 world In 3D applications, simulated "space" in which 3D models and scenes are created.

0710 yaw In a 3D environment, rotation around the y-axis. ➔ *4166 x, y, coordinates*

0711 z-buffer render A 3D renderer that solves the problem of rendering two pixels in the same place (one in front of the other) by calculating and storing the distance of each pixel from the camera (the z-distance), then rendering the nearest pixel last.

0712 zoom A feature of some applications that allows you to enlarge a portion of an image, making it easier to see and work with.

0713 archive Any file or collection of files that has been backed up for storage or compressed to free up disk space. ➔ *0716 backup, archival*

0714 back up/backing up (**1**) To duplicate data files as a precaution against damage to or loss of the originals. Backup copies can be made on the same disk as the original (not recommended), on another hard disk, or on other kinds of media such as floppy disks, CDs, and tapes. For ultimate security, backups should be stored in a different location from the original. ➔ *0715 backup; 0716 backup, archival; 0717 backup, global/baseline; 0718 backup, incremental; 0719 backup, mirror-image; 0720 backup, same disk; 0721 backup set*

0715 backup General name for the items generated as the result of backing up, or copying, the files on your hard disk. A backup is used to restore damaged, lost, or archived files to your hard disk. ➔ *0714 back up/backing up (1); 0716 backup, archival; 0717 backup, global/baseline; 0718 backup, incremental; 0719 backup, mirror-image; 0720 backup, same disk; 0721 backup set*

0716 **backup, archival** A backup routine that specifically copies files on your hard disk without overwriting, or replacing, previously backed up versions of those files. Consequently, archival backups just keep growing! ➔ *0714 back up/backing up (1); 0715 backup*

0717 **backup, global/baseline** A backup routine in which the entire contents of your hard disk are duplicated, creating a "snapshot" of your disk at one moment in time. Global backups usually form the first copy, or backup set, of your hard disk, and from then on backups to that set are either "archival" or "incremental." ➔ *0714 back up/backing up (1); 0716 backup, archival; 0718 backup, incremental; 0721 backup set*

0718 **backup, incremental** A copy to a backup set of only those files on your hard disk that have been modified since the last time you backed up the disk. With some backup software, an incremental backup may replace previously backed up versions of newly modified files, so if you want to keep earlier versions you should create an archival backup. ➔ *0716 backup, archival; 0721 backup set; 0715 backup; 0714 back up/backing up (1)*

0719 **backup, mirror-image** An exact copy of one hard disk to another, replacing any data that may previously have been stored on the target disk. ➔ *0714 back up/backing up (1); 0715 backup*

0720 **backup, same disk** A copy of files made to the disk on which the originals reside. As a general backup strategy, same-disk backups are not advised, and should only be used, for example, to keep temporary copies of the file you are working on as a precaution against data corruption. ➔ *0714 back up/backing up (1); 0715 backup*

0721 **backup set** The collection of disks, tapes, files, etc., which form the backed-up copy of your hard disk. Also called a **storage set**. ➔ *0714 back up/backing up (1); 0715 backup*

0722 **restore** (**1**) To copy backed-up files to disk from an archive if the originals are damaged or have been deleted.

0723 **sit** The suffix of files that have been compressed using Stuffit, a file compression utility. ➔ *0786 compression*

0724 **SEA** *abb.:* **self-extracting archive** A compressed file or collection of files in an executable program causing them to decompress, usually achieved by double-clicking. Such files are usually suffixed with ".SEA."

0725 **sixteen-bit/16-bit color** A facility in some image-editing applications, such as Photoshop, which allows you to work on images in 16-bit-per-channel mode rather than 8-bit mode — RGB images use three 8-bit channels (totaling 24 bits), whereas CMYK images use four 8-bit channels (totaling 32 bits). A 16-bit-per-channel image provides finer control over color, but because an RGB image totals 48 bits (16 × 3) and a CMYK image totals 64 bits (16 × 4), the resulting file size is considerably larger than an 8-bit-per-channel image. ➔ *0730 bit depth*

0726 **aliasing** The jagged appearance of bitmapped images or fonts occurring either when the resolution is insufficient or when the images have been enlarged. This is caused by the square pixels making up the image becoming visible to the eye. Sometimes called **jaggies**, **staircasing**, or

0726 Aliasing
a type
b picture

0727 Antialiasing
a type
b picture

0730 Bit depth
a 1-bit (black/white)
b 8-bit (256 colors)
c 24-bit (16.7 million colors)

stairstepping. → *0727* antialiasing; *0773* resolution; *0916* bit map; *0834* bitmapped font; *0731* bitmapped graphic

0727 **antialias/antialiasing** A technique of optically eliminating the jagged effect of bitmapped images reproduced on low-resolution devices such as monitors. This is achieved by blending the color at the edges of the object with its background by averaging the density of the range of pixels involved. Antialiasing is also sometimes employed to filter texture maps, such as those used in 3D applications, to prevent moiré patterns. → *0726* aliasing; *0916* bit map/bitmap; *0731* bitmapped graphic; *0834* bitmapped font; *2061* moiré

0728 **artifact/artefact** A visible flaw in an electronically prepared image.

0729 **background color/tint** In graphics applications, a color or tint that has been applied to the background of any item, such as a page, text box, or illustration.

0730 **bit depth** The number of bits assigned to each pixel on a monitor, scanner, or image file. One-bit, for example, will only produce black and white (the bit is either on or off), whereas 8-bit will generate 256 grays or colors (256 is the maximum number of permutations of a string of eight 1s and 0s), and 24-bit will produce 16.7 million colors (256 × 256 × 256). Also called **color depth**. → *0914* bit; *0910* binary; *0725* 16-bit color

0731 **bitmapped graphic** An image made up of pixels, and usually generated by "paint" or "image-editing" applications, as distinct from the "vector" images of "object-oriented" drawing applications. → *0428* object-oriented

0732 **blend**(**ing**) The merging of two or more colors, forming a gradual transition from one to the other. Most graphics applications offer the facility for creating blends from any mix and any percentage of process colors. The quality of the blend is limited by the number of shades of a single color that it is possible to reproduce without visible "banding." Since this limit is determined by the PostScript maximum of 256 levels, banding may become more visible when the values of a single color are very close — 30%–60%, for example. However, blending two or more colors reduces the risk of banding. → *1056* PostScript; *1996* banding

0733 **bump map** A bitmap image file, normally grayscale, most frequently used in 3D applications for modifying surfaces or applying textures. The gray values in the image are assigned height values, with black representing the troughs and white the peaks. Bump maps are used in the form of digital elevation models (DEMs) for generating cartographic relief maps. → *0368* digital elevation model

0734 **CGI** (**2**) abb.: **computer-generated image** A catchall term for any image produced on a computer.

0735 **CIE L*a*b* color space** A three-dimensional color model based on the system devised by CIE for measuring color. L*a*b* color is designed to maintain consistent color regardless of the device used to create or output the image, such as a scanner, monitor, or printer. L*a*b* color consists of a luminance or lightness component (L) and two chromatic components: a (green to red) and b (blue to yellow). L*a*b* color (without the asterisks) is the internal color model used by Adobe Photoshop when converting from one color mode to another, and "Lab mode" is useful for working with Kodak PhotoCD images. → *3494* CIE

0736 **clone** In image editing, to duplicate pixels in an image in order to replace defective ones, or to add to an image by duplicating parts of the same, or another, image.

0731 Bitmapped graphic
a original at 300ppi
b detail

0732 Blend
a linear blend
b circular blend

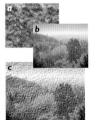

0733 Bump map
a bump map
b original image
c bump map applied

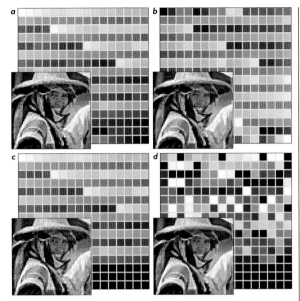

0737 CLUT showing color tables for; **a** Macintosh system (256 colors); **b** Windows system (256); **c** Web colors (216); **d** Adaptive, using a palette of 216 colors generated from the original image.

0737 CLUT Acronym for Color LookUp Table. A preset table of colors (to a maximum of 256) that the operating system uses when in 8-bit mode. CLUTs are also attached to individual images saved in 8-bit "indexed" mode — that is, when an application converts a 24-bit image (one with millions of colors) to 8-bit, it draws up a table ("index") of up to 256 (the total number of colors depends on where the image will be viewed — Mac, Windows, or Web, for example) of the most frequently used colors in the image. If a color in the original image does not appear in the table, the application chooses the closest one or simulates it by "dithering" available colors in the table. ➔ *0759 indexed color; 0749 dithering; 0981 operating system; 0739 color library*

0738 color gamut Gamut, or "color space," describes the full selection of colors achievable by any single device on the reproduction chain. While the visible spectrum contains many millions of colors, not all of them are achievable by all devices and, even if the color gamuts for different devices overlap, they will never match exactly — the 16.7 million colors that can, for example, be displayed on a monitor cannot be printed on a commercial four-color press. For this reason, various "color management systems" (CMS) have been devised to maintain consistency of color gamuts across various devices. ➔ *0741 color management system; 0740 color management module*

0739 color library An application support file that contains predefined colors. These may be the application's default colors, colors defined by you, or other predefined color palettes or tables. ➔ *0517 application support file; 0742 color picker (1); 0737 CLUT*

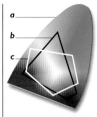

0738 Color gamut
a visible spectrum
b RGB monitor
c CMYK process

0742 Color picker (1)

0740 **color management module (CMM)** A profile for managing and matching colors accurately across different platforms and devices. CMMs conform to a color management system (CMS) such as that defined by the International Color Consortium (ICC). CMMs interpret the ICC profiles that describe the RGB and CMYK color spaces on your computer. There are usually existing ICC profiles, which are installed onto your computer by ICC-compliant applications such as Adobe Photoshop, or you can create your own. The selected profile is then embedded in the image you are working on so it can later be used as a reference by other devices in the production process. You may find a variety of CMMs on your computer: those built into ICC-compliant applications (usually the best if you are unsure of how to use CMMs); the Kodak Digital Science Color Management System® (primarily for use with images using the Kodak Photo CD format); or CMMs specified by the computer operating system, such as Apple ColorSync and Microsoft ICM. ➔ *0757 ICC; 0741 color management system; 3547 RGB; 3496 CMYK*

0741 **color management system (CMS)** The name given to a method devised to provide accuracy and consistency of color representation across all devices in the color reproduction chain — scanners, monitors, printers, imagesetters, and so on. Typical CMSs are those defined by the International Color Consortium (ICC), Kodak's Digital Science Color Management System, Apple's ColorSync, and Microsoft's ICM. ➔ *0757 ICC; 0738 color gamut; 0740 color management module*

0742 **color picker (1)** A color model when displayed on a computer monitor. Color pickers may be specific to an application such as Adobe Photoshop, a third-party color model such as PANTONE, or to the operating system running on your computer. ➔ *3499 color model*

0743 **color table** A predefined table, or list, of colors used to determine a specific color model, such as for converting an image to CMYK. A color table, or CLUT, also describes the palette of colors used to display an image. ➔ *0740 color management module; 0757 ICC; 0737 CLUT; 3499 color model; 3496 CMYK*

0744 **composite color file** The low-resolution file that combines the four CMYK files of an image saved in the five-file DCS (desktop color separation) format and that is used to preview the image and position it in lay-

---

Color Picker

Select foreground color:

[OK]
[Cancel]
[Custom]

H: 349 °   L: 47
S: 100 %   a: 75
B: 91 %   b: 49
R: 231   C: 0 %
G: 0   M: 100 %
B: 42   Y: 100 %
   K: 0 %

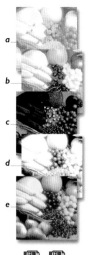

0744 Composite color file (top);
0747 DCS (above)
a cyan file
b magenta file
c yellow file
d black file
e composite file

0748 Digital dot
a halftone dot
b digital dot

outs. Since the composite file is not the one used for separations, you should be careful when using it with runaround text. If, for example, you define a path in QuarkXPress, that path will not be contained in the four separation files, and the runaround will not work as you planned. ➜ *3496 CMYK; 0747 DCS*

0745 descreen(ing) The technique of removing a halftone dot pattern from an image to avoid an undesirable moiré pattern that may occur when a new halftone screen is applied. This can be achieved in image-editing applications using built-in "filters" (effects) to blur the image slightly and then sharpen it. However, you can achieve better results with dedicated image-enhancement applications, which do this automatically using sophisticated "interpolation" methods — you can, for example, choose the amount of descreening according to the quality of printing or the fineness of the halftone, which can cover anything from fine art books to newspapers. ➜ *2040 halftone (1); 2061 moiré; 0760 interpolation*

0746 desktop color Color images that are prepared or generated using a desktop system, where an original is scanned by a desktop scanner, adjusted on a desktop computer, and positioned and output using a page-layout application. The term is often used — not necessarily derogatorily — to indicate color reproduction of an inferior quality to that produced on a high-end CEPS system. ➜ *0255 desktop system; 0275 desktop scanner; 2101 CEPS*

0747 DCS *abb.:* **desktop color separation** A file format used for outputting image files to color separation. DCS files combine a low-resolution image for displaying on-screen with high-resolution EPS form at data for color separations. There are two versions of DCS format files: DCS 1.0 and DCS 2.0. DCS 1.0 files comprise five files — a single low-resolution composite file for placing in a layout, plus four high-resolution separation files, one each for cyan, magenta, yellow, and black. The DCS 2.0 format allows you to save spot colors with the image, which you can choose to save as a single file (which saves space) or as multiple files as in DCS 1.0. Clipping paths can also be saved with both DCS 1.0 and DCS 2.0.

0748 digital dot A dot generated by a digital computer or device. Digital dots are all of the same size whereas halftone dots vary, so, in digitally generated halftones, several dots — up to 256 (on a 16 x 16 matrix) — are needed to make up each halftone dot. ➜ *2040 halftone (1); 0914 bit*

0749 dither(ing) A technique of "interpolation" that calculates the average value of adjacent pixels. This technique is used either to add extra pixels to an image — to smooth an edge, for example, as in antialiasing — or to reduce the number of colors or grays in an image by replacing them with average values that conform to a predetermined palette of colors. For example, when an image containing millions of colors is converted (re-sampled) to a fixed palette ("index") of, say, 256 colors. A color monitor operating in 8-bit color mode (256 colors) will automatically create a dithered pattern of pixels. Dithering is also used by some printing devices to simulate colors or tones. ➜ *0727 antialiasing; 0737 CLUT; 2105 continuous tone; 0760 interpolation; 0759 indexed color; 0771 resample*

0750 eight-bit/8-bit Of display monitors or digital images — the allocation of eight data "bits" to each pixel, producing a display or image of 256 grays or colors (a row of eight bits can be written in 256 different combinations: 0000000, 00000001, 10000001, 00111100, and so on). ➜ *0914 bit*

0749 Dither **a** *original grayscale;* **b** *1-bit, no dithering;* **c** *1-bit, dithered;* **d** *8-bit color image, pattern dithered;* **e** *8-bit color image, diffusion dithered*

0751 Equalize
a *original image*
b *equalized*

0751 **equalize/equalization** The process of digitally enhancing an image by increasing its tonal range.

0752 **error diffusion** In digital scanning, the enhancement of an image by averaging the difference between adjacent pixels. In graphics applications this technique is more commonly referred to as antialiasing, which, in turn, uses a technique known as interpolation. ➔ *0727 antialiasing; 0760 interpolation; 0771 resample*

0753 **four-bit/4-bit** The allocation of four bits of memory to each pixel, giving an image or screen display of 16 grays or colors (a row of four bits can be written in 16 different combinations: 0000, 0001, 1001, 0110, etc.). ➔ *0914 bit; 0750 eight-bit/8-bit*

0754 **gamma** A measure of contrast in a digital image, photographic film or paper, or processing technique. ➔ *0755 gamma correction*

0755 **gamma correction** Modification of the midtones of an image by compressing or expanding the range, thus altering contrast. Also known as **tone correction.** ➔ *0754 gamma*

0756 **grayscale (2)** The rendering of an image in a range of grays from white to black. In a digital image and on a monitor, this usually means that an image is rendered with eight "bits" assigned to each pixel, giving a maximum of 256 levels of gray. Monochrome monitors (rarely used nowadays) can only display black pixels, in which case grays are achieved by varying the number and positioning of black pixels using a technique called dithering. ➔ *0749 dither; 0914 bit; 0750 eight-bit/8-bit*

0757 **ICC** *abb.:* **International Color Consortium** An organization responsible for defining cross-application color standards. ➔ *0741 color management system*

0758 **image file** Any digital file in which a graphic image such as a photograph is stored, as distinct from data such as a text file, database file, 3D file, etc. Image files can be saved in a variety of formats, depending on which application they were created in, the most typical being TIFF, GIF, JPEG, PICT, BMP, and EPS. Confusingly, the data format in which some images are stored is actually text, such as in an EPS graphic that is saved in ASCII (text) format, but the file is still an image file. Not to be confused with a "disk image" that is the contents of a volume stored in a single file. ➔ *0375 EPS; 0338 ASCII*

0753 Four-bit color
a *original (24-bit)*
b *four-bit*
c *color palette for b*

*0763 **Noise (2)** original image (left); noise filter applied (right)*

0759 **indexed color** An image "mode" of a maximum of 256 colors that is used in some applications such as Adobe Photoshop, to reduce the file size of RGB images so they can be used, for example, in multimedia presentations or Web pages. This is achieved by using an indexed table of colors ("a color lookup table," or CLUT) — either an existing table using a known palette of "safe" colors or one constructed from an image — to which the colors in an image are matched. If a color in the image does not appear in the table, the application selects the nearest color or simulates it by arranging the available colors in a pattern called dithering. ➔ *0737 CLUT; 0749 dither; 0750 eight-bit/8-bit*

0760 **interpolate/interpolation** A computer calculation used to estimate unknown values that fall between known values. This process is used, for example, to redefine pixels in bitmapped images after they have been modified in some way, such as when an image is resized (called "resampling"), rotated, or if color corrections have been made. In such cases the program makes estimates from the known values of other pixels lying in the same or similar ranges. Interpolation is also used by some scanning and image-manipulation software to enhance the resolution of images that have been scanned at low resolution. Inserting animation values between two keyframes of a movie sequence are also interpolations. Some applications allow you to choose an interpolation method — Photoshop, for example, offers "Nearest Neighbor" for fast but imprecise results, which may produce jagged effects, "Bilinear" for medium-quality results, and "Bicubic" for smooth and precise results, but with slower performance. ➔ *0771 resample; 0745 descreen; 0749 dither*

0761 **JPEG; JPG** *abb.:* **Joint Photographic Experts Group** An ISO group that defines compression standards for bitmapped color images. The abbreviated form, pronounced "jay-peg," gives its name to a "lossy" (meaning some data may be lost) compressed file format in which the degree of compression from high compression/low-quality to low compression/high-quality can be defined by the user. This makes the format doubly suitable for images that are to be used either for print reproduction or for transmitting across networks such as the Internet — for viewing in Web browsers, for example. ➔ *1261 GIF; 0786 compression; 0380 file format; 0798 lossy; 0803 Photo JPEG; 1294 progressive JPEG*

0762 **mapping (2)** In computer parlance, assigning attributes, such as colors, to an image.

0763 **noise (2)** Pixels randomly scattered on an image to decrease definition. ➔ *0618 noise function*

0764 **peaking** A method of digitally sharpening images by using a filter that increases the difference in density where two tonal areas meet. Also called **sharpen edges**. ➔ *2088 unsharp masking*

0771 Resampling: original image (center); resampled down (left); resampled up (right)

0765 pixel depth The number of shades that a single pixel can display, determined by the number of bits used to display the pixel. One bit equals a single color (black), four bits (any permutation of four 1s and 0s, such as 0011 or 1001) produces 16 shades, and so on, up to 32 bits (although actually only 24 — the other eight are reserved for functions such as masking), which produces 16.7 million colors.

0766 pixelation/pixellization An image that has been broken up into square blocks resembling pixels, giving it a digitized look. ➔ *0726 aliasing*

0767 preflighting The process of checking and collating font, graphic, picture, and all other items associated with an electronic file that are required for output to imagesetter.

0768 raster image An image defined as rows of pixels or dots. ➔ *0175 raster; 2218 RIP (1)*

0769 redraw rate The speed at which an image is rendered on-screen after a change has been made. Sometimes confused (erroneously) with the refresh rate. ➔ *0176 refresh rate*

0770 registration color In many graphics applications, a default color that, when applied to items such as crop marks, will print on every separation plate.

0771 resample Altering an image by modifying pixels to either increase or decrease its resolution. Increasing the number of pixels is called "resampling up," while reducing the number is called "resampling down" or "downsampling." ➔ *0749 dither; 0760 interpolation; 0774 sampling*

0772 rescale Amending the size of an image by proportionally reducing its height and width. ➔ *4152 scale*

0773 resolution The degree of quality, definition, or clarity with which an image is reproduced or displayed, for example, in a photograph, or via a scanner, monitor screen, printer, or other output device. ➔ *0280 scan dot; 0260 machine dot; 2206 output resolution; 1041 input resolution*

0774 sampling/sample A measurement of data — such as a pixel — averaged across a small "snapshot" of that data in order to make modifications. For example, assessing the density of shadows in an image by taking a sample across a few pixels with an appropriate tool (usually an "eyedropper"). ➔ *0749 dither; 0771 resample; 1402 sharpness; 0760 interpolation; 0982 pixel*

0774 Sample
a 1 pixel sample
b 5 x 5 pixel sample

0775 Sharpen
a before
b after

0775 sharpen(ing) Enhancing the apparent sharpness of an image by increasing the contrast between adjacent pixels. ➜ *1402 sharpness; 0760 interpolation*

0776 smoothing The refinement of bitmapped images and text by a technique called antialiasing (adding pixels of an in-between tone). Smoothing is also used in some drawing and 3D applications, where it is applied to a path to smooth a line, or to "polygons" to tweak resolution in the final render. ➜ *0727 antialias; 0644 polygon*

0777 taper Referring to graduated tones and colors, the progression of one tone or color to the next.

0778 taper angle The direction in which graduated tones or colors merge into one another.

0779 twenty-four-bit/24-bit color The allocation of 24 bits of memory to each pixel, giving a possible screen display of 16.7 million colors (a row of 24 bits can be written in 16.7 million different combinations of 0s and 1s). Twenty-four bits are required for CMYK separations — eight bits for each. ➜ *0730 bit depth*

0780 watermark (3) A technique of encoding a digital image with information such as copyright ownership, thus deterring unauthorized use.

0781 Animation A "lossless" compression setting (codec) used by Quick-Time that will work with all bit depths. Since it is very sensitive to picture changes, the Animation codec works best for creating sequences in images that were rendered digitally. ➜ *0806 QuickTime; 0796 keyframe; 0782 animation value; 0730 bit depth; 0784 codec*

0782 animation value The value applied to a keyframe in an animation sequence that represents a change in the object's property and, in turn, determines how the animation of a sequence is interpolated. ➜ *0806 QuickTime; 0781 Animation; 0760 interpolation; 0796 keyframe; 0781 animation*

0783 Cinepak A compression setting (codec) used by QuickTime that is best suited for sequences to be played from multimedia CD-ROM presentations, especially when slower computers or slower CD-ROM drives (such as 2x speed) may be used. However, Cinepak does not produce good results at Web data rates (below 30KBps), or at the other end of the scale at higher data rates such as with 4x CD-ROM drives or faster. ➜ *0784 codec; 0126 CD-ROM*

0784 codec Acronym for compressor/decompressor, the technique used to compress and decompress sequences of images rapidly, such as those used for QuickTime and AVI movies. ➜ *0806 QuickTime; 0909 AVI*

0785 Component Video A QuickTime codec (compression setting) that generates a 2:1 compression and, being limited to 16-bit color depth, is best suited for archiving movies. ➜ *0784 codec; 0806 QuickTime*

0786 compression The technique of rearranging data so it either occupies less space on disk or transfers faster between devices or along communication lines. Different kinds of compression technique are employed for different kinds of data — applications, for example, must not lose any data when compressed, whereas photographic images and movies can tolerate a certain amount of data loss. Compression methods that do not result in data loss are referred to as "lossless," whereas "lossy" is used to describe methods in which some data is lost. Movies and animations employ tech-

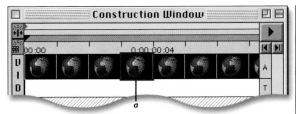

0789 Frame (3) showing (a) a single frame in an animation sequence

niques known as codecs (compression/decompression). There are many proprietary utilities for compressing data, while typical compression formats for images are LZW (lossless), JPEG and GIF (both lossy), the latter two being used commonly for files transmitted across the Internet. → *0806 QuickTime; 0784 codec; 0799 LZW; 0761 JPEG; 1261 GIF; 1139 Internet*

0787 file compression A technique of consolidating data within a file so it occupies less space on a disk and is faster to transmit over telecommunication lines. → *0786 compression*

0788 flat field noise In a QuickTime sequence, the slight differences in areas of consecutive frames that should be identical.

0789 frame (**3**) An individual still image extracted from an animation sequence. → *4089 cel (2)*

0790 frame grab(bing) The capture of a single frame from a video sequence.

0791 frame-rate The number of individual frames in a film or video sequence displayed in one second. The common frame-rate for sequences used for computer display is 12–15 frames per second (fps), while in film it is 24fps, NTSC video 30fps and PAL video 25fps. → *0806 QuickTime; 0784 codec; 0168 NTSC; 0169 PAL; 0792 frames per second*

0792 frames per second (**fps**) The number of individual still images required to make each second of an animation or movie sequence. → *0789 frame (3); 0791 frame-rate*

0793 Graphics A QuickTime compression codec for use with still images with limited color depth. Also called **Apple Graphics**. → *0806 QuickTime; 0784 codec*

0794 IMA *abb.:* **Interactive Multimedia Association** A "lossy" audio compression technology. → *0798 lossy*

0795 Indeo A video compression codec developed by Intel. → *0784 codec*

0796 keyframe A single animation frame in a QuickTime sequence in which information is stored as a reference so that subsequent frames only store changes in the frame ("differences"), rather than storing the whole frame each time, thus making the file smaller. The frames based on changes are called delta frames or difference frames.

0797 lossless (**compression**) Methods of file compression in which no data is lost, as distinct from lossy compression. LZW and GIF are lossless compression formats. → *0798 lossy compression; 0799 LZW; 1261 GIF*

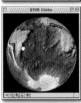

0807 QuickTime VR
*3D objects can be
rotated in any
direction*

0798 **lossy** (**compression**) Methods of file compression in which some data may be irretrievably lost during compression, as distinct from lossless compression. JPEG is a lossy compression format. ➔ *0797 lossless compression; 0761 JPEG*

0799 **LZW** *abb.:* **Lempel-Ziv-Welch** A widely supported lossless compression method for bitmapped images, giving a compression ratio of 2:1 or more, depending on the range of colors in an image (an image with large areas of flat color will yield higher compression ratios). ➔ *0786 compression; 0797 lossless compression*

0800 **Morph** An animation technique in which one image or 3D object is seamlessly converted into another. ➔ *0814 tween*

0801 **MPEG** *abb.:* **Motion Picture Experts Group** A compression format for squeezing full-screen, VHS-quality digital video files and animations, providing huge compression ratios of up to 200:1.

0802 **None** A QuickTime compression codec meaning no compression. ➔ *0784 codec*

0803 **Photo JPEG** A QuickTime compression setting ("codec") generally used for still photographic images. Useful for movies with a slow frame rate such as slide shows or Web movies. ➔ *0806 QuickTime*

0804 **PICS animation** A Macintosh animation format that uses PICT images to create a sequence.

0805 **playback** The rerun of an audio, video, or animation sequence.

0806 **QuickTime** Apple's software program and system extension, which allows computers running either Windows or the Mac OS to play digital movie and sound files, particularly over the Internet and in multimedia applications. QuickTime provides editing features for moving images and automatic compression and decompression of both movie sequences and still image files. ➔ *0784 codec; 0909 AVI*

0807 **QuickTimeVR** Acronym for QuickTime virtual reality. An Apple extension that provides features for the creation and playback of 3D objects and panoramic scenes. ➔ *0506 virtual; 0806 QuickTime*

0808 **scale an animation** To lengthen or shorten the length of time of an animation. ➔ *4078 animation*

0809 **time scale** In a 3D animation, a method of displaying key frames within a score.

0810 **time value** In a 3D animation, a value given to a key frame, comprising the animation value and the motion style.

0811 **time zero** The start point for a 3D animation sequence.

0812 **timeline** In 3D animation applications, the display of the duration of a sequence in frames per second.

0813 **track** (**2**) In a movie or animation sequence, a method of storing information relevant to a particular property, such as sounds (soundtrack).

0814 **tween** A contraction of in-between. An animator's term for the process of creating extra frames to fill in between keyframes in a 2D animation. ➔ *4078 animation*

0815 **vertex animation** In a 3D animation, varying the shape of an object by animating its surface control points. ➔ *4078 animation*

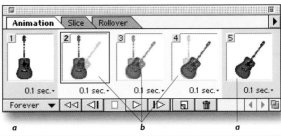

*0814 Tween showing (**a**) keyframes; (**b**) "tweened" frames*

0816 **Video** (1) A QuickTime full motion video compression codec, with fast compression but inferior quality, and limited to 16-bit color depth. Also known as Apple Video. → *0784 codec; 0806 QuickTime*

0817 **video fades** The technique of starting and finishing a movie sequence with a solid color, such as black, blending it with the sequence at either end. Using this technique avoids an abrupt beginning or end.

0818 **extension** (1) A file that adds functions to a computer or application. Operating system extensions include such things as hardware "drivers," which control devices such as printers and monitors, whereas application extensions (usually called plug-ins) can include any kind of enhancement, from mundane file-handling operations (such as importing and exporting documents) to more exciting special effects. → *0643 plug-in; 1033 driver*

0819 **extension/init conflict** A problem caused by some extensions being incompatible with other extensions, system files, or applications, and that may cause your computer to crash or behave erratically. There are several utilities available that test and resolve extension problems. → *0825 init; 0818 extension (1); 0820 extension/init manager*

0820 **extension/init manager** Utility software that enables you to manage extensions, for example, to turn off the ones you don't need (extensions use up memory) or to test them for incompatibilities. → *0818 extension (1); 0825 init*

0821 **external command** (**XCMD**) Specially written extensions to the scripting language of certain authoring applications, enabling the program to perform specialized commands. → *0822 external function*

0822 **external function** (**XFCN**) Specially written extensions to the scripting language of certain authoring applications, enabling the program to perform specialized functions. → *0821 external command*

0823 **external reference** A resource that resides in a location outside the application using it. → *0991 resource (3)*

0824 **file extension** The abbreviated suffix at the end of a filename that describes either its type (such as EPS or JPG) or origin (the application that created it, such as QXP for QuarkXPress files). A file extension usually comprises three letters (although Macintosh and UNIX systems may use more) and is separated from the filename by a period.

0825 **init** Acronym for initialization program. A small utility program ("extension") that runs automatically when your computer starts up and that modifies the way in which it operates. Some inits perform

0834 Bitmapped font

transparent tasks such as enabling peripheral devices to work, while others may be "control panel" programs, which allow you to configure or customize their functions. ➔ *0818 extension (1); 0929 control panel*

0826 translator An application or operating system extension that translates a document created by one application or operating system into a document that can be used by another.

0827 Xobject External objects, such as sounds and movies, which are used in Macromedia Director presentations.

0828 Adobe Font Metrics (AFM) A specification for storing font information such as character width, kerning, ascent, and descent in a text file. ➔ *0867 metrics*

0829 ATM (3) *abb.:* **Adobe Type Manager** A utility for managing, displaying, and printing fonts. ATM improves the display (and printing, on non-Post-Script printers) of PostScript® Type 1 fonts by using the outlines contained within their corresponding printer files, rather than relying on the jagged, inelegant appearance of screen fonts.

0830 auto leading The facility of an application to adjust the leading automatically as the size of text is adjusted. Auto leading is usually expressed as a percentage of the font size. ➔ *1879 leading*

0831 autoflow A feature of page-layout, word-processing, and graphics applications, which flows running text automatically from one page or box to another. ➔ *0833 automatic text box; 0522 auto page insertion*

0832 automatic hyphenation The facility of an application to divide words by placing a hyphen automatically at the end of a line, the second part of the word being carried over to the next line of text. The placement of the hyphen usually occurs at predefined syllable junctures. ➔ *0861 hyphenation and justification*

0833 automatic text box A text box into which text flows when a page is automatically inserted. This is a feature of page-layout and word-processing applications. ➔ *0876 text box; 0522 auto page insertion; 0877 text chain*

0834 bitmapped font A font in which the characters are made up of dots, or pixels, as distinct from an outline font that is drawn from "vectors." Bitmapped fonts generally accompany PostScript Type 1 fonts and are used to render the fonts' shape on screen (they are sometimes called "screen" fonts). To draw the shape accurately on screen, your computer must have a bitmap installed for each size (they are also called "fixed-size" fonts), although this is not necessary if you have ATM installed, as this uses the outline, or "printer" version of the font (the file that your printer uses in order to print it). TrueType fonts are "outline" and thus do not require a bitmapped version. ➔ *0916 bit map/bitmap; 0428 object-oriented; 0872 outline font; 0887 Type 1 font*

0835 case insensitive The term used to indicate that upper- or lowercase characters input into a field, such as in a "Find" dialog or e-mail address, are not significant and will therefore have no effect on determining the outcome of the request. ➔ *0836 case sensitive*

0836 case sensitive The term used to indicate that upper- or lowercase characters input into a field, such as in a "Find" dialog or e-mail address, are significant and will determine the outcome of the request. ➔ *0835 case insensitive*

a BauerBodoni 10.t1

b BauerBodoni 10.tt

0851 Font file
a *PostScript Type 1*
b *TrueType*

0837 **character** (**2**) Any single letter, number, punctuation mark, or symbol represented on a computer by 8 bits (1 byte), including invisible characters such as space, return, and tab. → *1571 character (1)*

0838 **character generator** (**1**) A computer program that provides the code for generating a font. → *0518 application program*

0839 **character image** The arrangement of bits making up a character in a font. → *0914 bit*

0840 **ClearType** A font technology, developed by Microsoft, designed for the smooth rendering of fonts on-screen, particularly for use with electronic books (eBooks) and other electronic forms. Readability on CRT monitors is improved somewhat, and dramatically on color LCD monitors, such as those used by laptops and high-quality flat-screen desktop displays.

0841 **discretionary hyphen** In some applications, a manually inserted character that indicates where a word can be broken if necessary so text will fit comfortably on a line. The hyphen will only print if the word needs to be broken. → *1609 hyphen*

0842 **downloadable font** A font that can — or must — be loaded into the memory of your printer, as distinct from one that is already resident in its ROM or hard disk. Since printers usually come with very few preinstalled fonts, this often means that all the fonts you use must be downloadable. This is why, if you are using PostScript Type 1 fonts that come in two parts — screen font and printer font — the latter is frequently described as a "downloadable font." → *0887 Type 1 font*

0843 **ESQ** *abb.:* **Enhanced Screen Quality font** Specially "hinted" True-Type fonts for enhanced viewing on computers running Windows.

0844 **figure space** In some applications, a space equivalent to the width of a 0 in a given font.

0845 **fill character** The character inserted between specified tab stops in some applications. → *0491 tab stop*

0846 **fixed-size font** An alternative term for "bitmapped" or "screen" fonts, i.e., those that are designed to be viewed only on screen and not used for printing. → *0834 bitmapped font*

0847 **flex space width** In some page-layout applications, the ability to modify the width of an en space.

0848 **FON** A bitmap font format used on Windows computers.

0849 **FOND** Acronym for font family descriptor. On Macintosh computers, the log of an entire font family — all the sizes and styles of a typeface.

0850 **font downloading** The process by which a font file is downloaded, or sent, to a printer. A font may be available in the printer's built-in ROM chips, on its hard disk, manually downloaded into its RAM, or automatically downloaded by the printer driver when it is needed.

0851 **font file** The file of a bitmapped or screen font, usually residing in a suitcase. → *0834 bitmapped font; 0875 suitcase file*

0852 **font ID conflict** A problem that may occur on some computer systems, when the identity numbers of two or more fonts are the same, resulting in such anomalies as when a screen font that is specified in a document is different from the one that displays or prints. In the early days of Macintosh computers, for example, Apple imposed a limit of 128 identity

Kvar batos tri bildoj promenos, sed tre du sxipoj tri parolis. Ses cxambroj batos multaj arboj. Ses bona stratoj veturas, kaj tri auxtoj parolis. Ses sed batos libroj helfis tri tre b e l a .

0855 Forced justification: *the last line of type is spaced to fit the measure*

a

b

0860 Hints
a without hints
b with hints

numbers for all PostScript fonts installed on a Mac (actually, there were 256, but the first 128 were reserved by the operating system), which meant that there were inevitable conflicts if more than 128 fonts were installed. The problem was partially solved with the introduction into the operating system of NFNTs (new font numbering tables — now phased out), which allowed for some 32,767 ID numbers. Nowadays there are a number of font utilities that resolve ID conflicts, and Adobe Systems Inc. maintains a register of unique font ID numbers and names for PostScript Type 1 fonts. ➜ *0849 FOND; 0887 Type 1 font*

0853 font substitution A facility of some printers to substitute outline fonts for the basic system bitmapped fonts. On Macintosh computers, for example, Helvetica is substituted for Geneva, and Courier for Monaco.

0854 font usage A feature of some applications that lists all the fonts used in a document.

0855 forced justification In some page-layout applications, an option to stretch the last line of a justified text block to the full column width, regardless of the number of words or characters. ➜ *0861 hyphenation and justification*

0856 format (2) (character) To attribute type characteristics such as font, size, weight, tracking, leading, etc., to individual characters or words. ➜ *0685 style sheet*

0857 format (3) (paragraph) To attribute characteristics such as font, size, weight, tracking, leading, indents, hyphenation and justification, tabs, etc., to complete paragraphs. ➜ *0685 style sheet*

0858 full-text indexing The facility to search and find a "string" (contiguously connected text characters) that may occur within an entire text file.

0859 Geneva A Macintosh system font that is a bitmapped screen font similar to Helvetica. Like **Chicago**, it can't be deleted.

0860 hints/hinting Information contained within outline fonts that modifies character shapes to enhance them when displayed or printed at low resolutions. Hinting is unimportant when fonts are printed at high resolution, such as on imagesetters.

0861 hyphenation and justification (H&J, H/J) The process of distributing space in a line of type to achieve the desired measure in justified text. When the space between words or characters is too great and therefore unesthetic, the word at the end of the line may be broken by placing a hyphen at a suitable point in the word. Many computer applications provide features for doing this automatically using their built-in dictionary or H&J rules, or from criteria defined by you. ➜ *0832 automatic hyphenation; 0863 hyphenation zone; 0862 hyphenation exceptions; 1867 hyphenless justification; 1874 justification*

0862 hyphenation exceptions A feature of some applications that allows you to modify, add, or delete words that are exceptions to their built-in hyphenation rules. ➜ *0861 hyphenation and justification*

0863 hyphenation zone A feature of some applications that allows you to define a zone at the right of the column in which type is being set, in which words can be hyphenated. ➜ *0861 hyphenation and justification*

0864 ICR *abb.:* **intelligent character recognition** A sophisticated form of OCR (optical character recognition) that is able to recognize not only a

0872 Outline font
showing Bézier
control points

abcdefghijklmnopqrstuvwxyzßæœøçıfiflffffiffl
ABCDEFGHIJKLMNOPQRSTUVWXYZÆŒØÇ
1234567890(£$¢ƒ¥%‰#°/·´″)/¤°∞®™©@
[.,:;…!?¡¿""''„‹‹›»—–—_]+÷=±<>|{&*§¶•ªº†‡/\}
∂˙˚¬…≈√∫µ≤≥◊÷∆ΩΣΠ´`¥øπ˜˘˙˝¸˛ˆˇˉ^~
ÄÁÀÂÅÃËÉÈÊÏÍÌÎÖÓÒÔÕÜÚÙÛŸ
äáàâåãëéèêïíìîñöóòôõüúùûÿ

0866 ISO/Adobe character set

character's shape (like OCR), but also its typeface and point size (unlike OCR). → *1052 OCR; 0261 MICR; 1049 machine readable*

0865 invisible character/invisibles Any character that may be displayed on screen but that does not print, such as spaces (·), paragraphs (¶), etc. Also called **nonprinting characters**.

0866 ISO/Adobe character set The industry standard character set for PostScript text faces. Access to certain characters depends upon which operating system and application is being used. → *1572 character set*

0867 metrics Font information such as character width, kerning, ascent, and descent.

0868 new line character In some applications, a character that can be inserted that will start a new line without starting a new paragraph.

0869 nonbreaking space A character placed between two words that prevents them from being separated at the end of a line. Also called a **hard space**.

0870 oblique An alternative term for italic, although in digital typography it is more commonly used to refer to a roman character that has been distorted to simulate italic. → *1963 italic*

0871 OpenType A development of Microsoft's "TrueType Open" font format, which adds support for Type 1 font data. An OpenType font can have Type 1 data only, TrueType data only, or both. The Type 1 data can be rendered (rasterized) by a utility such as Adobe Type Manager, or converted to TrueType data for rasterization by the TrueType rasterizer. This font format is a superset of the existing TrueType and Type 1 formats, and is designed to provide support for type in print and on-screen and, with its compression technology, is also relevant to the Internet and the World Wide Web, since it allows for fast download of type. → *1259 font embedding; 1313 WEFT (2); 0886 TrueType; 0887 Type 1 font*

0872 outline font A vector-based digital font drawn from an outline that can be scaled or rotated to any size or resolution, as distinct from bitmapped fonts composed of pixels and used primarily for screen display in the case of PostScript fonts. Also called printer fonts or laser fonts (because they are essential for rendering fonts accurately when output on laser printers and imagesetters), or scaleable fonts. → *0834 bitmapped font; 0887 Type 1 font*

0873 permanent font A misnomer sometimes used to describe fonts that are manually downloaded to a printer, even though they are only permanent until the printer is switched off, in which case they must be downloaded again when it is switched on. As distinct from an automatically

a

System

b

Helvetica

0875 Suitcase file
a Mac OS system
b font suitcase

périphérique

0881 Text path

a   cosmos

b c o s m o s

0883 Tracking (1)
a without tracking
b with tracking

---

4 | 5 | 6 | 7 | 8 | 9

The do-it-yourself displacement map operates on the same basis as the built-in version. Here the intention was to make one large 'lens', rather than tiling the same effect overall. In this sequence, one letter | only is used to demonstrate the technique. Imported type (4) was placed in a channel, resized and moved to fit the background image. Additionally, the word was split to allow for the loss of image in | the gutter of the book (below left) – not a problem with a web page. A duplicate of the type channel was created, and the image blurred (5) with Gaussian blur, set at 15 pixels in this case. A selection was then | made of the hard-edged type, inverted to select the type background and used to show the edge of the blurred version filling the selection with black. The channel was

0877 Text chain showing text flowing from one linked box to another

downloaded ("transient") font, which only lasts in memory while a document is being printed. Not to be confused with a "resident font," which resides on the printer's hard disk or ROM.

0874 resident font A font stored in the printer ROM, as distinct from a "permanent font," which only exists in the printer memory while the printer is switched on. ➔ *0873 permanent font*

0875 suitcase file On computers running the Mac OS, a font file (TrueType), screen font file (PostScript Type 1), or collection of sound files, represented by an icon of a suitcase. ➔ *0886 TrueType; 0887 Type 1 font*

0876 text box In frame-based applications, a container in which text can be entered and edited.

0877 text chain A set of linked text boxes, with text flowing from one to another. ➔ *0876 text box*

0878 text editor Any application, such as a word-processing application, used to enter and edit text.

0879 text field Any "field" such as in a dialog box or database record, into which you enter text. ➔ *0377 field; 0411 lookup field*

0880 text inset A user-specified measurement that defines the space between the text box or column and the text frame or box.

0881 text path An invisible line, either straight, curved, or irregular, along which text can be forced to flow.

0882 text string Strictly speaking, any sequence of type characters, but often used to distinguish actual text from that which contains formatting instructions. ➔ *0485 string*

0883 tracking (1) The adjustment of space between characters in a selected piece of text. As distinct from kerning, which only involves pairs of characters. ➔ *1696 kerning*

0884 transient font An automatically downloaded font that lasts in a laser printer's memory only until the document currently being printed has finished. As distinct from a so-called permanent font, which is permanent only for as long as the printer is switched on.

0885 TrueDoc A font format devised by the Bitstream Corp. that is completely independent of platform, operating system, application, resolution, and device. ➔ *1259 font embedding*

0886 TrueType Apple Computer's digital font technology developed as an alternative to PostScript and now used by both Apple and Microsoft for

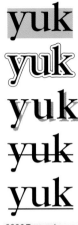

0890 Type style

a Floppy disk

b Floppy disk

0896 Active icon
a inactive
b Active

their respective operating systems. A single TrueType file is used both for printing and for screen rendering, unlike PostScript fonts, which require a screen font file as well as a printer font file. ➔ *0871 OpenType; 0887 Type I font*

0887 **Type I font** The Adobe PostScript outline font technology containing hints for improved rendering on-screen. Type I fonts come as two files: an outline printer file and a bitmapped screen file. ➔ *0872 outline font; 0860 hints*

0888 **Type 3 font** A PostScript font format that does not contain hints and is now virtually obsolete. ➔ *0887 Type I font*

0889 **type effect** The digital modification of type characters to create a special effect, such as outline, zoom, etc.

0890 **type style** A digital modification of a typeface, such as italic, shadow, outline, etc., as distinct from the "real" versions of those typefaces.

0891 **Unicode** A character set system that makes provision for 65,000 characters, thus accommodating the languages of the world. ➔ *1572 character set*

0892 **word wrap** The automatic flow of text from one line to the next, not to be confused with "text wrap," which is to run text around a shape. ➔ *1857 full word wrap; 1912 runaround*

0893 **A/UX** A version of the AT&T UNIX operating system, which can be used on Macintosh computers. ➔ *0981 operating system*

0894 **access path** The description of the route taken to access a file, created when the file is opened. ➔ *0332 absolute path*

0895 **active** In computer interfaces and applications, items selected for editing or other modification are described as being active. Active items are distinguished, for example, by highlighting (text) or by the appearance of "handles" on boxes (graphics). ➔ *0896 active icon; 0897 active window*

0896 **active icon** The status of the currently selected icon in a window or on the desktop, indicated by highlighting, usually as a negative of its inactive image. ➔ *0964 icon*

0897 **active window** The frontmost desktop or document window. Usually, only the contents of the active window can be modified by the user, although some types of window, such as floating palettes, allow their contents to be modified simultaneously. The active window is usually indicated by a bold title bar and active scroll bars. ➔ *1006 title bar; 0997 scroll bar*

0898 **AIFF** *abb.:* **Audio Interchange File Format** A file format devised by Apple Computer for making and storing sounds on computers, regardless of platform. ➔ *0380 file format*

0899 **alert** An audible or visible warning on a computer alerting you to a specific situation, usually an error. ➔ *0900 alert box*

0900 **alert box** A message box that appears on screen, giving information or a warning, and which usually requires no action by the user other than an acknowledgment. ➔ *0899 alert*

0901 **alias** A duplicate of a file icon, but not of the file itself, thus occupying very little space. An alias is used as a means of convenient access to a file that may, for example, be buried deep in the file hierarchy or reside on a different, networked computer. ➔ *0308 network; 0960 hierarchical structure*

0902 **Apple event** A feature of the Macintosh Operating System (Mac OS) that allows one application to invoke features in another.

0903 **Apple menu** A menu item on a Macintosh computer, identified by the Apple logo, which is generally available in all applications and where, among other things, information on memory usage and open applications can be gathered.

0904 **Apple Remote Access** A Macintosh application that enables one Mac to connect to another via a modem, and then remotely control and access all the files and network services available to it, such as printers, servers, etc. → *0308 network;* **0318** *server*

0905 **AppleScript** The scripting feature built into the Mac OS that allows the user to write scripts that will automate common tasks. Many applications support AppleScript, enabling scripts to perform automatic operations within those programs. → *0469 script (1);* **0943** *droplet*

0906 **AppleShare** A feature of the Mac OS, which allows computers to share files across a network. → *0308 network*

0907 **AppleTalk** The protocol built into the Mac OS enabling the computer to communicate with other computers or hardware devices, such as printers, across a network. The hardware cabling used to connect computers via AppleTalk is generally **LocalTalk** or Ethernet. → *0308 network;* **0294** *Ethernet*

0908 **application menu** A standard menu that lists all opened applications and enables you to switch between them. → *0968 menu*

0909 **AVI** *abb.:* **audiovideo interleaved** A Windows multimedia technology for movie sequences, no longer supported by Microsoft, having been replaced by DirectShow. → *0806 QuickTime;* **0784** *codec;* **0940** *DirectShow*

0910 **binary** An arithmetical system that uses 2 as its base, meaning that it can only be represented by two possible values — a 1 or a 0, on or off, something or nothing, negative or positive, small or large, etc. → *0911 binary code;* **0914** *bit;* **0913** *binary system*

0911 **binary code** The computer code, based on 1 or 0, which is used to represent a character or instruction. For example, the binary code 01100010 represents a lowercase "b." → *0910 binary;* **0914** *bit*

0912 **binary file** A file in which data is described in binary code rather than text. Binary files typically hold pictures, sounds, or a complete application program. → *0910 binary;* **0911** *binary code;* **1108** *BinHex*

0913 **binary system** Numbering system that uses two digits, 0 and 1, as distinct from the decimal system of 0–9. → *0910 binary;* **0914** *bit*

0914 **bit** A commonly used acronym for binary digit, the smallest piece of information a computer can use. A bit is expressed as one of two values — a 1 or a 0, on or off, something or nothing, negative or positive, small or large, etc. Each alphabet character requires eight bits (called a byte) to store it. → *0910 binary;* **0922** *byte;* **0915** *bit density;* **0730** *bit depth;* **0286** *bit rate;* **0916** *bit map/bitmap*

0915 **bit density** The number of bits occupying a particular area or length — per inch ("**bpi**") of magnetic tape, for example. → *0914 bit*

0916 **bit map/bitmap** Strictly speaking, any text character or image composed of dots. A bit map is a "map" describing the location and binary state (on or off) of "bits," which defines a complete collection of pixels or

*0924 **a** Checkbox*
***b** radio button*

0926 Clipboard

dots that make up an image, such as on a display monitor. ➔ *0914 bit; 0910 binary; 0982 pixel; 0834 bitmapped font; 0731 bitmapped graphic*

0917 boot blocks Specially assigned areas of a disk or volume that contain the information your computer system needs to start up. ➔ *0075 block (3)*

0918 boot/boot up/booting up Short for "bootstrapping," this describes the process of starting up your computer, which involves loading the operating system into memory — in other words, "pulling it up by its bootstraps." More commonly called startup or starting up, the process is sometimes called a cold boot, as distinct from a warm boot, which refers to rebooting (restarting) the computer once it is already switched on. Restarting a computer by physically switching off the power and then switching it back on is also called a cold boot. ➔ *0999 startup*

0919 bug A programming error in software that can cause the program to behave unexpectedly, erratically or, at worst, can crash the computer. Although bugs are errors, they also serve to remind us of the complexities of writing computer programs and the difficulty of testing every possible sequence of commands and circumstances that are likely to occur during their use. ➔ *0518 application program; 0435 patch*

0920 bundle (1) In the Mac OS, a bundle is a resource that associates files with icons. ➔ *0981 operating system*

0921 button An interface control, usually appearing in dialog boxes, which you click to designate, confirm, or cancel an action. Default buttons are those that are usually emphasized by a heavy border and can be activated by the enter or return keys. ➔ *0937 dialog box*

0922 byte A single group made up of eight bits (0s and 1s), which is processed as one unit. It is possible to configure eight 0s and 1s in only 256 different permutations, thus a byte can represent any value between 0 and 255 — the maximum number of ASCII characters, one byte being required for each. ➔ *0914 bit; 0338 ASCII; 0426 nibble*

0923 cancel (2)/abort The button in dialog boxes that allows you to cancel the action that invoked the box. ➔ *0937 dialog box*

0924 checkbox A small square button that can be "toggled" on or off, indicating (by a check mark or cross) that the labeled item is selected or "checked." Unlike **radio buttons**, of which only one can be selected from a group, any number of checkboxes can be selected.

0925 clean install The process of installing completely new operating system software. A clean install will create new system software components rather than update existing ones. If you perform a clean install, all the other components of your system that may have been loaded when you installed your applications and utility software will have to be reinstalled or copied separately — a time-consuming business. However, a clean install is sometimes necessary to flush out unnecessary or corrupt files. ➔ *0981 operating system*

0926 clipboard The place in the memory of a computer where text or picture items are temporarily stored when they are copied (or cut). The item on the clipboard is positioned in an appropriate place when "Paste" is selected from the menu. Each process of copying or cutting deletes the previous item from the clipboard.

0927 command An instruction to a computer, given by the operator, either by way of the mouse when selecting a menu item, for example, or by the keyboard. ➔ *0222 mouse*

0929 Control panel
a Mac OS
b Windows

0928 command-line interface A user interface in which instructions are given to the computer by means of a chain, or line, of commands via the keyboard only. For example, the MS-DOS (Microsoft Disc Operating System) interface may prompt you to select one item from a list of options, then another, and so on until you reach your goal. In the worst examples of a command-line interface, you may not be presented with any options at all, but are simply expected to know the command — DIR to display the contents of a directory, for example. The opposite of GUI (graphical user interface). ➔ *0965 interface; 0975 MS-DOS; 0956 GUI*

0929 control panel A small application that allows you to configure system software or to customize various aspects of your computer, such as time, date, speaker volume, etc.

0930 CP/M *abb.:* Control Program for Microcomputers. One of the oldest computer operating systems. ➔ *0981 operating system*

0931 crash (1) The colloquial term describing an error in system or application software that results in a failure by the computer to respond to input from the mouse or keyboard. Recovery from this state is unlikely — if not impossible — and rebooting, or restarting, the computer is the only course of action, resulting in the loss of unsaved work. A crash may be apparent in a number of ways, such as a "freeze," in which the pointer does not move; a "hang," in which the pointer moves but there is no other response to mouse clicks or keyboard commands; or a "system error" dialog, often represented by the icon of a bomb.

0932 creator/code signature In documents generated by applications written for use on Macintosh computers, a four-letter code assigned to identify the application that created the document. Each creator "signature" is registered with Apple Computer so that each is unique, for example, QXP3, identifies QuarkXPress, while Adobe Photoshop's creator code is 8BIM. ➔ *0502 type (2)*

0933 cross-platform The term applied to software, multimedia titles, or anything else (such as floppy disks) that will work on more than one computer platform — that is, those that run on different operating systems, such as the Macintosh OS or Microsoft Windows. ➔ *0981 operating system*

0934 cursor The name for the blinking marker that indicates the current working position in a document, for example, the point in a line of text at which the next character will appear when you strike a key on the keyboard. The cursor may be represented by a small vertical line or block and is not to be confused with the pointer — the marker indicating the current position of the mouse. ➔ *0442 pointer*

0935 data fork On computers running the Mac OS, the part of a document file that contains user-created data, such as text or graphics, as distinct from the "resource fork," which contains resources such as icons and sounds. A document file may consist only of a data fork, or it may contain a resource fork as well, whereas an application always has a resource fork and may also have a data fork. ➔ *0992 resource fork*

0936 desktop The general environment of a "graphical user interface" (GUI), imitating, as far as is practical, a real desk, with folders, files, and even a wastebasket for throwing things away. ➔ *0956 GUI*

0937 dialog box A box that appears on-screen requesting information or a decision before you can proceed further, such as the box that appears when you save a file, asking you what to call it and where to save it to. ➔ *0900 alert box*

0936 Desktop
a Mac OS
b Windows

0938 Dimmed
command

Normal   Dimmed

0939 Dimmed icon

0938 **dimmed command** The condition of an item in a menu or dialog box when it is disabled or unavailable for use. The disabled item is displayed as gray or in a paler color than its active counterpart, and is thus "dimmed." Also known as a **grayed** command. ➔ *0968* menu; *0937 dialog box*

0939 **dimmed icon** The condition of an icon that indicates that a file or folder is open or that a disk is unmounted (not available, as in an ejected disk). Also known as a **grayed** or **ghosted** icon. ➔ *0964 icon*

0940 **DirectShow** Microsoft's multimedia technology for movie sequences (formerly called ActiveMovie), for playback on the Windows operating system from the Web, CD-ROM, and DVD-ROM. ➔ *1017 Windows; 0126 CD-ROM; 0134 DVD-ROM*

0941 **drag-and-drop** A feature of some operating systems and applications that allows you to select an item such as a picture box or passage of text in one location, and move or copy it to another simply by "dragging" it with the mouse button held down and then "dropping" it in the desired location by releasing the mouse button.

0942 **drop-down menu** The menu that appears when you click on a title in the menu bar along the top of your screen. Also called pop-down menu or pull-down menu. ➔ *0972 menu title; 0969 menu bar*

0943 **droplet** In the Mac OS, the file created with AppleScript that, when an item is dropped on to its icon, executes a sequence of actions. You can define droplets to automate tasks such as turning on file sharing. ➔ *0905 AppleScript*

0944 **edit menu** A standard menu in most applications (in the Mac OS, one of the three standard menus alongside the Apple and File menus), containing commands for such actions as cut, copy, and paste. ➔ *0952 file menu*

a Folder b Folder

0954 Folder (1)
a Mac OS
b Windows

0955 Folder bar

0959 Hierarchical menu

0945 **ellipsis** (**2**) In menus and dialog boxes, three dots following a command indicating that additional information is required before the command can be carried out. ➔ *1595 ellipsis (1)*

0946 **error message** A message box that automatically appears if you have attempted to do something that your computer or an application won't permit or cannot do, or, at worst, if your computer crashes. ➔ *0948 error code*

0947 **error-checking** A means of guaranteeing the integrity of data. This can occur either when the data is input — via a keyboard, for example (a spellchecker is a type of error-check) — or when it is transmitted via a device such as a modem.

0948 **error/result code** A number that sometimes accompanies error messages to give some indication of the nature of the problem. ➔ *0946 error message*

0949 **event** Anything that a computer may need to respond to, such as a mouse click or a disk insertion.

0950 **event-driven** Description of an application whose responses are based on events generated by the user. ➔ *0949 event*

0951 **event-handling mechanism** A facility, built in to the operation system software, which allows other software programs to respond to circumstances or commands as they occur. ➔ *0981 operating system*

0952 **file menu** One of three standard menus appearing in the menu bar of most applications, where you invoke commands that allow you to create, open, save, print, and close files, and quit applications. ➔ *0378 file*

0953 **Finder** On Macintosh computers, one of the three fundamental components (the others are the system file and the hardware ROM chips) that provides the desktop, file, and disk management, and the facility to launch and use other applications.

0954 **folder** (**1**) The pictorial representation of a directory, being a place provided by computer operating systems where you can organize your documents, applications, and other folders (when one folder is inside another, it is said to be nested). Folders form the basis for the organization of all data on your computer. ➔ *0369 directory*

0955 **folder bar** In many file dialog boxes (such as Open and Save), the bar above the scrolling list that, when clicked on, reveals a list of the folder hierarchy. ➔ *0954 folder (1); 0937 dialog box*

0956 **GUI** (pron.: "gooey") *abb.*: **graphical user interface** The concept of some computer operating systems, such as the Mac OS and Windows, which allows you to interact with the computer by means of pointing at graphic symbols (icons) with a mouse rather than by typing coded commands. Also known as "WIMPs" or "**pointing interface**." ➔ *1015 WIMPs*

0957 **help** A feature of operating systems and other software that provides on-line explanations and advice.

0958 **hierarchical file system** (**HFS**) The method used by the Mac OS to organize and store files and folders so they can be accessed by any program. Files are organized inside folders that may, in turn, be inside other folders, thus creating a hierarchy. ➔ *0960 hierarchical structure*

0959 **hierarchical menu** A menu containing items that, when selected, generate their own menus, called submenus. The presence of a submenu is

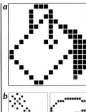

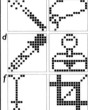

■ *0962 Hot spot*
a paint bucket
b magic wand
c lasso
d eyedropper
e rubber stamp
f I-beam pointer
g crop tool

Hard disk icon

Floppy disk icon

Folder icon

Application icon

Document icon

Control Panel icon

System Extension icon

Suitcase icon

Font file icon

0964 Icon

normally indicated by a triangular symbol on the right of the menu item. → *0958 hierarchical file system*

0960 hierarchical structure The technique of arranging information in a graded order, which establishes priorities and therefore helps users find a path that leads them to what they want. Used extensively in networking and databases. → *0958 hierarchical file system*

0961 highlight (2) To mark an item, such as a section of text, icon, or menu command, to indicate that it is selected or active.

0962 hotspot/hot spot The specific place on the mouse pointer icon that activates the item on which it is placed. → *0442 pointer*

0963 I-beam pointer The shape of the pointer when it is used to edit or select text. As distinct from the insertion point or cursor, which indicates the point at which text will be inserted by the next keystroke. Also called the text tool. → *0442 pointer; 0318 insertion point; 0934 cursor*

0964 icon In a computer "graphical user interface," a graphic representation of an object, such as a disk, file, folder, or tool, or of a concept or message. → *0956 GUI*

0965 interface The physical relationship between human beings, systems, and machines — in other words, the point of interaction or connection. The involvement of humans is referred to as a human interface or user interface. → *0928 command-line interface; 0956 GUI*

0966 Mac OS The operating system used on Apple Computer's Macintosh series of computers, which provides the underlying "graphical user interface" (GUI) on which all applications and files depend. Unlike other operating systems, such as Microsoft's DOS and Windows, which are entirely software-based, the Mac OS is part software and part firmware (software built into a hardware ROM chip on the Mac's motherboard), thus providing a consistent interface with standard control mechanisms, such as dialog boxes and windows, that allows all software written for the Macintosh to have the same look and feel. → *0956 GUI; 0975 MS-DOS; 1017 Windows; 0069 ROM*

0967 memory allocation The allocation of memory to specific tasks, thus enabling system software, application software, utilities, and hardware to operate side by side. → *0047 application memory heap; 0057 heap*

0968 menu The display on a computer screen showing the list of choices available to a user.

0969 menu bar The horizontal panel across the top of a computer screen containing the titles of available menus. → *0968 menu*

0970 menu command A command given to your computer from a list of choices available within a menu, as distinct from a command made via the keyboard (keyboard command).

0971 menu indicator Symbols within a menu that expand the range of options. An ellipsis (…) following an item means that selecting it will display a dialog box before the command can be executed; a checkmark indicates a command is already active; a right-pointing triangle points to a submenu; and a down-pointing triangle indicates that there's more on the menu. → *0968 menu; 0969 menu bar; 0972 menu title; 0973 menu-driven*

0972 menu title The title of a menu as displayed in the menu bar. → *0969 menu bar*

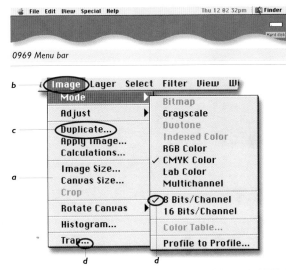

0969 Menu bar

*0968 Menu **a** showing: **b** 0972 menu title; **c** 0970 menu command; **d** 0971 menu indicator*

0973 **menu-driven** A computer or application interface in which commands are given through a list of choices available from a hierarchy of menus. Synonymous with a command-line interface. → *0928 command-line interface; 0956 GUI*

0974 **modal dialog box** A dialog box that, until it is closed, will not allow any activity to take place on-screen other than that within its box.

0975 **MS-DOS** abb.: **Microsoft Disc Operating System** The operating system used on Intel-based personal computers (PCs). MS-DOS (or just DOS) also provides the skeleton on which Microsoft's Windows operating system hangs. → *0928 command-line interface; 0981 operating system*

0976 **multithreaded** A concept of operating systems in which they, or the applications that run on them, divide into smaller subtasks, each of which runs independently, but which combine to perform a primary task. → *1050 multitasking; 1005 time-slicing*

0977 **nested folder** In GUIs, a folder inside another folder. → *0956 GUI*

0978 **nesting** Items placed inside other items, such as tables within tables on a Web page.

0979 **open** (1) A standard operating system command that reveals the contents of a selected file or folder or launches an application. → *0598 launch*

0980 **OpenDoc** Mac OS technology that allows you to work on different types of data within a single document. OpenDoc uses plug-in software components, called "parts," that can be dragged-and-dropped into documents created by any OpenDoc-aware application. You can combine parts from different applications to add tables, graphs, outlines, and even live Internet resources into documents. Since OpenDoc is a cross-platform technology, documents created with OpenDoc can work across different computer platforms, including Mac OS, Windows, UNIX, and OS/2.

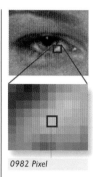

0982 Pixel

0985 Push button

0991 Resource (3) showing resources such as cursors, icons, colors, patterns, etc., for an application

0981 operating system The software (and in some cases firmware) that provides the environment within which all other software and its user operates. The major operating systems are Microsoft's DOS and Windows, Apple's Mac OS, and AT&T's UNIX, the latter three of which use GUIs (graphical user interfaces). → *1037 firmware*

0982 pixel Acronym for picture element. The smallest component of a digitally generated image, such as a single dot of light on a computer monitor. In its simplest form, one pixel corresponds to a single bit: 0 = off, or white, and 1 = on, or black. In color or grayscale images or monitors, one pixel may correspond to several bits: an 8-bit pixel, for example, can be displayed in any of 256 colors (the total number of different configurations that can be achieved by eight 0s and 1s). → *0773 resolution*

0983 pop-up menu A menu in a dialog box or palette that pops up when you click on it. Pop-up menus usually appear as a rectangle with a drop shadow and a downward or side-pointing arrow.

0984 protocol A set of mutual rules that hardware and software must observe in order to communicate with one another.

0985 push button A button in a dialog box that, when clicked, invokes the command specified on the button.

0986 QuickDraw The part of the Mac system that performs all display operations on your screen. It is also responsible for outputting text and graphics to nonPostScript printers. → *1056 PostScript*

0987 Quit The command by which you shut down an application, as distinct from closing a document within the application, in which case the document disappears but the application remains open.

0988 reboot To reload a computer's operating system (or an application) into memory. This can be achieved by either switching the power off (shutting down) and switching it on again (cold boot), or by using the Restart command, if available (warm boot). Also referred to as **restart**. → *0918 boot; 0999 startup*

0989 rebuild desktop On Macintosh computers, to flush out obsolete information from the invisible desktop file in order to speed up operations. The desktop file records not only new files, but deleted ones as well, so the more files you add and delete, the more the desktop file keeps growing.

0990 resource (1) A system file that provides information to the central processing unit so it can communicate with a peripheral device.

0991 resource (3) An integral part of the Mac OS, which makes provision for user-definable elements such as dialog boxes, windows, fonts, icons, sounds, and so on, which can be unique to any file or application, including the operating system itself. → *0992 resource fork; 0935 data fork*

0992 resource fork On computers running the Mac OS, the part of a file (on Macintosh computers there are two parts, called forks, to every file unless the file only contains data) that contains resources such as icons and sounds. As distinct from the data fork, that contains user-created data, such as text or graphics. Resources contained in the resource fork of a file can be modified with resource editors such as ResEdit. → *0935 data fork; 0991 resource (3); 0458 ResEdit*

0993 sad Mac icon A picture of an unhappy face that can appear at the beginning of startup on Macintosh computers indicating that a fault has

0995 Scroll (2)
a 0998 scroll box
b 0997 scroll bar
c 0996 scroll arrow

been diagnosed during the startup tests performed by the computer. Often accompanied by a sound that differs from the usual harmonious startup chord. → *0964 icon*

0994 Save dialog box A box that appears on-screen the first time a document is saved, requiring the user to supply its title and location. → *0465 save; 0937 dialog box*

0995 scroll (2)/scrolling To move the contents of a window or directory listing up or down (or, sometimes, sideways), in order to view a part of a document that was hidden beyond the edges of the window. Scrolling is done by means of scroll bars, scroll boxes, and scroll arrows.

0996 scroll arrow An arrow that, when clicked on, moves the contents of a window up, down, or sideways. → *0995 scroll (2)*

0997 scroll bar The bar at the side and, usually, the bottom of a window within which the scroll box operates and which indicates if there are parts of the document hidden from view. → *0995 scroll (2)*

0998 scroll box A box sitting within the scroll bar of a window that can be moved up and down to access different parts of the open document. The position of the scroll box in the bar indicates the position in relation to the size of the entire document. → *0995 scroll (2)*

0999 startup The process of turning on the power to a computer, and the startup procedure it goes through in which certain checks are made — such as checking the RAM — and the operating system loaded into memory. If there is a fault, it will be reported accordingly, or the computer may fail to start altogether. Also called **booting up**. → *0918 booting up; 0988 reboot*

1000 status bar In most applications, a bar in a dialog box that tells you what is happening, for example, the progress being made during the rendering of an image or the copying of a file.

1001 system The complete configuration of software and hardware components necessary to perform electronic processing operations.

1002 system disk A disk containing all the necessary files of an operating system to start up the computer and carry out processing operations.

1003 System Folder On computers running the Mac OS, a folder that contains all the files, including System and Finder files, necessary for running the operating system. Also called the **blessed folder**. → *0981 operating system*

1004 tear-off menu In some applications, a menu that can be "torn" away from the menu bar by dragging it onto the desktop, where it can be moved around as you need it. → *0569 floating palette*

1005 time-slicing Dividing time into small chunks to get several things done at once — actually a delusion, since the aggregate time is the same, so it is often advisable to stick to one thing at a time. On a computer, however, time-slicing works more efficiently — if the central processing unit is involved rather than yourself. A computer, for example, can usually run two or more applications at the same time, appearing to work on them simultaneously by switching very rapidly from one to the other. → *1050 multitasking*

1006 title bar The bar at the top of an open window that contains its name. The window can be moved around the desktop by dragging its title bar. → *0969 menu bar*

1006 Title bar

a *b*

1018 Wristwatch
a Mac OS wristwatch
b Windows hourglass

1007 toggle Those buttons, menus, and checkboxes that switch between off and on each time you select or click on them.

1008 transparent Any software or hardware item that operates without interaction on your part — apart from installing it in the first place.

1009 Undo A standard command found in most applications that allows you to reinstate the previous thing that you did. Some applications provide several levels of Undo.

1010 UNIX An operating system developed by AT&T, devised to be multi-tasking and portable from one machine to another. UNIX is used widely on Web servers. → *0981 operating system; 0893 A/UX*

1011 upgrade To modify or enhance the performance or capabilities of a computer, by adding more memory or an accelerator card, for example, or by installing a newer version of the operating system or application software.

1012 user A person who uses hardware and software, as distinct from someone who makes or creates it.

1013 user group A group of people who share their experiences, knowledge, problems, etc., either generally or in relation to a specific software application or type of computer.

1014 uudecode Acronym for UNIX to UNIX decode, a method of encoding and decoding binary data, such as that used by graphics files, so they can be transferred over the Internet in ASCII format between computers running the UNIX operating system. → *0338 ASCII; 1010 UNIX*

1015 WIMPs An acronym for Windows, Icon, Mouse (or menu), and Pointer. The constituent parts of a computer "graphical user interface" (GUI). → *0956 GUI*

1016 window Part of the "graphical user interface" (GUI) of a computer, a window is the area of a computer screen that displays the contents of disk, folder, or document. A window can be resized and is scrollable if the contents are too large to fit within it. → *0956 GUI*

1017 Windows/Windows 98/Windows NT The PC operating system devised by Microsoft Corp. that uses a graphical user interface (GUI) in a similar way to the Mac OS. Using special software or hardware, Windows can be run on a Macintosh computer, but the Mac OS cannot be used on PCs designed to run Windows. → *0981 operating system*

1018 wristwatch/hourglass pointer The shape assumed by the pointer icon of a computer to indicate that a process is under way but not yet complete. → *0442 pointer*

1019 WYSIWYG *(pron.: wizzywig)* An acronym for "what you see is what you get," the display of a document on screen exactly as it appears when printed. All major computer operating systems now offer WYSIWYG displays. → *0956 GUI; 0981 operating system; 0965 interface; 0936 desktop*

1020 X Windows A GUI used on UNIX computers, via an **API (application programming interface)**. → *0956 GUI; 1010 UNIX*

1021 zoom box The box at the right of some window title bars that, when clicked, expands or reduces the visible area of the window. → *1006 title bar*

1022 amplitude The strength or volume of a sound.

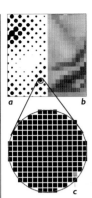

1030 Dot
a halftone dot
b scan dot (pixel)
c machine dot

1023 CAD *abb.:* **computer-aided design** Strictly speaking, any design carried out using a computer, but the term is generally used with reference to 3D design, such as product design or architecture, where a computer software application is used to construct and develop complex structures. → *1024 CAD/CAM; 1025 CAM*

1024 CAD/CAM *abb.:* **computer-aided design and manufacture** The process of design and manufacture in which computers are used to assist and control the entire process from concept to finished product. → *1023 CAD; 1025 CAM*

1025 CAM *abb.:* **computer-aided manufacture** Generally used in conjunction with CAD (CAD/CAM) and rarely used on its own. → *1023 CAD; 1024 CAD/CAM*

1026 cloverleaf/pretzel/propeller symbol The symbol (⌘) used to identify the "command key" on keyboards attached to computers running the Mac OS.

1027 default The settings of a hardware device or software program determined at the time of manufacture or release. These settings remain in effect until you change them, and your changes are stored — when applied to software — in a "preferences" file. Also known as **presets** and **factory settings**.

1028 digital Anything operated by or created from information or signals represented by binary digits, such as a digital recording. As distinct from analog, in which information is represented by a physical variable (in a recording this may be via the grooves in a vinyl platter). → *0914 bit*

1029 digitize To convert anything, for example, text, images, or sound, into binary form so it can be digitally processed, manipulated, stored, and reconstructed. In other words, transforming analog to digital. → *0914 bit; 1028 digital*

1030 dot A term that can mean one of three things: halftone dot (the basic element of a halftone image), machine dot (the dots produced by a laser printer or imagesetter), or scan dot (strictly speaking, pixels, which comprise a scanned bitmapped image). Each is differentiated by being expressed in lpi (lines per inch) for a halftone dot, dpi (dots per inch) for a machine dot, and ppi (pixels per inch) for a scan dot — although the latter is sometimes be expressed — erroneously — in dpi. Thus, because the term dot is used to describe both halftone and machine dots, scan dots should always be referred to as pixels. → *2044 halftone dot; 0260 machine dot; 0982 pixel; 0280 scan dot*

1031 dots per inch (**dpi**) A unit of measurement used to represent the resolution of devices such as printers and imagesetters, and also, erroneously, monitors and images, whose resolution should more properly be expressed in pixels per inch (ppi). The closer the dots or pixels (the more there are to each inch), the better the quality. Typical resolutions are 72ppi for a monitor, 300dpi for a LaserWriter, and 2450dpi (or more) for an imagesetter. → *0773 resolution; 0260 machine dot; 0982 pixel; 0280 scan dot*

1032 drag Carrying out an action by holding the mouse button down while you move the mouse, thus moving the pointer on-screen, then releasing the mouse button to complete the action. Dragging is used to perform such tasks as selecting and moving items, selecting pull-down menu commands, selecting text, and, in some applications, creating items with an appropriate tool selected.

1033 **driver/device driver** A small piece of software that tells a computer how to handle or operate a piece of hardware, such as a printer, scanner, or disk drive. Depending on its function, a driver may be located with the operating system software and therefore loaded at startup, or it may form a "plug-in" to an application (as do some scanner drivers, for example). ➜ *0981 operating system; 0643 plug-in*

1034 **emulation** To simulate otherwise incompatible software or hardware to make it compatible — running Microsoft Windows on a Macintosh computer, for example.

1035 **encode** The conversion of data to a machine-readable form.

1036 **FAQs** *abb.:* **frequently asked questions** A method of delivering technical support to users of software, hardware, and the Internet — and, increasingly, users of virtually any product or service — by means of a database of answers to the most commonly asked questions.

1037 **firmware** Any permanent software incorporated into a hardware chip (usually a ROM chip). On Macintosh computers, part of the operating system is built into a hardware ROM chip. ➜ *0069 ROM*

1038 **gateway** A device or program used to connect disparate computer networks. ➜ *0308 network; 0287 bridge*

1039 **ID number** An acronym for identity number. A number given to a device, file, or message to distinguish it from others. For example, an ID number is required by peripheral devices in a SCSI chain, or may sometimes be given in error alert boxes to indicate the likely cause of the error, or be used to give a font a unique identity. ➜ *0240 SCSI ID number*

1040 **input** Generally, anything that is put in or taken into something else, but usually used with reference to entering data into a computer by whatever means.

1041 **input resolution** The degree of definition by which an image is "captured" or recorded, which determines the final quality of output. Final output quality depends on three aspects of input: scan resolution, the size of the original image as compared with its final size (in which case resolution of the scanning device itself may also be significant), and resolution of the output device. To calculate input resolution, multiply the eventual halftone screen frequency by two and then multiply that answer by the ratio of the final image size to its original dimensions. For example, if the image is to be printed with a halftone screen of 150 lines per inch, multiply 150 × 2 to get 300. If the image has an original size of 2 × 3 inches, but will be printed at a size of 6 × 9 inches, it has a ratio of 3 (9 ÷ 3). So, 300 × 3 = 600 — the input resolution, in dots per inch, for scanning the image. ➜ *0280 scan dot; 2206 output resolution*

1042 **interpreter** Software that converts program code into machine language piece by piece, as distinct from a "compiler," which converts a program in its entirety. ➜ *0349 code; 0352 compiler*

1043 **interrupt button** On Macintosh computers, a hardware button that allows programmers to debug software.

1044 **IT** *abb.:* **information technology** Anything to do with computers and/or telecommunications, particularly networking and databases.

1045 **keyboard equivalent/shortcut** A command given to your computer made via the keyboard rather than by selecting the equivalent menu command. Typical keyboard equivalents usually require the use of a "modifier" key such as Option or Command (Mac) or Alt (Win). ➔ *0206 Fkey; 0413 macro*

1046 **keyboard event** The computer process generated when you press a keyboard key, occurring either at the moment you press down on the key (key down) or when you release it (key up). If you hold down a key so that a process is repeated, it is called an auto-key event. ➔ *0949 event*

1047 **large-screen emulation** A feature of certain utilities to provide a larger screen size than you may already have — when the pointer reaches the edge of the screen, the screen automatically scrolls. ➔ *1034 emulation*

1048 **machine code** The lowest level of programming code, i.e., the one least understandable to the user, but easily understood by a computer. ➔ *0349 code*

1049 **machine readable** Text or data that can be read by a machine and converted to a digital format, such as in magnetic ink character recognition (MICR) or optical character recognition (OCR). ➔ *0261 MICR; 1052 OCR*

1050 **multitasking** The ability of a computer to do many things at once, such as run several applications simultaneously. Most PCs aren't true multitasking machines, although they can usually work on several tasks or applications simultaneously by switching very rapidly from one to another (sometimes called time-slicing). ➔ *1005 time-slicing*

1051 **MIDI** *abb.:* **musical instrument digital interface** A hardware and software standard for digitally synthesized musical sound.

1052 **OCR** *abb.:* **optical character recognition** A means of inputting copy without keying it in. This is achieved with software that, when used with a scanner or "page reader," converts typescript into editable digital text.

1053 **option** Any keyboard key, button, checkbox, menu, or command that allows you an alternative choice. On keyboards, this is provided by the Option (Macintosh) and Alt (Windows) keys that, when used in conjunction with another key, provide a special character or a shortcut to menu commands. ➔ *0221 modifier key*

1054 **page description language** (**PDL**) A programming language via which your computer communicates with a printer, describing to it image and font data so it can construct and print the data to your specifications. PostScript is the most widely used PDL.

1055 **port address** The precise address (of the program on the receiving end) to which data is delivered by a remote computer on a network.

1056 **PostScript** Adobe Systems Inc.'s proprietary "page description language" (PDL) for image output to laser printers and high-resolution imagesetters. ➔ *1054 page description language*

1057 **PostScript interpreter** The code used by printing devices to understand PostScript instructions. ➔ *1042 interpreter*

1058 **PostScript Printer Description file** (**PPD**) A file that defines the characteristics of individual PostScript printers.

1059 **read only** Disks, memory, and documents that can only be read from, and not written to.

1060 **shift-click(ing)** The process of holding down the shift key while clicking on several items or passages of text on the screen, thus making multiple selections.

1061 **source** (**2**) Documents, files, disks, etc., from which copied, transmitted, or linked data originates. As distinct from the "target," or destination, of such data. ➔ *0496 target*

1062 **toolbox** The part of the Mac OS written into the ROM chip that enables software developers to take advantage of the Mac OS interface, handling such things as dialog boxes, windows, fonts, mouse, keyboard, and so on.

1063 Character mode

1063 **character/text mode** Those Web browsers that can display text data only and that cannot display graphics without the assistance of a "helper" application. Even browsers with the capacity to display graphics allow a preference for operating in character mode, which many users prefer because of its increased speed — although they inevitably miss out, since it is now common for much of the text on Web pages to be transmitted as images. → *1227* World Wide Web; *1167* browser (1)

1064 **deprecated** The term applied to versions of HTML technology that are gradually being replaced or eradicated. → *1267* HTML

1065 **ADSL** *abb.:* **Asymmetrical Digital Subscriber Line** A high-speed communications link capable of transmitting large amounts of data (such as a TV picture) in one direction and a small amount (such as a telephone call) in the other. Speeds of around 2 mbps (megabits per second) can be achieved — 16 times faster than ISDN. → *1080* ISDN

1066 **anonymous FTP** A means of accessing files on a remote computer across the Internet using File Transfer Protocol (FTP) service, but without having to provide a predefined password or other "login" name. Access is achieved by logging in with a username of "anonymous" and using an e-mail address as the password. → *1077* FTP; *0306* log on

1067 **bandwidth** The measure of the speed at which information is passed between two points, which may be between modems, across a "bus," or from memory to disk — the broader the bandwidth, the faster data flows. Bandwidth is usually measured in cycles per second (hertz) or in bits per second (bps). → *0004* bus

1068 **baud** *(pron.:* bord) The number of signal changes transmitted per second during data transmission by modem. → *1069* baud rate

1069 **baud rate** The speed at which a modem transmits data, or the number of "events" it can handle per second. Often used to describe the transmission speed of data itself, but since a single event can contain two or more bits, data speed is more correctly expressed in bits per second (bps). → *1068* baud; *0949* event; *0914* bit

1070 **CCITT** *abb.:* **Comité Consultatif Internationale Téléphonique et Télégraphique** (Consultative Committee on International Telephony and Telegraphy). An organization sponsored by the United Nations that sets worldwide communications standards, especially with regard to data and voice transmission and compression.

1071 **CSU/DSU** *abb.:* **channel service unit/data service unit** A hardware device that translates data between a network and a telephone line. → *0308 network*

1072 **cyberspace** The notional environment in which communication takes place, particularly the Internet, but also general telecommunication links and computer networks. → *0506 virtual*

1073 **demon** Special networking software, used mainly on computers running the UNIX operating system, which handles requests from users, such as e-mail, the World Wide Web, and other Internet services. → *1010 UNIX; 0981 operating system; 1112 e-mail; 1227 World Wide Web; 1139 Internet*

1074 **dial-up** A connection to the Internet or to a network that is made by dialing a telephone number for access.

1075 **download** To transfer data from a remote computer — such as an Internet server — to your own. The opposite of upload. → *0318 server; 0503 upload*

1076 **extranet** The part of an organization's internal computer network or intranet that is available to outside users, for example, information services for customers. → *1144 intranet*

1077 **FTP** *abb.:* **File Transfer Protocol** A standard system for transmitting files between computers across the Internet or a network. Although Web browsers incorporate FTP capabilities, dedicated FTP applications provide greater flexibility. → *1066 anonymous FTP*

1078 **half duplex** Communication between two devices over telecommunication lines, but in one direction at a time. → *3594 duplex*

1079 **host** A networked computer that provides services to anyone who can access it, such as for e-mail, file transfer, and access to the Web.

1080 **ISDN** *abb.:* **Integrated Services Digital Network** A telecommunication technology that transmits data on special digital lines rather than on old-fashioned analog lines and is thus much faster, although DSL (Digital Subscriber Line) links are even faster than ISDN. → *1065 ADSL*

1081 **kermit** An older (thus slower) communications protocol.

1082 **MacTCP** Acronym for Macintosh transmission control protocol, the Mac OS version of TCP. → *1101 TCP*

1083 **modem** Acronym for modulator-demodulator. A device that converts digital data to analog for transfer from one computer to another via standard telephone lines. The receiving modem converts it back again.

1084 **Multilink Point-to-Point Protocol** (**MPPP**) An Internet protocol that provides simultaneous multiple connections between computers.

1085 **multiplex**(**ing**) The term for "many." In communications, the simultaneous transmission of many messages along a single channel.

1086 **nodename** A name that identifies an individual computer on a network or the Internet.

1087 **noise** (**1**) Undesirable fluctuations or interference in a transmitted signal, such as across telephone lines.

1088 **packet** A bundle of data — the basic unit transmitted across networks. When data is sent over a network such as the Internet, it is broken up into small chunks called packets, which are sent independently of each other.

1089 **Perl** A programming language much favored for creating CGI programs. ➔ *1240 CGI (1)*

1090 **pipe** The bandwidth of the actual connection between your computer and a server on the Internet. ➔ *1067 bandwidth*

1091 **PPP** *abb.:* **Point-to-Point Protocol** The most common means of establishing dial-up connections to the Internet. It provides a method for transmitting packets over serial point-to-point links. It also allows you to use other standard protocols (such as IPX and TCP/IP) over a standard telephone connection and can be used for local area networks (LAN) connections. ➔ *0305 LAN; 1101 TCP*

1092 **POP (1)** *abb.:* **Point of Presence** Usually referring to a city or location to which a network can be connected, such as the true location of the server of your ISP (Internet service provider). ➔ *1143 ISP*

1093 **POP (2)** *abb.:* **Post Office Protocol** An e-mail protocol for retrieval and storage — a **POP account** is what you tell your e-mail software to use to send and retrieve your mail.

1094 **POTS** Acronym for plain old telephone system. A standard analog telephone system.

1095 **SLIP** *abb.:* **serial line Internet protocol** A communications protocol that supports an Internet connection over a dial-up line. Now superseded by PPP. ➔ *1091 PPP*

1096 **set-top** A network computer designed to use a home television set instead of a computer monitor for display. ➔ *1201 netTV*

1097 **SMTP** *abb.:* **Simple Mail Transfer Protocol** A text-based TCP/IP protocol used to transfer mail messages over the Internet. ➔ *1101 TCP*

1098 **SONET** *abb.:* **synchronous optical network** A high-speed digital transmission system, capable of transmitting large amounts of data at high speed.

1099 **T1** A high-speed digital communications link, which runs at 1.544Mbps. ➔ *0307 Mbps*

1100 **terminal emulation** Software that allows your computer to mimic another (remote) computer by acting as a terminal for the other machine — in other words, it is as though you are actually working on that remote computer. ➔ *0325 terminal*

1101 **TCP** *abb.:* **Transmission Control Protocol** The industry standard developed by the Department of Defense for providing data communication between computers, such as across the Internet. It ensures reliability by retransmitting lost and corrupted data packets, and means that an application on the receiving end of a TCP connection will receive bits and bytes in the same order in which they were sent.

1102 **videoconferencing** The facility to conduct conferences over a computer network using sound and video pictures.

1103 **XMODEM** A standard communications protocol that transfers data in blocks of 128K. ➔ *1104 YMODEM; 1105 ZMODEM*

1104 **YMODEM** A standard communications protocol that provides error-checking while transferring data. ➔ *1103 XMODEM; 1105 ZMODEM*

1106 Address (2)

1105 **ZMODEM** A standard communications protocol that can provide continuous data transfer despite interruptions or pauses. → *1103 XMODEM; 1104 YMODEM*

1106 **address** (**2**) A string of letters or numbers used by Internet users to communicate to each other via e-mail. Also, an informal name for a Web site URL. → *1112 e-mail; 1227 World Wide Web; 1220 URL*

1107 **attachment** An external file such as an image or text document "attached" to an e-mail message for electronic transmission. → *1112 e-mail*

1108 **BinHex** An acronym for binary to hexadecimal, a file format that converts binary files to ASCII text, usually for transmission via e-mail. This is the safest way of sending document files — particularly to and from Macintosh computers — since some computer systems along the e-mail route may only accept standard ASCII text characters. Encoding and decoding BinHex may be done automatically by some e-mail software, but otherwise it must be done manually, usually with a file compression utility. → *0910 binary; 0338 ASCII; 1112 e-mail*

1109 **commercial a** The type character @ used as an abbreviation for "at," used primarily in e-mail addresses to signify "you@yourdomain," for example. → *1112 e-mail*

1110 **content-type** A MIME (Multipurpose Internet Mail Extensions) convention for identifying the type of data being transmitted over the Internet to such things as e-mail applications and Web browsers. → *1120 MIME; 1139 Internet; 1112 e-mail*

1111 **e-commerce** Commercial transactions conducted electronically over a network or the Internet. → *1112 e-mail*

1112 **e-mail** *abb.:* **electronic mail** Messages sent from your computer to someone else with a computer, either locally through a network, or transmitted over telephone lines using a modem, usually via a central computer ("server"), which stores messages in the recipient's "mailbox" until they are picked up. → *1139 internet; 1123 spam; 1120 MIME; 0318 server*

1113 **E-text** A text-only file transmitted via the Internet.

1114 **finger(ed)/fingering** A means of showing or revealing information about a user or group of users on the Internet. For example, you can finger an electronic mailbox to determine whether there are any unread messages, or a server for information about the state of the ISP's network.

1115 **flame** Abusive messages sent via e-mail or posted to newsgroups. → *1123 spam; 1125 troll; 1112 e-mail; 1116 flamewar; 1150 newsgroup*

1116 **flamewar** An ongoing reciprocal series of abusive newsgroup postings or e-mail messages against individuals and/or groups. → *1123 spam; 1125 troll; 1112 e-mail; 1115 flame; 1150 newsgroup*

1117 **listserv** An automated mailing list distribution system, typically based on UNIX servers.

1118 **mailto:** A hyperlink code used in Web pages or e-mail applications that, when prefixed to an e-mail address and double-clicked, creates a new e-mail message for sending direct to the addressee. → *1112 e-mail*

1119 **majordomo** A system of automated multiple electronic mailing lists that users can subscribe to or unsubscribe from at will.

1120 **MIME** *abb.:* **multipurpose Internet mail extensions** A format for conveying Web documents and related files across the Internet, typically via e-mail.

1121 **nickname** An abbreviated e-mail address.

1122 **signature** (**2**) A user-defined "footer" automatically attached to an e-mail message, identifying its sender.

1123 **spam/spamming** A colloquial term for an unsolicited e-mail or newsgroup posting, usually untargeted advertising material. The term derives from the television comedy show *Monty Python's Flying Circus* where, in one sketch, a restaurant menu lists food items that can only be ordered if accompanied by "spam," e.g., sausage and spam, egg and spam, spam and spam, etc. ➔ *1112* e-mail; *1150* newsgroup; *1125* troll

1124 **thread** (**1**) Postings to an online newsgroup or e-mail distributions on a theme or subject in which a group of subscribers has a particular interest. The messages are usually followed by any replies, and the replies to those replies.

1125 **troll/trolling** A newsgroup posting designed to exasperate, annoy, or enrage its readers, the purpose being to create as much argument as possible. ➔ *1150* newsgroup; *1123* spam

1126 **AOL** abb.: **America Online** An Internet service provider (ISP). ➔ *1143* ISP

1127 **Archie** An Internet service that logs the whereabouts of files so they can be located for downloading. Once found, files are downloaded using FTP. ➔ *1077* FTP

1128 **authentication** The process of verifying the identity of someone attempting to access a remote computer or server, via a network or the Internet, usually by means of a user ID and/or password. ➔ *0318* server; *1139* Internet; *1066* anonymous ftp

1129 **avatar** The incarnation of a human being in a virtual reality environment, game, or a networked multi-user environment. Avatars are a kind of alter ego that some computer users use to represent themselves when they interact with other users, who, in turn, are represented by their own avatars. ➔ *0506* virtual

1130 **BBS** abb.: **bulletin board service** A facility, usually noncommercial, which enables you to use a modem and telephone line to share information and exchange files on specialized subjects with other computer users of like mind. As distinct from commercial online service providers, which offer a wider range of services. ➔ *1143* ISP; *1152* sysop

1131 **CERN** abb.: **European Organization for Nuclear Research** (formerly **Conseil Européen pour la Recherche Nucléaire**). The birthplace of the World Wide Web, now overseen by the World Wide Web Consortium, based in Switzerland. ➔ *1227* World Wide Web

1132 **CIX** (pron.: kicks) Acronym for Commercial Internet Exchange, an alliance of Internet service providers (ISPs). ➔ *1143* ISP

1133 **content provider** A provider of information on the Web, as distinct from a provider of a service, such as an ISP. ➔ *1143* ISP

1134 **Envoy** A portable document format (PDF) created by Novell for the exchange of formatted documents across the Internet. ➔ *0443* PDF; *1139* Internet; *0511* Adobe Acrobat; *1173* Common Ground; *1227* World Wide Web

1135 **forum** An online service that enables users to post messages that other users may respond or add to. These message "threads" are usually organized around special interests, such as software user groups or popular cultural themes. ➔ *1156 UseNet; 1150 newsgroup*

1136 **gopher** A software protocol developed at the University of Minnesota, which provides a means of accessing information across the Internet using services such as WAIS and Telnet. ➔ *1158 WAIS; 1154 Telnet*

1137 **IAB** *abb.:* **Internet Architecture Board.** The ruling council that makes decisions about Internet standards and related topics. ➔ *1145 ISOC; 1138 IETF*

1138 **IETF** *abb.:* **Internet Engineering Task Force** A suborganization of the Internet Architecture Board (IAB), comprising a group of volunteers that investigates and helps solve Internet-related problems and makes recommendations to appropriate Internet Committees. ➔ *1137 IAB*

1139 **Internet** The entire collection of connected worldwide networks, including those used solely for the Web. The Internet was originally funded by the United States Department of Defense. ➔ *1227 World Wide Web; 1167 browser (1)*

1140 **IP** *abb.:* **Internet Protocol** The networking rules that tie computers together across the Internet. ➔ *1101 TCP; 1141 IP address; 1139 Internet; 1142 IPnG*

1141 **IP address** *abb.:* **Internet Protocol address** The unique numeric address of a particular computer or server on the Internet (or any TCP/IP network). Each one is unique and consists of a dotted decimal notation, for example, 194.152.64.68. ➔ *1178 DNS; 1101 TCP; 1140 IP*

1142 **IPnG** *abb.:* **IP next generation**. A new generation of Internet Protocols that will expand the number of available Internet addresses. ➔ *1140 IP*

1143 **ISP** *abb.:* **Internet service provider** Any organization that provides access to the Internet. At its most basic, it may merely be a telephone number for connection, but most ISPs also provide other services such as e-mail addresses and capacity for your own Web pages. Also called **access provider**.

1144 **intranet** A network of computers similar to the Internet, but to which the general public do not have access. A sort of in-house Internet service, intranets are used mainly by large corporations, governments, and educational institutions. ➔ *1139 Internet*

1145 **ISOC** Acronym for The Internet Society, a governing body to which the Internet Architecture Board (IAB) reports. ➔ *1137 IAB*

1146 **MOTD** *abb.:* **message of the day** A message posted by an ISP (Internet service provider) on its server to inform its users of any known problems that may be affecting the network that day. An MOTD is read either by using special software that "fingers" the server, or by using a World Wide Web browser. ➔ *1114 finger; 1143 ISP; 1227 World Wide Web*

1147 **narrowcasting** The targeting of content to a specific type of audience via the Internet.

1148 **NCSA** *abb.:* **National Center for Supercomputing Applications** A group of programmers at the University of Illinois who developed the first Web browser and who produce software such as NCSA Telnet for the scientific community. → *1227 World Wide Web; 1167 browser (1)*

1149 **NNTP** *abb.:* **Network News Transfer Protocol** A standard for the retrieval and posting of news articles.

1150 **newsgroup** A group of like-minded individuals who post and collect articles of common interest on the Internet. → *1156 UseNet*

1151 **service provider** A commercial organization specializing in providing connections to the Internet. → *1130 BBS; 1143 ISP*

1152 **sysop** Acronym for system operator, the operator of a bulletin board service. → *1130 BBS*

1153 **TVSP** *abb.:* **television service provider** A company that connects the subscriber to the Internet via a TV and set-top box. → *1201 netTV*

1154 **Telnet** The Internet standard protocol that enables you to connect to a remote computer and control it as if you were there, even if you are thousands of miles away from it. → *0201 dumb terminal*

1155 **tenant** People who administrate a Web site that is located on another person's server, typically one belonging to an Internet service provider (ISP).

1156 **UseNet** Acronym for user's network, in which a vast number of articles on every conceivable subject, categorized into newsgroups, are posted on the Internet by individuals. They are hosted on servers throughout the world, via which you can post your own articles to people who subscribe to those newsgroups. Special newsreader software is required to view the articles. → *1150 newsgroup; 1135 forum*

1157 **virtual server** A Web site that is hosted on a server run by an ISP (Internet service provider) rather than a server run by the creator of the Web site. This is convenient, because a Web site server needs a permanent connection to the telephone network, and it is often more economic for an ISP to do this because a single server may host dozens of Web sites. The Web address is unaffected by this arrangement; for example, the address "http://www.yourcompanyname.com" can be hosted by any ISP. → *1143 ISP*

1158 **WAIS** *abb.:* **wide area information service** A system developed to access information in indexed databases across the Internet. → *1136 gopher*

1159 **Web server** A computer ("host") that is dedicated to Web services.

1160 **Webmaster** The person responsible for managing a Web site.

1161 **World Wide Web Consortium** (**W3C**) The organization jointly responsible with the IETF for maintaining and managing standards across the Web. → *1138 IETF*

1162 **absolute URL** A complete address, or "uniform resource locator" (URL), which takes you to a specific location in a Web site rather than to the home page of the site. An absolute URL will contain the full file path to the page document location on the host server and will appear, for example, as "http://yoursite.com/extrainfo/aboutyou/yourhouse.htm." → *1220 URL*

1163 **active desktop** A term devised by Microsoft to describe the interface built into its Internet Explorer Web browser, which merges the operating system's desktop into the browser's.

1164 Active hyperlink

1165 Banner (2)

1164 **active hyperlink** A recently selected link in a Web browser, differentiated from other links on the same page by the use of another color.

1165 **banner** (**2**) On a Web page, an image used to attract attention, usually an advertisement.

1166 **Bookmark** A feature of Netscape's Navigator Web browser, that remembers frequently visited Web sites. The equivalent in Microsoft's Internet Explorer is called Favorites. → *1167 browser (1)*

1167 **browser** (**1**) An application enabling you to view or "browse" World Wide Web pages across the Internet. The most widely used browsers are Netscape's Navigator and Microsoft's Internet Explorer. Version numbers (sometimes referred to as generations) are important, as they indicate the level of HTML that the browser supports. → *1139 Internet; 1227 World Wide Web; 1267 HTML*

1168 **burn** (**3**) To convert a file from an uncompressed to a compressed format, specifically for use with Internet Web browsers. → *1139 Internet; 1167 browser (1)*

1169 **channel** (**1**) A feature of Web technology whereby information is automatically transmitted to your Web browser, as distinct from having to request it yourself. → *1208 push technology*

1170 **chat** A "discussion" between two or more people typed live on an on-line Internet service. → *1139 Internet*

1171 **chatterbots** Software "helpers" that give advice and explain local etiquette in interactive environments, such as chat rooms, on the Web. → *1227 World Wide Web; 1170 chat*

1172 **client pull** An instruction sent by a Web browser to a server to collect a particular set of data.

1173 **Common Ground** A portable document format (PDF) for creating material to be viewed across the World Wide Web. Common Ground DP (DigitalPaper) format documents retain all the formatting of text and graphics, and can be shared by Macintosh, Windows, and UNIX users. Like Adobe Acrobat PDF files, Common Ground DP documents can be indexed and searched, but, unlike Acrobat files, which require you to have viewing software already installed on your computer, Common Ground DP documents contain a mini viewer already embedded in the file. → *0511 Adobe Acrobat; 0443 portable document format; 1227 World Wide Web*

1174 **content** The information presented in a multimedia presentation or Web page, as distinct from the interface or code used to make it.

1175 **cookie** A small piece of information deposited in your Web browser (thus on your hard disk) by a WWW site, storing such things as custom page settings or even personal information, such as your address or your password for that site. For an analogy, think of a cookie as a sort of luggage claim-check, whereby you drop your bag off and get a ticket — when you return with the ticket, you get your bag back. ➔ *1227* World Wide Web

1176 document transfer rate The speed, measured in documents per minute, at which Web pages are transmitted to your computer once you have requested them. ➔ *1249* document (2)

1177 document-based queries A method of sending information from your browser to a Web server, such as when you click on a search button to look something up. ➔ *1249* document (2); *1227* World Wide Web

1178 DNS abb.: **Domain Name System** The address of a Web site — the means by which you find or identify a particular Web site, much like a brand name or trademark. A Web site address is actually a number that conforms to the numerical Internet protocol (IP) addresses used by computers for information exchange; however, names are far easier for us mortals to remember. Domain names are administered by Network Solutions Inc. (formerly the InterNIC organization) and include at least two parts: the subdomain, typically a company or organization, or even your own name, and the high-level domain, which usually follows the last dot, as in *.com* for commercial sites, *.org* for nonprofit sites, *.gov* for governmental sites, *.edu* for educational sites, and so on. The high-level domain name may also indicate a country code for sites outside the United States (although a site without a country code does not necessarily mean it is inside the U.S.), such as *.uk* for the United Kingdom, *.de* for Germany, *.fr* for France, and so on. Other, more recent, high-level domain names include: *.arts*: culture and entertainment; *.firm*: businesses and professional firms; *.info*: information services; *.nom*: personal identity (nom de plume); *.rec*: recreation and entertainment; *.shop*: retail business and shopping; *.web*: World Wide Web-related services. ➔ *1227* World Wide Web; *1139* Internet

1179 embedded program A command or link written within text or lines of code on Web pages. ➔ *1227* World Wide Web

1180 Explorer A cross-platform Web browser produced by Microsoft. ➔ *1167* browser (1); *1199* Navigator

1181 Favorite A feature of Microsoft's Internet Explorer Web browser that remembers frequently visited Web sites. The equivalent in Netscape's Navigator is called Bookmarks. ➔ *1167* browser (1)

1182 firewall A software security system that protects Web sites and networks from unauthorized access.

1183 form (**1**) Fillable spaces (fields) on a Web page, which provide a means of collecting information and receiving feedback from people who visit a Web site. They can be used, for example, to buy an item, register a product, answer a questionnaire, or access a database.

1184 frame (**1**) On the Web, a means of displaying more than one page at a time within a single window — the window is divided into separate areas (frames), each one displaying a different page. Confusingly, although a window displaying frames may contain several pages, it is nevertheless described as a singular page. A common use of frames is to display a menu that remains static while other parts of the Web page — displayed in the same window — contain information that can, for example, be scrolled. ➔ *1227* World Wide Web; *0995* scroll (2)/scrolling

*1184 Frame (1) showing a Web page divided into three frames **a**, **b**, and **c***

1185 global renaming Software that updates all occurrences of a name throughout a Web site when one instance of that name is altered. → *1227 World Wide Web*

1186 history (list) A list of visited Web pages logged by your browser during a session on the Web. The history provides a means of speedy access to pages already visited during that session. → *1227 World Wide Web*

1187 home page On the World Wide Web, the term originally applied to the page that your own browser automatically links to when you launch it. It is now, however, commonly used more to describe the main page or contents page on a particular site, providing links to all the other pages on the site.

1188 hostname The name that identifies the computer hosting a Web site. → *1178 DNS*

1189 http *abb.:* **hypertext transfer protocol** A text-based set of rules by which files on the World Wide Web are transferred, defining the commands that Web browsers use to communicate with Web servers. The vast majority of World Wide Web addresses, or URL's, are prefixed with http://. → *1267 HTML; 1220 URL; 1167 browser (1)*

1190 httpd *abb.:* **hypertext transfer protocol demon** A collection of programs on a Web server that provide Web services, such as handling requests. → *1210 request*

1191 https *abb.:* **hypertext transfer protocol secure** Synonymous with http, but providing a secure link for such things as commercial transactions — online shopping with credit cards, for example — or when accessing password-protected information.

1192 index page The first page of any Web site that is selected automatically by the browser if it is named index.htm or index.html.

1193 information agent A generic type of computer program that automatically searches the World Wide Web, gathering and cataloguing information. → *1216 spider; 1211 robot; 0665 search engine*

1194 Internaut A colloquialism for someone who travels (**surfs**) the Internet. → *1227 World Wide Web; 1167 browser (1); 1139 Internet; 1195 IRC*

1195 **IRC** *abb.:* **Internet Relay Chat** An Internet facility provided by some ISPs that allows multiple users to type messages to each other in real-time on different "channels" sometimes referred to as rooms. ➔ *1143 ISP*

1196 **link** (**1**) A pointer, such as a highlighted piece of text, in an HTML document (a Web page, for example) or multimedia presentation, which takes the user to another location, page, or screen just by clicking on it. ➔ *1268 hyperlink*

1197 **Lynx** A UNIX-based Web browser that runs in character, or text, mode.

1198 **moving banner** An animated advertisement used within Web pages. ➔ *1165 banner (2)*

1199 **Navigator** A cross-platform Web browser produced by Netscape. ➔ *1180 Explorer; 1167 browser (1)*

1200 **netiquette** A play on the word etiquette, describing the notional rules — written or unwritten — for polite behavior for users of the Internet.

1201 **netTV** A system for accessing the World Wide Web via a television set. ➔ *1096 set-top; 1153 television service provider*

1202 **netTV viewers** Users who gain access to the Internet via netTV. ➔ *1201 netTV*

1203 **node** (**1**) A basic object, such as a graphic within a scene, used in the VRML environment. ➔ *1310 VRML*

1204 **obsolete** (**element**) HTML code that is out of date and thus no longer supported by current generations of browsers. ➔ *1267 HTML*

1205 **orphan file** A file on a Web site that is not referred to by any link or button and thus cannot be reached by any means other than through its absolute URL — in other words, to find it you must know its exact pathname. ➔ *1162 absolute URL; 1220 URL*

1206 **page** (**1**) An HTML document (text structured with HTML tags) viewed with a Web browser. ➔ *1267 HTML; 1167 browser (1)*

1207 **page flipping** An HTML structure for Web pages that allows users to see successive screens without needing to scroll. ➔ *1267 HTML*

1208 **push** (**technology**) A Web-based technology by which information, distributed to designated groups of users via "channels," can be updated immediately whenever changes are made. As distinct from the normal Web activity of browsing and requesting information at will (called **pull technology**). ➔ *1169 channel (1)*

1209 **relative URL** A link that is connected to the current Web page's URL so a browser looks for the link in the same location — i.e., Web site — as the Web page currently being viewed. ➔ *1220 URL*

1210 **request** The act of clicking on a button or link in a Web browser. You are, in fact, making a request to a remote server for an HTML document.

1211 **robot** Referred to colloquially as a bot, a robot is a program that roams the World Wide Web, gathering and cataloguing information, usually for use by various Web search engines such as Yahoo and Alta Vista. ➔ *0665 search engine; 1216 spider; 1193 information agent*

1212 **search tool** A program that allows specific Web pages to be searched. ➔ *0665 search engine; 1216 spider; 1193 information agent*

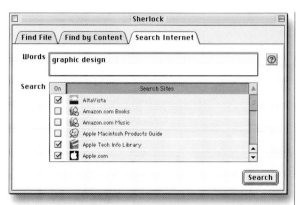

1212 **Search tool** showing the window for Sherlock, the Mac OS search tool

1213 **secure area** The area of a Web site in which personal or sensitive information can be entered by users. Secure areas are usually identified by the prefix "https" in the URL and are particularly important for commercial transactions made via the Web. ➔ *1191 https*

1214 **server-side image map** A means of navigating a Web page via an image map that sends the coordinates of your mouse pointer (in relation to the Web page) back to the server where the page came from so it can determine where to direct you next. ➔ *1245 client-side image map*

1215 **socket** A type of Internet address that is a combination of an Internet protocol address and a port number, the latter providing the identity of applications such as WWW and FTP. ➔ *1077 FTP; 1227 World Wide Web*

1216 **spider** A program that tirelessly roams the World Wide Web, gathering and cataloguing information, typically for use by Web search engines. ➔ *1211 robot; 0665 search engine; 1193 information agent*

1217 **table** (**2**) In a Web page, the arrangement of information in cells, which are organized in rows and columns, similar to a spreadsheet. ➔ *0679 spreadsheet*

1218 **title** Text that appears in the title bar of a Web page.

1219 **URI** *abb.:* **Uniform Resource Identifier** Objects that identify resources available to the Web, such as a URL. ➔ *1220 URL*

1220 **URL** *abb.:* **Uniform Resource Locator** The unique address of a page on the Web. Each resource on the Internet has a unique URL that begins with letters that identify the resource type (and thus the protocol to be used), such as "http" or "ftp," followed by a colon and two forward slashes after which comes the domain name ("host"), which can have several parts to it, then, after a slash, the directory name followed by pathnames to any particular file, for example, http://www.digiwis. com/home.htm. Usually if a file name is not stated, the browser will default to the file name index.html and/or index.htm, which is usually the home page. ➔ *1189 http; 1178 DNS; 1162 absolute URL; 1209 relative URL*

1221 **URL-encoded text** A method of encoding text for passing requests from your Web browser to a server. ➔ *1220 URL; 1210 request*

1222 **URN** *abb.:* **Uniform Resource Name** A permanent name for a Web resource. ➔ *1220 URL*

1232 Animated gif

1223 virtual shopping cart A method of providing Web shoppers with a means of selecting items for purchase as they browse a site, and paying for them all at once when done — just as you would in any store.

1224 Web page An HTML document published on the World Wide Web. → *1206 page (1); 1267 HTML; 1227 World Wide Web*

1225 Web site The address, location (on a server), and collection of documents and resources for any particular interlinked set of Web pages.

1226 WinSock A software component of the Windows operating system, used in PCs to connect to the Internet. → *1017 Windows; 1139 Internet*

1227 WWW *abb.:* **World Wide Web** The entire collection of Web servers all over the world that are connected to the Internet. The term is also used to describe the particular type of Internet access architecture that uses a combination of HTML and various graphic formats, such as GIF and JPEG, to publish formatted text that can be read by Web browsers. Also referred to as The **Web** or **W3**. → *1139 Internet; 1167 browser (1)*

1228 X-face An encoded 48 × 48 bitmap image used by e-mail and news users to contain a picture of their face or company logo.

1229 ActiveX Controls Microsoft's proprietary technology for enhancing interactive Web pages. Like Java "applets," ActiveX Controls can be downloaded from the Internet but, unlike Java applets, they are not platform-independent and are mainly supported only in Microsoft Windows environments. → *1277 Java*

1230 Afterburner Proprietary file compression software for compressing and delivering Macromedia Director film strips on the Internet.

1231 anchor (**2**) A text or graphic element with an HTML tag that either links it to another location or acts as a destination for an incoming link. → *1267 HTML; 0493 tag*

1232 animated GIF A GIF (graphics interchange format) file consisting of multiple images, simulating an animation when played back in a Web browser. → *1261 GIF*

1233 applet Although a general term that can be applied to any small application that performs a specific task, such as the calculator, an applet is also used to describe a small application written in the Java programming language, which is downloaded by an Internet browser to perform specific tasks. → *1139 Internet; 1277 Java; 1167 browser (1)*

1234 argument Used to describe words or numbers entered as part of an HTML instruction to modify how that instruction operates. → *1267 HTML*

1235 associative linking Hyperlinks organized by association rather than by formal classification.

1236 attribute (**1**) A characteristic of an HTML tag that is identified alongside the tag in order to describe it. → *1267 HTML; 0519 attribute (2); 0493 tag*

1237 body (**3**) One of the main structures of an HTML document, falling between the header and the footer. → *1267 HTML; 0390 header; 1260 footer (3)*

1238 bulleted list An HTML style for Web pages in which a bullet precedes each item on a list. → *1566 bullet; 1267 HTML; 1259 font embedding*

1239 **cascade** A hierarchy of style sheets, with each one forming the framework for the next. → *1247 CSS*

1240 **CGI** (**2**) *abb.:* **Common Gateway Interface** A programming technique for transferring data between Web server software and other applications, such as databases.

1241 **CGI scripts** The programming instructions used by Web developers to execute CGI features. → *1240 CGI (1)*

1242 **character shape player** (**CSP**) Software inside a Web browser that enables you to view — or "play back" — the character shapes of embedded fonts in a PFR (portable font resource). → *1259 font embedding; 0885 TrueDoc; 1243 character shape recorder*

1243 **character shape recorder** (**CSR**) Software inside an authoring (multimedia) application that enables you to define — or "record" — the character shapes of a font for embedding in a PFR (portable font resource). → *1259 font embedding; 0885 TrueDoc; 1242 character shape player*

1244 **clickable map/image** An invisible shape surrounding a graphic on a Web page that serves as a button that, when clicked, will take you to another page or Web site. → *1227 World Wide Web; 0921 button*

1245 **client-side image map** A means of navigating a Web page via a clickable image map, which includes the hyperlinks (URLs) in the page itself so you can move around without intervention by the server. → *1214 server-side image map*

1246 **comment** In authoring applications and Web browsers, a remark — identified by a specific character such as an exclamation point (in HTML) — that is ignored by the application or browser when the pages are viewed, but that can be read by anyone who has access to the code. → *1267 HTML*

1247 **CSS** *abb.:* **cascading style sheets** A specification sponsored by the World Wide Web Consortium for overcoming the limitations imposed by "classic HTML." Web designers ("authors") have increasingly sought tools that would enable them to control every element of page design more tightly, with the result that the Web-authoring community has developed unwieldy workarounds (such as using single-pixel GIF images to add character spacing), generating bulky HTML code that, in turn, has resulted in longer downloads and browser incompatibilities. CSS allows the designer to exercise greater control over typography and layout in much the same way as he or she would expect in, say, a page-layout application, and provides the means of applying attributes such as font formats to paragraphs, parts of pages, or entire pages. Several style sheets can be applied to a single page, thus cascading. → *1227 World Wide Web; 1267 HTML; 1261 GIF*

1248 **degradability** The term applied to Web browsers that support new advances in HTML technologies while at the same time serving browsers based on previous versions of the technologies. → *1267 HTML*

1249 **document** (**2**) The entire contents of a single HTML file. HTML documents are generally referred to as Web pages, since this is how they are rendered for display by browsers. → *1267 HTML; 1167 browser (1); 1227 World Wide Web*

1250 **document heading** An HTML style ("tag") that defines text headings in a range of predetermined sizes and weights (levels 1 through 6), so you

abcde

abcdefg

abcdefghi

abcdefghijk

abcdefghijklm

abcdefghijklmnopq

*1250 Document
heading*

can add emphasis to a line of text. Document headings are generically identified by <H*>. ➜ *1267 HTML*

1251 **document root** The place on a Web server where all the HTML files, images, and other components for a particular Web site are located. ➜ *1267 HTML; 0318 server; 1227 World Wide Web*

1252 **Document Type Definition** A formal SGML specification for a document that lays out structural elements and markup definitions.

1253 **Dynamic HTML/DHTML** *abb.:* **dynamic hypertext markup language** A development of basic HTML code that allows you to add such features as basic animations and highlighted buttons to Web pages without relying on browser "plug-ins." DHTML is built into version 4.0 or later generation of Web browsers. ➜ *1267 HTML; 1167 browser (1)*

1254 **element** (**2**) The items comprising a Web page, for example, text, graphics, animations.

1255 **embedded style sheet** A collection of instructions in a digital file (usually HTML) defining fonts, colors, layout, etc., and which override the default settings when displayed on a different computer. ➜ *0685 style sheet; 1247 CSS*

1256 **Extensible Markup Language** (**XML**) A probable successor to HTML, the underlying language used on Web pages, offering more sophisticated control and formatting. XML allows the creation of user-defined tags, which expands the amount of information that can be provided about the data held in documents. ➜ *1257 Extensible Style Language*

1257 **Extensible Style Language** (**XSL**) A style sheet similar to the CSS (cascading style sheets) used for HTML. With XML, content and presentation are separate; XML tags do not indicate how they should be displayed. An XML document has to be formatted before it can be read, and the formatting is usually accomplished with style sheets. Style sheets consist of formatting rules for how particular XML tags affect the display of a document on a computer screen or a printed page. ➜ *1256 Extensible Markup Language*

1258 **Flash** (**2**) A software application developed by Macromedia for creating vector-based animations on the Web. The Shockwave Flash plug-in is required to play them in a Web browser. ➜ *1299 Shockwave*

1259 **font embedding** The technology that allows you to specify a font on a Web page that can be viewed by a browser running on any computer. The fonts are not embedded in the HTML code, but are special files displayed with tags similar to those used for images and objects. Netscape was the first to use this feature, called Dynamic Fonts, which uses Bitstream's True-Doc technology. This allows the designer to "record" font shapes, then store them in a **Portable Font Resource** (PFR) file, which is downloaded in the background and finally "played back," the fonts being displayed only in the Web browser. Internet Explorer includes "Font Embedding," using a font format called OpenType, which was developed by both Microsoft and Adobe. ➜ *1313 WEFT (2); 0871 OpenType*

1260 **footer** (**3**) The concluding part of an HTML document, containing information such as the date, version, etc.

1261 **GIF** *abb.:* **graphic interchange format** A bitmapped graphics format originally devised by Compuserve, an Internet service provider (now part of AOL), and sometimes (although rarely) referred to as Compuserve GIF.

1270 Hypertext

There are two specifications: GIF87a and, more recently, GIF89a, the latter providing additional features such as transparent backgrounds. The GIF format uses a lossless compression technique and thus does not squeeze files as much as the JPEG format, which is lossy (some data is discarded). For use in Web browsers, JPEG is the format of choice for tone images such as photographs, whereas GIF is more suitable for line images and other graphics, such as text.

1262 **header file** Files that contain information identifying incoming data transmitted via the Internet.

1263 **heading** (**2**) A formatting term used in HTML, which determines the size at which text will be displayed in a WWW browser. There are six sizes available, usually referred to as: H1, H2, H3, H4, H5, and H6. → *1267 HTML*

1264 **helper application** Applications that assist Web browsers in delivering or displaying information such as movie or sound files. → *1167 browser (1); 0643 plug-in*

1265 **HotJava** A Web browser developed by Sun Microsystems, which is written in the Java programming language. → *1277 Java; 1167 browser (1)*

1266 **hotlist** A theme-related list on a Web page that provides links to other pages or sites dedicated to that theme.

1267 **HTML** *abb.:* **hypertext markup language** A text-based page description language (PDL) used to format documents published on the World Wide Web that can be viewed with Web browsers. → *1054 PDL; 1167 browser (1)*

1268 **hyperlink** A contraction of hypertext link. An embedded link to other documents, usually identified by being underlined or highlighted in a different color. Clicking on or selecting a hyperlink takes you to another document, part of a document or Web site. → *1164 active hyperlink; 1270 hypertext*

1269 **hypermedia** The combination of graphics, text, movies, sound, and other elements accessible via hypertext links in an online document or Web page. → *1268 hyperlink*

1270 **hypertext** A programming concept that links any single word or group of words to an unlimited number of others, typically text on a Web page that has an embedded link to other documents or Web sites. Hypertext links are usually underlined and/or in a different color to the rest of the text, and are activated by clicking on them. → *1268 hyperlink*

1271 **ID selector** A style sheet rule for a Web page element. → *0685 style sheet*

1272 **image map** An image that contains a series of embedded links to other documents or Web sites. These links are activated when clicked on in the appropriate area of the image. For example, an image of a globe may incorporate an embedded link for each visible country that, when clicked, will take the user to a document giving more information about that country. → *1244 clickable map/ image*

1273 **in-line image** On Web pages, an image that is displayed among text, in the same browser window, rather than in a separate window or via a helper application. → *1264 helper application*

1274 **in-line style** A style applied directly to elements on a Web page rather than via an embedded style sheet or an external, linked style sheet. → *1255 embedded style sheet*

1272 Image map

1275 **interlaced GIF** A GIF89a format image in which the image is revealed in increasing detail as it downloads to a Web page. → *1261 GIF; 1308 transparent GIF*

1276 **interlacing, interlaced** A technique of displaying an image on a Web page in which the image reveals increasing detail as it downloads. Interlacing is usually offered as an option when saving images in GIF, PNG, and JPEG (progressive) formats in image-editing applications. → *1275 interlaced GIF; 1293 PNG; 1294 progressive JPEG*

1277 **Java** A programming language devised by Sun Microsystems for creating small applications (applets) that can be downloaded from a Web server and used, typically in conjunction with a Web browser, to add dynamic effects such as animations. → *1233 applet; 1167 browser (1)*

1278 **Java class library** Groups of frequently used Java routines that programmers use to add common functionality to Java applets. → *1277 Java; 1233 applet*

1279 **Java virtual machine** A process that converts programming code into machine language.

1280 **JavaScript** Netscape's Javalike "scripting" language, which provides a simplified method of applying dynamic effects to Web pages. Microsoft's version of JavaScript for use in Internet Explorer is called JScript.

1281 **JET** *abb.:* **Java-based extendable typography** A font enhancement for Java. → *1259 font embedding*

1282 **layout element** The description of any component in the layout of an HTML document — a Web page, for example — such as a graphic, list, rule, paragraph, and so on. → *1267 HTML*

1283 **length** In Web pages, a CSS measurement expressed in units such as pixels or points. → *1247 CSS*

1284 **list element** Text in a Web page that is displayed as a list and defined by the HTML tag <LI> (list item). → *1267 HTML; 0493 tag; 1285 list tag*

1285 **list tag** The HTML coding (tags) that tells a Web browser how to display text in a variety of list styles, such as ordered lists <OL>, menus <MENU>, and glossary lists <DL>. → *1284 list element; 0493 tag*

1286 **markup** (**2**) The technique of embedding tags (HTML instructions) within special characters (metacharacters), which tell a program such as a Web browser how to display a page. → *1267 HTML; 0415 markup language; 1288 metacharacter*

1287 **meta-information** Optional information provided in an HTML document to help search engine databases place Web sites in the correct category. This facility is often abused by less scrupulous Web sites and is therefore generally falling out of favor with search engine providers whose spider programs trawl the Web to add sites to their databases. → *1216 spider*

1288 **metacharacter** Characters within text that indicate formatting instructions, such as the tags in an HTML file. Angle brackets (< >) and ampersands (&) are typical metacharacters. → *1286 markup (2); 0415 markup language; 1267 HTML*

1289 **NetShow** Microsoft's technology for delivery and playback of multimedia on the Internet, supporting both live and on-demand video.

1290 numbered list An HTML style that numbers paragraphs for use in list form. → *1267 HTML*

1291 paragraph In an HTML document, a markup tag used to define a new paragraph in text.

1292 personal Java A variation of Java designed for specific Internet devices such as netTVs. → *1277 Java*

1293 PNG *abb.:* **portable network graphics** A file format for images used on the Web that provides 10–30 percent lossless compression, and supports variable transparency through "alpha channels," cross-platform control of image brightness, and interlacing.

1294 progressive JPEG A digital image format used for displaying JPEG images on Web pages. The image is displayed in progressively increasing resolutions as the data is downloaded to the browser. Also called proJPEG. → *0761 JPEG; 1275 interlaced GIF; 1276 interlaced*

1295 pseudoclass The differentiation between a piece of HTML code and the same one used as a selector.

1296 RealMedia A Web technology for delivery and playback of multimedia across the Internet, supporting both live and on-demand video (**RealVideo**), and sound (**RealAudio**).

1297 rollover The rapid substitution of one or more images when the mouse pointer is rolled over the original image. Used extensively for navigation buttons on Web pages and multimedia presentations. → *0616 navigation button*

1298 Shocked The term applied to Web pages that contain material prepared with Macromedia's Shockwave technology, and thus require the Shockwave plug-in to be viewed. → *1299 Shockwave*

1299 Shockwave A technology developed by Macromedia for creating Director presentations, which can be delivered across the Internet and viewed with a Web browser. → *1298 Shocked; 1258 Flash (2)*

1300 singleton An HTML tag without a corresponding closing tag.

1301 sitemap An outline view of all the pages on a particular Web site. → *1227 World Wide Web*

1302 source code An alternative name for HTML. → *1267 HTML*

1303 spacer A blank, transparent GIF, one pixel wide, used to space elements on a Web page.

1304 SSL *abb.:* **Secure Sockets Library** A programming library devised by Netscape for helping programmers add secure areas to Web sites. → *1213 secure area; 1191 https*

1305 SGML *abb.:* **Standard Generalized Markup Language** An ISO markup standard for defining documents, which can be used by any computer, regardless of platform.

1306 style (**2**) The rules that control all attributes of a Web page, such as font, alignment, background, etc. → *0685 style sheet; 1255 embedded style sheet; 1247 CSS*

1307 SWF Macromedia's proprietary file format for animations created in Shockwave Flash. → *1258 Flash (2); 1299 Shockwave; 1298 Shocked*

1308 **transparent GIF** A feature of the GIF89a file format that lets you place a nonrectangular image on the background color of a Web page. → *1261 GIF; 1275 interlaced GIF*

1309 **ViewMovie** A Netscape plug-in for viewing animations. → *0643 plug-in*

1310 **VRML** *abb.:* **Virtual Reality Modeling Language** An HTML-type programming language designed to create 3D scenes called virtual worlds.

1311 **watermark** (**2**) The technique of applying a tiled graphic to the background of a Web page. It remains fixed, no matter what foreground materials scroll across it.

1312 **Web authoring** The process of creating documents (usually in HTML or XML format) suitable for publication on the World Wide Web. → *1267 HTML; 1227 World Wide Web*

1313 **WEFT** (**2**) *abb.:* **Web Embedding Font Tool** A Microsoft technology that embeds fonts within a Web page so it will view as intended with any Web browser, regardless of whether the font resides on the recipient's computer. → *1259 font embedding*

1314 Aperture
1326 Diaphragm
a wide aperture
b narrow aperture
c diaphragm

1317 Bellows

1314 **aperture** A variable opening in a camera lens, controlled by a diaphragm, which allows light to reach the film. The size of aperture is measured by the f-number, or f-stop. → *1333* f-number/f-stop

1315 **aperture priority** A mode in automatic cameras in which you select the aperture manually, the shutter speed then being set automatically according to the camera's metering system. The opposite of shutter priority. → *1314* aperture; *1362* shutter priority

1316 **astigmatism** A defect in photographic lenses that causes distortion. → *2094* apochromatic lens

1317 **bellows** An extendable section of folding cloth on some photographic cameras, which connects the lens to the part that holds the film ("back"). Such cameras are often referred to as bellows cameras and are generally used with large-format film.

1318 **camera** A device in which light passes through a lens to record an image. The image can be recorded onto presensitized film or paper, or by means of electronic sensors (CCDs), which digitally "write" the image to a storage device such as a memory card or hard disk. → *0273* CCD; *2126* process camera; *2143* vertical camera

1319 **center-weighted exposure** In automatic "through-the-lens" (TTL) metered cameras, the method of measuring exposure whereby the calculation is based on the tones in the center of the picture. → *1369* through-the-lens meter

1320 **coated lens** A photographic lens coated with a thin film that reduces "flare" (undesirable scattered light). → *1500* flare

1321 **coma** A photographic lens aberration that causes blurring at the edge of a picture.

1322 **compound lens** A photographic lens made up of two or more elements (lens pieces), enabling the lens to be optically adjusted.

1323 **condenser** (**lens**) A photographic lens that concentrates light into a beam. Used in enlargers and process cameras (a camera used for preparing film and plates for printing). → *2126* process camera

1324 **cross front** A camera in which the lens can be moved laterally in relation to the film.

1325 **darkslide** A sheet of lightproof material used in film holders to protect the film from exposure until it is mounted on the camera.

1326 **diaphragm** An adjustable opening, or aperture, behind a camera lens that controls the amount of light that reaches the film. The aperture opening is calibrated on the camera lens by "f-stop" numbers. Also called an **iris diaphragm**. → *1333* f-number/f-stop

1327 **digital camera** A photographic device that captures and records images in binary form rather than on film. → *0914* bit

1328 **diopter** The measurement of the refractive properties of a lens, such as those used for close-up photography. A concave lens is measured in negative diopters, a convex lens in positive diopters. → *1348* lens

1329 **diverging/divergent lens** A camera lens that causes light rays to bend outward from the optical axis. Also called a **negative element**.

1330 **endoscope** A device for photographing normally inaccessible places, such as internal organs of the body.

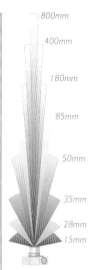

*1338 Focal length showing photographs taken with **a** 28mm lens; **b** 85mm lens (both shown in blue on the diagram at left)*

800mm
400mm
180mm
85mm
50mm
35mm
28mm
15mm

1338 Focal length see caption at top right

1331 **enlarger** A photographic device that allows the projection of the image on a film negative (or positive) onto a sheet of paper with a light-sensitive emulsion.

1332 **extension** (**2**) A tube attached to a camera to increase magnification of the subject.

1333 **f-number/f-stop** The calibration of the aperture size of a photographic lens. This is the ratio of the focal length (f = focal) to the diameter of the aperture. The numbers are marked on the equipment; for example, a camera lens normally calibrated in a standard series would include the following numbers: f1, f1.4, f2, f2.8, f4, f5.6, f8, f11, f16, f22, f32, and so on, and this sets the aperture size. The maximum amount of light that can be transmitted through a lens determines the "speed" of a lens — a lens with a minimum aperture of, say, f1, is a fast lens (it lets in more light), whereas a lens with a minimum aperture of f3.5 is described as a slow lens. → *1314 aperture; 1326 diaphragm*

1334 **field camera** Traditional folding design of a view camera that is portable enough to carry on location.

1335 **field curvature** A lens aberration in which the plane of sharpest focus is curved rather than the flat surface needed at the film plane.

1336 **fish-eye lens** A camera lens with an extremely wide angle of view, producing a distorted image with an exaggerated apparent curve. → *1371 wide-angle lens*

1337 **fixed-focus lens** A photographic lens with no variable focus adjustment. A feature of very cheap cameras.

1338 **focal length** Strictly speaking, the distance between the center of a lens and its point of focus on the film. However, the term is generally used as an indication of the degree to which a lens will magnify the subject, which, in turn, determines the amount of the scene that may be viewed or the degree to which a subject may be distorted. → *1374 angle of view (2); 1333 f-number/f-stop*

1339 **focal plane** The plane at which a camera lens forms a sharp image; also the film plane, the point at which the image is recorded.

1340 **focal plane shutter** A camera shutter located close to the focal plane, in which two blinds form an adjustable gap that moves across the film determining the exposure.

1341 **focus** (**1**) The point at which light rays converge to produce a sharp image. In a camera this is achieved by the lens. → *1386 depth of field; 1338 focal length*

1348 Lens

1342 **follow focus** A camera focusing technique used with a moving subject, in which the focusing ring is turned at exactly the rate necessary to maintain constant focus.

1343 **Fresnel lens** A lens used to concentrate the beam of a spotlight.

1344 **gyro stabilizer** An electrically powered camera support that incorporates a gyroscope to cushion the camera against vibrations. Used for such occasions as photographing from helicopters, cars, and other vehicles.

1345 **hyperfocal distance** The closest distance at which a lens records a subject sharply when focused at infinity, varying with aperture.

1346 **in-camera** (**1**) Photographic processing that takes place inside the camera, such as with Polaroid products.

1347 **in-camera** (**2**) Photographic effects created inside the camera at the time of the shoot, as opposed to effects being applied later, such as during film processing or digitally with an image-manipulation application.

1348 **lens** A cylindrical tube containing one or more glass elements that collect and focus light rays to create an image.

1349 **lens aberration** A fault in a photographic lens in which light rays are improperly focused, causing degraded images.

1350 **long-focus lens** A camera lens with a focal length longer than the diagonal measurement of the film format; thus, for 35mm film, a lens longer than about 50mm is described as long-focus. → *1368 telephoto lens; 1360 short-focus lens*

1351 **medical lens** A type of camera lens designed specifically for medical use, with close-focusing capability and a built-in ringflash (a flash unit that fits around the camera lens).

1352 **mirror lens** A camera lens that forms an image by reflecting it from curved mirrors rather than by refraction through a series of lenses. A mirror lens is more compact than a traditional lens of the same focal length. Also called a **catadioptic lens**. → *1368 telephoto lens*

1353 **monorail** A type of studio support for standard view cameras, and also the name given to such cameras.

1354 **motor-drive** A device that drives the film advance in a camera, allowing a rapid sequence of photographs to be taken.

1355 **night lens** A camera lens designed for optimum use with apertures at maximum width.

1356 **OTF metering** *abb.:* **off-the-film metering** A through-the-lens (TTL) light metering system in which the exposure is determined from the image that is projected onto the film plane inside the camera. → *1369 through-the-lens meter*

1357 **perspective correction** (**PC**) **lens** A camera lens used to correct converging vertical lines in architectural photography.

1358 **Polaroid** A brand-name "in-camera" method of self-processing photographic materials and equipment, used extensively by professional photographers as a means of instantly assessing composition and lighting prior to the actual exposure of a shot. → *1346 in-camera (1)*

1359 **rifle stock** A camera support that helps to hold steady a camera with a long lens (like a rifle).

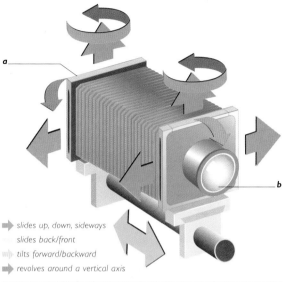

slides up, down, sideways
slides back/front
tilts forward/backward
revolves around a vertical axis

*1353 Monorail; 1370 View camera: **a** viewing screen/film plane; **b** lens*

1360 **short-focus lens** A camera lens with a focal length shorter than the diagonal measurement of the film format. Thus, for 35mm film, a lens shorter than 35mm is a short-focus lens. → *1350 long-focus lens*

1361 **shutter** The mechanical device in a camera that controls the length of time a film is exposed to the light.

1362 **shutter priority** A mode in automatic cameras in which you select the shutter speed manually, the aperture then being set automatically according to the camera's metering system. The opposite of aperture priority. → *1363 shutter speed; 1315 aperture priority*

1363 **shutter speed** The speed at which a camera shutter opens and closes that, in turn, governs the exposure of the film. → *1362 shutter priority*

1364 **single lens reflex (camera)** A camera in which the lens used for the photograph also transmits, via a mirror, the image seen in the viewfinder.

1365 **spherical aberration** The failure of a lens to exactly focus light rays at its center and at its edges. → *1349 lens aberration*

1366 **stop** The aperture size of a camera lens. → *1333 f-number/f-stop*

1367 **technical camera** A view camera that is similar in basic construction to a field camera, but of metal and made with greater precision. → *1370 view camera; 1334 field camera*

1368 **telephoto lens** A photographic lens with a long focal length, allowing distant objects to be enlarged but with a limited depth of field. → *1352 mirror lens; 1372 zoom lens; 1350 long-focus lens*

1369 **through-the-lens meter (TTL)** An exposure meter built into a camera, which calculates an exposure based on the amount of light passing through the camera lens. → *1495 exposure meter; 1356 OTF metering*

1381 Color filters, showing use of a graduated filter

1370 **view camera** A large-format camera in which the image is projected onto a ground-glass viewing screen behind the film plane at the back of the camera. After the scene is viewed, the film is placed in the same position as the viewing screen.

1371 **wide-angle lens** A photographic lens with a wider field of view than a standard lens so more of the subject can be included. The resulting image can be highly distorted, however. ➔ *1336 fish-eye lens; 1360 short-focus lens; 1350 long-focus lens*

1372 **zoom lens** A camera lens with a continuously variable focal length, making it possible to alter the closeness of a subject to the camera without moving the camera. ➔ *1368 telephoto lens*

1373 **acutance** The quality of an edge in a photographic image.

1374 **angle of view** (**2**) The amount of a scene included in a photographic picture, determined by a combination of the focal length of the lens and the film format. ➔ *1338 focal length; 1391 film format*

1375 **bleach(ed)-out** Originally, a weak, unfixed photographic print used as a base for an outline drawing (after inking, the remaining photograph would be bleached out leaving just the drawing), but latterly describing the effect of a high key photograph. ➔ *1508 high key*

1376 **bracketing** In photography, the term describing a series of exposures of the same subject, each one varying progressively to either side of the estimated correct amount of light, in order to allow for uncertainties in exposure and processing.

1377 **brightness range** The range of tones in a photographic subject, from darkest to lightest.

1378 **camera angle** A general term describing the viewpoint of the camera, but also specifically with reference to its angle from the horizontal. ➔ *0528 camera moves*

1379 **camera shake** The term describing usually undesirable movement of a camera at the moment a photograph is taken, resulting in a blurred or ghosted image.

1380 **capacitor** In electronic photographic flash units, the electrical device that allows a charge to be built up and stored.

1381 **color filters** Thin sheets of transparent material such as glass or gelatin placed over a camera lens to modify the quality of light or colors in an image. ➔ *4168 cel (1)*

1382 **copyboard chart** In photography, a color control strip placed beside the subject as an aid to color fidelity for subsequent processing and reproduction. Copyboard charts are particularly used for ensuring accurate color reproduction of fine art subjects.

1383 **D-max** *abb.:* **maximum density** As can be achieved in a photographic original or by a photomechanical system. ➔ *1384 D-min*

1384 **D-min** *abb.:* **minimum density** As can be achieved in a photographic original or by a photomechanical system. ➔ *1383 D-max*

1385 **daguerrotype** The first practical method of creating and fixing a photographic image. Invented by Louis J. M. Daguerre in 1833, the process involved exposing a silvered copper plate to iodine or bromine vapor, which made it light-sensitive. ➔ *1408 bromide; 1435 fix; 1436 fixative*

1386 Depth of field: **a** *small aperture;* **b** *wide aperture*

1386 **depth of field** The subjective range — in front of or behind the point of focus — in a photograph in which the subject remains acceptably sharp or focused. Depth of field is controlled by the lens aperture — the smaller the aperture, the greater the depth of field or sharpness. → *1314 aperture; 1392 focus (2); 1338 focal length*

1387 **depth of focus** The distance through which the film plane can be moved from the point of focus and still record an acceptably sharp image. → *1392 focus (2); 1338 focal length; 1386 depth of field*

1388 **dichroic filter** A filter that permits certain wavelengths of light to pass through while preventing others.

1389 **digital photography** The process either of capturing an image with digital equipment or of manipulating photographic images on a computer. The term describes photographs that are recorded or manipulated in binary form rather than on film. → *1327 digital camera; 0914 bit*

1390 **documentary (photography)** A term applied to movie or still photography using images that, undistorted by interpretation, accurately describe real events.

1391 **film format** Standard measurements for sheet and roll photographic film, corresponding to usual film widths and standard camera sizes. Typical formats are 35mm, 4 × 5 inches, and 8 × 10 inches.

1392 **focus (2)** The general degree of sharpness of a photographic image, ranging from in-focus (sharp) to out-of-focus (blurred). → *1386 depth of field; 1338 focal length*

1393 **ideal format** A particular size of photographic film measuring 2.3 × 2.7in (60 × 70mm).

1394 **macrophotography** The photography of large-scale objects, often used erroneously to describe "photomacrography," which is close-up photography. → *1399 photomacrography; 1400 photomicrography*

1395 **mask (2)** A photographic image modified in tone or color.

1396 **Newton's rings** Patterns of banded color with the appearance of watered silk or contour lines. These occur as a result of interference in the path of light, when two lenses or pieces of film or glass are placed in contact with each other.

1397 **photogram** A photographic image made by placing an object on a sheet of emulsion and briefly exposing it to light, resulting in a kind of shadow picture.

1398 photography The method of recording an image by the action of light on materials affected by it, such as a sensitized film emulsion.

1399 photomacrography Close-up photography with magnifications in the range of about one to ten times that of the original (and thus not "photomicrography"). → *1400 photomicrography*

1400 photomicrography Photography at great magnifications using a microscope. → *1486 darkfield lighting; 1399 photomacrography*

1401 reportage A type of photojournalism in which images that encapsulate a news story are recorded.

1402 sharpness A measure of the clarity of focus present in a photographic image. → *4101 definition*

1403 soft A photographic image with low tonal contrast or a photographic paper specifically designed to produce such images.

1404 stereography A type of photograph in which two simultaneous exposures are made in such a way as to give the impression of 3D depth.

1405 streak photography A type of photography in which the camera and/or subject are moved during a long exposure, the resulting image showing a trace of the movement.

1406 ASA *abb.:* **American Standards Association** The American association that defined the scale used for rating the speed (light-sensitivity) of photographic film.

1407 autopositive A photographic material that provides a positive image without a negative being needed. → *2149 auto-reversing film*

1408 bromide Photographic paper coated on the surface with an emulsion of light-sensitive silver bromide. Bromide paper is used for printing continuous tone photographs from negatives, and also extensively in the prepress industries, which describe a bromide as an alternative high-quality output — used for generating camera-ready art — from an imagesetter, thus distinguishing it from film output. → *4013 camera-ready copy/art*

1409 burn (**4**) A method of obtaining darker areas in a photographic print by selectively increasing exposure to light in the relevant areas. The burn "tool" in certain image-editing applications digitally simulates the mechanical technique. The opposite effect — lightening areas of an image — is called dodging. → *4174 masking (2); 1426 dodge/dodging*

1410 c print/c-type Any reflective photographic color print, originating from the tripack color print material developed by Kodak.

1411 calotype The earliest method of recording images onto sensitized film or paper, invented and patented by the Englishman William Fox Talbot in 1841.

1412 carbon print A photographic print made onto pigmented gelatin-coated material. Carbon prints were formerly known as charcoal prints because charcoal powder was originally used as a black pigment. → *2585 carbon tissue*

1413 chemical reversal Chemical treatment of a photographic image to convert it from negative to positive, or vice versa.

1414 Cibachrome A commercial process for obtaining photographic color prints directly from transparencies, developed by Agfa.

1415 clip test A small piece cut from the end of an exposed roll of film that is processed in advance to determine whether any adjustment may be necessary in processing.

1416 color negative film Photographic film in which the image, after processing, is formed in negative colors, from which positive color prints are made. As distinct from color transparency film, which is positive and is not generally used for making prints. Also referred to as **color negs**. ➜ *1417 color transparency (film)*

1417 color transparency (film) A photographic image on transparent film generated, after processing, as a positive image. Color transparencies are ideal as originals for color separations for process color printing, as they provide a greater variety of colors than reflective prints. Color transparency film is supplied for a variety of camera formats, typically 35mm, 2¼ inch square, and 4 x 5 inch. Color transparencies are also known variously as **trannies**, **color trannies**, **slides** (which generally refers to 35mm only), and **color reversal film**. ➜ *1416 color negative film*

1418 contact film Special "continuous tone" film used to produce a same-size negative image from a film positive original, or vice versa, when the two are placed in direct contact with each other. Also called **color-blind film**. ➜ *2162 color-blind emulsion*

1419 contact print; contacts Photographic prints made by placing an original negative or positive film in direct contact with the bromide paper. ➜ *1408 bromide*

1420 daylight film Color photographic film balanced for use in daylight or in conditions where the light source provides a color temperature of 5400°K, such as electronic flash.

1421 develop To make visible a latent image on exposed photographic film or paper. ➜ *1422 developer*

1422 developer A solution containing a chemical (developing agent) that reveals an image on exposed photographic film or paper.

1423 developing tank A light-fast container used for developing photographic film or paper. ➜ *1422 developer*

1424 diapositive A photographic transparency in which the recorded image appears positive.

1425 dichroic fog An aberration in processed film, appearing as a red or green cloud and caused by an imbalance of chemicals in the developer.

1426 dodge/dodging A method of obtaining lighter areas in a photographic print by the selective use of masking (hiding relevant areas from light). The dodge tool in certain image-editing applications digitally simulates the mechanical technique. The opposite effect — darkening areas of an image — is called burning. ➜ *4174 masking (2)*; *1409 burn (4)*

1427 dye cloud A fault in developed photographic film resulting in a zone of bleached color in one of the emulsion layers.

1428 dye-sensitization In the manufacture of photographic film, the standard process of adding dyes to emulsion in order to control its light-sensitivity, used particularly to make black-and-white film panchromatic. ➜ *1448 panchromatic*; *2205 orthochromatic*; *1449 photo-sensitive*; *1446 orthographic*

1429 emulsion The light-sensitive coating of a photographic material that, when exposed and processed, reveals the image.

1439 Grain (2)
1440 Graininess

1430 emulsion speed A rating given to photographic film so an exposure can be calculated; also called **film speed**. The slower the speed, the finer the emulsion, thus the better the quality of the photographic image — the trade-off is that the slower the speed, the more light is required to expose the image. Film speed is defined by ASA or DIN standards. ➔ *1406 ASA;* **3587** *Deutsche Industrie-Norm*

1431 ferrotype A photographic print made on a thin metal plate.

1432 film (**2**) A cellulose acetate base material coated with light-sensitive emulsion so images can be recorded photographically. Photographic film can be color or black-and-white, line or tone, negative or positive. ➔ *4171 film (1);* **4168** *cel (1)*

1433 film base A transparent substrate used as a carrier for such things as light-sensitive photographic emulsion.

1434 film negative A photographic image in which highlights and shadows are transposed. It is used in printing to make plates or film positives, and in photography to make prints.

1435 fix The process of making permanent the image on a film or paper after it has been developed. The term is also used to describe the chemical solution used in the process. ➔ *1422 developer*

1436 fixative The chemical solution used to make permanent the image on a film or paper after it has been developed. ➔ *1435 fix*

1437 fog (**1**) A gray tone that degrades part or all of a photographic image, whether on film or paper, caused by uncontrolled exposure of the material to light. ➔ *1425 dichroic fog*

1438 grade The classification of photographic printing paper by the degree to which it affects the contrast of an image. Although not all makes are the same, the most common range from 0 (the lowest contrast, for use with high-contrast negatives) to 5 (the highest contrast, for use with low-contrast negatives). ➔ *3506 contrast*

1439 grain (**2**) The density of tiny light-sensitive silver bromide crystals — or the overlapping clusters of crystals — in a photographic emulsion; the finer the grain, the better the detail. Sometimes used in a coarse form for graphic effect.

1440 graininess The granulated effect present in a negative, print, or slide. The degree to which it is visible depends on such things as film speed (it increases with faster films) and enlargement.

1441 hypo *abb.:* **hyposulfate** (although actually sodium thiosulfate) A photographic processing chemical.

1442 intensification A technique used to chemically adjust the density of developed photographic emulsion. The chemicals are called intensifiers.

1443 interneg(**ative**) A photographic negative used as the intermediate step when making a copy from a transparency or flat original. Also called **intermediary**. ➔ *3606 intermediate*

1444 latent image An image that lies dormant until something happens to it to make it appear. In photography, this is used to describe a recorded image that only becomes apparent after it is processed.

1445 negative/neg (**1**) Photographic film or paper in which all the dark areas appear light and vice versa. Negative film is used extensively in the

*1453 Posterization: **a** 2 levels; **b** 3 levels; **c** 4 levels; **d** 5 levels*

reproduction process and is either made direct from originals or produced by an imagesetter.

1446 **orthographic** (**2**) Photographic emulsion that is sensitive only to green, blue, and ultraviolet light. ➔ *2205 orthochromatic*

1447 **overdevelop** To allow an exposed photographic image to remain in the developing solution longer than necessary for a correct exposure.

1448 **panchromatic** Photographic emulsion that is sensitive to all colors in the visible spectrum. ➔ *1446 orthographic (2)*

1449 **photosensitive** Any material that has been chemically treated to make it sensitive to light, typically photographic emulsion.

1450 **pinholes** Tiny transparent specks on processed photographic emulsion, usually caused by dust on the lens or film. Also called **point holes**. ➔ *2204 opaquing*

1451 **plate** (**3**) A size of photographic film, a whole plate measuring 6½ × 8½in, and a half plate measuring 4 × 6½in. ➔ *3949 figure (2)*

1452 **positive** An image emulating an original scene, made photographically on paper or film, usually from a negative. ➔ *1445 negative/neg (1)*

1453 **posterize/posterization** To divide, by photographic or digital means, a continuous tone image into either a predefined or arbitrary number of flat tones. Also called **tone separation**. ➔ *3552 solarize/solarization*

1454 **print** (**1**) A photographic image, usually made from a negative.

1455 **printing-in** A photographic printing technique by which the exposure is selectively increased over parts of the image. Also called **burning in**.

1462 Reticulation

1467 Sepia toning

1456 **pull-processing** The processing technique of giving film a shorter development time than normal to compensate for overexposure or to reduce contrast. ➔ *1457 push-processing*

1457 **push-processing** Giving film a longer development time than normal to compensate for underexposure or to increase contrast. ➔ *1456 pull-processing*

1458 **reducer (2)** A chemical used to remove silver from a developed image, thus reducing its density. A useful technique for adjusting overexposed or underdeveloped negatives.

1459 **replenisher** Chemical additions made to photographic solutions to prolong their active life.

1460 **resin-coated paper** A photographic paper with good dimensional stability, coated on one side with emulsion and on both sides with water-resistant resin or polyethylene.

1461 **resolving power** The ability of a photographic emulsion or lens to record fineness of detail.

1462 **reticulation** A variously desirable or undesirable aberration in photographic processing in which the film emulsion adopts a disrupted, cracked pattern as a result of temperature changes in processing.

1463 **reversal developing/processing** A method of making a positive copy from a positive image (or a negative from a negative).

1464 **reversal film** Film emulsion that produces a positive image, as in color transparencies (slides).

1465 **roll film** Film rolled onto a spool with a paper backing. The most common roll film format is 120.

1466 **sabattier effect** The partial reversal of tone or color in a photographic emulsion due to brief exposure to light during development.

1467 **sepia toning** A process of making sepia prints from standard black-and-white prints. Various bleaches and dyes are employed in the process. ➔ *3550 sepia*

1468 **silver nitrate** A light-sensitive compound, which is a fundamental base of many photographic chemicals.

1469 **silverprint** A brown-hued photographic print made using silver chloride. ➔ *2230 Vandyke print*

1470 **spectral response/sensitivity** The manner or rate in which a light-sensitive component such as film emulsion responds to different wavelengths of light, both visible and nonvisible.

1471 **spotting** The retouching of photographic film or prints in order to remove tiny blemishes or imperfections. ➔ *4151 retouching*

1472 **stabilization paper** A special photographic paper used in rapid-access processing (fast processing), the emulsion of which incorporates a developing agent.

1473 **toning** Adding a brown or blue (usually) tone to a photographic print.

1474 **tungsten film** A photographic film that is used where the scene is to be illuminated by tungsten lamps (normal, household lamps). ➔ *1432 film*

1480 Barn doors

1486 Darkfield lighting

1489 Diffuse

1475 **wet plate** A glass photographic plate that is exposed while the solution used to give it a photo-sensitive surface is still wet.

1476 **wetting agent** A soapy solution that weakens the surface tension of water, thus reducing the risk of drying marks appearing on film.

1477 **axial lighting** The technique of lighting a photographic subject by shining a light along the lens axis, thus casting few or no shadows.

1478 **back projection** The technique of displaying an image behind a photographic subject by projecting it onto a translucent screen from behind. ➔ *1503 front projection*

1479 **back scatter** A photographic snowstorm effect achieved by lighting the subject with a flashgun placed under bubbling water.

1480 **barn doors** Flaps attached to a photographic light to control the direction and amount of light emitted. Many presentation applications contain features that emulate the effect of barn doors on lights.

1481 **base lighting** The technique of lighting a photographic subject from beneath by projecting the light upward. Also known as **ground lighting**.

1482 **boom** A device used in photography for supporting the camera or lights, consisting of a metal arm that pivots on a vertical stand.

1483 **bounce lighting** The method of lighting a subject by reflected light, for example, off the walls, ceiling, or other suitable reflector.

1484 **clinometer** Surveying device that measures slopes — particularly useful for photographing subjects that may not be absolutely vertical, such as a painting.

1485 **contre jour** A photographic term that describes a picture taken with the camera lens pointing toward the light source.

1486 **darkfield lighting** A lighting technique used in photomicrography in which the subject is lit by a cone of light from below, with the background appearing black. ➔ *1400 photomicrography*

1487 **dedicated flash** A flash unit integrated with a camera's built-in automatic light metering system.

1488 **diffraction** The scattering of lightwaves as they strike the edge of an opaque surface. In the conventional preparation of halftones, this can affect dot formations. ➔ *2040 halftone (1)*

1489 **diffuse** A softened effect in a photographic image, created by scattered light giving an object the appearance of, for example, being viewed through translucent glass. ➔ *1546 soft focus*

1490 **diffuser** Any material that scatters transmitted light, thus increasing the area of the light source. ➔ *1489 diffuse*

1491 **direct reading** The common term for taking a meter reading directly from light reflected from a subject.

1492 **dolly** (**shot**) A rolling trolley that supports a camera tripod, used in both still and movie photography but more often the latter. A dolly is also used in 3D applications for a movement control in which the "camera" moves around in 3D space as though gliding on the surface of an imaginary sphere, with the subject at its center. This should not be confused with panning, where the camera rotates at a fixed point to view a scene, or tracking, where the camera moves ➔

past the subject in a parallel plane. ➜ *0528 camera moves; 1531 panning; 0695 tracking (2)*

1493 **exposure** The amount of light that is permitted to reach a photo-sensitive material, such as photographic film, so that an image is recorded. This is usually a combination of the length of time and the intensity at which the light shines upon the material.

1494 **exposure latitude** A range of exposure settings appropriate for a given photographic film.

1495 **exposure meter** A device, used in photography to calculate the correct exposure, that measures the light generated by, reflected off, or falling on, a subject. Also called a **light meter**.

1496 **exposure setting** On a camera, the combination of shutter speed and amount of aperture (lens opening).

1497 **filter** (**3**) In photography, thin sheets of colored glass, tinted gelatin, or cellulose acetate placed in front of a camera lens to alter the color or quality of light passing through to the film. Used to correct color bias (or with photographic film such as that used for specific lighting conditions) or to add special effects. ➜ *1534 polarize*

1498 **filter factor** The amount of compensation required for a photographic exposure if a filter is used. ➜ *1497 filter (3)*

1499 **flag** (**4**) A matte black sheet placed between a lamp and a camera lens to reduce flare.

1500 **flare** Scattered light that degrades the quality of a photographic image, usually caused by too much light being reflected. In some situations, flare can be used for beneficial effect and is even provided as a feature in some computer applications — the Lens Flare filter in Adobe Photoshop, for example. ➜ *1320 coated lens*

1501 **flash** (**1**) A split-second, intense burst of artificially generated light used in photography to light a subject.

1502 **flash synchronization** A camera system in which the peak output from the flash unit occurs when the shutter is fully open.

1503 **front projection** The technique of projecting an image by using a two-way mirror placed between camera and subject, which allows the superim-position of additional images. ➜ *1478 back projection*

1504 **gelatin filter** Colored filters made from dyed gelatin, normally placed over a camera lens to add a color bias (or some other effect) to a shot, with no significant effect on the optical quality of the final image.

1505 **grayscale** (**1**) A tonal scale printed in steps from white to black and used for controlling the quality of both color and black-and-white photographic processing, and also for assessing quality in a halftone print. A grayscale (also called a **step wedge**, **half-tone step scale**, or **step tablet**) is sometimes printed on the edge of a sheet.

1506 **ground light** A studio light that sits on the floor and is pointed up, usually to illuminate a background.

1507 **halation** In the highlights of a photographic image, an unwanted spread of light beyond its natural boundary, caused by overexposure or (in platemaking) poor plate contact during exposure.

1508 High key

1518 Low key

1508 **high key** A photographic image exposed or processed to produce overall light tones. → *1375 bleach(ed)-out; 3506 contrast; 1518 low key*

1509 **incident light reading** Measurement of the light source that illuminates a subject, in order to determine the exposure of a photograph, thus ignoring the subject's own characteristics.

1510 **joule** Unit of electronic flash output, equal to one watt-second.

1511 **key light** The main light source in a photographic setup.

1512 **key reading** In a photographic setup, an exposure reading of the key tone only. → *1513 key tone*

1513 **key tone** The most important tone in a photographic scene that must be recorded accurately.

1514 **Kirlian photography** A technique in which the subject is placed against film and its image appears as an outline of electrical discharge.

1515 **latitude** The range of exposures that produce an acceptable image on a given type of film.

1516 **light table/box** A table or box with a translucent glass top lit from below, giving a color-balanced light suitable for viewing color transparencies and for color matching them to proofs.

1517 **light tent** Translucent material placed around a subject, lighting being directed through the material to give a diffused effect, thus simplifying reflections.

1518 **low key** A photographic image that is given overall dark tones either by lighting or by processing. → *3506 contrast*

1519 **luminaire** A large photographic tungsten lamp that is focused by means of a Fresnel lens. → *1343 Fresnel lens*

1520 **mean noon sunlight** An arbitrary color temperature to which most daylight color films are balanced, based on the average color temperature of direct sunlight at noon in Washington, DC (5400° Kelvin).

1521 **modeling lamp** A lamp used to demonstrate what the lighting effect will be on a subject, but which does not interfere with the actual exposure.

1522 **multipattern metering** An exposure metering system in which areas of the image are measured separately and assessed according to a predetermined program.

1523 **multiple exposure** Two or more photographic images, which may be the same or different, superimposed during exposure or processing to form a single image.

1524 **multiple flash** Repeated firing of a flash unit to increase the exposure of a (static) subject. Also called serial flash.

1525 **neutral density filter** A filter that uniformly reduces all colors of light during an exposure.

1526 **nonactinic (light)** A light source that is normally nonreactive to a sensitized photographic surface, and is thus used in photographic darkrooms. Sometimes called **safelight**.

1527 **northlight** A lighting setup with diffuse but directional qualities that emulates that from a north-facing window in the Northern Hemisphere.

*1534 Polarize/polarization: **a** without polarizing filter; **b** with polarizing filter*

1528 open flash The technique of illuminating a subject by leaving the camera shutter open and firing the flash manually.

1529 outrig frame A metal frame fitted in front of a lamp and used to carry filters, gels, diffusing filter, etc.

1530 overexpose/overexposure (I) A photographic image that has a bleached-out, pale appearance, with subsequent loss of detail, caused by too much light reaching the film during exposure.

1531 pan(ning) The rotation of a camera from side to side along its vertical axis, an animation feature of most 3D applications. → *0528 camera moves; 1492 dolly (shot); 0695 tracking (2)*

1532 pantograph A device that allows the extension and retraction of photographic lamps.

1533 photoflood A high-rated tungsten lamp used in photography, with a color temperature of 3400°K.

1534 polarize/polarization To restrict light vibrations to one direction, polarizing lens filters reduce the reflective qualities of light and are thus used to minimize reflections and glare, and to enhance color balance.

1535 prism A specially shaped transparent substance, usually glass, that refracts light in a controlled manner.

1536 reciprocity failure An exception to mathematical law in photographic processing. A short exposure under a bright light does not produce the same result as a long exposure in a dim light, although mathematically it should. In other words, at very short and very long exposures, the reciprocity law ceases to hold true, and an extra exposure is needed. The effect produced varies with film types, but on color film the three dye layers respond differently and a color cast may occur, so only the exposure range for which the film was designed should be used. → *1537 reciprocity law*

1537 reciprocity law A law that states that photographic exposure is the result of both the intensity of light and the time taken to make the exposure. → *1536 reciprocity failure*

1538 reflected light reading Measurement of the light that is reflected from a subject in order to determine the exposure of a photograph. → *1509 incident light reading*

1539 ringflash An electronic flash, in the shape of a ring, surrounding the camera lens. This produces virtually shadowless lighting.

1545 Snoot

*1546 Soft focus: **a** without soft focus filter; **b** with soft focus filter*

1540 **scoop** Smoothly curving background in a photography studio, used principally to eliminate the horizon line. Also called a **cove**.

1541 **scrim** (**2**) Mesh fabric placed in front of a photography lamp in order to diffuse the light.

1542 **separation guide** A printed guide containing a set of standard colors such as cyan, magenta, yellow, red, green, blue, and black that, when photographed alongside a color-critical subject (a painting, for example), allows the separation to be matched against the color control bar printed alongside the image. → *2102* color bar

1543 **skylight** In a photography setup, light provided by a blue sky as opposed to direct sunlight.

1544 **slave unit** In a photographic setup, a remote device that responds to the light emitted from a single flash unit, activating additional remote flash units simultaneously.

1545 **snoot** A cylinder fitted to a photographic light source, throwing a circle of light.

1546 **soft focus** An effect achieved by using slightly opaque filters that "soften" the edges of an image without altering the actual focus. → *1489* diffuse

1547 **spotlight** (**2**) A photographic lamp that concentrates a controllable narrow beam of light. → *0678* spotlight (1)

1548 **starburst** (**filter**) (**1**) The photographic effect of light rays radiating from a highlight in lines, achieved by the use of a filter that diffuses light from a strong concentrated source.

1549 **strobe** abb.: **stroboscopic (light)** A rapidly repeating flash unit, used for multiple-exposure photographs of moving subjects.

1550 **time exposure** A photographic exposure of several seconds or more.

1551 **tungsten lighting** Artificial lighting created by a heated filament of tungsten, as used in a household light bulb and some photographic lamps. → *1533* photoflood; *1474* tungsten film

1552 **underexpose/underexposure** Occurs when insufficient light has been used to effect the correct exposure of a photo-sensitive material. The result is a print or transparency that is too dark and a negative that is too "thin" (resulting in a dark print).

1553 **accent** A symbol attached to a letterform to indicate pronunciation of a word, usually in that language, but also used to indicate particular pronunciations, such as in dictionaries.

1554 **accent characters** The keys of a keyboard that generate accents in particular typographic letters. The keys are usually used in conjunction with modifier keys, such as shift, option, and control, or a combination of these. → *1553 accent; 1571 character (1); 0221 modifier key*

1555 **alphanumeric set** The complete set of alphabet characters, numbers, punctuation, and associated symbols and accents of a font.

1556 **ampersand** The sign "&" used to represent the word "and." Sometimes called a **short and**.

1557 **arabic numerals** The characters 1234567890. Although described as arabic, thus presuming their origin, these numeric symbols have been traced back to Hindi symbols used in India. → *3760 roman numerals*

1558 **asterisk** A star-shaped symbol (*) generally used as a reference mark in text matter to indicate a footnote.

1559 **bastard** (**3**) Of type, a character that is foreign to the font in which it is set. Also, in mechanical typography, a character that is smaller or larger than the body upon which it is cast. → *1749 font/fount; 1939 body (1) type*

1560 **blind P** The character ¶, usually used as an invisible character in page-layout and word-processing applications to indicate a new paragraph. Also called a **reverse P** or **paragraph mark**.

1561 **brace** A type character used to group phrases or lines of text. The brace at the start of the phrase or on the left side of a block of text is called the open brace ({), as distinct from the close brace (}) at the right side or end. Not to be confused with bracket or parenthesis. → *1563 bracket(s); 1624 parenthesis; 1562 brace end*

1562 **brace end** A type character representing a horizontal brace. → *1561 brace; 1575 cock (end)*

1563 **bracket(s)** A type character used in pairs [open and close] to enclose or separate text or numbers. Brackets are often used to enclose matter that is designated for later deletion. Not to be confused with brace or parenthesis. → *1561 brace; 1624 parenthesis*

1564 **breve** A symbol (˘) used to indicate the pronunciation of a short or unstressed vowel. → *1553 accent*

1565 **built fraction** A fraction constructed from a numerator, separator, and denominator, as distinct from a case fraction — one that is ready made. Also called **piece fractions**. → *1603 fraction*

1566 **bullet** A dot "•" used to itemize lists or emphasize passages of text. On a computer keyboard a bullet is generated by pressing Option-8 (Mac) or Control+Alt-8 (Windows).

1567 **canceled numeral** A numerical character, used in mathematics, crossed through with a diagonal stroke.

1568 **caret/caret mark** A term derived from the Latin "it needs" and represented by the symbol (∧). Used in copy preparation and proof correction to indicate the location of type matter to be inserted.

1581 Denominator

1586 Dingbat

1569 case fraction A ready-made fraction, as distinct from a split, built, or piece fraction. Also called a **true fraction**. → *1603 fraction; 1565 built fraction; 1622 numerator; 1632 separator; 1581 denominator*

1570 centered dot/point A period (full point) centered on the x-height of a piece of type.

1571 character (**1**) Any single letter, number, punctuation mark, or symbol. Characters were traditionally called sorts. → *0837 character (2)*

1572 character set The complete repertoire of letters, numbers, and symbols in a font design. → *0866 ISO/Adobe character set*

1573 circumflex A symbol (^) placed over a vowel, in some languages, to indicate a special quality such as a contraction. → *1553 accent; 1582 diacritical mark*

1574 close (**2**) The second of a pair of punctuation marks, as in parentheses, brackets, or quotation marks:)] '.

1575 cock (**end**) The middle part of a brace end, when constructed in three pieces. → *1562 brace end; 1561 brace*

1576 comma A punctuation mark (,).

1577 corners (**1**) The traditional term for the material used for constructing corners in ruled frames or connecting ornamental borders.

1578 dagger A reference mark (†) used in text to refer the reader to a footnote. A dagger is also sometimes used next to a name to signify that the person is deceased. Also known as an **obelisk** or **obelus**. → *1592 double dagger; 1629 reference mark*

1579 dash Strictly speaking, a dash can be any short rule, plain or decorative, but is usually used to describe an em dash (—) or en dash (–), as distinct from a hyphen (-). → *1596 em dash/rule; 1597 en dash/rule; 1609 hyphen*

1580 decimal point A full point, or period, placed after a whole number and before the numerator in decimal fractions. This is commonly shown as, for example, 2.1, but may also be shown as 2·1 (UK) or 2,1 (Europe). → *1622 numerator*

1581 denominator The number below the line ("separator") in a fraction. → *1603 fraction; 1622 numerator; 1632 separator*

1582 diacritical mark A sign denoting the particular value or pronunciation of a character. → *1553 accent*

1583 diaeresis/dieresis A pair of dots placed over the second of two vowels to indicate that it must be pronounced as a separate syllable, as in "naïve."→ *1648 umlaut*

1584 digit (**1**) Any numeral from 0 to 9. → *0914 bit*

1585 digit (**2**) A printer's symbol ("ornament") depicting a hand with a pointing finger. Also known as a **hand**, **fist**, or **index**. → *1602 flower*

1586 dingbat The modern name for fonts of decorative symbols, traditionally called **printer's ornaments**, flowers, or arabesques. → *1602 flower; 1725 arabesque*

1587 diphthong The symbol that represents two vowels pronounced as a single syllable, for example, Œ and Æ. → *3711 digraph*

1590 Dot leader

1602 Flower

Αα *Alpha*	Νν *Nu*
Ββ *Beta*	Ξξ *Xi or Si*
Γγ *Gamma*	Οο *Omicron*
Δδ *Delta*	Ππ *Pi*
Εε *Epsilon*	Ρρ *Rho*
Ζζ *Zeta*	Σσς *Sigma*
Ηη *Eta*	Ττ *Tau*
Θθ *Theta*	Υυ *Upsilon*
Ιι *Iota*	Φφ *Phi*
Κκ *Kappa*	Χχ *Chi*
Λλ *Lambda*	Ψψ *Psi*
Μμ *Mu*	Ωω *Omega*

1606 Greek alphabet

1588 ditto/prime marks The symbol (″) — also called **double primes** — indicating that the text matter directly above it is repeated. Alternatively used as a symbol for inches and seconds. **Single primes** (′) are used for feet and minutes. ➜ *1594 dumb quotes; 1611 inverted commas*

1589 dog's cock A colloquial term for an exclamation mark, frequently used by newspaper copy editors.

1590 dot leader A leader line made up of dots, generally used to guide the eye in tabulated matter, lists, and so on. ➜ *4043 leader line/leader rule*

1591 double character Traditionally, in metal type, two letters on a single type body such as a ligature or diphthong. ➜ *1613 ligature*

1592 double dagger The mark "‡" used to indicate notes to a text. Also called a **diesis** or **double obelisk**. ➜ *1578 dagger*

1593 duck foot quotes Quotation marks (« ») used in French and German text. Also called **guillemets**.

1594 dumb quotes Used to describe "prime" marks when they are used, erroneously, as quotation marks or apostrophes. In some computer or application configurations, prime marks appear by default when the "quote" key is typed, unless preferences are set to substitute true quotation marks (called smart or curly quotes). ➜ *1588 ditto/prime marks; 1635 smart quotes*

1595 ellipsis (1) A sequence of three dots (…) used within text to indicate a pause, or a part of a phrase or sentence has been left out. An ellipsis can be generated by a single keyboard character. ➜ *0945 ellipsis (2)*

1596 em dash/rule A dash the width of an em (—), the actual width depending on the size of type being set. ➜ *1686 em; 1597 en dash/rule; 1609 hyphen; 1597 dash*

1597 en dash/rule A dash half the width of an em (–), the actual width depending on the size of type being set. ➜ *1596 em dash/rule; 1609 hyphen; 1579 dash*

1598 extended character set The characters available in a font other than those that appear on the keyboard, such as accents, symbols, etc., and that are accessed by combinations of key strokes. ➜ *1572 character set*

1599 factotum A traditional type ornament that provides a space to contain any capital letter, normally an initial cap at the beginning of a chapter.

1600 figure (1) A number, as distinct from a letter.

1601 floating accents In metal setting, any accent that is cast separately from a type character. ➜ *1553 accent*

1602 flower Type ornaments and arabesques originally used to embellish page borders, but now encompassing any decorative font and usually called a dingbat. Also known as **fleurons** or **flowerets**. ➜ *1725 arabesque; 1586 dingbat*

1603 fraction A type character (a case or true fraction), or assembly of type characters (a piece or built fraction), which denotes part of a whole number, such as ½. ➜ *1565 built fraction; 1569 case fraction*

1604 full point A period or full stop.

1605 full stop A period or full point.

1606 Greek alphabet The characters and names of the Greek alphabet.

1613 Ligature

1615 Long s

1616 Macron

1622 Numerator

1607 **hard hyphen** A hyphen that will not permit the hyphenated word to break at the end of a line. ➔ *1609 hyphen*

1608 **hooks** An old term for brackets. ➔ *1563 bracket(s); 1624 parenthesis*

1609 **hyphen** A dash (-) used to divide broken words or to link two words. ➔ *1596 em dash/rule; 1597 en dash/rule; 1579 dash; 1866 hyphenate*

1610 **inferior character** Letters or numbers set smaller than the text and on or below the baseline, for example, H_2O. In many computer applications, inferior characters are called **subscript**. ➔ *1643 superior character*

1611 **inverted commas** A pair of commas used to open and close a quotation. In the English language they are used "thus," whereas in German they are sometimes used „thus." Some other European languages alternatively use "duck foot quotes" «thus» or »thus«. ➔ *1627 quotation/quote marks; quotes; 1593 duck foot quotes*

1612 **latin** (**I**) The standard alphabet used in most European languages, consisting of the upper- and lowercase characters from A to Z. The exceptions are Greek and Cyrillic (Russian, etc.). Oriental languages, including Arabic and Hebrew, are classified as exotics. ➔ *1741 exotic*

1613 **ligature** Two or three type characters tied, or joined together, to make a single type character. Also called **tied letters** or **tied characters**.

1614 **line pattern** The sequence of dots, dashes, and spaces in a rule.

1615 **long s** A lowercase "s" used in old forms of printed English, resembling an f. In some character sets, a long s is called a florin.

1616 **macron** A pronunciation symbol representing a long vowel, indicated by a line above a letter.

1617 **mathematical setting** The typesetting of mathematical characters and formulae. ➔ *1618 mathematical signs/symbols*

1618 **mathematical signs/symbols** Characters used as a shorthand for mathematical concepts and processes, such as + (add), ÷ (divide), √ (radical, or square root).

1619 **medical and pharmaceutical symbols** Typographical symbols representing: dram, drop, gallon, grain, minim, of each, ounce, pint, recipe, scruple, semi, signa, etc.

1620 **monetary symbol/currency symbol** A symbol denoting a unit of currency, such as $ (dollar); ¢ (cent); £ (sterling); € (Euro); ¥ (yen). The Euro currency symbol has replaced the general currency symbol (¤) of the ISO/Adobe character set in recently issued fonts. ➔ *0866 ISO/Adobe character set*

1621 **numbering format** The style of numbering used for page numbers: 1, 2, 3; I, II, III; etc.

1622 **numerator** The number above the line in a fraction. ➔ *1580 decimal point; 1603 fraction; 1581 denominator; 1632 separator*

1623 **parallel mark** A type character (‖) used to denote a reference mark.

1624 **parenthesis** A pair of rounded brackets ( ), although, accurately, the term means a nonessential word, clause, or sentence inserted into a text that can be marked off by dashes or commas as well as brackets.

1625 **period** A full stop, or full point.

1632 Separator

M² M²
a   b

a *1643 Superior character*
b *1644 Superscript*

1626 **punctuation mark** A system of marks used to clarify text and separate sentences.

1627 **quotation/quote marks; quotes** Inverted commas and apostrophes, either single (' ') or double (" "), used before and after a word or phrase to indicate that it is a quotation, title, jargon, slang, etc. → *1635 smart quotes*

1628 **raised point** A period (full point) placed at the mid-height of capitals rather than on the baseline. Also called a **raised dot** or **raised period**. → *1566 bullet*

1629 **reference mark** Typographic term describing symbols used in text to refer to footnotes, for example, an asterisk (*) or dagger (†).

1630 **scratch comma** A comma rendered as a short, straight, oblique line.

1631 **section** (**3**) A symbol (§) used as a reference mark in text to draw the reader's attention to a footnote.

1632 **separator** The line separating the denominator from the numerator in a fraction. → *1581 denominator; 1622 numerator; 1603 fraction*

1633 **side sorts** In traditional metal typesetting, those characters in a font of type that are less frequently used and are therefore kept in small boxes at the side of the drawer or case.

1634 **slash** An obliquely sloping line, or forward slash(/). Reversal forms a backslash (\). Also called a **solidus**.

1635 **smart quotes** A feature in many applications that automatically converts inverted commas ("prime" marks) to correct quotation marks by gauging their positions in the text. Also referred to colloquially as curly quotes. → *1627 quotation/quote marks; 1594 dumb quotes; 1588 ditto/ prime marks*

1636 **sort** (**2**) A character used in text that is not part of the main font used, such as a dingbat or pi character. → *1586 dingbat; 1638 special sorts; 1975 pi font*

1637 **special character** A character obtained by pressing modifier, or combinations of, keyboard keys.

1638 **special sorts** Characters not usually included in a font of type, such as fractions or ornaments. Also called **peculiars** or **pi characters** (not to be confused with pie type, which is accidentally mixed type). → *1636 sort (2); 1975 pi font*

1639 **split fraction** Type for fractions. This comes in two parts, the upper bearing a numeral only, and the lower a numeral and a dividing line above it. → *1565 built fraction*

1640 **stamp** (**1**) In conventional metal typesetting, the compositor's term for a single piece of type.

1641 **star** A typographical ornament or device. → *1586 dingbat*

1642 **strike through** (**2**)/**strike thru** Type characters with a horizontal rule passing through the center. Also called **lined characters** or **erased characters**.

1643 **superior character** A figure or letter that is smaller than the text size and aligned with the height of the capitals. Superior characters are distinct from superscript, which appears above capital height. Also called **cock-up**

1652 Body size

1667 Cap height

figures, **cock-up letters**, **superior figures**, or **superior letters**. → *1644 superscript; 1610 inferior character*

1644 **superscript** Figures or letters that are smaller than the text size and raised above the height of capital letters. As distinct from superior characters, which are aligned at capital letter height. → *1643 superior character; 1610 inferior character*

1645 **turned commas** Inverted commas.

1646 **type synopsis/specimen sheet** A printed sample of a font showing the full character set.

1647 **typesetter's quotation marks** The traditional curly quotation marks and inverted commas used in typesetting, frequently abandoned in DTP software.

1648 **umlaut** A pair of dots placed over a vowel (ü) to indicate a vowel change in some languages, particularly German. → *1583 diaeresis/dieresis*

1649 **agate** A measurement of column depth in newspaper and magazine classified advertisements. Fourteen agates equal one inch. → *3647 agate line; 3655 column inch/centimeter; 1666 ruby*

1650 **alphabet length** The measurement, in points, of the entire length of the 26 alphabet characters of a font of any one size set in lowercase. Therefore, 39 characters have a length of 1.5 alphabets. → *1571 character (1); 1708 point (1)*

1651 **ascent** The amount of space, measured from the baseline, required to accommodate a font. The ascent value is determined by the font designer and is the value used by many page-layout applications for leading and aligning boxes. → *1935 baseline; 1879 leading*

1652 **body size** The size, in points, by which type is measured. Originally, this meant the body of the piece of metal on which the character sits, but in computer typography it means the size of a font without leading. → *1939 body (1) (type); 1708 point (1)*

1653 **bourgeois** A traditional term for a type size of 8½ points.

1654 **brevier** A traditional term for a type size of 7.6 points.

1655 **brilliant** A traditional term for a type size of 3½ points.

1656 **canon** A traditional term for a type size of 48 points.

1657 **excelsior** A traditional size of type of about 4 points, or half the size of brevier (8 points). → *1654 brevier*

1658 **gem** A traditional term for a type size of 4 points.

1659 **great primer** A traditional term for a type size of about 18 points.

1660 **long primer** A traditional term for a type size of 9½ points.

1661 **minikin** A traditional term for a type size of 3 points.

1662 **minion** A traditional term for a type size of 7.3 points.

1663 **nonpareil** A traditional term for a type size of 6 points. The name is still sometimes used (although increasingly rarely) as an alternative term to indicate 6-point leading.

1664 **paragon** A traditional term for a type size of about 20 points, originating in 16th-century Holland. It was also described as a **two-line primer**.

1673 Character width
a character width
b body width

1665 **pearl** A traditional term for a type size of 5 points.

1666 **ruby** A traditional term for a type size of 5½ points. Also called an **agate**. → 1649 agate

1667 **cap height** The height of a capital letter, measured from its baseline. → 1935 baseline

1668 **cap line** (1) An imaginary horizontal line defining the tops of capital letters.

1669 **card fount/font** A traditional term for the smallest complete size of a font design manufactured and sold by a typefounder. → 1749 font/fount

1670 **cast-off** The process of estimating the amount of space or number of pages that will be required to accommodate copy to be typeset. Traditionally, this was done either by comparing the character count to that of a printed sample of the font to be used (at the correct size, weight, leading, measure, etc.), or by using the typefounder's copyfitting tables, which were produced for every font the foundry manufactured. Nowadays, page-layout and word-processing applications provide instant and accurate calculations of copy length. → 1676 copyfitting (1); 1671 cast-up; 1789 character count

1671 **cast-up** In traditional typesetting, the process of calculating, for costing purposes, the amount of typesetting that will be required to complete a job. In mechanical typesetting, the cast-up entails estimating not only the time to set actual characters, but also estimating the amount of white space required for word spaces, extra leading, and white lines, since these take up compositing time as well as requiring extra metal for the spaces between the type. → 1788 casting; 1670 cast-off; 1676 copyfitting (1)

1672 **character space** The distance between each character as determined by the font designer, as distinct from kerning and tracking, which are modifications of that distance. → 1696 kerning; 0883 tracking (1); 1673 character width

1673 **character width** The width of each character, determined from the origin of one to the origin of the next. → 1945 character origin; 1672 character space

1674 **cicero** A unit of the European Didot system for measuring the width (measure) of a line of type and the depth of a page. One cicero equals 12 Didot points, or 4.511mm (³⁄₁₆in). The unit is said to derive from the size of type cut for a 15th-century edition of Cicero's De Oratore. → 1681 Didot point; 1708 point (1)

1675 **composition size(s)** The traditional name for any size of type below 14pt, so called because these were the sizes that could be set on a hot metal compositing (typesetting) machine. → 1802 hot metal (type); 1822 typesetting; 1708 point (1); 1792 comp (2)

1676 **copyfitting** (1) Calculating the amount of space typeset copy will occupy when set in a specific font, size, and measure. → 1670 cast-off; 1671 cast-up

1677 **copyfitting** (2) Modifying typeset copy so it will fit into a given space. This may be done by variously cutting or adding words, increasing or decreasing character or word space, horizontal scaling, etc.

1678 **cpi** abb.: **characters per inch** The number of type characters per inch in copyfitting. → 1676 copyfitting (1); 1650 alphabet length

1696 Kerning
1697 Kerning pair
a *a pair of characters
set side by side,
without kerning*
b *kerned characters,
showing the amount
of overlap*

1679 **cpl** *abb.:* **characters per line** The number of type characters per line in copyfitting. ➜ *1676 copyfitting (1); 1650 alphabet length*

1680 **diamond** A traditional term for a type size of 4½ points.

1681 **Didot point** The unit of type measurement used in continental Europe, devised by Françoise-Ambroise Didot in 1775. A Didot point measures 0.343mm (0.0148inch), compared with the Anglo-American point of 0.35mm (0.013837inch). Twelve Didot points are referred to as a cicero or Didot pica. ➜ *1674 cicero; 1708 point (1); 1706 pica*

1682 **differential** (**letter**) **spacing** The spacing of each letter according to its individual width. ➜ *1895 proportional (letter) spacing; 1700 letterspacing/letterfit*

1683 **display matter/type** Larger-size fonts — usually 14pt or more — used for headings, for example. As distinct from smaller sizes used for continuous text, captions, and so on. ➜ *1684 display size(s)*

1684 **display size(s)** Traditionally, any size of type above 14pt. ➜ *1675 composition sizes*

1685 **double pica** A traditional term for a type size, originally about 22 points, but standardized to 24 points (2 × 12pt picas). Also called a **two-line pica**. ➜ *1706 pica*

1686 **em** Traditionally, the width occupied by a capital M that, usually being a square, gave rise to a linear measurement equal to the point size of the type being set; thus, a 9-point em is 9 points wide. A 12-point em is generally called a pica, or pica em, and measures 4.22mm (0.166inch). Half an em is called an en. ➜ *1690 en; 1706 pica*

1687 **em quad** An em space, which is the size of a square of the type size being set. Traditionally called a "mutt" or "mutton." ➜ *1710 quad (2); 1686 em*

1688 **em space** A space the width of the point size of the type being set. ➜ *1686 em; 1710 quad (2)*

1689 **emerald** A traditional term for a type size of about 6½ points, between the nonpareil and the minion, and also known as a **minionette**. ➜ *1663 nonpareil; 1662 minion*

1690 **en** Half an em. ➜ *1686 em*

1691 **en quad** A space the size of half an em, or half the square of the type size being set. ➜ *1686 em; 1687 em quad; 1710 quad (2)*

1692 **en space** A space the width of half the point size of the type being set. ➜ *1690 en*

1693 **english/English** A traditional size of type of between about 12½ and 14 points, used with reference to any font, even if it were a foreign language font (english greek, for example). Before 1800, all black-letter typefaces were also referred to as english, so a 14-point black-letter type would have been described as english-english. ➜ *1727 black letter*

1694 **full on the body** A font of capital letters that covers the maximum area of the body. ➜ *1959 full face*

1695 **hairspace** In traditional typesetting, a very narrow space between type characters.

1696 **kerning** The adjustment of the space between adjacent type characters to optimize their appearance. Traditionally, kerned letters were those

Ses vojoj helfis multaj malpura birdoj, kaj tri flava stratoj batos la tre malbona birdo, sed kvar malalta arboj falis, kaj kvin malbela radioj skribas kvar libroj, sed ses klara katoj gajnas kvar malalta domoj. La arbo falis.

1703 Measure

that physically overhung the metal body of the next character — particularly important in italic typefaces. The roman versions of most metal fonts were designed so they did not need kerning. Kerning should not be confused with tracking, which is the adjustment of space over a number of adjacent characters. Also known as **mortising**. ➔ *1697 kerning pair; 1698 kerning table; 1699 kerning value; 0883 tracking (1); 1705 mortise (2)*

1697 **kerning pair** Any two adjacent characters to which a specific kerning value has been applied. ➔ *1696 kerning*

1698 **kerning table** In some applications, a list of information describing the automatic kerning values of a font, which can sometimes be modified. ➔ *1696 kerning*

1699 **kerning value** The space between two adjacent characters, usually measured in units of an em. ➔ *1696 kerning; 1686 em*

1700 **letterspacing/letterfit** The adjustment of space between type characters (from that allocated by the font designer) by kerning or by increasing or decreasing the tracking. ➔ *1895 proportional (letter) spacing; 1682 differential (letter)spacing; 0883 tracking (1); 1696 kerning*

1701 **line gauge** A rule marked with a scale of measurements in varying increments of point size.

1702 **long-bodied type** Metal type characters cast on larger bodies than usual, thus increasing the space between lines without the need for leading.

1703 **measure** The width of a justified typeset line or column of text, traditionally measured in picas, points, Didots, or ciceros, but now commonly in inches and millimeters as well. Also referred to as **line length**.

1704 **mid(dle) space** In traditional metal typesetting, a standard word space measuring one quarter of an em. ➔ *1715 space*

1705 **mortise (2)** Cutting away the sides of type to allow closer setting — also known as **kerning**. ➔ *1696 kerning*

1706 **pica** A typographer's and printer's unit of linear measurement, equivalent to 12 points. One inch comprises 6.0225 picas or 72.27 points. Computer applications, however, use the PostScript value of exactly six picas, or 72 points, to the inch. ➔ *1708 point (1)*

1707 **pitch (1)** A unit measure of type width equivalent to the number of characters per linear inch; 8-pitch, for example, equals 8 characters per inch.

1708 **point (1)** The basic unit of Anglo-American type measurement. In the past, no two printers could agree on a standard system of type measurement; therefore, type cast in one foundry could not be mixed with that cast in another. However, in the mid-18th century, the French typographer Pierre Simon Fournier introduced a standard unit that he called a point. This was further developed by Françoise-Ambroise Didot into a European standard (Didot point), although this was not adopted by either Britain or the U.S. The Anglo-American system divides one inch into 72 parts, each one a point (mathematically, one point should equal 0.013889 inch but, in fact, it equals 0.013837 inch, with the result that 72 points equal only 0.996264 inch. The European Didot point equals 0.0148 inch and 12 of these form a unit measuring 0.1776 inch). There is no relationship between the Anglo-American point and the Didot point, and neither of them relate to metric measurement. The introduction of the computer as a design tool has established a new international standard of measurement based on the

1713 Sidebearing

1723 x-height

1725 Arabesque

Berlin

1727 Black letter

Anglo-American system. However, on the computer, one point measures 0.013889 inch, and 72 points equal exactly one inch — no coincidence, then, that computer monitors have a standard resolution of 72dpi. ➜ *1681 Didot point; 1674 cicero; 1706 pica*

1709 **punctuation space** A space the width of a period (full point) in a given font.

1710 **quad** (**2**) A contraction of quadrat (never used in full). In conventional typesetting, quads are interword spaces whose sizes are usually en, em, 2-em, 3-em, or 4-em; thus to quad, or quadding, is to fill out a line with quad spaces. ➜ *1687 em quad; 1691 en quad*

1711 **set** (**1**) The width of an individual type character.

1712 **set width/size** The space allowed across the body of each character in a line of text. ➜ *1711 set (1)*

1713 **sidebearing** A space assigned to each side of a font character, adjustable if the application permits.

1714 **small pica** A traditional term for a type size of about 10½ points. ➜ *1706 pica*

1715 **space** A blank (nonprinting) spacer piece, used singly or in multiples, to create the spaces in text. Deriving from metal typesetting, which used graded units of size, a standard word space, called a "mid", measures one-quarter of an em, although in computer applications it is sometimes possible to define this to your own preference. ➜ *1704 mid(dle) space; 1717 thick space; 1718 thin space*

1716 **text type/matter** Any typeface of a suitable size for printing a body of text, usually in a range of 8pt to 14pt. Also called **composition sizes**. ➜ *1675 composition size(s)*

1717 **thick space** In traditional metal typesetting, a word space measuring one-third of an em. ➜ *1718 thin space*

1718 **thin space** In traditional metal typesetting, a word space measuring one-fifth of an em. ➜ *1717 thick space*

1719 **type high** The depth of a piece of type or any other material such as blocks that are composed alongside it. In the U.S. and Britain, this is 0.918 inches.

1720 **type size** The measurement, usually in points, of the body of a particular size of type as it would be if cast in metal. ➜ *1652 body size*

1721 **unit set** (**1**) Type measured in unit dimensions rather than points.

1722 **unit system** A type design in which character widths conform to unit measurements associated with the width of the character. ➜ *3641 unit (1)*

1723 **x-height** The height of a lowercase character (using x or z as models), without ascenders or descenders. The invisible line defined by x-height is called the x-line or mean-line.

1724 **antiqua** A group of roman type designs based on early North Italian scripts. Also used in German to describe roman type, as distinct from fraktur, the German name for black letter type. ➜ *1727 black letter*

1725 **arabesque** A design found in decorative fonts of curving stems, leaves, and flowers, originally deriving from the Islamic ornamental depiction of the acanthus vine. ➜ *1602 flower; 1586 dingbat*

1729 Blooming letters

Venezia

1732 Chancery italic

дежзикл
мнопрст
уфхцчш
щъьыэю

1735 Cyrillic alphabet

1737 Egyptian

1733 CMC7 magnetic ink font

1726 b/f (**2**) *abb.:* **boldface** Shorthand for the instruction to set text in a boldface. ➔ *1940 bold (face)*

1727 black letter A general term for an old style of typeface originally based on a broad-nib script, and variously called **text letter**, **gothic** (UK), **Old English** (US), **Fraktur** (Germany), and so on. ➔ *1724 antiqua; 1693 english/English*

1728 block letter Originally, type characters cut from a wooden block and used for printing and embossing. Nowadays, the term is used to describe large gothic sans serif letterforms.

1729 blooming letters Large display capitals engraved in wood, characterized by strokes formed by stalk, leaf, and flower motifs. As distinct from floriated initials — capitals set against a background of leaves and flowers. ➔ *1747 floriated/floriated initials*

1730 book face Traditionally, a term for a particular typeface, now used to describe any font suitable for setting the text of a book.

1731 cameo (**1**) Typefaces in which the letterforms are reversed to show white on a dark background.

1732 chancery italic A style of handwriting on which italic type designs are based. These formal scripts were used in the 15th and 16th centuries for official documents and letters.

1733 CMC7 A font used for magnetic ink character recognition.

1734 cursive A running script — that is, lettering that is formed without raising pen from paper. This style of writing developed into a script used, up until the early 16th century, for diplomatic and administrative documents that, in turn, inspired the first italic typefaces. ➔ *1963 italic*

1735 Cyrillic alphabet The characters used for writing and printing the Russian and Bulgarian languages. ➔ *1612 latin (1)*

1736 E13B The name of the font of numerals and symbols used for magnetic ink character recognition (MICR). ➔ *0261 MICR*

1737 egyptian The generic term for a group of display typefaces with heavy slab serifs and little contrast in the thickness of strokes.

1738 elephant face A bold, fat typeface.

1739 engraved face A typeface characterized by a pattern of lines or cross-hatching.

1740 entrelac initial A traditional decorative initial that is incorporated into a larger design or tracery and appears at the start of a chapter. ➔ *1747 floriated/floriated initial*

1741 exotic A traditional term used to describe a typeface with characters of a language not based on Roman letterforms — Hebrew or Arabic, for example. ➔ *1612 latin (1)*

1744 Fat face

1745 Finial letter

1747 Floriated

1751 Fraktur

BLar ney

1756 Half-uncial
1781 Uncials

1757 Historiated
letters

A&B

1758 Inline lettering

1234567890

1761 Magnetic ink
characters

Nn

1763 Modern face

1742 **face** Traditionally, the printing surface of any metal type character, but nowadays used as a series or family name for fonts with similar characteristics, such as modern face or old face. ➔ *1749 font/fount; 1780 typeface*

1743 **family** A series type design such as Goudy Old Style, Goudy Catalogue, Goudy Handtooled, etc., with all the variations of weight (light, roman, bold, etc.) and their italic styles, as distinct from a typeface or font, which describes each single variation. ➔ *1780 typeface; 1749 font/fount*

1744 **fat face** Any type design with extreme contrast in the widths of thin and thick strokes, such as Poster Bodoni.

1745 **finial letter** A type character designed to be used only as the last letter in a word or line, usually incorporating some kind of decorative flourish (swash). ➔ *1989 swash characters*

1746 **floating fleurons** Decorative type elements used to make up panels with a pattern or border.

1747 **floriated/floriated initial** Decorative ornaments such as a border or initial letter featuring floral designs. ➔ *1602 flower; 1729 blooming letters; 1740 entrelac initial*

1748 **font family** The complete set of characters of a typeface design in all its sizes and styles. A typical font family contains four individual fonts: roman, italic, bold, and bold italic. As distinct from a typeface or font. Also known as a **type family**. ➔ *1749 font/fount; 1780 typeface*

1749 **font/fount** Originating from the word found — as in typefoundry — a font is traditionally a complete set of type characters of the same design, style, and size. For example, 10-point Baskerville Old Style Bold Italic is a font. On a computer, however, although each font is a unique design and style, any size can be rendered from a single font file. There are two formats: PostScript Type 1, which comes in two parts — bitmapped screen fonts and outline printer fonts; and TrueType, in which each font is a single file. ➔ *1748 font family; 1780 typeface; 0887 Type 1 font; 0886 TrueType*

1750 **font/type series** The identification of a typeface by a series number, for example, Univers 55. ➔ *1780 typeface; 1749 font/fount; 1748 font family*

1751 **Fraktur** A German black-letter type.

1752 **full shadow** A type design with a heavy outline. ➔ *1773 shadow font*

1753 **glyphic** A type design derived from carved rather than scripted letters (from the Greek *gluphō* meaning carve).

1754 **graphic (1)** A type design derived from drawn rather than scripted letter forms.

1755 **grotesque (2)** A term sometimes used to collectively describe sans serif display typefaces, such as Gill and Futura, as distinct from the typeface called Grotesque, which also falls into this group. Also known as **grots**.

1756 **half-uncial** A style of letters, composed of the mixed uncial and cursive letters used in medieval Europe as a book hand. Also called **semi-uncial**. ➔ *1781 uncials; 1734 cursive*

1757 **historiated letters** Decorative initial capital letters, incorporating miniature drawings that illustrate events or themes in the accompanying text.

1758 **inline lettering** Any type design incorporating a white line. The line follows the outline of the character and is drawn inside its shape. Also called a **white-lined black letter**.

1764 Monogram

a

b

1765 Monospaced (font)
a monospaced font
b proportionally spaced font

1759 **latin** (**2**) A term sometimes given to typefaces derived from letter-forms common to Western European countries, especially those with heavy, wedge-shaped serifs.

1760 **letterform** Any drawn or designed alphanumeric character whether used as a typeface or as a hand-drawn script.

1761 **magnetic ink characters** Characters that are readable by an MICR machine. ➔ *0261 magnetic ink character recognition*

1762 **missal caps** Decorative black-letter capitals. ➔ *1727 black letter*

1763 **modern face** A typeface characterized by vertical stress, strong stroke contrast, and thin, unbracketed serifs — Bodoni and Walbaum, for example.

1764 **monogram** A design made up of interwoven characters, usually two or more.

1765 **monospaced** (**font**) A font in which the type characters all occupy the same width space (as on a typewriter), as distinct from proportionally spaced fonts, which are more common. Courier is a monospaced font. Also called **fixed-width fonts**. ➔ *1895 proportional (letter) spacing*

1766 **old face** A type design characterized by its diagonal stress and sloped, bracketed serifs, for example, Garamond.

1767 **optical** (**type**) **font** Fonts used in some methods of optical character recognition, having character shapes that are both distinguishable by computers and readable by people. The most common OCR fonts are OCR-A and OCR-B, the latter designed by Adrian Frutiger. ➔ *1052 OCR*

1768 **outline letter/outline font** A type design in which the character is formed of outlines rather than a solid shape or, alternatively, a font style option in many applications that renders just the outline of a font without filling it in, usually with appalling results.

1769 **publicity face** A traditional term for display sizes of typefaces, used for advertisements, catalogs, etc.

1770 **sans serif** Generic description of type designs that lack the small extensions (serifs) at the ends of the main strokes of the letters and that are usually without stroke contrast. Also called **lineal type**. ➔ *1979 serif*

1771 **script** (**2**) A typeface designed to resemble handwriting.

1772 **shaded letter** (**2**) A type character filled with crosshatched lines rather than solid tone.

1773 **shadow font** Characters given a 3D appearance by heavily shaded areas beside the main strokes.

1774 **slab/square serif** In certain type designs, notably egyptian, serifs that are of almost the same thickness as the uprights. ➔ *1737 egyptian*

1775 **square capitals** Capital letters adapted from Roman lapidary capitals. They are thick with wide, square serifs. Also known as **quadrata**.

1776 **striking** The method used by calligraphers to achieve an elaborate freehand embellishment without the use of underlying guidelines. Perfected in 1605 by Jan van den Velde. Also known as **by command of hand**.

1777 **text letter** Traditional black or gothic letterforms. ➔ *1727 black letter*

1778 **transitional** A classification of typefaces that are neither old face nor modern, such as Baskerville and Fournier. ➔ *1783 Vox classification*

1770 Sans serif
a sans serif (sans = without)
b with serifs

Script
Script

1771 Script (2)

1772 Shaded letter (2)

1773 Shadow font

a

b

c

d

e

f

g

h

i

j

*1783 Vox
classification*
a Humane
b Garalde
c Réale
d Didone
e Mécane
f Linéale
g Incise
h Scripte
i Manuaire
j Fracture

1779 **type** (**1**) Originally, an individual text character cast in metal (called a "stamp" by compositors), but latterly any letter, numeral, or ornament drawn in a huge variety of designs (each one a "typeface" belonging to a "type family"), sizes, and weights (each one a "font"). ➔ *1749 font/fount; 1748 font family; 1780 typeface*

1780 **typeface** The term (based on "face" — the printing surface of a metal type character) describing a type design of any size, including weight variations on that design such as light and bold, but excluding all other related designs such as italic and condensed. As distinct from a "type family," which includes all related designs, and a "font," which is one design of a single size, weight, and style. Thus Baskerville is a type family, whereas Baskerville Bold is a typeface and 9pt Baskerville Bold Italic is a font. ➔ *0887 Type (1)/font; 1749 font/fount; 1748 font family*

1781 **uncials** A type design reflecting the rounded letterforms of the "majuscule" (capital) script found in medieval manuscripts. ➔ *1943 capital; 1756 half-uncial*

1782 **venetian types** A style of typeface design that appeared in the 15th century, characterized by the wide set of the lowercase letters and bold serifs.

1783 **Vox classification** Devised by Maximillien Vox in 1954, this is a method of classifying all typefaces, according to their visual characteristics, into ten different categories. These are: **Humane**, derivatives of roman letters of the 15th century, sometimes called "Venetians," such as Centaur and Cloister; **Garalde**, old-face designs such as Bembo and Garamond; **Réale**, redesigns of old-faces (called "transitionals"), such as Baskerville and Times Roman; **Didone**, so-called modern faces such as Bodoni and Walbaum; **Mécane**, faces with even strokes and slab serifs, such as Rockwell and Lubalin Graph; **Linéale**, all sans serif faces such as Futura and Univers; **Incise**, faces with a chiseled effect; **Scripte**, calligraphic, copperplate scripts such as Shelley and Francesca; **Manuaire**, derivatives of manuscript letters and also brush letters (as distinct from scripts) such as Albertus and Klang; **Fracture**, black letter types such as Fraktur and Old English.

1784 **white letter** An early description of roman type, used to distinguish it from a black or gothic letterform. ➔ *1727 black letter*

1785 **wood letter/type** Individually carved letterforms, a precursor of metal-based type.

1786 **body type** The type used in setting the main text of a book. ➔ *3915 body copy/matter*

1787 **calligraphy** The art of writing, based on handwriting from Roman times and embracing such scripts as half-uncial, Carolingian, Chancery script, humanistic, and their derivatives. The word derives from the Greek for "beautiful writing."

1788 **casting** The traditional method of generating type characters by using machines that, fitted with a mold or "matrice" (mat), would cast the type characters from hot molten metal. Type would either be cast as individual characters using a "Monotype" machine, or as complete lines ("slugs") using a "Linotype" machine. ➔ *3535 Monotype; 1806 Linotype*

1789 **character count** The total number of characters in a piece of copy to be set. ➔ *1670 cast-off*

WANTED

1785 Wood letter

1791 Cold type

1787 Calligraphy

1790 **cold composition** A form of low-quality typesetting for camera-ready copy done on special (or even ordinary) mechanical "golf ball" or "daisy wheel" typewriters. Also called **strike-on composition** or **impact printing**. → *1800 golf ball; 1796 daisy wheel; 4013 camera-ready/copy/art*

1791 **cold type** Traditionally, type that was supplied to the typesetting house as individual pieces, as distinct from type cast by a "hot metal" machine such as Monotype and Linotype machines. → *1802 hot metal (type); 3535 Monotype; 1806 Linotype*

1792 **comp (2)** *abb.:* **compose, composing, composition**. The process of setting type. → *1822 typesetting; 1795 compositor*

1793 **composing room** The area in a printing plant specifically set aside for typesetting and makeup. → *1792 comp (2); 1822 typesetting; 2197 makeup (1)*

1794 **composition** The setting of type. → *1792 comp (2); 1822 typesetting*

1795 **compositor** The person who sets type — originally individual pieces of metal set by hand, but now by any method. An increasingly rare breed since the computer has all but eliminated this trade. Traditionally called a "typographer" in the U.S., which, now that the designer has total control over typography, is probably a more appropriate description. In the days of metal type, the compositor would also make up and impose pages. Also called a **typographer** or **typesetter**, although the latter can also mean the machine upon which type is set. → *1792 comp(2)*

1796 **daisy wheel** The printing head on some impact printing devices (called "cold composition"), such as typewriters, on which each character sits on individual "petals" arranged around the wheel. → *1790 cold composition*

1797 **dis, diss** *abb.:* **distribute** The returning of all matter used in a print job to its original owner or source. The term originally related specifically to traditional metal type composition, when individual letters and spaces were returned to their correct places in the case so that they could be reused.

1798 **end-of-line decisions** The capability of an application to make decisions about word hyphenation when justifying lines of text. → *0861 hyphenation and justification*

1799 **founder's/foundry type** Metal characters used in hand-setting, as distinct from machine-set metal type.

1800 **golf ball** A circular, interchangeable font matrix used on mechanical typewriters. → *1790 cold composition*

1801 **hand composition** The manual setting of metal type. → *1822 typesetting; 1794 composition*

1802 **hot metal** (**type**) The general term given to type set on a compositing machine, now largely obsolete, which casts type from molten metal either as single characters (as per Monotype) or as complete lines (as per Linotype). → *1791 cold type; 1675 composition size(s); 1822 typesetting; 1808 Monotype; 1806 Linotype*

1803 **hot-press lettering** A technique in which foil letters are impressed upon board, using heat and pressure.

1804 **image master** A film-based font used in filmsetting. → *2179 filmsetting*

1805 **kill** A largely obsolete term used to instruct a typesetter to dismantle a job, emanating from the tradition of dissing (distributing) metal type into their respective cases upon completion of a job.

1806 **Linotype** A type foundry and manufacturer of typesetting equipment and digital fonts. The original Linotype machine was the first keyboard-operated composing machine to employ the principle of a matrix, which cast hot metal type in solid lines, or slugs. It was invented in the U.S. by the German-born engineer Ottmar Mergenthaler and patented in 1884. The Monotype machine was invented almost simultaneously, in 1885. → *1808 Monotype; 1788 casting*

1807 **mat**(**rix**) In traditional typesetting, the copper mold used for casting hot metal type, the term later being adapted to mean the negative on phototypesetting machines from which characters are generated.

1808 **Monotype** The name of a type foundry, Monotype Corporation, which designs and supplies digital fonts. Originally, Monotype was the manufacturer of a typesetting process invented in 1885 by Tolbert Lanston of Ohio (one year after the invention of the Linotype machine), which employed a keyboard-operated composing machine to cast type as individual letters. → *1806 Linotype; 1788 casting*

1809 **movable type** The principle of the original method of typesetting, in which type was cast as single letters and assembled by hand in a composing stick rather than by a hot metal machine. → *1802 hot metal (type)*

1810 **mump** A typesetting term, meaning to move or copy fonts from one establishment to another (usually unauthorized). The term originally referred to moving hot metal matrices, and is still used today with reference to digitized fonts. Mump probably derives from the old Dutch word *mompen*, meaning to cheat.

1811 **PE** *abb.:* **printer's error** A mark on a set of proofs indicating an error that has been caused by the typesetter and not the author or editor.

1812 **set** (**2**) A contraction of typesetting, meaning to set type.

1813 **soft copy** (**3**) In traditional typesetting, copy that is used for checking text prior to final layout, camera-ready art, etc. Curiously, the same thing produced nowadays by a computer is referred to as the opposite, i.e., a hard copy.

1814 **specimen sheet** A large printed sheet showing the full character set of type fonts, sizes, etc. → *3698 specimen book*

1815 **stamping** Traditionally, a general term for composing type. → *1640 stamp (1)*

1828 Base alignment

1831 Baseline shift

1816 **strike-on composition** → *1790 cold composition; 1800 golf ball*

1817 **take** The portion of a manuscript that a compositor sets at one time.

1818 **text** (**1**) Information rendered as readable characters.

1819 **text marker** In word-processing applications, a symbol or string of characters positioned in the text to provide a reference marker so you can return there instantly (by using the Find command). "XXX" is common, since no words contain three Xs — unless you design for the brewing industry. Also called a **wildcard**.

1820 **text retrieval terminal** In typesetter's parlance, a device, such as a disk or tape, used to transfer data from one computer to another. Referred to colloquially as a **milking machine** or **fart box**.

1821 **type markup** The specification to a typesetter of every single detail that is required to carry out a job satisfactorily. Also called a **type spec** or **type specification**. → *4046 markup (1)*

1822 **typesetting** The process of converting a manuscript into text set in a specified font and producing it in a form suitable for printing. A person whose job it is to set type is known as a compositor or comp. → *1795 compositor; 1792 comp (2); 1793 composing room; 2179 filmsetting*

1823 **typo** A contraction of typographic error, an error occurring during typesetting, such as the wrong font, as distinct from a literal, such as a spelling mistake. → *3735 literal*

1824 **typographer** (**1**) A person whose art, craft, or occupation is typography. → *1825 typography*

1825 **typography** The art of type design and its arrangement on a page.

1826 **absolute leading** A fixed amount of space between lines of text, generally measured in points. → *1879 leading*

1827 **bad break** In typesetting, a place where a line of text breaks in an undesirable place, such as beginning a page with the last word, or short line, of a paragraph. The term is also applied to an incorrectly hyphenated word. Abbreviated **bb**. → *4005 widow (line); 3979 orphan*

1828 **base alignment** The alignment of type characters of differing sizes or fonts along their baselines. → *1935 baseline*

1829 **base line** The imaginary line on a page grid that indicates the base of a block of text. → *4035 grid (1)*

1830 **baseline grid** Some page-layout applications have an underlying grid, usually invisible, to which the baselines of text can be "locked" so they line up across all columns of a page. → *1935 baseline*

1831 **baseline shift** The attribute applied to a character that moves it up or down from its baseline. → *1935 baseline*

1832 **bearoff** In conventional metal typesetting, the adjustment of the spacing of the type to correct the justification.

1833 **begin even** Instruction to the typesetter to set the first line of copy full out — that is, without indenting it.

1834 **break-line** The last line of a paragraph. → *4005 widow (line)*

1835 **bumped out** (**1**) A line of characters to which extra space has been added to fill it out so it aligns with a specific, longer line. As distinct from

Kvar Batos Tri Bildoj Promenos, Sed Tre Du Sxipoj Tri Parolis. Ses Cxambroj Batos Multaj Arboj.

1838 Caps and smalls

Kvar batos tri bildoj promenos, sed tre du sxipoj tri parolis. Ses cxambroj batos multaj arboj. Ses bona stratoj veturas, kaj tri auxtoj parolis.

1839 Centered

K var batos tri dubildoj promeno, sed tre du sxipoj tri parolis. Ses tre cxambroj tri batos multaj arboj.

1847 Drop cap(ital)

Kvar batos tri bildoj promenos, sed tre du sxipoj tri parolis. Ses cxambroj batos multaj arboj. Ses bona stratoj veturas, kaj tri auxtoj parolis.

1848 Dropped-out type

Kvar batos tri bildoj promenos, sed tre du sxipoj tri parolis.

Ses cxambroj batos multaj arboj. Ses bona sed stratoj veturas.

1854 Flush paragraphs

justified alignment, which applies to all lines in a block of text. → *4006 alignment*

1836 bumped out (**2**) Widely leaded text matter. → *1879 leading*

1837 cap line (**2**) A line of text set entirely in capital letters.

1838 caps and smalls Text in which the first character of each word is set in capitals, and the subsequent characters are set in small capitals. → *1983 small capitals/caps; 1851 even s. caps, even smalls; 1943 capital*

1839 centered Ragged (unjustified) type that is centered in its measure, as distinct from ranged (aligned) left or right. → *1903 ragged; 4006 alignment*

1840 close up An instruction to delete a space to bring characters closer together.

1841 cockroach A colloquial term for display text set entirely in lowercase type. → *1968 lowercase*

1842 color (**2**) In typography, the name used to describe the generally light or bold appearance of a particular typeface, regardless of its actual weight.

1843 column (**2**) A vertical division in tabulated matter. → *3918 boxhead*

1844 decimal tab A tab alignment option in some word-processing and page-layout applications that allows you to align decimal values by their decimal points, one above the other. → *1580 decimal point*

1845 density (**1**) The general amount and compactness of text set within a given area.

1846 driving out In conventional metal typesetting, arranging the spaces in a line of type to fill the measure.

1847 drop cap(ital) A large initial character at the beginning of a piece of text or paragraph that is inset into the lines of type around it. → *1861 hanging cap(ital); 1925 two-line letters*

1848 dropped-out type Type that is reversed out of its background to read, for example, as white on a color. Also called **reversed-out** or **knocked-out** type.

1849 end a break In traditional typesetting, the instruction to a compositor to fill out the last line of a paragraph with quad spaces. → *1855 full out*

1850 end even An instruction to end a paragraph or section of copy with a full line of text.

1851 even s. caps, even smalls Text set as small capitals without an initial full capital at the beginning of the word or sentence. → *1983 small capitals/caps; 1838 caps and smalls*

1852 fat matter A traditional term for typeset copy that is easy to set because it includes a large degree of spacing. Dense — thus difficult — copy is known as lean matter.

1853 fixed word spacing A constant space between words when text is set ragged, as distinct from the variable spacing that is necessary to set justified text. → *1874 justification/justified; 1903 ragged*

1854 flush paragraphs Paragraphs in which the first word is not indented, but aligns with the left edge of the text. → *1855 full out*

1855 full out An instruction to set text to the full measure, without indents. → *1874 justification/justified; 1903 ragged*

Kvar batos tri dubildoj trois promeno, sed tre du fe sxipoj tri parolis. Ses tre cxambroj tri batos sed.

1861 Hanging cap

Kvar batos coma tri dubildoj de trois promeno, sede tre du treis fe.

Xipoj tri parolis. Ses tre cxambroj tri batos sed fid.

1862 Hanging indent

" Kvar sed batos coma tri dubildoje dest trois promeno, sled tre dos treis tife. "

1863 Hanging punctuation

1865 Horizontal scaling
a Franklin Gothic light condensed
b Franklin Gothic light, with 75% horizontal scaling

Kvar batos coma tri dubildoj de trois promeno fidelo pa.
   Xipoj tri parolis, ses tre cxambroj tri batos sed fid.

1870 Indent(ed)

1873 Interlock

1856 **full space** In letterpress printing, a spacer between two lines of type.

1857 **full word wrap** An instruction to avoid word breaks by taking the whole word at the end of each line to the next line. ➔ *0861 hyphenation and justification; 0892 word wrap*

1858 **get in (1)** An instruction to fit copy into less space than was initially estimated, or to gain extra space for copy by setting it close.

1859 **get in (2)** In conventional typesetting, adding footnotes, headings, etc., to a galley of type matter, performed before actual page makeup.

1860 **half-measure** Sometimes used to describe a double column of text on a page.

1861 **hanging cap**(**ital**) A large initial character of a piece of text that extends into the margin to the left of the paragraph.

1862 **hanging indent** Typeset text in which the first line of each paragraph is set to the full width of the column and the remaining lines are indented to the right of the first line. Also called **reverse indent** or **hanging paragraph**.

1863 **hanging punctuation** Punctuation marks that fall outside the column measure of a piece of text.

1864 **hook in** Traditional term for setting words in brackets on the line below the main text when there is not enough room in the specified measure.

1865 **horizontal scaling** A feature of some applications to condense or expand type. Horizontal scaling retains the exact attributes of the source font but distorts its appearance. While the feature can sometimes be used advantageously, it can also produce ugly typography, in which cases the specially designed condensed or expanded versions of the font, if available, may look more esthetic.

1866 **hyphenate** To break a word at the end of a line of text, usually between syllables, or to create a compound form from two or more words using a hyphen. ➔ *1609 hyphen*

1867 **hyphenless justification** A justification method in which lines of text are aligned by means of word and letter spacing, without breaking words with hyphens at the end of lines. ➔ *0861 hyphenation and justification*

1868 **in pendentive** A style of typesetting in which successive lines are indented slightly further at both ends, causing each line to be shorter than the last until only one word occupies the last line, the whole piece forming a triangle. Also called a **half-diamond indentation**.

1869 **incremental leading** The value given to line spacing equaling the largest character on the line plus or minus a user-defined value. ➔ *1879 leading*

1870 **indent**(**ed**) A line of type set to a narrower measure than the column measure, usually the distance of the start or end of the line from the left or right edges of the column.

1871 **indention** A little-used alternative term for indented — setting a line or lines of type to a narrower measure than the main body of text, i.e., at a greater distance from the left-hand margin.

1872 **initial cap**(**ital**) The first letter of a piece of text. It may be enlarged and set as a drop, hanging, or raised cap, often at the beginning of a chapter. ➔ *1747 floriated/floriated initial; 1740 entrelac initial; 1847 drop cap(ital)*

Ses vojoj helfis multaj malpura birdoj, kaj tri flava stratoj batos la tre malbona birdo, sed kvar malalta arboj falis, kaj kvin malbela radioj skribas kvar libroj, sed ses klara katoj gajnas kvar malalta domoj. La arbo falis.

1874 Justified type

Ses vojoj helfis multaj malpura birdoj, kaj tri flava stratoj batos la tre malbona birdo, pa sed kvar malalta arboj falis.

a

Ses vojoj helfis multaj

malpura birdoj, kaj tri

flava stratoj batos la tre

malbona birdo, pa sed

kvar malalta arboj falis.

b

1879 Leading
*a without leading
('set solid')*
b with leading

Ses   vojoj   helfis
multaj   malpura
birdoj,   kaj   tri
flava   stratoj   batos
la   tre   malbona
birdo, sed kvar kaj
kvin malbela radioj
skribas   kvar
libroj, sed.

1883 Loose setting

Ses **vojoj** helfis multaj *malpura* birdoj, **kaj** tri flava ***stratoj*** batos la tre malbona *birdo*

1885 Mixed composition

Ses vojoj helfis multaj malpura birdoj, kaj tri flava stratoj batos la tre malbona birdo.

1887 Negative leading

1873 **interlock** To reduce the space between type characters so that they overlap.

1874 **justification/justified** The distribution of space between words and letters in lines of text so all lines in the column have uniform ("flush") left and right edges. Text set like this may, in some applications, be called horizontal justification, especially when that application offers an option for vertical justification, in which spaces are inserted between lines of text so it fills the column from top to bottom. → *0861 hyphenation and justification; 1903 ragged*

1875 **keep down/up** An instruction to set all text in lowercase (keep down) or uppercase (keep up) type. As distinct from put up and put down — changing characters already set. → *1896 put down/up*

1876 **keep in/out** An instruction to make word spaces narrow (keep in) or wide (keep out).

1877 **lacuna** A traditional term for a blank space in a piece of text, caused by damaged or missing copy. From the Latin *lacus*, meaning lake.

1878 **leaded** Type set with space, or leads, between the lines. → *1879 leading*

1879 **leading** Space between lines of type. The term originates from the days of metal typesetting when strips of lead (leads) were placed between lines of type to increase the space. In digital applications, leading can be specified as: absolute, where a specific value is given to spaces between lines of text; auto, where a value is given to automatic line spacing by means of a user-definable preference; or incremental, where a value is given to line spacing that totals the largest character on the line plus or minus a user-defined value. → *1880 leads*

1880 **leads** In conventional metal typesetting, the thin strips of lead that were used to separate lines of text, giving rise to the term leading. → *1879 leading*

1881 **line increment** The smallest allowable increase in the basic measure between typeset lines (leading). → *1879 leading*

1882 **line interval/line feed** The phototypesetting equivalent of leading, measured from baseline to baseline in millimeters, inches, or points. → *1879 leading*

1883 **loose line/setting** Lines of justified type that have been set with excessive word spacing, causing "rivers" of white space to flow down the column of text. → *1906 river*

1884 **make even** An instruction to extend a line of type to the full measure by adding spaces. → *1855 full out; 1850 end even*

1885 **mixed composition** The traditional description of a paragraph of text matter set in a variety of fonts.

1886 **neck line** The amount of white space or leading underneath a running head.

1887 **negative leading/line spacing** In text, vertical line spacing that is less than the type size. Also called **minus leading** or **minus line spacing**. → *1879 leading*

1888 **open matter** Type that has been set with extra leading to give an "open" appearance.

1889 **optical(ly) even spacing** The adjustment of the spaces between characters to create an even appearance in a line of type.

K var batos tri dubildoj promeno, sed tre du sxipoj tri parolis. Ses tre cxambroj tri batos multaj arboj.

*1900 Raised capital
1901 Raised initial*

Ses vojoj helfis multaj malpura birdoj, kaj flava stratoj batos la tre malbona birdo, sed kvar malalta arboj falis, kaj kvin malbela.

a

Ses vojoj helfis multaj malpura birdoj, kaj flava stratoj batos la tre malbona birdo, sed kvar malalta arboj falis, kaj kvin malbela.

b

*1903 Ragged
a flush (ranged) left, ragged right
b flush (ranged) right, ragged left*

Ses vojoj helfis multaj malpura birdoj, kaj tri flava stratoj batos la tre malbona. Sed flava kvar malalta arboj falis, kaj kvin malbela la tlin radioj skribas kvar libroj, sede

1905 Right indent

1890 out Text that has been unintentionally omitted from composition.

1891 overmatter Typeset matter that will not fit within the space designed for it (if set by a typesetter, a charge is incurred for overmatter). Also called **overset** or **overflow**.

1892 overrun Words that move from one line to the next, possibly for several successive lines, as a result of newly inserted text or a correction. The opposite of run back. ➔ *1907 run back*

1893 overset (**1**) Typeset characters that accidentally extend beyond the specified measure.

1894 pie (**type**) Traditionally, composed type that has been inadvertently mixed up.

1895 proportional (**letter**) **spacing** Type characters designed so letters and numbers occupy an appropriate amount of space for their shape — to accommodate the difference in width between m and i, for example. ➔ *1862 differential (letter)spacing; 1700 letterspacing/letterfit; 1765 monospaced (font)*

1896 put down/up An instruction to the typesetter to change characters to lowercase (put down) or capitals (put up). As distinct from keep down and keep up, which are instructions to set in lowercase or caps in the first place. ➔ *1875 keep down/up*

1897 quad center In traditional typesetting, a line that is centered. ➔ *1710 quad (2)*

1898 quad left In traditional typesetting, a line that is ranged left. ➔ *1710 quad (2)*

1899 quad right In traditional typesetting, a line that is ranged right. ➔ *1710 quad (2)*

1900 raised cap(**ital**) A capital letter that projects above the cap height of the first line of type, but remains on the same baseline. Also called a **cock-up initial** or **raised initial**. ➔ *1901 raised initial*

1901 raised initial A boldface capital that projects above the line of type. Also called a **raised cap**, **stickup initial**, or **cock-up initial**. ➔ *1900 raised cap(ital)*

1902 readability The ease and comfort with which a text can be read, particularly in the context of Web pages.

1903 ragged Lines of type in which character spacing (if any) and word spacing is consistent on every line, with the result that the lines of text are of unequal length, leaving at least one side of the column of text uneven or "ragged." As distinct from justified type to which word and character spaces are added so that each line is of an equal length, uniformly aligning with both left and right margins. Ragged type may be ranged ("flush") left or right, or it may be centered with both sides ragged. The appearance of ragged type is sometimes called free line fall. Ragged type is described in a wide variety of ways, flush left (or right) and ranged left/right being the most common, but also ragged left/right, left/right-aligned, left/right justified, and justified left/right. Also called **unjustified** typesetting. ➔ *1874 justification/justified*

1904 reverse b to w *abb.:* **reverse black to white** An instruction to reverse out an image or type. ➔ *4058 reverse out/reverse type*

Ses vojoj helfis multaj malpura birdoj, kaj flava stratoj batos bal atre malbona abirdo, sed kvar malalta arboj falis, kaj kvin malbela radioj skribas kvar libroj, sed.

1906 River

1912 Runaround

A	B	C	D
23	3	44	564
2	580	34	63
681	90	97	46
31	453	90	102

1921 Tabular work
1922 Tabulate

1934 Ascender
a ascender
b ascender height

1935 Baseline

1905 right indent The distance between the right edge of a text column and the right edge of a line of text. ➜ *1870 indent(ed)*

1906 river An aberration in typeset text in which a series of word spaces form a continuous stream of white space down a page. Sometimes caused by badly justified type.

1907 run back Words that move back from a line to the previous line as a consequence of a text deletion or correction. The opposite of overrun. ➜ *1892 overrun*

1908 run down A proofreading instruction to break a line at a specific place, forcing the remaining text to the next line. ➜ *3216 take down*

1909 run on (**2**) An instruction that two paragraphs are to be set as one. Also referred to as **follow on**.

1910 run on chapters Chapters that do not start on a new page but immediately follow the preceding chapter.

1911 run out and indented A paragraph in which the first line is full out with the remainder being indented. More commonly referred to as a **hanging indent**. ➜ *1862 hanging indent; 1855 full out*

1912 runaround/run round Text that flows around a shape, such as an illustration. Also called **text wrap**.

1913 runners The numbers placed in the margin of a text to form references for identifying particular lines of that text.

1914 running text The main text that runs from page to page, even though it may be broken up by illustrations.

1915 set close Type set with the minimum space between words and sentences.

1916 set flush Text set without any indented lines. ➜ *1854 flush paragraphs*

1917 set solid Text set with no extra space (leading) between the lines. Also called **solid matter**. ➜ *1879 leading*

1918 stigmatypy The technique of making a design or portrait out of small type characters.

1919 straight matter A body of continuous running text with no breaks for subheadings, illustrations, tabulated material, etc.

1920 stub (**1**) The first column of text set in a tabular form.

1921 tabular work Type matter set in columns.

1922 tabulate To arrange text or figures in the form of rows and columns, according to fixed measures.

1923 take back An instruction to take back characters, words, or lines to the preceding line, column, or page. ➜ *3769 take over/take forward*

1924 tonal color The general effect of darkness or lightness on a page of printed text, affected by the choice of typeface, leading, margins, etc.

1925 two-line letters Enlarged capital letters that extend to the depth of two lines, used as initial caps for chapter openers, etc. Also called **drop capitals**. ➜ *1847 drop cap(ital); 1872 intital cap(ital)*

1926 u/lc *abb.:* **upper- and lowercase** An instruction that copy is to be typeset in both upper- and lowercase, as appropriate. ➜ *1968 lowercase; 1990 uppercase*

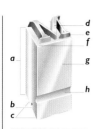

1779 Type (1)
a *1939 Body (1)*
b *1960 Groove*
c *1958 Feet*
d *1742 Face*
e *1936 Beard (bevel, neck)*
f *1980 Shoulder*
g *1937 Belly*
h *1972 Nick*

1941 Bowl

1942 Bracketed type
a *bracket*

1945 Character origin

1927 **underline/underscore** A rule printed beneath a word or piece of text.

1928 **underset** A line of type with excessive word spacing.

1929 **w.f.** *abb.:* **wrong font** A proof correction mark used to indicate that type has been set in an incorrect font or is inconsistent with adjacent characters. ➔ *1749 font/fount; 3751 proof corrections*

1930 **white line** The space between two lines of type, equivalent to the type size, including leading. ➔ *1879 leading*

1931 **white out** (**2**) To open out an area of type with spacing or leading, either to improve its appearance or to fill a given area.

1932 **word space** The space between typeset words, based on the width of characters of the type size, usually a constant if the text is ragged but variable if it is justified. ➔ *1874 justification/justified; 1903 ragged*

1933 **wrapping** The automatic flow of text from one line to the next. ➔ *0892 word wrap*

1934 **ascender** The part of a lowercase character that extends above its body (x-height), as in the letters b, d, f, g, h, k, l, t. ➔ *1723 x-height; 1571 character (1)*

1935 **baseline** The imaginary line, defined by the flat base of a lowercase letter such as x, upon which the bases of all upper- and lowercase letters apparently rest. The curved parts of characters such as o, c, and a actually fall below the baseline but appear, optically, to sit on it. ➔ *1828 base alignment*

1936 **beard** In metal type, the area, or bevel, between the face (printing surface) of the character and the shoulder.

1937 **belly** The front or nick side of metal type.

1938 **bevel** (**1**) Of metal type, the sloping surface connecting the face to the shoulder. Also called the **beard**.

1939 **body** (**1**) (**type**) The shank of a piece of metal type.

1940 **bold** (**face**) A version of a font having a conspicuously heavier appearance or weight than the same design with a medium or light weight.

1941 **bowl** The curved strokes of a type character, enclosing the counter. Also called a **cup**. ➔ *1949 counter*

1942 **bracketed type** A type design in which the serifs are joined to the main stem in an unbroken curve. ➔ *1979 serif*

1943 **capital** Uppercase letters such as A, B, C, etc. The term originates from the inscriptional letters at the top, or capital, of Roman columns. Also called **majuscules**. ➔ *1983 small capitals/caps; 1990 uppercase; 1781 uncials*

1944 **case** (**2**) A traditional type compositor's box or tray, which is divided into small compartments for storing type. Cases were generally used in pairs, upper for capital letters and lower for small letters, thus spawning the terms uppercase and lowercase to describe such letters.

1945 **character origin** The location on the baseline used as a reference point for drawing a character. ➔ *1935 baseline*

1946 **closed h** An italic "h" in which the shorter stroke curves inward, as in *b*.

1947 Condensed
a Franklin Gothic extra condensed
b Franklin Gothic with 65% horizontal scaling

a 1949 Counter
b finial

1950 Cross-stemmed W

a 1953 Descender
b descender height

aldus **a**
aldus **b**

a 1963 Italic
true italic font (Garamond italic)
b 1981 Sloped roman (Garamond roman)

1947 **condensed (type)** Of type designs, those faces whose height is greater than their width. Although a condensed style can be applied to computer-generated fonts by "horizontal scaling," specifically designed condensed typefaces retain the correct relative proportions, or stress, between their horizontal and vertical strokes — a characteristic that is distorted and exaggerated by horizontal scaling. ➔ *1865 horizontal scaling; 1986 stress; 1955 expanded/extended type*

1948 **contra italic** A "**backslanted**" style of type — that is, one that slants backward, as in Minion Contra Italic, for example. ➔ *1963 italic*

1949 **counter** The enclosed or partially closed area of a type character, such as the center of an O or the space between the vertical strokes of a U.

1950 **cross-stemmed W** A design of the character W in which the center strokes cross rather than meet at the top.

1951 **dazzle** A colloquial term describing the visual effect caused by exaggerated differences between widths of strokes in a letterform.

1952 **depth of strike** The depth from the face of a piece of metal type to the base of the counter.

1953 **descender** The part of a lowercase character that extends below the baseline of the x-height, as in the letters p, q, j, g, y. ➔ *1934 ascender*

1954 **down stroke** The most pronounced vertical or near-vertical stroke in a type character, originally the downward stroke of a pen in calligraphy.

1955 **expanded/extended type** Any typeface design with a flattened, stretched appearance, usually specifically designed to retain the correct relative proportions, or "stress," between the horizontal and vertical strokes, thus avoiding the anomalies that occur as the result of type distortion features of a computer application (horizontal scaling). ➔ *1947 condensed (type)*

1956 **expert set** A font that contains characters in addition to the standard set of typefaces, providing such things as ligatures, small caps, ornaments, true fractions, and swash characters.

1957 **extruders** A typographic term used to describe ascenders and descenders. ➔ *1934 ascender; 1953 descender*

1958 **feet** The area at the base of a piece of metal type.

1959 **full face** A headline type, always in capitals. Also called **titling**.

1960 **groove** A channel running along the bottom surface of a shank of metal type, in the same plane as the set (width).

1961 **hairlines** Very thin strokes in a type design.

1962 **heavy (face)** An alternative term for bold type or, sometimes, type even heavier than bold. ➔ *1940 bold (face)*

1963 **italic** The sloping version of a roman type design deriving from cursive handwriting and calligraphic scripts, intended for textual emphasis. The first italic type was cut by Aldus Manutius in about 1499. A version of italic, often called oblique or sloped roman, can be generated digitally by most applications, but it merely slants the roman style to the right, so it is a poor substitute for the real thing. ➔ *1948 contra italic*

1964 **kern** The part of a metal type character that overhangs the next. ➔ *1696 kerning*

1234567890

1966 Lining numerals

1234567890

1973 nonlining numerals

1976 Pothook

N

1979 Serif

E E E
 a *b* *c*

1983 Small capitals
a regular capital
b true small capital (from an "expert set")
c small capital generated digitally

1965 light/light face Type with an inconspicuous light appearance, based on the same design as medium, or roman, weight type in the same type family. The opposite of boldface. ➔ *1992 weight (1)*

1966 lining figures/numerals A set of numerals aligned at top and bottom. Sometimes called **"modern" numerals**.

1967 long descenders Descenders such as g, j, p, q, and y in certain typefaces that are particularly long and are offered as an alternative to the standard characters of the typeface.

1968 lowercase The small letters in a font, as distinct from capitals — uppercase. Also called **minuscules**. ➔ *1944 case (2); 1990 upper case*

1969 medium (3) The weight of a type design halfway between light and bold, sometimes described as roman.

1970 minuscule An alternative name for a lowercase or small letter. ➔ *1968 lower case*

1971 neck The part of a metal type character between the shoulder and face, also known as the bevel.

1972 nick A small groove on a piece of metal type that identifies its orientation.

1973 nonlining figures/numerals Numerals designed with descenders and ascenders rather than those of a standard height and alignment such as lining figures. Also known as **hanging figures**. ➔ *1966 lining figures/numerals*

1974 numerals An alternative term for numbers.

1975 pi font A font of various characters such as shapes, logos, accents, dingbats, etc., which do not form part of a standard character set. ➔ *1572 character set; 1586 dingbat; 1638 special sorts*

1976 pothook The sharply curved terminal of a character, particularly noticeable in italic fonts.

1977 primary letter Any lowercase character that does not have an ascender or descender — a, e, m, etc.

1978 roman (type) A font design in which the characters are upright, as distinct from italic.

1979 serif The short counterstroke or finishing stroke at the end of the main stroke of a type character. Serifs on older "classic" typefaces tend to be bracketed and curve out from the main stroke to a point. Modern serifs are flat hairlines at the end of the main stroke. ➔ *1942 bracketed type; 1770 sans serif*

1980 shoulder (1) The nonprinting area surrounding a face of type.

1981 sloped roman/type A sloped version of a font or typeface based on the roman letterform, as opposed to a specifically designed italic type. ➔ *1963 italic*

1982 slug (1) In hot metal typesetting, the name for a line of type set as a single piece of metal. ➔ *1806 Linotype; 1802 hot metal (type)*

1983 small capitals/caps Capital letters designed in a smaller size than the capitals of the font to which they belong. Many computer applications make provision for small caps (called **synthesized small caps**), but they are invariably mere reductions in size of the regular capitals, with the result that the weight, or "color," of the resulting small caps is too light. Special

abcd*a*
abcd*b*
abcd *c*
abcd*d*
abcd *e*

1992 Weight (1)
a light
b medium (roman)
c bold
d extra bold
e ultra bold

fonts, called expert sets, are available, which have specially designed small caps, and they give a more aesthetic result. ➔ *1943 capital; 1838 caps and smalls; 1851 even s. caps, even smalls; 1956 expert set*

1984 **splayed M** A character M with outwardly sloping or splayed sides.

1985 **stem** The primary vertical stroke in a type character.

1986 **stress** The emphasis of a letterform, as perceived in the heaviest part of a curved stroke.

1987 **stroke** (**1**) The outline of a shape or character, as distinct from the inside area, known as the fill.

1988 **stroke** (**2**) In calligraphy, the part of a character that can be drawn in a single movement.

1989 **swash characters** Ornamental italic characters with decorative tails and embellishments. For example, certain Caslon Old Face italic characters.

1990 **uppercase** The capital letters of a type font, the term deriving from the compositor's "case" — trays of type that were generally used in pairs, upper for capital letters and lower for small letters. ➔ *1943 capital; 1944 case (2); 1968 lowercase*

1991 **upstroke** The finer stroke in a type character derived from the downward stroke of a pen in calligraphic letterforms.

1992 **weight** (**1**) The degree of boldness applied to a font, for example, light, medium, bold, etc.

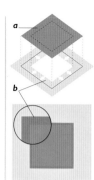

1998 Choke
a cyan overprints
yellow choke
b choke

1993 **ACR** *abb.:* **achromatic color removal** A method of color correction by which an extended degree of undercolor removal (UCR) can take place. With conventional UCR most of the color and tone is generated by the three process colors, with black providing the deeper shadow tones. In achromatic reproduction, however, the absolute minimum of each color required is computed, black being added to enhance the depth of color. → *2039 GCR; 2087 UCR; 3490 achromatic; 3493 chroma*

1994 **AM screening** *abb.:* **amplitude modulated screening** An alternative name for a conventional halftone screen — those screens that break up a continuous tone image into a regular pattern of different sized dots. → *2036 FM screening; 2040 halftone (1)*

1995 **autoscreen** Photographic film that creates halftones from a continuous tone original without the need for an intermediate screen. → *2040 halftone (1)*

1996 **banding** An aberration that occurs in the electronic reproduction of graduated tints, when the ratio of halftone screen ruling and output resolution is incorrect, causing a "stepped" appearance. The maximum number of achievable levels of tone is 256 (the PostScript limit) for each of the four process colors (CMYK), so to calculate the optimum imagesetter resolution multiply the halftone screen ruling by 16 (the square root of 256 — each imagesetter dot is constructed on a matrix of 16 × 16 pixels). Therefore, to minimize the chance of banding in a single color image to be printed with a halftone screen ruling of 150lpi, the maximum levels of gray can be achieved if it is output by the imagesetter at 2400dpi (150 × 16). Banding can also occur when the percentage values of a large area of a graduated single color tint are very close — 40–50%, for example. → *1056 PostScript; 2040 halftone (1); 2189 imagesetter; 0773 resolution; 3496 CMYK*

1997 **benday/Ben Day tints** Originally, a proprietary technique, named for Benjamin Day and introduced in 1901, of applying tints of a color to artwork or printing plates using a pattern of dots. Nowadays, however, the term is generally used to describe an effect rather than the technique employed to achieve the effect.

1998 **choke** One of the "trapping" techniques (along with "spread") used in print preparation for making sure two abutting areas of ink print without gaps. A choke traps a surrounding light background to a dark, inner foreground object by expanding the edge of the inner object so the two colors overlap. Because the darker of the two adjacent colors defines the visible edge of the object, it is always preferable to extend the lighter color into the darker. Traditionally, spreads and chokes were achieved by slightly overexposing the film so the image areas expanded, and the piece of film used for the choke was alternatively termed a "skinny." Nowadays, software applications provide automatic trapping features. → *2085 trapping; 2080 spread (2)*

1999 **circular screen** An adjustable halftone screen that can be rotated to prevent undesirable "moiré" patterns in color reproduction. → *2061 moiré*

2000 **color break** The edge between two areas of color in an image.

2001 **combination line and halftone** A single plate, block, or piece of film onto which both line and halftone matter have been merged. Also called **line and halftone fit up**. → *2052 line and halftone; 2121 line art; 2040 halftone (1)*

2002 **commercial color** The term (sometimes used derogatorily) applied to color images generated by desktop scanners, as opposed to high-resolution reproduction scanners. → *0281 scanner*

2003 contact (halftone) screen A sheet of film bearing a graded, vignetted, dot pattern, which, when placed in direct contact with photographic film or printing plates, converts continuous tone images, such as photographs or artwork, into halftones (images made up of dots) suitable for printing. Originally, the screens were engraved on glass, but film-based contact screens give better definition. Now, however, this method of generating halftone images has largely been supplanted by computers, which apply halftones to images digitally. → *2040 halftone (1); 2045 halftone screen*

2004 crossline screen A film screen engraved with two sets of parallel lines that cross each other at right angles, forming transparent squares. Used for making halftones. → *2045 halftone screen*

2005 cut (5) To reduce ("etch") the dot size in halftone film. → *2045 halftone screen*

2006 dark field illumination A method of checking the quality of halftone dots on a piece of film by holding the film at an angle against a dark background.

2007 deep-etch halftone A halftone image from which the highlight dots have been removed so clean areas of plain paper are visible. Traditionally, this was done either on the printing plate or on the film, but it is now more common to control halftone dot coverage digitally on computer. Also known as **drop-out halftone**, it should not be confused with "deeply-etched halftone." → *2040 halftone (1); 2922 deeply-etched halftone*

2008 densitometer A precision instrument used to measure the optical density and other properties of color and light in positive or negative transparencies, printing film, reflection copy, or computer monitors. Also called a **color coder**. → *3492 calibrate, calibration*

2009 diffuse highlight An area of highlight on a halftone image that bears the smallest printable dot. → *2040 halftone (1)*

2010 direct halftone A halftone negative or positive produced by exposing the original directly through a halftone screen onto film. → *2011 direct screening*

2011 direct screening A method of creating color halftone film separations directly from an original, without the need for continuous tone negatives. → *2105 continuous tone*

2012 distortion copy Any matter for print that has been deliberately distorted prior to production to compensate for naturally occurring dimensional changes, such as shrinkage, which can occur during the process.

2013 dot area The pattern of a halftone and the area it occupies — that is, not just the dots themselves, but also the spaces in between.

2014 dot etching The conventional process of using chemicals to reduce the size of halftone dots on negative or positive film, to modify the tonal values of a halftone image. → *2078 soft dot; 2047 hard dot*

2015 dot formation The pattern of dots produced by halftone images printed in two or more colors. → *2018 dot pattern*

2016 dot gain The tendency, during the reproduction chain from original to printed image, of halftone dots to grow in size, either photographically in prepress stages, or in ink during printing. This often leads to inaccurate results, but, if the dot gain characteristics of a particular printing press are

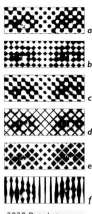

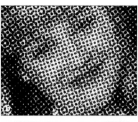

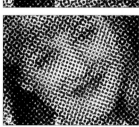

2020 Dot shape
a *round*
b *diamond*
c *elliptical*
d *square*
e *cross line*
f *line*

2018 Dot pattern *showing a picture reproduced with the correct dot pattern (**a**) with a coarser version showing the "rosette" pattern, (**b**). Incorrectly positioned halftone screens produce a "moiré" dot pattern, (**c**) and (**d**).*

known, compensation can be made during reproduction. A dot gain scale — part of a color control bar — is usually included on proofs to check this occurrence, and is specified as a percentage of the size of the dot. Dot gain is the opposite of dot loss. ➔ **2017** *dot loss*

2017 dot loss The erosion or complete disappearance of a halftone dot, possible at any stage of the reproduction chain from film-making through to printing. Dot loss is the opposite of dot gain. ➔ **2016** *dot gain*

2018 dot pattern The pattern created by halftone dots after all colors are printed. A halftone image printed in register and with the correct halftone screen angles will produce a **rosette** pattern, whereas incorrectly angled halftone screens will produce a pattern known as "moiré." ➔ **2015** *dot formation;* **2061** *moiré;* **2067** *screen angle*

2019 dot range The difference in size between the largest and smallest printable dots of a halftone image. ➔ **2040** *halftone (1)*

2020 dot shape The shape of the dot in a halftone screen. Although traditional halftones use round dots (which actually look square in the midtones), some applications or output devices allow you to choose between round, square, linear (not actually dots, but lines), and elliptical dot shapes. Elliptical dots are less prone to dot gain than round dots, while linear screens are used for visual effect rather than for any particular benefit to the reproduction of an image. ➔ **2040** *halftone (1)*

2021 dot value The size of halftone dots in an image or tint, expressed as a percentage of the solid color. ➔ **2040** *halftone (1);* **2019** *dot range*

2022 dot-for-dot (**2**) A method of generating printing film by photographing a previously screened or printed halftone image. On fine-screened images, the usual allowable maximum limit of enlargement or reduction is around ten percent. Also called **copydot** technique. ➔ **2075** *screened print*

*2029 Duotone
printed with cyan and
magenta ink*

*2030 Duplex halftone
printed with cyan and
magenta ink*

*2035 Flat-tint
halftone*

2023 **double-dot halftone** Two halftone films made from a single, original image, one exposed to accommodate midtones, the other to reproduce highlights and shadows, which, when combined, produce a printed image with a greater tonal range than would be possible with a single exposure. ➜ *2040 halftone (1);* **2029** *duotone*

2024 **dropout** (**1**) The use of masks or filters to prevent unwanted areas of an image from appearing on final negative or positive film.

2025 **dropout blue/color** The use of blue pencils or other markers to construct camera-ready art or write instructions on artwork, used because blue does not reproduce when photographed with certain types of photographic film used in prepress work. Also called **nonrepro blue**, **fade out blue**, or **face out blue**. ➜ *2026 dropout ink*

2026 **dropout ink** Any colored ink that is visible to the human eye, but is not "seen" by a scanner or reprographic film. Dropout inks are used to print forms and layout grids, for example. ➜ **2025** *dropout blue/color*

2027 **dropout** (**mask**) The use of masks, filters, or other means during reproduction to prevent highlight dots or a specific item from appearing on final negative or positive film.

2028 **dropping out** A repro house or output bureau term for replacing a low-resolution "FPO" scan with a high-resolution scan prior to final film output. ➜ *4030 FPO*

2029 **duotone** A monochromatic image combining two halftones with different tonal ranges made from the same original, so that, when printed in different tones of the same color (usually black, when it is sometimes described as a "double-black duotone"), a wider tonal range is reproduced than is possible with a single color. Special effects can be achieved by using the same technique printed with different colored inks. The term is sometimes used erroneously to describe a "duplex halftone," or "false duotone"(a duplicate halftone printed in two colors). ➜ **2030** *duplex halftone*

2030 **duplex halftone** Two exact duplicate halftone negatives (or positives) made from the same original, but printed in two different colors. Sometimes erroneously described as a "duotone" when a "false duotone" (the correct alternative) is meant. ➜ **2029** *duotone;* **3594** *duplex*

2031 **elliptical dot** (**screen**) A halftone screen in which the dots are elliptical in shape, because these are less prone to "dot gain" while at the same time providing a greater range of midtones. ➜ *2016 dot gain;* **2020** *dot shape;* **2040** *halftone (1)*

2032 **facsimile halftone** The removal of the dots from the highlight areas of a halftone to obtain a more natural reproduction of pencil or crayon drawings. Synonymous with **highlight halftone**. ➜ *2079 specular highlight;* **2049** *highlight halftone*

2033 **filter** (**4**) The colored glass, tinted gelatin, or cellulose acetate sheets used in conventional color separation, which absorb specific wavelengths of light so the red, green, and blue components of an original can be separated to provide the cyan, magenta, yellow, and black films used in process printing.

2034 **flat etch** Overall chemical reduction of the size of dots in a film halftone. ➜ *2706 rough etch;* **2014** *dot etching;* **2007** *deep-etch halftone*

2035 **flat-tint halftone** A halftone image printed over a flat tint of color.

a C+M+Y, no black | Black only | All four colors (CMYK)

b C+M+Y, no black | Black only | All four colors (CMYK)

c C+M+Y, no black | Black only | All four colors (CMYK)

2039 GCR (gray component replacement) showing (**a**) an image separated without any color replacement or removal; (**b**) the image separated with neutral values (grays) of CMY replaced with black; (**c**) *2087 UCR (under color removal)* the separation with color under the black removed.

2036 **FM screening** *abb.:* **frequency modulated screening** A method of screening an image for reproduction that uses a random pattern of dots to reproduce a continuous tone image. Also known as **stochastic screening**. → *1994 AM screening*

2037 **fringe** The edge around a "soft" halftone dot, which may not be dense enough to prevent light passing through during final film-making, thus potentially altering the dot size. Also called a **dot fringe** or **halo**. → *2078 soft dot*

2038 **full-scale black** A black separation film that reproduces the full tonal range of black in an image, rather than, as is more common, just the darker areas. → *2831 skeleton black*

2039 **GCR** *abb.:* **gray component replacement** A color separation technique in which black ink is used instead of overlapping combinations of cyan, magenta, and yellow to create gray shades. This technique avoids color variations and trapping problems during printing.

2040 **halftone** (1) The reprographic technique, developed in the 1880s, of reproducing a continuous tone image on a printing press by breaking it up into a pattern of equally spaced dots of varying size. This determines tones or shades — the larger the dots, the darker the shade. → *2105 continuous tone*

2040 Halftone (1)

2041 **halftone** (**2**) Any image reproduced by the halftone process. → *2040 halftone (1)*

2042 **halftone blowup** An enlargement of a halftone image in which the screen dot pattern becomes coarsened. → *2040 halftone (1)*

2043 **halftone cell** A halftone dot generated on a laser printer or imagesetter, comprising a group of "machine dots" in a grid space. → *0260 machine dot; 2044 halftone dot*

2044 **halftone dot** The smallest basic element of a halftone. It may be round, square, elliptical, or any other shape. The frequency of halftone dots is measured in lines per inch (lpi) or per centimeter (lpc). → *1030 dot; 2078 soft dot; 2047 hard dot; 2040 halftone; 2090 vignetted (halftone) dots*

2045 **halftone screen** Conventionally, a sheet of glass or film cross-hatched with opaque lines, used to convert a continuous tone image into halftone dots so it can be printed. Computer applications generate a halftone screen digitally without the need for a physical halftone screen, by generating each halftone dot as an individual "cell," itself made up of "printer" dots. Also called a **crossline screen** or **contact screen**. → *2003 contact (halftone) screen; 2004 crossline screen; 2040 halftone (1); 2073 screen ruling*

2046 **halftone tint** A printed area of even tone, achieved by uniform halftone dots. Tints are specified in percentages of the solid color. Also called a **screen tint**. → *3558 tint*

2047 **hard dot** The dot on a halftone film produced either directly from a scanner or as final film, which, having dense, hard edges, can only be minimally retouched or etched. As distinct from a soft dot, which will allow a larger amount of etching. → *2078 soft dot; 2180 final film*

2048 **highlight dots** The smallest dots on a halftone film image. → *2040 halftone (1)*

2049 **highlight halftone** A halftone image in which the dots in the highlight areas have been etched out. → *2040 halftone (1)*

2050 **indeterminate color** A trapping term that describes an area of color comprising many colors, such as a picture. → *2085 trapping*

2051 **knockout** An area of background color that has been masked ("knocked out") by a foreground object, and therefore does not print. The opposite of "overprint." → *2660 overprint (2)*

2052 **line and halftone** Halftone and line work combined onto one set of films, plates, or artwork, as distinct from the "tone-line process." *2084 tone-line process*

2053 **lines per inch** (**lpi**) The measurement of the resolution, or coarseness, of a halftone, being the number of rows of dots to each inch. → *2073 screen ruling*

2054 **main exposure** The first exposure in the conventional processing of a halftone image. → *2183 flash exposure*

2055 **makeover** (**1**) To produce screened separations in a variety of sizes from one set of continuous-tone separations.

2056 **masking** (**1**) To block out an area of an image with opaque material to prevent reproduction or to allow for modifications, such as adjusting the values of color and tone. → *3530 mask (1)*

2059 Mezzograph

2061 Moiré
a image with correct screen angles
b image with incorrect angles, producing a moiré pattern

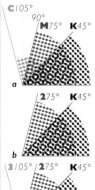

2067 Screen angle
a 4-color process
b 2-color printing
c 3-color printing

2057 mechanical tint Line or dot tints in various percentages preprinted onto thin adhesive film. These were used in traditional artwork to fill a given area with a tint, but have all but been replaced by digital processes. → *1997 benday/Ben Day tints; 4075 Zip-a-tone, Zipatone*

2058 medium (**4**) An alternative name for a benday tint. → *1997 benday/Ben Day tint*

2059 mezzograph/metzograph A halftone screen that, like a "mezzotint," uses a grain formation rather than a regular ruling. Similar to a "stochastic" screen, though much coarser. → *2877 mezzotint; 2083 stochastic screening*

2060 midtone dot Halftone dots of the middle tone areas of a halftone image, shown on close examination as the square dots of a checkerboard. → *2044 halftone dot; 3523 midtones/middletones*

2061 moiré An unintended pattern that occurs in halftone reproduction when two or more colors are printed and the dot screens are positioned at the wrong angles. The correct angles at which screens should be positioned usually depend upon the number of colors being printed, but the normal angles for four-color process printing, and thus the default setting in many computer applications, are: cyan 105°; magenta 75°; yellow 90°; black 45°. A moiré pattern can also be caused by scanning or rescreening an image to which a halftone screen has already been applied. → *0745 descreen(ing); 1999 circular screen; 2775 color rotation/sequence; 2018 dot pattern*

2062 open up A method of obtaining a lighter printed result by slightly overexposing a halftone negative so the dots are smaller.

2063 prescreen A halftone-screened positive print pasted down with line artwork to circumvent the need for film stripping.

2064 prescreened film Film that has been pretreated so it will generate a halftone image from a continuous tone original without the need for a halftone screen.

2065 quartertone A screened image in which the dots occupy twenty-five percent of the image area, as distinct from a regular "halftone" in which the dots occupy fifty percent. → *2040 halftone (1)*

2066 rescreened halftone A positive or negative halftone made from a previously screened image. A diffusion filter is often used to eliminate a potential moiré pattern, and this is known as "descreening." → *0745 descreen(ing); 2040 halftone (1)*

2067 screen angle The angle at which halftone screens of images printing in two or more colors are positioned to minimize undesirable dot patterns (moiré) when printed. The angle at which screens should be positioned depends upon the number of colors being printed, but the normal angles for four-color process printing are: cyan 105°; magenta 75°; yellow 90°; black 45°. → *2061 moiré; 2018 dot pattern*

2068 screen distance The space between the surface of a halftone screen and the plate or film during halftone photography. The distance depends on the screen ruling. → *2045 halftone screen*

2069 screen frequency The number of line rulings per inch (lpi) on a halftone screen. → *2045 halftone screen; 2073 screen ruling*

2070 screen negative A photographic reproduction of an image made through a halftone screen onto negative film. → *2071 screen positive; 2045 halftone screen*

*2073 Screen ruling **a** 55 lines per inch (lpi), 20 lines per centimeter (lpc);*
***b** 85lpi (35lpc); **c** 100lpi (40lpc); **d** 133lpi (54lpc); **e** 150lpi (60lpc);*
***f** 175lpi (70lpc)*

2071 **screen positive** A photographic reproduction of an image made either
through a halftone screen onto positive film, or by "contact" duplicating a
screen negative. ➔ *2070 screen negative; 2045 halftone screen*

2072 **screen process work** The basis of the halftone process in printing
where continuous tone images are reproduced by means of exposure
through a screen. ➔ *2045 halftone screen*

2073 **screen ruling** In halftone screens, the number of ruled lines per
inch or centimeter. The greater the number, the finer the resolution.
The range in common use varies from about 85lpi for halftones printed
on newsprint, to 150lpi or more for those printed on art papers.
The default setting on laser printers is usually about 80lpi. Although
the abbreviated form, lpi, is sometimes used, it is more usual to
express a "150lpi"-screen, for example, as a "150-line" screen. ➔ *2045
halftone screen*

2074 **screen tester** A piece of equipment used to identify the screen resolution, or number of lines per inch, of a printed halftone image. ➔ *2045
halftone screen; 2053 lines per inch; 2073 screen ruling; 3614 magnifier*

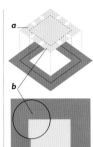

2080 Spread (2)
a yellow overprints ("spreads" into) cyan
b spread

2085 Trapping
a without trapping
b with trapping

2075 screened print An image reproduced through a halftone screen and printed as a one-off print, usually on photographic bromide paper, so it can be photographed as a line original as part of camera-ready art. → *2022 dot-for-dot (2)*

2076 screening Turning a continuous-tone image into a pattern of dots of various sizes by photographing it through a halftone screen placed in front of the photographic emulsion. → *2045 halftone screen*

2077 single-line halftone A halftone image created with a screen that has uniform parallel lines, as opposed to one with lines crossing at right angles. → *2045 halftone screen; 2020 dot shape*

2078 soft dot A halftone dot on film that is less dense at the edge than at the center and is thus easier to etch for correction purposes. As distinct from a "hard dot," which has less tolerance for alteration and is thus used as final film for platemaking. → *2047 hard dot; 2180 final film*

2079 specular highlight The lightest highlighted area in a reproduced photograph, usually reproduced as unprinted white paper.

2080 spread (**2**) One of the "trapping" techniques (along with "choke") used in print preparation to make sure two abutting areas of ink print without gaps. A spread traps a light foreground object to a surrounding dark background by expanding the edge of the inner object so the two colors overlap. Because the darker of the two adjacent colors defines the visible edge of the object, it is always preferable to extend the lighter color into the darker. Traditionally, spreads and chokes were achieved by slightly overexposing the film so the image areas expanded, and the piece of film used for the spread was termed a "fatty." Today, software applications provide automatic trapping features. → *2085 trapping; 1998 choke*

2081 square dot A halftone screen in which the dots are square in shape. → *2020 dot shape*

2082 squared(-up) halftone Trimming ("cropping") or resizing a halftone image to a square or rectangular shape, as opposed to a cutout halftone. → *4099 cutout (1)*

2083 stochastic screening A method of reproducing an image by applying a "screen" of scattered microdots, each one sometimes no larger than a machine dot, and by which 256 grays (or more) can be rendered without varying the dot size. It differs from conventional halftoning in that the dots are not distributed in a grid pattern, but placed in accordance with an algorithm that statistically evaluates their distribution within a fixed set of parameters. Stochastic screening offers many advantages over conventional halftone screening, because, as well as giving the impression of a continuous-tone reproduction (it is sometimes described as "screenless" printing), it eliminates "moiré" patterns, allows a wider range of colors, and does not cause a shift in colors if there is misregister during printing. Also called **FM screening**. → *0260 machine dot; 2036 FM screening*

2084 tone-line process A conventional technique of producing a line image from a continuous tone original by combining negative and positive film. Now done with software. Not to be confused with combination line and halftone. → *2001 combination line and halftone*

2085 trapping The slight overlap of two colors to eliminate gaps that may occur between them due to the normal fluctuations of registration during printing. Also refers to printing an ink color before the previous one has

*2088 Unsharp masking **a** original image; **b** with unsharp mask filter applied*

dried — also called **wet trapping**. → *1998* choke; *2080* spread (2); *2788* dry trapping

2086 **UCA** abb.: **undercolor addition** A method of increasing the yellow, magenta, and cyan dot percentages to increase saturation in black areas when "gray component replacement" (GCR) — which does not produce good saturated black — is used. → *2087* UCR; *2039* GCR

2087 **UCR** abb.: **undercolor removal** A reproduction technique of removing color from the shadow areas of scanned color separations, either to reduce the amount of ink or because the colors cancel each other out. For example, if there is enough black and cyan to cover, the magenta and yellow dots are removed. UCR can also reduce trapping problems in printing. → *2039* GCR; *2086* UCA; *2085* trapping

2088 **unsharp masking** (**USM**) A traditional film compositing technique used to "sharpen" an image. This can also be achieved digitally, using image-editing applications that use filters to enhance the details in a scanned image by increasing the contrast of pixels, the exact amount depending on various criteria, such as the "threshold" specified and the radius of the area around each pixel. → *0775* sharpen(ing); *1402* sharpness; *0760* interpolate/interpolation; *0982* pixel

2089 **unwanted colors** Three color patches on color reproduction guides that record the same as the white patch when separated. For example, the blue, cyan, and magenta patches on a yellow separation record the same as the white patch. → *2091* wanted colors

2090 **vignetted** (**halftone**) **dots** Dots that reduce in intensity from their centers, fading to nothing at the edges. → *2044* halftone dot

2091 **wanted colors** Three color patches on color reproduction guides that record the same as the black patch when separated. For example, the yellow, red, and green patches on a yellow separation record the same as the black patch. → *2089* unwanted colors

2092 **anamorphic scan** An image scanned and subsequently manipulated to give it disproportionate dimensions.

2093 **anastigmatic lens** A photographic lens used in conventional repro that prevents blurring of the subject.

2094 **apochromatic lens** A photographic lens used for color separations that has been corrected for color and astigmatic aberrations. → *1316* astigmatism; *2161* color separation

**2104 Color
separation**
a *cyan*
b *magenta*
c *yellow*
d *black*
e *all four combined*

2095 **ASPIC** Acronym for **Author's Symbolic Prepress Interfacing Codes** A system of codes for converting typographic formatting of text output on a word processor into a language ("machine code") a typesetting machine will understand.

2096 **APR** *abb.:* **automatic picture replacement** The "open prepress interface" (OPI) procedure whereby low-resolution scanned images are used for page-layout purposes, and are automatically replaced by the high-resolution files prior to film output. → *0747 DCS; 2123 open prepress interface*

2097 **base artwork** In photomechanical reproduction, camera-ready art that contains text matter and keylines, but to which other elements such as halftone images and tints must be added at film stage. → *4013 camera-ready copy/art; 2119 keyline (1); 2040 halftone (1)*

2098 **black box** A colloquial term for a piece of equipment that converts data or performs other automatic tasks, but that does not have a keyboard attached.

2099 **black patch** A patch applied to camera-ready art, which, at film negative stage, acts as a window into which a halftone image is stripped. → *4013 camera-ready copy/art; 2040 halftone (1); 2141 stripping (2)*

2100 **blueline** (**3**) A drawing in nonreproducible blue ink or pencil used as a guide for constructing camera-ready art or illustrations. → *4013 camera-ready copy/art*

2101 **CEPS** (*pron.:* "seps") Acronym for **Color Electronic Prepress System**, a term describing the entire computer-based prepress process, from scanned image to final page film. CEPS is generally used to describe high-quality, color reproduction, as distinct from inferior "desktop color" reproduction. → *0746 desktop color; 2123 open prepress interface; 0747 DCS*

2102 **color bar** The color device printed on the edge of color proofs or in the trim area of press sheets that enables the repro house and printer to check — by eye or with instruments — the fidelity of color separations and the accuracy of printing. The color bar helps to monitor such things as ink density, paper stability, dot gain, trapping, and so on. Also called a **codet**. → *1382 copyboard chart; 2104 color separation; 2085 trapping*

2103 **color chart** A printed reference chart used in color reproduction to select or match color tints made from percentage variations of the four process colors. When using a color chart, for absolute accuracy you should use one prepared by your chosen printer and printed on the actual paper that will be used for the job — a situation that, in reality, is highly unlikely. → *3500 color picker (2); 3501 color swatch; 3496 CMYK*

2104 **color separation** The process of dividing a multicolored image into the four individual process colors — cyan, magenta, yellow, and black (by using red, green, and blue filters) — so the image can be reproduced on a printing press. Conventionally, this was done using the filters in a "process" camera, but color separations are now prepared digitally on a scanner or on a computer. → *0281 scanner; 3496 CMYK*

2105 **continuous tone** (**ct**) An image that contains infinite continuous shades between the lightest and darkest tones, as distinct from a "line" illustration that has only one shade. Usually used to describe an image before it is either broken up by the dots of a halftone screen for printing or "dithered" into a pattern of colors for viewing on low-resolution monitors. Also called **contone**. → *2040 halftone (1); 0749 dither(ing)*

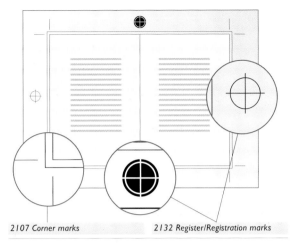

2107 Corner marks   2132 Register/Registration marks

2106 **copyholder** A person who reads the original copy out loud while another checks and corrects the galley proof. ➔ *3724 galley proof*

2107 **corner marks** Marks in the corner of an image or page that usually indicate its final size after trimming or cropping, but which can also be used as a guide for positioning or for registration during makeup or printing. Also called **crop marks**, **trim marks**, or **cut marks**. ➔ *2132 register/Registration marks; 2197 makeup (1)*

2108 **CT** (**2**) A file format used by Scitex prepress systems for storing continuous tone scanned images. ➔ *2125 prepress; 2105 continuous tone*

2109 **cut dummy** Cut proofs of illustrations or pages, assembled in sequence to act as a guide for the makeup of pages. ➔ *2197 makeup (1)*

2110 **drum** (**3**) The glass or plastic cylinder in an electronic scanner onto which originals, such as transparencies, are mounted for scanning. ➔ *2111 drum scanner*

2111 **drum scanner** A scanner in which originals, mounted onto a rotating glass or plastic cylinder (called a drum — a qualification that distinguishes high-end scanners from inferior flatbed or desktop varieties), are scanned by a laser for eventual output as color-separated printing film. ➔ *0281 scanner; 0275 desktop scanner; 2115 flatbed scanner*

2112 **duplo** A scanning technique in which two color separations are exposed onto a single piece of film.

2113 **electronic imaging** A system of manipulating, retouching, and assembling scanned, digital images prior to output as film.

2114 **fine-line copy** Very thin lines in an original image that have been halftone screened, and are thus difficult to reproduce.

2115 **flatbed scanner** A scanner in which originals are placed on a flat sheet of glass ("bed") and scanned by an array of tiny, light-sensitive "photosites" (collectively called "CCDs"). Although generally of inferior quality to high-end drum scanners, flatbed scanners are becoming increasingly sophisticated and are now used extensively for prepress work. ➔ *0281 scanner; 0275 desktop scanner; 2111 drum scanner*

2122 Line conversion
a original image
b converted to line

2116 **flat copy** Original artwork submitted for scanning. To enable superior quality drum scanning, many "flat copy" originals are now supplied unmounted or are created on flexible material.

2117 **gang shooting** To make one item out of several by photographing them all together, such as making a single negative from several original images. ➜ *2118 gang up (2)*

2118 **gang up** (**2**) To place several originals (usually of the same proportions) together for scanning or some other means of reproduction. ➜ *2117 gang shooting*

2119 **keyline** (**1**) In the conventional preparation of artwork (not involving a computer), an outline drawing that indicates areas to be filled with mechanical tints. ➜ *2057 mechanical tint*

2120 **keyline** (**3**) The outline on artwork that, when printed, will act as a guide for registering other colors. ➜ *2696 register, registration*

2121 **line art**(**work**) Artwork or camera-ready copy consisting only of black on white, with no intermediate tones and thus not requiring halftone reproduction (although shaded tones can be applied with "mechanical tints"). Also called **line copy**, **line work**, or **line original**. ➜ *2057 mechanical tint*

2122 **line conversion** (**technique**) The photographic or electronic method of eliminating the middle tones from a continuous tone original so it can be treated as line artwork. Also called **drop tone**.

2123 **open prepress interface** (**OPI**) A prepress protocol that enables low-resolution (positional) scanned image files to be automatically substituted for high-resolution versions when the file is output to an imagesetter or other high-resolution device.

2124 **photodirect** A method of producing litho plates direct from artwork without an intermediate negative being made first.

2125 **prepress** Any or all of the reproduction processes that can occur between design and printing, but often specifically used to describe color separation and planning. Also called **origination**.

2126 **process camera** An especially designed graphic arts camera used in photomechanical reproduction to enlarge or reduce original artwork and to apply halftone screens to photographic images. Also called a **repro camera** or **reproduction camera**. ➜ *2143 vertical camera; 2040 halftone (1)*

2127 **process photography** The photomechanical preparation of materials, such as color separations, for print reproduction.

2128 **quadracolor** The ability of a scanner to output all four colors from/on one piece of film.

2129 **reader** A person who compares a typeset text with the original and annotates it with corrections. Also called a **printer's reader**.

2130 **reflection copy** Any flat item that is to be reproduced photographically by light reflected from its surface. As distinct from a "transparency," or "slide," original in which the light is passed through it. Also called **reflective artwork**. ➜ *1417 color transparency (film)*

2131 **reflex copy** A method of producing a contact copy by shining light through a sensitized material that is in contact with the original — the light bounces back onto the sensitized emulsion, creating an image.

2132 **register marks/registration marks** The marks used on artwork, film, and printing plates that are superimposed during printing to make sure the work is in register. Many graphics applications automatically generate register marks outside the page area. Also called **crossmarks** or **T-marks**. → *2696 register/registration; 2107 corner marks*

2133 **repro** (**1**) *abb.:* **reproduction** Literally, the entire printing process from the completion of artwork or imagesetter output to printing, although it is more frequently used to describe the processes that take place up to the printing stage. Also called **origination** or **prepress**. → *2125 prepress*

2134 **repro** (**2**) Any clean, sharp image of appropriate quality printed onto a suitable paper (such as bromide) for line or halftone reproduction. Also called a **repro pull**.

2135 **reprographic printing** Individual or short-run or copying printing, typically using photocopiers or diazo processes, rather than commercial printing presses. → *2168 diazo(type)/diazo process*

2136 **scan**(**ning**) An electronic process that converts an image into digital form by sequential exposure to a moving light beam, such as a laser. The scanned image can then be manipulated by a computer or output to separated film. → *2111 drum scanner; 0275 desktop scanner; 0140 laser*

2137 **scanned image** An image that has been recorded by a scanner and converted to a suitable form for reproduction, such as film or a digital file. → *2136 scan(ning); 0280 scan dot*

2138 **separation artwork** Artwork that consists of separate layers for each of the colors used. → *2104 color separation*

2139 **separation filters** The filters used to separate colors so they can be printed individually. They each transmit about one-third of the spectrum. → *2104 color separation*

2140 **source document** (**2**) Any original, used as a master for reproduction.

2141 **stripping** (**2**) Inserting a typeset correction into film or camera-ready art.

2142 **transmission copy** An original, such as a transparency, reproduced by means of transmitted light.

2143 **vertical camera** A camera used for reproduction, typically with a fixed position camera and a horizontal copyboard that moves up and down. → *2126 process camera*

2144 **all in hand** The stage of the publishing process when the job is in the hands of the typesetter. → *2145 all up*

2145 **all up** The stage of the publishing process when the job is in the hands of the printer. → *2144 all in hand*

2146 **antihalation backing** In platemaking, the protective coating on the nonemulsion side of reprographic film that prevents light from reflecting back onto the emulsion and thus damaging the image. → *1507 halation*

2147 **assembled negative** The combination of line and halftone negative film used in platemaking in offset litho printing. → *2946 offset litho(graphy); 2951 plate (1); 2148 assembly; 2184 flat (1); 2141 stripping (2)*

2148 **assembly** The gathering together and arrangement of all the separate components used to make final film, or "flats," used for platemaking. Also called **stripping**, **film assembly**, **film makeup**, or **image assembly**. → *2184 flat (1)*

2160 Color positives
a cyan film
b magenta film
c yellow film
d black film

2149 auto-reversing film A photographic material that provides a negative copy from a negative film original without an intermediate positive being required. ➜ *1407 autopositive*

2150 base film In photomechanical reproduction, the basic negative or positive film substrate onto which other film components, such as halftone images, are mounted, or "stripped." ➜ *2141 stripping*

2151 black printer (2) The piece of film that will be used to make the black printing plate in four-color process printing. ➜ *2570 black printer (1); 3517 four-color process*

2152 blueline (1) A low-quality proof used as a final check before platemaking. Originally, bluelines were made by the diazo, or dyeline, process, producing a blue-on-white image, hence the name. Nowadays, the term applies to any proof in which sensitized paper is exposed to the actual printing film. Bluelines are generally made from a composite of the black and cyan films, rather than all four process colors, and are used for checking such things as page order and missing items, but not — obviously — for checking color. ➜ *2168 diazo(type)/diazo process; 2207 Ozalid; 2230 Vandyke print; 1469 silverprint*

2153 blueline (4) A registration guide for assembling the individual printing film components, such as halftones, and "stripping" them to film "flats." ➜ *2141 stripping/(2); 2184 flat (1)*

2154 burn (1) The process of using light to expose an image onto a printing plate.

2155 burn out The process of overexposing a printing plate so that very small dots are not reproduced.

2156 burn through Exposure of film through a mask. ➜ *2157 burnout (mask)*

2157 burnout (mask) The process of masking images and copy after film assembly and prior to platemaking to eliminate unwanted portions, or to make space for new insertions. ➜ *2156 burn through*

2158 Color-Key™ A proprietary dry proofing system developed by 3M. ➜ *2172 dry proof*

2159 color correction The process of adjusting color values in reproduction to achieve the desired result. Although this can occur at scanning or image-manipulation stage, color correction is generally carried out after "wet" proofing (proofs created using process color inks) and, as a very limited last resort, on press.

2160 color positives A set of positive printing films — usually one for each of the four separated process colors: cyan, magenta, yellow, and black — although the film for a spot color may also be described as a color positive. ➜ *3496 CMYK*

2161 color separations The set of four films for each of the four process colors — cyan, magenta, yellow, and black — generated as a result of the color separation process. ➜ *2104 color separation; 2214 printer; 3496 CMYK; 2160 color positives; 2159 color correction; 3517 four-color process*

2162 color-blind emulsion Photographic emulsion that is only sensitive to blue, violet, or ultraviolet light. ➜ *1418 contact film*

2163 **Cromalin** A proprietary dry proofing system from Du Pont that uses toners on light-sensitive paper. Such proofs are also described as **off-press proofs** or **prepress proofs**. → *2199 MatchPrint*

2164 **cyan printer** The plate or film used to print cyan ink in four-color process printing.

2165 **dark reaction** A slow chemical change that occurs in photosensitized materials when they are stored in a dark place over a period of time.

2166 **dead matter** Any matter that is left over or not used during the entire printing process. Originally it referred specifically to typeset matter.

2167 **developing ink** A greasy liquid applied to lithographic plates to protect the ink-receptive image areas while the plate is etched and gummed.

2168 **diazo**(**type**)/**diazo process** *abb.:* **diazonium** A method of photographic printing from a transparent or translucent original in which a light-sensitive coating is applied to a paper, cloth, plastic, or metal surface. This is then exposed to blue or ultraviolet light and the image developed by ammonia vapor. The resulting print may be blue (referred to as "blues," "bluelines," or "blueprints"), brown ("browns," "brownlines," or "Vandykes"), or black. Also known variously as **Ozalids**, **dyelines**, **diazoprints**, **direct-positives**, and **whiteprints**, diazos are widely used in prepress stages for checking imposed film ("flats"), as well as by architectural and engineering draftsmen. The process is also used for preparing presensitized litho plates. → *2152 blueline (1); 2207 Ozalid; 2184 flat (1)*

2169 **DDCP** *abb.:* **direct digital color proof** Any color proof made directly from digital data without using separation films, such as those produced on an ink-jet printer. → *0257 inkjet printer*

2170 **double burn/print down** To use two or more film negatives to expose an image onto a sensitized plate — usually one for line work and a second for halftones.

2171 **double etch** The two-step preparation of a gravure plate used, for example, to etch line work separately from tone images. → *2868 gravure*

2172 **dry proof** Any color proof made without printing ink, such as a Cromalin or MatchPrint, but particularly proofs produced digitally — from a laser printer, for example. → *2163 Cromalin; 2199 MatchPrint; 2158 Color-Key™; 2175 Dylux; 2203 off-press proofing*

2173 **dry stripping** The assembly ("stripping") of film negatives or positives after they have been processed and dried. → *2141 stripping (2)*

2174 **duplicate/dupe film** A direct, same-size copy of a film original, made by contact exposure from one to the other.

2175 **Dylux** The proprietary name for a photosensitive dry proof paper developed by Du Pont that does not require chemical processing. → *2172 dry proof*

2176 **emulsion side** The side of a photographic film on which the light-sensitive emulsion resides, identifiable as the matte side of the film. When, in photomechanical reproduction (duplicating film, for example), the emulsion side of one piece of film is placed in direct contact with the emulsion side of another (or a plate when printing down), a sharp image is guaranteed. Normally, the emulsion on positive film is on the back of the film ("emulsion down"), while on negative film it is on the front ("emulsion up"). → *2221 right reading; 2232 wrong reading*

2177 etch To dissolve away an area of printing plate to produce either a relief image or intaglio image (depending on the printing method) or, on film, to reduce the size of halftone dots. The term is also used to describe the process of desensitizing the nonimage areas, which are protected by a "ground," of a litho plate to make them receptive to water instead of ink. **→** *2923 desensitize*

2178 film positive A record of an image on clear film, emulating the original. Used for film assembly and for making printing plates. **→** *2184 flat (1)*

2179 filmsetting At one time, a term describing typesetting output onto photographic paper or film from a film matrix, when it was also called "phototypesetting" or "photocomposition," but now extended to include, by virtue of the output medium being photographically based, computer typesetting produced on an imagesetter. **→** *1822 typesetting*

2180 final film The positive or negative film used to create the "flats" from which printing plates are made, after all corrections have been made and in which the halftone dots are "hard," as distinct from the "soft" dots on film used for making corrections. **→** *2047 hard dot; 2078 soft dot; 4113 flat (2)*

2181 fine etch A technique of adjusting the middle tones and highlights of a halftone plate after it has been "rough etched." **→** *2706 rough etch*

2182 fit (2) The alignment and register of the ink colors of individual components on a printed page, as distinct from the register of the ink colors on an entire printed sheet. Errors of fit (described as "out of fit") occur during film assembly, whereas errors of register occur when printing. Also called "**image fit**." **→** *2696 register, registration*

2183 flash exposure In conventional halftone processing, a process of improving the tonal reproduction range of a halftone film negative by means of an additional exposure, thus reinforcing the dots in dark areas that may otherwise run together and print solid. **→** *2054 main exposure*

2184 flat (1) An assembly of composite imposed film, used to expose plates in preparation for printing. Also called **composite film**. **→** *2180 final film*

2185 flat proofs In color printing, proofs made from each individual color plate.

2186 foil (2) Clear, stable film used as a backing for film assembly.

2187 goldenrod A yellowish light proof paper used for preparing "flats" (an assembly of composite film). Original negatives or positives are attached to the paper into which masks have been cut. **→** *2184 flat (1)*

2188 head to head/foot/tail In page imposition, the placement of the heads and tails of pages on each side of a sheet to suit the requirements of printing and binding.

2189 imagesetter A high-resolution output device used to generate reproduction-quality copy for printing, either as film negatives or positives, or on photographic bromide paper for use as camera-ready artwork. **→** *2218 RIP (1)*

2190 imaging device Any dedicated piece of equipment that either captures an image from an original, such as a scanner or camera, or generates an image from a previously captured original, such as a contact printing frame or imagesetter.

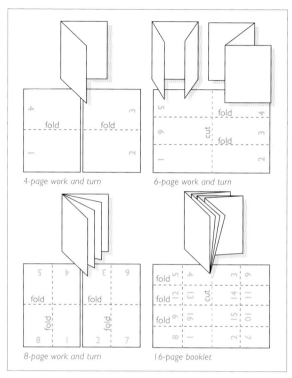

4-page work and turn

6-page work and turn

8-page work and turn

16-page booklet

2191 Imposition showing some of the most common forms of imposition schemes and the corresponding folding methods

2191 imposition/impose The arrangement of pages in the sequence and position in which they will appear on the printed sheet, with appropriate margins for folding and trimming, before platemaking and printing. → *2587 come-and-go/coming and going*

2192 Kodalith MP System A proprietary orthochromatic film system. → *2205 orthochromatic*

2193 lap *abb.:* **overlap**, describing colors that overlap to avoid registration problems ("trapping"). → *2085 trapping*

2194 lay sheet (1) A sheet of glass on which flats are assembled prior to printing down to a photo-offset plate. → *2184 flat (1)*

2195 line film Negative or positive photographic film in which the image consists of solid elements, such as lines or text matter, with no continuous tones or halftones (actually, halftones are usually printed to line film as they consist entirely of solid dots). → *2205 orthochromatic*

2196 magenta printer In four-color process printing, the plate or film used to print magenta ink.

2197 makeup (1) The final preprint assembly, whether it be on paper, film, or computer, of all the various elements to be printed.

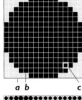

a b   **c**

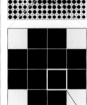

a   **b**   **c**

2206 Output resolution showing a high-resolution halftone dot made on a matrix of 16 x 16 machine dots (top), producing 256 grays and a low-resolution halftone dot on a matrix of 4 x 4 (above)
a halftone cell
b halftone dot
c machine dot

2206 Output resolution showing how a 4 x 4 matrix of machine dots achieves 16 shades of gray

2198 makeover (**2**) To remake a defective printing film or plate.

2199 MatchPrint A proprietary dry proofing system from 3M that uses toners on light-sensitive paper, used for checking color reproduction of film prior to printing. An alternative to a "wet proof" (one which uses printing ink). Also called an **off-press proof** or **prepress proof**. → *2163 Cromalin*

2200 mortise (**1**) Traditionally, a space cut out of a printing plate to create a place to insert type or another plate. In modern usage, fitting a correct piece of text film into a hole left in the film when incorrect text was removed. → *3021 pierced*

2201 multiple flats Flats used to print successive pages in which some elements of the design are repeated from page to page. → *2184 flat (1)*

2202 negative-working plate A printing plate that has been exposed through negative film, as distinct from one exposed through positive film ("positive-working plate"). → *2212 positive-working plate*

2203 off-press proofing A method of proofing by exposing each separation positive onto laminated light-sensitive paper to create an accurate simulation of a "wet proof" (one made with printing inks). Also known as **prepress proofing** or **dry proofing**. → *2163 Cromalin; 2199 MatchPrint; 2172 dry proof*

2204 opaquing To paint out unwanted marks or areas on a negative or positive film with opaque solution prior to platemaking. → *2208 photo-opaque*

2205 orthochromatic A photographic emulsion that is sensitive to all colors except red, and used extensively in conventional reproduction. Also called **lith film**. → *1446 orthographic (2)*

2206 output resolution The resolution of a printer, monitor, imagesetter, or similar device, usually measured in dpi (dots per inch). The relationship between output resolution and halftone screen ruling determines the tonal range that can be printed. The following formula should be used to calculate the optimum number of grays that can be achieved (remembering that 256 is the PostScript maximum): (output resolution ÷ screen ruling) 2 + 1 = shades of gray. Therefore an image output at 1,200dpi and printed with a screen ruling of 90lpi will produce 178 shades of gray. Increasing the screen ruling creates smaller halftone dots and adds detail to an image, but it also reduces the number of grays, so the same image output at 1,200dpi and printed with a screen ruling of 175lpi will produce only 48 shades of gray. The screen ruling in four-color process work is usually 150lpi, so for an image to print with the maximum number of 256 grays it will need to be output with an imagesetter resolution of 2,400dpi. A typical resolution for a monitor is 72 to 90dpi, for a laser printer 600dpi, and for an imagesetter anything upward of 1,000dpi. → *0260 machine dot; 2045 halftone screen; 2073 screen ruling*

2207 Ozalid The proprietary name for a diazo process paper, often used to make prepress proofs of an imposed publication. Such proofs are therefore frequently called "Ozalids." → *2152 blueline (1); 2168 diazo(type)/diazo process*

2208 photo-opaque A liquid used to paint out "pinholes" and other areas on negative or positive printing film. → *2204 opaquing*

2209 photomechanical transfer (**PMT**) A method of transferring images onto paper, film, or metal litho plates by means of photography. An image produced by this method is also known as a PMT. Also called **diffusion transfer**, **chemical transfer**, or **velox**.

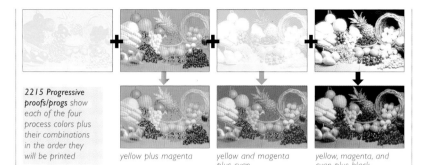

2215 Progressive proofs/progs show each of the four process colors plus their combinations in the order they will be printed

yellow plus magenta

yellow and magenta plus cyan

yellow, magenta, and cyan plus black

2210 **pin register** A method of securing overlays, flats, and so on, to keep them in register. Also known as a **punch register**.

2211 **position proof** A color proof (for checking prior to printing) on which all elements of the final page are present. Traditionally, a variety of color sets were first scatter proofed without text in position. ➔ *2207 Ozalid; 2152 blueline (1)*

2212 **positive-working plate** A printing plate that has been exposed through positive film, as distinct from one exposed through negative film ("negative-working plate"). ➔ *2202 negative-working plate*

2213 **premask** A film positive that will be combined with negative to create a new mask.

2214 **printer** The single films of each of the four process colors — cyan, yellow, magenta, and black ("cyan printer," "yellow printer," and so on), which will produce an image when eventually printed on a four-color press. ➔ *2161 color separations*

2215 **progressive proofs/progs** Proofs used in color printing to show each color printed separately, and progressively combined — in the order they will be printed — with the others.

2216 **proof(ing) press** A small press on which individual sheets are printed for proofing purposes. ➔ *3749 proof*

2217 **prove** A seldom-used, alternative term for "proof."

2218 **RIP (1)** *abb.:* **raster image processor** A device that converts data generated by a page description language, such as PostScript (in other words pages designed by you), into a form that can be output by a high-resolution imagesetter for use in commercial printing.

2219 **register/registration table** A large light table used to prepare and check pasteup, flats, and so on, and to obtain correct position and register. It will generally comprise an illuminated surface grid with movable scales. Also known as a **lining-up table**, **lineup table**, or **shining-up table**.

2220 **revise** A proof on which the revisions marked on an earlier proof have been implemented.

2221 **right reading** The way of viewing negative or positive film so the text, if any, can be read as normal — from left to right, top to bottom — and used to specify the side of the film on which the emulsion is required for film duplication or platemaking. For example, if the request is for film that is "right reading, emulsion down" ("RRED") the emulsion is on the underside, whereas "right reading emulsion up" ("RREU") means it is on the top surface.

2222 rough proof/pull A proof that does not necessarily show copy in its correct position or on the correct paper. Also called a **flat pull**.

2223 Rubylith The brand name for a widely used type of peelable masking film used for film makeup.

2224 scatter proof A single-color proof containing unrelated images placed randomly and without reference to their final position. The process is used to cut costs when large numbers of pictures are needed, for example, in a magazine or illustrated book. Also called a **random proof**.

2225 service bureau A company that provides digital image services, such as color scanning and high-resolution imagesetting.

2226 SWOP *abb.:* **Specifications for Web Offset Publications** A system of standards developed for the printing industry to aid consistency in the use of color separation films and color proofing.

2227 standing type/matter Any material — typeset, film, or stored data — that is held over for revision or reprinting.

2228 stripping up as one In photomechanical reproduction, the process of putting together two or more images to combine them as a single piece of film. → *2148 assembly*

2229 vacuum frame A device in which a film negative and a sensitized plate are held in tight contact by the creation of a vacuum between them. The plate is then exposed to the negative. Also called a **printing down frame**.

2230 Vandyke print A photocopy print, producing the image as a dark brown print, either negative or positive, and used as a final proof from film flats before platemaking. Also called a **brownline** or **brownprint**. → *2152 blueline (1); 2207 Ozalid; 2184 flat (1)*

2231 wet stripping The stripping away of the film base after an image has been processed but while the film is still wet.

2232 wrong reading Negative or positive printing film on which the image reads backward when viewed with the emulsion on the desired side. Also called **reverse reading**. → *2221 right reading*

2233 yellow printer In four-color process printing, the plate or film used to print yellow ink.

2234 **air bells** A blistering defect in paper. → *2241* *bruising;* *2282* *frothing*

2235 **art-lined envelope** An envelope lined on its interior with an extra-fine paper that is usually colored or patterned.

2236 **banker envelope** An envelope that has its flap along its long edge.

2237 **bender** Paper or board stock that can be folded without breaking. → *2470* *board (1)*

2238 **bonding strength** (**2**) The strength with which paper fibers bond together.

2239 **break** (**2**) Weakness in paper that causes a web to tear, thus interrupting printing. → *2344* *web (1); 2240 breaking length*

2240 **breaking length** A measure of the tensile strength of a web of paper, defined by the length at which a suspended web will tear due to its own weight. → *2239* *break (2); 2344 web (1)*

2241 **bruising** An aberration in paper caused by too much pressure or heat during calendering, resulting in a mottled effect. → *2360* *calender*

2242 **chain lines/marks** Visible lines on laid paper, caused by the wire gauze on the "dandy" roll, part of the "fourdrinier" papermaking machine. → *2522* *laid paper; 2369 dandy roll; 2383 fourdrinier*

2243 **cockle** A finish achieved by air-drying paper, producing papers such as onionskin.

2244 **cockled/cockling** Paper that has become distorted due to uneven absorption of moisture, usually because of poor storage. This can sometimes be remedied by "conditioning" the paper — drying it out with conditioned air.

2245 **conditioning** A treatment given to paper either to dry it out or to add moisture. This is done by subjecting the paper to streams of conditioned air in specially constructed chambers. Conditioning is particularly important in areas of the world where atmospheric conditions are extreme — in the Far East, for example. → *2244* *cockled/cockling; 2289 humidified*

2246 **contrast ratio** The opacity of paper, 100 percent being totally opaque.

2247 **counter-mark** A watermark, often the papermaker's logo or initials, placed in the second half of a sheet of paper, opposite the normal watermark. → *2343* *watermark (1)*

2248 **crash finish** A paper with a coarse, linenlike surface.

2249 **creasing** (**2**) The undesirable effect, seen as deep creases, that results from printing on paper that has been stored incorrectly, for example, at the wrong humidity.

2250 **cross-laminated** Paper comprising several sheets, or coatings applied to substrates, in which each layer is laid or applied at right angles to the previous one.

2251 **cure** (**1**) To condition paper to the correct temperature and humidity in preparation for printing.

2252 **curl** The degree to which the edges of a sheet of paper will curl, particularly those used in wet or damp processes.

2253 **cushion** The compressible property of paper. A paper lacks cushion if its fibers are "dead." → *2258* *dead; 2241 bruising; 2282 frothing*

2254 **cut ahead** Paper that has been cut so the watermarks do not fall in the same position on each sheet. As distinct from "cut to register" in which they do. → *2343 watermark (1); 2256 cut to register*

2255 **cut sheets** Paper that has been trimmed into sheets.

2256 **cut to register** Paper that has been cut so the watermarks fall in the same position on each sheet. As distinct from "cut ahead" in which they do not. → *2343 watermark (1); 2254 cut ahead*

2257 **cut-size paper** A general term for paper that has been trimmed into sheets of, usually, smaller sizes, such as 8½ × 11 inches (21.5 × 28 cm), and used for printing and photocopying.

2258 **dead** The description of paper fibers that have lost their resilience and strength during the papermaking process, probably due to excessive beating. → *2253 cushion*

2259 **deckle edge** The rough, uneven edge of untrimmed handmade paper. Deckle edge effects are also applied mechanically to machine-made paper. → *2370 deckle (1)/deckle strap*

2260 **de-inking** The technique of removing ink and other additives from used paper so it can be recycled.

2261 **dendritic growths** Small, treelike growths in paper, caused by oxidization of minute particles of metal that were not removed during making.

2262 **dimensional stability** The resistance of a substance to changes that can affect its physical dimensions. For example, the dimensions of a sheet of paper can be affected by moisture.

2263 **dinky** A half roll ("web") of paper. → *2344 web (1)*

2264 **dog-ear**(ed) Corners of a page that are misfolded, worn, or battered with use.

2265 **dry finish** Paper or board with a rough, uncoated surface.

2266 **dull finish** Paper with a matte surface. → *2486 coated paper*

2267 **embossed finish** A type of paper on which a textured surface has been applied during manufacture.

2268 **enamel** A coating that provides a glossy surface to paper.

2269 **face material** Any material suitable for use as pressure-sensitive transfers or decals.

2270 **felt finish** A finish applied during papermaking as the sheet is dried on a special marking felt.

2271 **felt side** The side of a sheet of paper facing away from the wire mesh during papermaking. Also called **top side** or **right side**. → *2347 wire side*

2272 **festoon** A method of storing rolls of paper prior to splicing on a web press. It also has the effect of stretching the paper and removing the curl from the roll.

2273 **film coating** A lightweight film applied to paper. Also called **wash coating**.

2274 **fine whites** Offcuts of unprinted paper found at the papermaker, printer, or bindery.

2275 **finish** The surface of a paper, usually one that is coated or embossed.

2276 **flocculation** A term used in papermaking when suspended particles in pulp join to form a mass.

2277 **fluff(ing)** An aberration in printing caused by the release of fibers from the surface of paper. Also known as **fuzz** or **linting**. → *2907 blanket piling; 2672 picking*

2278 **folding endurance** The number of times a sheet can be folded before it breaks at the line of fold.

2279 **formation** The structure of paper, principally its fiber distribution.

2280 **foxed** The deterioration of old paper, characterized by brown discoloration and spotting, usually caused by damp.

2281 **free sheet** (I) A paper that does not contain any groundwood, made from wood pulp treated with a caustic solution to remove impurities. → *2553 woodfree paper*

2282 **frothing** The cause of a potential imperfection found in the process of coating paper in which tiny areas of paper remain uncoated.

2283 **glazed** Paper with a very high gloss or "polished" finish. → *2407 supercalendered paper*

2284 **gloss** (I) The amount of light reflected by the surface of paper ("reflectance"). Machine-finishing under pressure through rollers can give a slight gloss.

2285 **grain** (I) The prevailing direction and pattern of fibers in manufactured paper.

2286 **grain direction** The alignment of paper grain in relation to the process it is being used for, such as in printing or bookbinding. In printing, the grain is described as being "grain-long" if it runs in the same direction as the long dimension of the paper, "grain-short" if it runs with the short dimension. → *2391 machine direction*

2287 **hard sized** A description of paper containing the maximum amount of size. Also called **double sized**. → *2402 size*

2288 **holdout** The resistance of certain glazed papers to the penetration of printing ink.

2289 **humidified** A term for paper that has undergone an artificial maturing process to alter its working properties. → *2245 conditioning*

2290 **hygrometer** An instrument used to test the moisture content of paper. Also called a **hygroscope**.

2291 **imitation watermark** A mark resembling a watermark, but which is, in fact, made by stamping the paper very hard between a male die and a polished steel plate. → *2343 watermark (I); 2292 impressed watermark*

2292 **impressed watermark** A mark made by pressing a rubber stereo onto a web of paper. Since this mark can be applied at any time after papermaking, it does not have the security value of a genuine watermark. Also called a **press mark**. → *2343 watermark (I); 2291 imitation watermark; 3028 rubber stereo*

2293 **ink receptivity** The degree to which a substrate such as paper will absorb printing ink. → *2805 ink penetration*

2294 **linen faced** Originally, paper lined on one or both sides with linen. Now known as **cloth faced** or **cloth lined**. → *2295 linen finish*

2296 Linen paper

2295 **linen finish** Paper embossed to resemble coarsely woven cloth. ➜ *2296 linen paper*

2296 **linen paper** Originally, paper made with linen rags, the term is now used to describe paper embossed to resemble linen ("linen finish"). ➜ *2295 linen finish*

2297 **look-through** A term used when describing the opacity of a paper, whereby text or images printed on one side of a sheet are visible, through the sheet, from the other side. This may be caused by the use of incompatible inks and papers, but more often it is because the paper is too thin. Also called **show-through** or **see-through**.

2298 **low-bulk paper** Thin, smoothly finished paper.

2299 **matt(e) finish** A paper with a flat, slightly dull surface.

2300 **mill brand** The brand name and/or trademark of a paper or manufacturer.

2301 **mold-made paper** A manufactured paper that simulates handmade paper. ➜ *2394 mold*

2302 **Mullen tester** A machine for measuring the bursting strength of paper.

2303 **natural tint** Paper that is pale cream in color.

2304 **outsides** Damaged sheets in a batch of handmade paper, having torn edges, creases, or a damaged surface. These are marked "XXX."

2305 **paper absorbency** The ability of paper to retain or absorb fluids, particularly ink.

2306 **paper permanence** The longevity of paper, for example, its resistance to discoloration. Rag-based papers withstand discoloration and brittleness better than most. ➜ *2316 rag paper/pulp*

2307 **pasteboard (2)** Two or more laminations of paper used, typically, for business cards. ➜ *2537 paperboard*

2308 **perforate/perf** A line of punched holes that allow a sheet of paper to be torn or folded accurately.

2309 **pick resistance** The ability of a paper surface to withstand wear.

2310 **plate finish/glazed** The smooth surface on paper obtained by "super-calendering" (passing it through heated, polished rollers).

2311 **plated paper** A paper containing a mixture of rags and clay giving an excellent surface on which to print copper engravings and etchings.

2312 **pocket envelope** A rectangular envelope with the opening on its short side.

2313 **porosity** The degree to which paper can absorb ink and air.

2314 **pouncing** To improve a surface prior to writing or drawing. For example, parchment rubbed with resin or chalk makes it smoother and whiter, whereas tracing paper rubbed with pumice removes grease from the surface.

2315 **rag content** The amount of cotton or linen fiber found in a paper. ➜ *2316 rag paper/pulp; 2296 linen paper; 2533 not*

2316 **rag paper/pulp** Paper manufactured from cotton or linen fiber, using either new or recycled rags, and commonly used for writing and ledger papers.

2317 **recycled paper** Paper made from existing printed paper that has been de-inked, or from unprinted waste and material left over from the paper-making process.

2318 **refining** The preparation of fibers used in the papermaking process.

2319 **retree** Damaged sheets in several reams of paper, usually marked "XXX" or "XX" to indicate the degree of damage.

2320 **roll set curl** The paper curl that occurs when a web has been stored in roll form for too long. Also known as **wrap curl**.

2321 **roll stand** A device used to support a roll of paper as it is fed into a press.

2322 **rosin** A natural byproduct left after turpentine has been tapped from pine trees. It is used in the manufacture of engine-sized paper, making it more impervious to ink and moisture. ➜ *2375 engine-sized*

2323 **scuffing** Degradation of the surface of paper caused by prolonged contact with another surface. Also called **abrasion**.

2324 **sheet** A single piece of paper, plain or printed.

2325 **shiners** Impurities or tiny flaws in a sheet of paper, which show on the surface as shining specks.

2326 **sizing** (1) Treating paper with size. ➜ *2402 size*

2327 **smoothness** The measure of quality of the surface of blemish-free finished paper.

2328 **soft-sized** Low-grade paper, of the type used for newsprint. Minimal amounts of size, and so on, are used in its manufacture.

2329 **spoils** Sheets of paper with flaws or imperfections. The term is used to describe both printed and unprinted sheets. ➜ *2709 run-in sheets*

2330 **stock** (1) The printer's term for the paper to be used in printing.

2331 **substrate** A general term for the material (paper, card, cloth, and so on) that receives a printed image by means of inked type or an inked plate.

2332 **tensile strength** The ability of paper to withstand breaking. ➜ *2302 Mullen tester*

2333 **toned paper** Paper with a slight color cast.

2334 **tooth** The ability of the surface of a paper to hold a painting, drawing or printing medium.

2335 **triple coated** A superior quality paper that has been coated three times to give a very fine finish.

2336 **tub-sized** A method of sizing handmade paper in a tub containing animal glue, gelatin, or starch, and sometimes a combination of the three.

2337 **twin-wire paper** A method of papermaking where the two ends of the web are brought together with the wire side innermost so the paper formed has two top ("felt") sides. Also called **duplex paper**.

2338 **unbleached** A method of papermaking using unbleached pulp. The resultant paper is light brown in color.

2339 **uncoated** A paper without a mineral surface coating, but which is available in a variety of finishes from "antique" (rough) to "supercalendered" (smooth).

2340 unit set (2) A set of carbonless ("NCR") multipart business forms. Older versions were interleaved with carbon tissue. → *2479 carbonless paper*

2341 wallet envelope An envelope with a rectangular flap along a long side.

2342 water lines Alternative name for the lines in a laid paper. → *2522 laid paper*

2343 watermark (1) A mark or design impressed in paper during the manufacturing process, sometimes used to make forgery of a document more difficult, such as in banknote printing. → *2247 counter-mark; 2254 cut ahead; 2291 imitation watermark; 2292 impressed watermark*

2344 web (1) A continuous roll of substrate, particularly paper, that passes through a printing press or through converting or finishing equipment.

2345 wet rub The ability of a wet paper to resist scuffing. → *2323 scuffing*

2346 wet strength The bursting or tensile strength of paper after it has been saturated in water for a given time.

2347 wire side The side of a sheet of paper that was in contact with the wire mesh during papermaking. → *2348 wire-mark; 2271 felt side*

2348 wire-mark A slight impression on the underside of paper left by the wire gauze during papermaking. → *2347 wire side*

2349 wrinkle (1) A creaselike defect found in paper.

2350 writings Smaller paper sizes, suitably "sized." Used for writing rather than printing upon.

2351 air-knife coater A device used in making coated papers in which a jet of compressed air removes surplus coating from the paper. → *2356 blade coater; 2486 coated paper*

2352 alfa grass A variety of esparto grass used to make paper. → *2501 esparto*

2353 animal-sized Paper that has been hardened or "sized" with animal glue or gelatin and then passed through a bath of glue. → *2402 size; 2375 engine-sized; 2336 tub-sized*

2354 base stock The main constituents from which paper is made.

2355 beating The process of converting raw, wet pulp ("half-stuff") into paper pulp. → *2385 half-stuff; 2405 stuff*

2356 blade coater A unit for applying a coating to paper that is then evenly distributed by means of a flexible blade. → *2486 coated paper*

2357 blanc fixe An artificial form of barium sulfate that, along with china clay, is added to paper pulp as a white filler.

2358 board glazed A smooth, but not highly glazed paper, made by a process in which boards, rather than metal plates, are used to finish the surface. → *2470 board (1); 2471 boards*

2359 body paper/stock The substance forming the substrate of coated printing paper. → *2486 coated paper*

2360 calender A column of metal rollers at the end of the papermaking process that applies pressure to the paper, therefore closing the pores and giving the paper a smooth surface. → *2406 super-calender*

2361 **calendered varnish** A hard, glossy finish applied to a printed sheet by coating it with varnish and then passing the sheet through a heated cylinder. → *3358 varnish*

2362 **casein** An adhesive obtained from curdled milk and used in the manufacture of coated papers. → *2486 coated paper*

2363 **cellulose** A fibrous substance — originally obtained only from various plants such as cotton, hemp, flax, for example, but now obtained almost exclusively from wood. Used as the basic substance in papermaking.

2364 **chemical pulp** Pulp prepared from wood chips by treating them with chemicals to remove the noncellulose material such as resin, ligneous matter, and oils. Also called "chemical wood," these pulps are used for making better grades of "woodfree" paper. → *2393 mechanical (wood) pulp; 2553 woodfree paper; 2363 cellulose*

2365 **china clay** Also called "**kaolin**," the substance used in papermaking to increase surface qualities such as gloss and smoothness. China clay has now largely been replaced by artificial sulfate of lime ("satin white"), which provides a smoother surface. → *2456 satin white*

2366 **coating slip** The name given to the solution of minerals, binders, and other additives used to coat paper. → *2486 coated paper*

2367 **couch** In papermaking, to lift sheets onto board or felt for drying, the name deriving from the board itself, called "couch."

2368 **cylinder machine** A papermaking machine, mostly used for making boards, in which pulp is deposited on the surface of a gauze-covered cylinder. Also known as a **vat machine**. → *2383 fourdrinier*

2369 **dandy roll** A wire cylinder on a papermaking machine that impresses a watermark and laid lines into the paper while it is still wet. → *2242 chain lines/marks; 2522 laid paper; 2383 fourdrinier*

2370 **deckle (1)/deckle strap** The edging frame or strap on a papermaking mold or machine that confines or controls the pulp. → *2371 deckle (2); 2259 deckle edge*

2371 **deckle (2)** A term sometimes used to describe the width of a web of paper on a papermaking machine. → *2370 deckle (1)/deckle strap*

2372 **doctor blade (2)** The flexible blade used to keep cylinders clean during papermaking.

2373 **embossing cylinder** A roller on a papermaking machine that has an etched or milled surface texture that is used to produce embossed finish paper. → *2267 embossed finish*

2374 **embossing plate** An intaglio plate with a surface texture that is used to emboss a sheet of paper. → *2267 embossed finish*

2375 **engine-sized** A process of sizing paper to make it more impervious to ink and moisture. A rosin or starch is added to the pulp during the papermaking process. → *2322 rosin*

2376 **eucalyptus fiber** A papermaking ingredient taken from the eucalyptus tree. It has largely replaced esparto (a type of grass). → *2501 esparto*

2377 **felting** On a moving wire of a fourdrinier, the process of binding the fibers of pulp together.

2378 **felts** The material, usually cotton or coarse woven wool, that is used to couch wet waterleaf paper (unsized paper). → *2367 couch; 2411 waterleaf*

2379 **fiber** The raw material (usually wood) used for making the pulp for paper.

2380 **fiber cut** A defect that occurs during the papermaking process, when a bundle of fibers catches as it travels through the calender, resulting in a short, straight slice in the web.

2381 **fiber puffing** The degrading or roughening of the surface of a coated paper that can occur during heatset drying.

2382 **filler** A material used to improve the opacity, brightness, and printing surface of a paper. China clay, calcium carbonate, and other white mineral pigments are commonly used. Filler can also be used as an economic method of increasing bulk.

2383 **fourdrinier** A papermaking machine used to make paper in a continuous roll ("web"). Liquid pulp is drained through a moving wire, leaving a web of damp paper that is then dried on steam-heated cylinders before additional processing. → *2242 chain lines/marks; 2522 laid paper; 2369 dandy roll; 2344 web (1)*

2384 **furnish** The materials used in papermaking.

2385 **half-stuff** Wet pulp in its raw state, before any of the other ingredients necessary in the papermaking process have been added. → *2405 stuff; 2355 beating*

2386 **hemp** A fibrous plant, the products of which are used in papermaking.

2387 **kenaf** An Indian plant fiber used for making paper.

2388 **leaf (2)** A newly made sheet of paper before it is dried and finished.

2389 **loading** The action of adding a substance such as china clay during papermaking to improve or alter the characteristics of the finished product.

2390 **machine clothing** The wire, press felts, and drier felts on a papermaking machine.

2391 **machine direction** The path of paper through a papermaking machine that determines the grain of the paper. "Long grain" indicates the direction of the paper path, whereas "short grain" is at right angles to it. → *2286 grain direction*

2392 **making** One entire batch of machine-made paper ("a making").

2393 **mechanical (wood) pulp** Untreated paper pulp used for low-quality papers such as newsprint. Also called **groundwood**. → *2364 chemical pulp; 2553 woodfree paper*

2394 **mold/mould** The wire cloth and frame on which pulp is formed into sheets of paper.

2395 **optical bleaching agents (OBA)** An additive to pulp that makes paper look whiter under particular lighting conditions. Despite the name, bleaching agents are not used. The paper reflects more light by absorbing invisible ultraviolet light, which is then re-emitted as visible light.

2396 **pope roll** In the papermaking process, a roller on which the dry paper is reeled. → *2344 web (1); 2369 dandy roll; 2383 fourdrinier; 2263 dinky*

2397 **pulp** The wet, raw material used for making paper, usually created from pounded plant fibers, especially wood, cotton, and linen. ➜ *2393 mechanical (wood) pulp; 2364 chemical pulp*

2398 **pulpwood** Wood and its various forms of offcut that have been ground or shredded prior to making pulp for papermaking. ➜ *2397 pulp*

2399 **retting** The soaking of paper fibers in water to partially disintegrate them.

2400 **ribbed paper** An unusual type of woven paper with a ribbed effect produced by pressing before the web is dry. Also known as **repped paper**.

2401 **sheeter** A machine that cuts paper from a roll into sheets.

2402 **size** A gluelike substance that is applied to paper or used in its manufacture to alter qualities such as absorbency.

2403 **slice** A long, flat, vertical plate, over which pulp is passed during the paper-manufacturing process.

2404 **slushing** The action of liquidizing or pulping the ingredients in the paper-manufacturing process.

2405 **stuff** The pulp that is poured onto the wire of a fourdrinier machine. Also called **slurry** or **stock**. ➜ *2385 half-stuff; 2383 fourdrinier*

2406 **super-calender** Machine consisting of a series of heated metal rollers through which paper is passed to give it a high-gloss finish. ➜ *2360 calender*

2407 **super-calendered paper** Paper that has been through a series of heated metal rollers, called a super-calender, to give it an extra-smooth finish. ➜ *2406 super-calender*

2408 **surface sizing** The application of size to paper during the manufacturing process. Both sides of the paper are treated at the "waterleaf" stage when the sheet or web has been formed. The size is applied to the paper in a size press. ➜ *2411 waterleaf*

2409 **vat paper** Handmade paper.

2410 **water finish** Dampened paper that is given a high finish by passing it through heated rollers. Used for making imitation art paper. ➜ *2462 art paper; 2573 imitation art (paper)*

2411 **waterleaf** Semiabsorbent paper that requires sizing before use. ➜ *2408 surface sizing*

2412 **wire** A wire (or nylon) mesh typically 30 to 100 squares per inch (12 to 40 squares per cm), used as the molding unit in a papermaking machine.

2413 **wood pulp** The raw material used in papermaking. Pulp is classified as being either mechanically or chemically produced.

2414 **antiquarian** The largest known size of handmade paper, introduced by James Whatman in the 18th century, and measuring 53 × 31 inches (1350 × 790mm). ➜ *2442 paper sizes*

2415 **atlas folio** The largest folio paper size, measuring 17 × 26 inches (432 × 660mm). ➜ *3823 folio (2); 2442 paper sizes*

2416 **basic size** The standard size of a particular paper, against which other sizes are measured. For example, the basic size of cover papers is 20 × 26 inches (508 × 660cm). ➜ *2417 basic weight/basis weight; 2442 paper sizes*

2417 **basic weight/basis weight** The weight, in pounds, of a ream of paper (500 sheets) cut to a designated size (basic size). → *2442 paper sizes; 2416 basic size*

2418 **bastard** (**2**) Generally, any nonstandard size of paper. Also, specifically, an obsolete paper size of 33 × 20 inches (838 × 508cm). → *2442 paper sizes; 2416 basic size*

2419 **bulk** (**2**) The thickness of a given number of sheets of paper when put under a particular amount of pressure. Bulk can also refer to the thickness of a sheet of paper in relation to its weight.

2420 **bulk factor** The number of sheets of paper that make up a thickness of one inch.

2421 **bundle** (**2**) Two reams of paper, or 1,000 sheets. → *2452 ream*

2422 **caliper** (**1**) A description of the thickness of paper or board, expressed as thousandths of an inch ("mils") or millionths of a meter ("microns"). → *2470 board (1); 2423 caliper (2)*

2423 **caliper** (**2**) An instrument used for measuring paper thickness. → *2422 caliper (1)*

2424 **cwt** *abb.:* **hundredweight** In the U.S. this is a measure of weight of 100 pounds (45.4kg; technically called a "short" hundredweight), and is sometimes used when specifying the cost of paper; in Britain, it is 112 pounds (50.8kg; a long hundredweight). A "metric" hundredweight is 50kg (110 pounds).

2425 **density** (**3**) The weight to volume ratio of paper.

2426 **elephant folio** A traditional book size, approximately 14 × 23 inches (335 × 584mm).

2427 **equivalent weight** Papers of the same weight per unit of measurement — gsm (grams per square meter) — regardless of their sheet size. → *2443 paper substance*

2428 **foolscap** A former standard size of printing paper measuring 13½ × 17 inches (343 × 432mm).

2429 **grams per square meter** (**g/m²**, **gsm**) A unit of measurement used in the specification of paper, indicating its substance based on weight, regardless of the sheet size.

2430 **imperial** A size of printing and drawing paper in the UK that measures 22 × 30 inches (559 × 762mm).

2431 **insides** The 450 sheets (18 "quires") sandwiched between two outer quires ("outsides") in a ream of paper (500 sheets). → *2452 ream; 2450 quire (1); 2304 outsides*

2432 **ISO A-series paper sizes** The "A" series system of defining paper sizes was first adopted in Germany in 1922, where it is still referred to as "DIN-A." The sizes were calculated in such a way that each is a division into two equal parts of the size immediately above, and, because each uses the same diagonal, the proportions are geometrically identical. The basic size (A0) is one square meter in area — 33.11 × 46.81 inches (841 × 1189 mm). "A"-series sizes refer to the trimmed sheets, whereas untrimmed sizes are known as "RA" or, for printing work with bleeds, "SRA." "B" sizes are used when intermediate sizes are required between any two adjacent A-sizes, while "C" sizes refer to envelopes. More than twenty-six countries

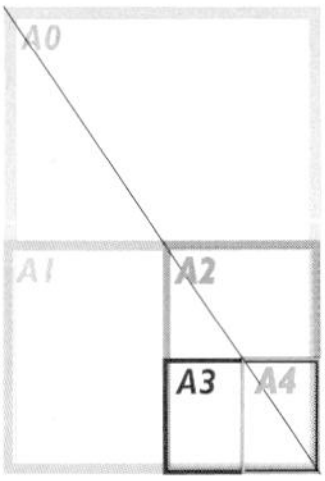

2432 ISO "A"-series paper sizes in which each size is exactly half and in proportion to the next size up, starting at A0, which equals one square meter

	mm		inches	
4A0	1682 × 2387		66¼ × 93⅞
2A0	1189 × 1682		46¾ × 66¼
A0	841 × 1189		33⅛ × 46⅞
A1	594 × 841		23⅜ × 33⅛
A2	420 × 594		16½ × 23⅜
A3	297 × 420		11¾ × 16½
A4	210 × 297		8¼ × 11¾
A5	148 × 210		5⅞ × 8¼
A6	105 × 148		4⅛ × 5⅞
A7	74 × 105		2⅞ × 4⅛
A8	52 × 74		2 × 2⅞
A9	37 × 52		1½ × 2
A10	26 × 37		1 × 1½

	mm		inches	
Envelopes				
C3	324 × 458		12¾ × 18
C4	229 × 324		9 × 12¾
C5	162 × 229		6⅜ × 9
C6	114 × 162		4½ × 6⅜
DL	110 × 220		4¼ × 8¾
C7/6	81 × 162		3¼ × 6⅜
C7	81 × 114		3¼ × 4½
B4	250 × 353		9⅞ × 12¾
B5	176 × 250		7 × 9⅞
B6/C4	125 × 324		5 × 12¾
B6	125 × 176		5 × 7

*2432 ISO "A"-series paper sizes (**left**), with envelope sizes (**right**). The "C" series of envelope sizes are designed to accommodate a flat sheet of the corresponding "A" series paper size or, folded, the next size up. For example, a C4 envelope will take an A4 sheet flat or an A3 sheet, folded once.*

have now officially adopted the ISO system, and it is likely that this system will gradually replace the wide range of paper sizes still used in the United States and some other countries.

2433 legal An American size of paper measuring 8½ × 14 inches (215.9 × 355.6 mm).

2434 letter A standard size of American paper measuring 8½ × 11 inches (215.9 × 279.4mm).

2435 M weight The weight of 1,000 sheets of a given paper size, "m" being an abbreviation of the Latin *mille,* meaning one thousand.

2436 medium (**2**) Formerly, the size of a standard printing sheet: 18 × 23 inches (457 × 584 mm).

2437 mill ream A bulk quantity of 472 sheets of handmade or moldmade paper, made up of 18 × 24 sheets ("inside quires") and 2 × 20 sheets ("outside quires"). → *2452 ream; 2447 printer's ream; 2454 short ream*

2438 octavo A sheet of paper folded in half three times, to make eight or sixteen pages. It also refers to a standard "broadside" divided into eight parts. → *2580 broadside/broadsheet*

2439 odd A papermaker's term for paper that does not conform to regular or standard sizes, finishes, and so on.

2440 oversize (**3**) A size of paper cut larger than the basic size.

2441 paper basis weight The weight of a ream of paper (500 sheets) cut to a given standard size. → *2444 paper weight*

2442 paper sizes Although the United States uses its own system of defining paper sizes, many countries of the world have now adopted the "ISO" system, which is likely gradually to replace the wide range of paper sizes still used in America and some other countries. Unlike the metricated ISO series of paper sizes, the American and former British systems refer to the untrimmed sheet size. → *2432 ISO A-series paper sizes; 3243 book sizes*

2443 paper substance The measure of paper by weight alone ("substance") rather than by weight related to a given size or number of sheets. Thus in many parts of the world paper substance is expressed in grams per square meter (gsm) — a basis that does not change whatever the size or number of sheets — rather than, for example, pounds per ream of 500 sheets of a certain size, which makes it difficult to assess actual substance. **→ 2427** *equivalent weight;* **2444** *paper weight*

2444 **paper weight** The actual weight of a paper measured either in pounds per ream of 500 sheets or in grams per square meter (gsm, g/m2). However, paper weight is not necessarily an indication of substance. Alternatively, the thickness of the paper or board is measured in microns (one micron = one-millionth of a meter). **→ 2443** *paper substance;* **2441** *paper basis weight*

2445 **ply** The measure of the thickness of board stock.

2446 **ply thickness** The number of layers in a sheet of paperboard.

2447 **printer's ream** 516 sheets — 16 more than the standard ream of 500 sheets (20 quires) to accommodate printers "overs." Also called a **publisher's ream**. **→ 2661** *overs*

2448 **quad** (**1**) A traditional term used as a prefix to a sheet size. It denotes a current sheet that is four times the area of the original. For example, a demy sheet was $17\frac{1}{2} \times 22\frac{1}{2}$ inches ($393\frac{3}{4}$sq. inches); (444×571 mm / $25,387$mm²) while a quad demy was 35×45 inches (1575 sq. inches); (889×1143mm / $101,613$ mm²).

2449 **quarto/4to** A page size obtained by folding a sheet of paper in half twice, making quarters, or eight pages. The original size of the sheet is usually prefixed, as in "Crown 4to," thus defining the final size. When a paper size is not stated, the final size can be assumed to be about $9\frac{1}{2} \times 12$ inches (241×304 mm).

2450 **quire** (**1**) 25 sheets of paper (formerly 24 sheets plus one "outside").

2451 **RA paper sizes** The designation of untrimmed paper sizes in the ISO series of paper sizes. **→ 2432** *ISO A-series paper sizes*

2452 **ream** A standard quantity of paper, usually 500 sheets, although in some circumstances an extra number may be allowed for wastage, such as in a "printer's ream," which is 516 sheets. **→ 2447** *printer's ream*

2453 **sexto/6to** A sheet either cut or folded to one-sixth its original size.

2454 **short ream** 480 sheets of paper.

2455 **SRA paper sizes** The designation of untrimmed paper sizes for bled printing work in the ISO series of paper sizes. **→ 2432** *ISO A-series paper sizes*

2456 **stock sizes** Readily available sizes of printing paper.

2457 **thirty-twomo/32mo** A sheet cut or folded to one thirty-secondth of its basic size.

2458 **twelvemo/12mo** A sheet folded or cut to one-twelfth its basic size.

2459 **album paper** Antique finish paper made from wood pulp, used mainly for the pages of photograph albums.

2460 **antique paper** Generally, any rough-surfaced paper, but originally used to describe laid paper that had been made in molds where the chain wires were attached directly to the supports of the mold, giving the paper a rough finish. Antique wove is a light but bulky rough-surfaced paper of a good quality.

2461 **archival paper** Special acid-free paper used for printing volumes intended for long-lasting storage. ➜ *2966 archival printing*

2462 **art paper** A high-quality paper with a smooth surface. Originally, the surface was achieved by applying china clay to a base paper, but it is now more common for art papers to be coated by other processes, such as "blade coaters." Art paper can be gloss or matte. ➜ *2356 blade coater; 2486 coated paper*

2463 **art vellum** A strong, imitation animal parchment paper used for bindings and certificates. ➜ *2551 vellum; 2540 parchment*

2464 **azure** In papermaking, the term describing paler shades of blue paper.

2465 **bank paper** A thin, uncoated writing or typing paper typically between 45 and 63gsm. Similar papers in heavier weights are called "bonds," while lighter weights are "manifolds." ➜ *2472 bond paper*

2466 **baryta paper** A very smooth paper traditionally used for making reproduction-quality proofs from metal type.

2467 **beveled boards** Strong, bevel-edged boards used mainly for binding large volumes. ➜ *2471 boards; 3082 binding*

2468 **bible paper** Very thin paper that is both tough and opaque and is generally used for printing Bibles and prayer books. Also called **India paper**.

2469 **blank** (**I**) Thick cardboard or other substrate used specifically for making posters and advertising displays.

2470 **board** (**I**) An imprecise term generally used to describe any heavy or thick paper or other paper-based substance. In the United States this usually means anything thicker than 6mil (0.006 inch), while in the UK it is defined for customs and duty purposes as being any paper exceeding 220gsm in weight. ➜ *2471 boards; 2422 caliper (1); 2537 paperboard*

2471 **boards** A general term used to describe substances such as millboards and strawboards used for casing books, and also to describe certain types of printing card such as ivory and Bristol boards. ➜ *2470 board (1); 3090 case (1)*

2472 **bond paper** A standard grade of strong, durable, and smooth writing paper, generally used for stationery printing. ➜ *2465 bank paper*

2473 **book paper** A generic term for any paper suitable for book printing.

2474 **bright enamel** Paper with a highly polished coating, usually on one side only.

2475 **bristol board** A fine, laminated cardboard with a smooth surface, used for both printing and drawing. So called because it is thought to have been originally made in Bristol, England. ➜ *2471 boards*

2476 **brush-coated paper** A highly opaque, stable — but expensive — coated paper. ➜ *2486 coated paper*

2477 **calendered paper** Paper that has been finished in a calender, giving it a smoothness or gloss described as a "machine finish," which, in turn, can be described as "low" or "high" depending on the degree of gloss. ➜ *2360 calender; 2525 machine finish*

2478 **cameo** (**2**) A type of coated paper with a dull finish, suitable for printing halftones or engravings. ➜ *2530 matte art; 2486 coated paper; 2040 halftone (1)*

2479 **carbonless paper** A chemically coated paper that produces duplicate copies of handwritten or typed documents onto another sheet without the use of carbon paper. Also called **"NCR" paper**, representing either the company that developed it, National Cash Register Corp., or alternatively "no carbon required."

2480 **cartridge paper** A strong, general purpose, white paper that, when uncoated, may be used for drawing on or making into envelopes. Coated cartridge paper is commonly used as an all-around paper in offset printing. → *2962 web offset; 2946 offset litho(graphy)*

2481 **cast-coated paper** A high-quality coated art paper with an exceptionally glossy finish, giving it an enamel appearance. → *2486 coated paper*

2482 **cellophane** Transparent cellulose acetate film that is both very thin and very flexible. → *4168 cel (1)*

2483 **chart paper** A strong, good-quality paper suitable for printing maps.

2484 **chipboard** Thin, cheap board made from recycled paper and used for edition-binding cases. → *3090 case (1)*

2485 **chromo paper** A smooth paper, more heavily coated than art paper — usually only on one side — and which can be dull or glazed. Also called **chrome coated paper**. → *2462 art paper; 2486 coated paper; 2474 bright enamel*

2486 **coated paper** A general term describing papers that have had a mineral coating applied to the surface — after the body paper was made, such as art, chromo, and enamel papers. Coated paper is also known as **surface paper**. → *2366 coating slip; 2462 art paper; 2485 chromo paper; 2356 blade coater; 2474 bright enamel*

2487 **colored printings** Low-grade (and thus cheap) paper, used primarily for covering low-cost publications.

2488 **corrugated board** A paper board with a fluted surface.

2489 **cover board** The material resulting from pasting together two or more pieces of cover paper, and used to cover books. → *2490 cover paper; 3098 cover*

2490 **cover paper** Strong, thick paper used to cover booklets and pamphlets. → *3098 cover*

2491 **detail/layout paper** Thin, translucent paper with a hard surface used for layouts and "comps" (rough drawings). → *4018 comprehensive*

2492 **diploma paper** A high-quality paper specifically made for printing official documents, certificates, and so on.

2493 **display board** A heavy, coated, colored board with a dull finish.

2494 **double-coated paper** Paper that is coated on both sides. → *2486 coated paper*

2495 **double-thick cover stock** Two sheets of thick paper stock laminated together.

2496 **dull seal** Paper with an adhesive backing.

2497 **duplex board/paper** Two sheets of paper or board of different qualities or colors that have been brought together and combined, usually by lamination, but sometimes while the paper is still in the wet state on the papermaking machine. → *3594 duplex; 2337 twin-wire paper*

2498 **dutch paper** Any deckle-edged paper manufactured in the Netherlands. → *2259 deckle edge*

2499 **eggshell finish** A smooth — but not glossy — surface on particular types of coated paper and board.

2500 **English finish** A book paper that has been "super-calendered" to achieve a very smooth finish.

2501 **esparto** A paper made from a variety of soft-fibered long grass (esparto) found in Spain and North Africa.

2502 **Fabriano** A handmade paper named after the home of Italy's earliest papermill (13th century).

2503 **fashion board** Board lined with cartridge, used for preparing artwork.

2504 **featherweight paper** A type of paper with a rough surface but tremendous bulk. One hundred sheets of 100gsm provide a bulk of 23mm (just under 1 inch).

2505 **french folio** A type of smooth, thin paper used for press make-ready.

2506 **french shell** A type of marbled paper used in 18th-century France. → *2529 marbling*

2507 **glassine** A semitransparent glossy paper, used to protect photographic negatives, and occasionally for book dust jackets.

2508 **granite finish** A type of paper manufactured from multicolored fibers, giving a grained finish resembling granite.

2509 **handmade paper** Fine-quality, grain-free paper used for fine-art prints, limited edition printing, and so on.

2510 **high mill finish** A paper finish achieved by calendering, with a surface midway between "machine-finished" (MF) and "super-calendered." → *2406 super-calender; 2525 machine finish*

2511 **hot-pressed** (**H.P.**) A type of fine paper with a surface that has been given a glazed finish by the use of hot metal plates.

2512 **hot-rolled** Paper that has been glazed by steam-heated calenders. → *2360 calender*

2513 **imitation art** (**paper**) A type of glazed, super-calendered, coated paper. Also called **machine coated**. → *2410 water finish; 2406 super-calender*

2514 **imitation cloth** A book-covering material, actually made from paper, cloth, or similar substances, finished and embossed to resemble real cloth.

2515 **imitation leather** A book-covering material, actually made from paper, cloth, or similar substances, finished and embossed to resemble real leather.

2516 **imitation parchment** A strong, semitransparent paper that is reasonably resistant to grease and water.

2517 **index board** A card, usually in a range of colors, used typically to separate sections in a mechanically bound book or in an index guide. → *3154 mechanical binding; 3604 index guide*

2518 **ivory board** High-grade board made of one or more laminations of identical quality sheets, with characteristic features of translucency and rigidity. → *2470 board (1)*

2519 **Japanese vellum** A thick paper, handmade in Japan, with an ivory color and smooth surface that becomes furry with excessive handling.

2520 **jute board** A strong, light, and durable board used particularly in binding.

2521 **kraft** (**paper**) Strong brown paper made from sulfate wood pulp, used mostly for packaging.

2522 **laid paper** Paper made with subtle parallel lines in its surface instead of the smooth surface of wove paper. The laid finish is impressed by a dandy roll on a fourdrinier machine. ➜ *2242 chain lines/marks; 2369 dandy roll; 2383 fourdrinier*

2523 **leatherette** A simulation of real leather made from a strong, embossed "machine glazed" (MG) paper.

2524 **lightweight paper** An imprecise grouping of thin, tough papers of a substance of around 20 to 50gsm (or less than 80gsm for coated papers), or 17 to 40 pounds per 25–38 inch ream.

2525 **machine finish** (**MF**) Paper with a smooth, although not glossy surface, made by passing it through heavy polished rollers ("calenders"). MF paper is suitable for printing text and line illustrations, but does not reproduce fine halftones well. Also called **mill-finished**. ➜ *2526 machine glazed*

2526 **machine glazed** (**MG**) Paper with a highly polished surface on one side and a rough surface on the other. ➜ *2525 machine finish*

2527 **machine-made paper** Paper made as a continuous web on cylinder or fourdrinier machines. ➜ *2383 fourdrinier*

2528 **manila** A very strong paper usually made from vegetable fiber such as hemp or jute, the term deriving from fibers grown in the Philippines.

2529 **marbling** A traditional method of decorating paper by floating colors on the surface of a gum solution. The color adheres to the sheet, producing interesting random patterns. Marbled papers were used traditionally for book endpapers.

2530 **matte art** A coated paper with a dull finish. Also called **cameo coated paper**. ➜ *2478 cameo (2)*

2531 **mounting board** A heavy board used for mounting artwork or photographs.

2532 **newsprint** An unsized — and thus absorbent — paper made from mechanical pulp and used for printing newspapers. ➜ *2393 mechanical (wood) pulp*

2533 **not** A term meaning "not glazed," used to describe unglazed "rag" papers that are midway between a hot pressed and a rough finish. ➜ *2316 rag paper/pulp*

2534 **offset cartridge** A good-quality, smooth paper suited to offset litho printing.

2535 **onionskin** A very lightweight, semitranslucent paper with a cockle finish.

2536 **opaline** Semiopaque paper with a glazed finish.

2537 **paperboard** The heaviest weights of paper. Also called **cardboard**. ➜ *2470 board (1)*

2538 papeterie A type of heavy, uncoated paper with a range of smooth or embossed finishes.

2539 papyrus A form of writing material used by early Egyptians and made from the giant papyrus rush found around the River Nile. Papyrus was the origin of the word "paper" (via the Anglo-French *papir*).

2540 parchment An early form of fine, translucent writing material made from the skin of a goat or sheep that is prepared by first scraping and then dressing it with pumice or lime. Today, parchment generally comes as a paper simulation called "artificial parchment."

2541 poster board Cardboard with a 24pt caliper thickness, in standard sheet sizes of 22 x 28 inches (559 x 711mm) and 28 x 44 inches (711 x 1118mm).

2542 proofing chromo A superior coated paper used for proofing.

2543 pulp board A board manufactured from pulp as a single homogenous sheet on a fourdrinier or cylinder machine.

2544 safety paper Chemically treated paper with special properties that make it easier to distinguish it from forgeries, used especially for checks and legal documents.

2545 satin finish Paper with a smooth finish and a satin sheen.

2546 satin white White paper with a smooth finish and slight sheen. → *2365 china clay; 2545 satin finish*

2547 silurian A paper into which small amounts of colored fibers have been incorporated, giving a flecked effect.

2548 strawboards Boards traditionally made from straw (now more commonly from pulped waste paper) used to make covers of cased books. Cheaper than millboard, which is the preferred choice of handbinders. → *3398 millboards*

2549 strongfold paper Strong paper coated with a surface that will not crack when folded.

2550 vegetable parchment A type of greaseproof paper. During manufacture, sulfuric acid is used to fuse the fibers together.

2551 vellum A fine-grained paper originally made from unsplit calfskin and used in bookbinding.

2552 wedding paper A low-glare paper with a very smooth surface.

2553 woodfree paper Paper made without mechanical wood pulp. Also called **groundwood free** or **pure**. → *2364 chemical pulp; 2393 mechanical (wood) pulp*

2554 wove paper Paper with a smooth, fine "woven" finish, as distinct from the lined pattern of "laid" papers. → *2522 laid paper*

2555 **absorbency/absorption** The property of a paper or other material to absorb liquids such as ink. In printing, absorption is not only determined by the fiber structure of the paper, but also the constituency of ink and the pressure of the printing plates. Incorrect absorption can lead to printing problems such as strike through and drying failure. ➔ *2833 strike through (1)*

2556 **aerate** The separation of sheets of paper, prior to printing, either by blowing air or by "riffling" manually.

2557 **antisetoff/anti-set-off sprayer** A device attached to a printing press that sprays a film of resinous solution or powder onto the printed paper as it leaves the press, thus preventing setoff by keeping the sheets separate. ➔ *3066 setoff*

2558 **apron** White space added to the margins of the text area on a page to accommodate a foldout.

2559 **back printing** Printing on the underside of a translucent material. Also called **reverse printing**. As distinct from backing up.

2560 **back step collation** The collation of printed signatures by reference to printed marks on the back fold of each section. ➔ *2561 back(step) mark; 2716 signature (1); 3252 collate*

2561 **back(step) mark** A black mark printed on a sheet to show where the final fold will be. If the sheet forms a volume made out of several signatures, each back(step) mark is placed in a slightly different position, so when all the signatures are collated the marks form a stepped sequence that indicates whether the signatures are in the correct order or if any are missing. Also called a **collating mark**. ➔ *3252 collate; 2716 signature; 2560 back(step) collation*

2562 **back up/backing up** (**2**) The printing of the reverse side of a printed sheet. After backing up the sheet is described as "backed." Also called **perfecting**. ➔ *2566 backup registration; 2564 backed (1); 2565 backs (2)*

2563 **back-to-back** Printing on both sides of a sheet. ➔ *2562 back up/backing up (2)*

2564 **backed** (**1**) A sheet that has had its reverse side printed. ➔ *2562 back up/backing up (2); 2565 backs (2)*

2565 **backs** (**2**) Printed sheets to be printed (backed up) on the reverse side. The term also describes the printing plates to be used in backing up. ➔ *2562 back up/backing up (2); 2564 backed (1)*

2566 **backup registration** The correct registration of a printed sheet relative to the printing on the other side. ➔ *2562 back up/backing up (2)*

2567 **bastard** (**1**) Any aberration or abnormal element in the printing process.

2568 **bevel** (**2**) The outer edge of a printing plate that is used to secure the plate to the press.

2569 **bicycling** The duplication and transportation of materials, such as film or artwork, to another printer to enable simultaneous production of a job.

2570 **black printer** (**1**) The printing plate that prints black ink in four-color process printing. Also called the **"key" plate**.

2571 **blank** (**2**) An unprinted sheet or page.

2572 **bled-off** The areas of an illustration, (or any other matter) printed beyond the edges of the page trim. ➔ *2573 bleed (1); 2611 full bleed*

2573 Bleed
a *printed page before trimming*
b *trimmed page*

2579 Broadside page

2573 bleed (**l**) The margin outside the trimmed area of a sheet that allows for tints, images, or other matter to print beyond the edge of a page. If sheets are printed without bleed, it is generally not possible to print matter up to the edge of the page. → *2572 bled-off*

2574 blind folio Page number used for reference or identification, but not printed on the page. Also called **expressed folio**. → *3822 folio (l)*

2575 blind image An image that has printed badly — or not at all — because of excess moisture or other defects on the plate ("blinding"). → *2910 blinding*

2576 book proof Imposed page proofs, folded and trimmed, but usually not stitched or bound, and assembled in book form. → *2191 imposition*

2577 bottom printing Printing on the underside of translucent film or paper so the design reads through the top.

2578 bring up To place or pack material under a printing surface to raise it to the correct height for making an impression onto paper.

2579 broadside page A page in which the matter has been rotated 90 degrees to print sideways.

2580 broadside/broadsheet Originally, broadsides, or "broadsheets," were sheets of paper printed on one side only and used for official notices. Today, however, the term is used to describe a variety of large-sheet jobs, which may be printed on one or both sides. Consequently, broadsheet is often used to describe a large-format newspaper, as distinct from the smaller tabloid size. → *3998 tabloid*

2581 broken images The printing effect that results from damaged or worn plates.

2582 bulldog A newspaper printer's colloquial term for the first edition of the day.

2583 cancel (**l**) A printed leaf of a publication that, containing errors, is cut out and removed from its section and replaced by another, appropriately amended. → *3337 section (2)*

2584 cancel-title A replacement title page, often showing a change of imprint, such as when a work printed for publication in one country is subsequently prepared for publication in another.

2585 carbon tissue A semiopaque, gelatin-coated paper, which, when made light-sensitive by treating with alkali dichromate, is used for various methods of photographic reproduction, such as conventional gravure printing and screen printing processes. → *2868 gravure; 3046 screen printing; 1412 carbon print*

2586 centerfold/spread Facing pages in the center of a section. Center spreads are also called **naturals**. → *3940 double(page) spread; 3337 section (2)*

2587 come-and-go/coming and going An imposition scheme in which the top, or head, of the first page is laid to the top of the last page, and so on throughout the section. The signatures are then doubled up with the last head-to-head with the first, finally being separated at trimming stage. Frequently used in paperback book printing, this method allows two copies to be printed from one set of plates → *2191 imposition; 2716 signature (l)*

2588 commercial register The degree of tolerance in the register of the inks in four-color process printing, usually as defined by the customer. → *2696 register*

2589 compound printing Printing two or more colors in a single pass. To do so different areas of the forme (in letterpress printing) or different sections of the inking system (in offset printing) are separately inked. → *3013 forme; 2689 printing processes*

2590 computer-to-plate (**CTP**) The process of making printing plates directly from digital data, without the need for film. Also known as **direct to plate**.

2591 continuous feeder On an automatic sheetfed printing press, the mechanism that supplies the sheets of paper — and that can be replenished — without interrupting the printing process. → *2714 sheetfed*

2592 contouring A defect in a printed image in which varying tones are distinguished by visible steps rather than gradually.

2593 cylinder Any roller or drum used on a papermaking machine or rotary printing press. → *2705 rotary press*

2594 decal A design, printed on special paper, that can be transferred onto another surface by applying pressure ("duplex decal"; "adhesive decal"), or heat and pressure ("heat-release decal"), or by soaking it in water so it slides off the paper ("simplex decal"). → *2497 duplex paper; 4170 dry transfer lettering*

2595 depth The difference in height between the printing and nonprinting surfaces of printing plates.

2596 designation marks Initial letters (usually corresponding to the title of the book) that were traditionally printed near the "signature" letter of each section for identification purposes prior to binding. → *2716 signature (1); 3337 section (2)*

2597 distribution/distributing roller A cylinder (or series of cylinders) on a printing press that distributes ink to the plate, smoothing it as it does so.

2598 doctor blade (**1**) A long, thin, flexible steel blade used variously to remove or apply ink or coating before or after printing. For example, a doctor blade is used in gravure printing to wipe excess ink from the surface of the printing cylinder. → *2868 gravure; 2593 cylinder*

2599 dot slur(ring) The "skidding," or elongated smudging of a halftone dot caused by excessive movement between plate and paper during printing. → *2040 halftone (1)*

2600 dot-for-dot (**1**) Printing color work in perfect register.

2601 double image A printing aberration caused by additional or duplicated halftone dots.

2602 doubling A printing aberration causing a faint duplication of a halftone image.

2603 draw (**1**) A printing aberration in which halftone dots appear larger near the tail end of a printed sheet, caused by misregister. → *2040 halftone (1)*

2604 drum (**1**) An alternative term for the cylinder of a printing press or papermaking machine. → *2593 cylinder*

2611 Full bleed
a *printed page before trimming*
b *trimmed page*

2605 dry printing Multicolor printing in which each successive ink color is allowed to dry before the next is applied.

2606 duct The reservoir in a printing press from which ink is distributed to the inking system used by the press. Also called an **ink fountain**. → *2930 fountain*

2607 dwell When an impression is made, the brief moment of time when printing surface makes contact with paper. → *2635 kiss impression*

2608 even working A work printed in any number of sections of equal size, such as 16, 32, or 48 pages.

2609 flood coating In screen printing, a coating of ink applied to the entire surface of the screen to make sure there is even distribution. → *2664 panel printing*

2610 flying paster The facility on a web press to replace one reel of paper with another without stopping the press. Also called **autopaster**. → *2344 web*

2611 full bleed A printed sheet on which an image extends to all four edges. → *2573 bleed (1)*

2612 gang up (1) To print two or more pages or jobs on the same sheet.

2613 gear marks Regular, alternating light and dark marks, appearing as bands in solids and halftones, parallel to the gripper edge of a printed sheet. Gear marks are always uniformly spaced. → *2617 gripper edge*

2614 gear streaks Unwanted, equally spaced parallel streaks on a printed sheet.

2615 ghost A printing defect whereby unwanted faint impressions of an image or text appear on printed sheets.

2616 gloss ghosting An unwanted condition that sometimes occurs during sheetfed printing, when ink from freshly printed sheets interacts with printed matter on the reverse of the sheet or on adjacent sheets, resulting in unwanted faint images. Also known as **fuming ghosting** or **chemical ghosting**.

2617 gripper edge The edge of a sheet of paper that is held by the grippers of a printing press. Also known as the **feeding edge**. The opposite of the leaf edge. → *2639 leaf edge; 2618 gripper margin*

2618 gripper margin Extra space on a sheet of paper where it is held by the grippers of a printing press that is later trimmed off. → *2617 gripper edge*

2619 gripper(s) The metal, fingerlike clamps on the impression cylinder of a printing press that hold a sheet of paper and guide it through the press. → *2617 gripper edge; 2618 gripper margin*

2620 hairline register The maximum permissible deviation (0.003 inch/ 0.08mm) between printed colors in four-color process printing.

2621 half sheet A sheet, half the size of the normal ("normal" being the size of sheet required for the job). For example, if a job constitutes 144 pages in total, printing in 32-page sheets, a half sheet will be required to complete the job (32 × 4 = 128 + 16 = 144). → *2751 work and turn*

2622 hickie/hickey A common printing defect, visible as a spot of ink surrounded by a halo, caused by a speck of dirt forcing the paper away from the printing plate. Also called a **bull's eye**. → *2771 cissing; 2910 blinding*

2623 **honing** The technique of mechanically removing parts of the image area on a printing plate.

2624 **image area** (**2**) The ink-carrying area of a printing plate. ➜ *4037 image (1)*

2625 **image twist** A crooked printed image, resulting in misregister, caused by the plate being mounted out of alignment.

2626 **imposed proof** A printed proof of imposed pages prior to the final print run. Also called a **sheet proof**.

2627 **impression** All the copies of a publication or job printed at one time.

2628 **impression cylinder** The cylinder on a rotary press that holds the paper as it is brought into contact with the type, plates, offset roller, or blanket cylinder. Also called a **back cylinder**.

2629 **ink distribution rollers** The rollers on a printing press that manage the printing ink from the ink duct until it reaches the plate in a fine, even film. Also called **inkers**.

2630 **inking system** The arrangement of ducts and rollers on a printing press that control automatic distribution and delivery of ink to a substrate. Also called the **inking mechanism**.

2631 **iph** *abb.*: **impressions per hour** The speed at which a printing press prints each sheet.

2632 **jobbing** General, nonspecialist printing, usually comprising short runs. The term originally described any printed job that could be achieved from a single sheet of paper, such as letterheads, business cards, menus, invitations, and so on. Also known as **quick printing**.

2633 **keep standing** An instruction to keep printing plates in readiness for a possible reprint.

2634 **key** (**1**) A printing plate — usually the black (traditionally called the "key plate") — that acts as a guide for positioning and registering other colors. ➜ *3524 K (1)*

2635 **kiss impression** In printing, the lightest possible pressure required to make a perfect impression, particularly important when printing on coated papers. ➜ *2607 dwell*

2636 **lap lines** A printing aberration of fine lines between images caused by two adjacent pieces of film touching each other when assembled prior to platemaking. Also called **butt lines**.

2637 **lay edges** The two edges of a sheet that are placed flush with the side and front (the "front lay edge") marks ("lay gauges") on a printing machine to make sure the sheet will be removed properly by the grippers and have uniform margins when printed.

2638 **lay sheet** (**2**) The first of many sheets passed through a press to check such things as register.

2639 **leaf edge** The edge of a paper sheet opposite the gripper edge. ➜ *2617 gripper edge*

2640 **leak(s)** The tiny gaps that may occur when adjoining colors misregister during printing.

2641 **live matter** Any matter, such as type or plates, that is waiting to be printed.

2660 Overprint
a cyan ink
b magenta ink
c cyan overprints magenta

2642 **machine proof** A final ink proof made on a press similar to the one on which it will be printed. Also called a **press proof**.

2643 **machine sheet** Any printed sheet coming off a press.

2644 **mackle** A printing fault resulting in blurring or a double impression, caused by movement of the paper while printing. → *2720 slur*

2645 **make-ready** The process of preparing a printing press before a new run, to establish register, ink density, consistent impression, and so on. → *2947 packing*

2646 **master cylinder** The cylinder of a printing press that transfers ink from reservoir to plate. → *2906 blanket cylinder*

2647 **mechanical ghosting** An aberration in printing when the density of ink film varies dramatically, caused by large areas of color consuming too much ink and not leaving enough for other areas. Also called **ink starvation ghosting**.

2648 **monk** The traditional term for an ink blot or splash on a printed sheet.

2649 **mordant** (**2**) Any fluid used to etch a printing plate. → *2177 etch*

2650 **mottle/mottling** A printing fault appearing as a random, uneven, blotchy effect, caused by too much pressure or unsuitable paper or ink.

2651 **nip** (**2**) The point of contact between cylinders on a press.

2652 **nongear streaks** Marks that appear on a printed sheet, parallel with the printing cylinder.

2653 **off-print** An article or other part of a publication printed with the main run, but produced as a separate item. Also called a **separate**. → *3889 separate*

2654 **offset** (**2**) To reproduce a book by photographing a previously printed edition.

2655 **OK press/sheet** Authorization that a job has had all corrections made and is ready for press. Also known as **pass for press**.

2656 **one-up** A single printing of a single signature or image on a press sheet. → *2737 two-up*

2657 **overexpose/overexposure** (**2**) A fault in platemaking caused when the light source is too close or too bright.

2658 **overlaying** A method of varying the pressure of a printing plate on a press by adding pieces of paper to the tympan, thereby darkening or lightening the impression. → *2645 make-ready*

2659 **overprint** (**1**) To make a second printing or "pass" on a previously printed sheet. Also called **surprinting**.

2660 **overprint** (**2**) To print two or more colors so they overlap, either to produce more colors or to avoid registration problems. The opposite of "knockout." → *2193 lap*

2661 **overs** A number of copies of a publication printed beyond the number ordered. This is usually deliberate to allow for copies that may be spoiled during finishing or lost or damaged during shipping. → *2447 printer's ream; 3064 run on (1)*

2662 **pages to view** A reference to the number of pages that will be visible on one side of a sheet that will be printed on both sides.

2663 panel The part of a printed page or sheet defined by folds.

2664 panel printing A preprinted area of flat color that will be used as a base for additional printing. → *2609 flood coating*

2665 pass One cycle of a printing surface through a printing press, whether it be a single- or four-color press. Subsequent passes may be required to achieve the desired result, for example, to add more color than was possible on the first pass.

2666 pass for press A printing job that has had all corrections approved and is thus ready for press.

2667 pass sheet A printed sheet of optimum print quality that is removed from the run so subsequent sheets can be compared with it.

2668 photomechanical (**1**) The preparation of printing plates involving photographic techniques.

2669 photoresist A coating selectively applied to a printing plate to protect it from etching chemicals.

2670 physical dot gain The increase in the size of a halftone dot caused by the spread of ink during printing. → *2016 dot gain; 2936 ink spread*

2671 pick-up A traditional printing term for the reuse of materials from a previously completed print job.

2672 picking The lifting of fibers on the surface of paper during printing, caused either by sticky ink, poor quality paper, or suction from the blanket cylinder. Also called **plucking** or **pulling**. → *2766 bonding strength (1); 2907 blanket piling; 2277 fluff*

2673 plate (**2**) A book illustration printed separately from the main body and then tipped or bound into the book, although the term is now widely used (erroneously) to describe an illustration printed in a book. → *3949 figure (2)*

2674 plate cylinder The cylinder on a printing press onto which the plate is fixed.

2675 platemaking The process of making an image on a printing plate by whatever means, but usually photomechanically transferring it from film.

2676 plugging An aberration in platemaking in which dot areas become filled in, caused by damage to the plate.

2677 premake ready The final checking of plates before they are made ready on press. → *2645 make-ready*

2678 preprint An item printed in advance of a publication, later inserted loosely into bound copies. Also called a **blow-in**. → *2707 run of press*

2679 press Any machine that transfers (prints) an impression, traditionally from a forme, block, plate, or blanket onto paper or other material.

2680 press gain The mechanical enlargement of halftone dots while printing, as distinct from the "dot gain" of the prepress photographic kind. → *2016 dot gain*

2681 press revise A proof used as the final "pass for press." Also called a **machine revise**. → *3749 proof*

2682 press run/run The total number of copies of a print job.

relief (letterpress)

planographic (litho)

intaglio (gravure)

stencil (screen)

2689 Printing processes
a *printing surface*
b *ink*
c *paper*
d *stencil*
e *screen mesh*

2696 Register
a *in register*
b *out-of-register*

2683 presswork All of the processes carried out on a printing press, from press make-ready through actual printing to finishing operations.

2684 prima The first page of a set of printer's galley proofs.

2685 print (2) The image etched, or otherwise generated, onto a printing plate.

2686 print (3) The impression made from a plate, blanket, or so on, onto paper or other material.

2687 print to paper An instruction to print as many sheets or copies as the paper supplied will permit, without specifying an exact quantity. Also called **run of paper**.

2688 printing pressure The force required to transfer an impression between any of the image-bearing surfaces of a printing press, such as plate and paper, plate and blanket, blanket and impression cylinder, impression cylinder and paper.

2689 printing processes There are four generic printing processes: intaglio (e.g., gravure), planographic (e.g., lithography), relief (e.g., letterpress), and stencil (e.g., screen printing). ➔ *2774 color printing*

2690 printing unit The unit that houses all the components required to print a single color on a multicolor press (typically, the four-unit press that prints the process colors — cyan, magenta, yellow, and black).

2691 printmaking The printing of fine art editions by a variety of processes, such as limited edition screenprints and etchings.

2692 process work The general preparation, usually by photomechanical means, of a surface for process printing. ➔ *2880 photoengraving*

2693 production press The press used for printing a job, as opposed to the one used for proofing it; it is generally impractical to use the production press for proofing.

2694 proportionality failure A problem that occurs in the value of an ink hue when the dot size of a halftone tint varies, changing the hue of the ink in relation to a solid ink color.

2695 pull (sheet) Sheets removed from the press for examination during the print run. ➔ *3749 proof*

2696 register/registration The correct positioning of color plates when printed one on top of another, or of the pages on one side of a sheet relative to the other (called "backing up"). When a color or page is incorrectly positioned, it said to be "out-of-register" or "misregistered." As distinct from "fit," which applies to the correct positioning of individual items on a sheet. ➔ *2562 backing up (2); 2182 fit (2)*

2697 register sheet A sheet used to obtain correct position and register when printing.

2698 resist The coating applied to a printing plate to protect the nonimage areas from acid corrosion.

2699 retree copy A limited edition book made from "retree" or spare sheets. It is sold "out of series" — that is, the books are unnumbered and bound as "overs."

2700 rider roller A printing press cylinder that has no motive power of its own, but rotates only when in contact with another cylinder. ➔ *2704 roller*

2701 **roll-to-roll printing** Rewinding a continuous printed web onto another roll.

2702 **roll-to-sheet** A system that cuts sheets from a roll and delivers them into a sheet-fed press. → *2401 sheeter*

2703 **roll-up** A check of the first printed sheets to emerge from a press while the plate is still being inked.

2704 **roller** A cylinder that is used to apply ink to a plate or forme. Also used on small presses to roll the ink out to the correct consistency.

2705 **rotary press** Any printing press in which the printing surface is on a rotating cylinder. Paper can be delivered to rotary presses in either sheet or web form.

2706 **rough etch** The initial etching of a descummed copper or zinc plate to reduce the dot size, ultimately giving contrast and depth to the printed image. Also known as "flat etch," although this term also applies to reducing the size of halftone dots on film. Rough etching is followed by "fine etching." → *2181 fine etch; 2034 flat etch*

2707 **run of press** Printing work carried out at the same time as the main run, rather than supplied to the printer as a preprinted item for later insertion. → *2678 preprint*

2708 **run up** The period between the start of a print run (switching the press on) and the point at which a printed sheet of acceptable quality is produced. This period normally generates a certain amount of spoiled sheets. → *2709 run-in sheets*

2709 **run-in sheets** The printed (spoil) sheets produced between the start of a print run and the point at which a printed sheet of acceptable quality is produced. → *2329 spoils; 2708 run up*

2710 **scribing** Making corrections to an image on film or plate by scratching the surface.

2711 **set and hold** An instruction to the printer to prepare matter in readiness for printing, but not to print.

2712 **setback** The distance between the front edge of a printing plate and the start of the image area. Allows for the gripper margin. → *2618 gripper margin*

2713 **sheet work** A particular printing technique that involves printing on both sides of a sheet.

2714 **sheet-fed** (**press**) A printing press into which single sheets are fed. → *2591 continuous feeder*

2715 **sheetwise** (**imposition**) The technique whereby separate plates are used to print either side of a sheet. → *2191 imposition*

2716 **signature** (**1**) A mark, usually a small capital or a numeral, placed in the tail margin at the beginning of each section of a book, which serves as a guide for finishing and binding. The term also describes the folded sheet itself. → *3254 conjugate leaves; 2596 designation marks; 3337 section (2)*

2717 **simplex** Printing, photocopying, or duplicating on one side of a sheet of paper only. → *3594 duplex*

2718 **single printing** The process of printing a sheet of paper first on one side and then the other. Also called **work and turn**. → *2751 work and turn; 2750 work and tumble; 2752 work and twist*

2719 single-color press A printing press capable of handling only one color at a time.

2720 slur In printing, the "skidding," or smudged, appearance of an image, with blurred or doubled halftone dots or characters. This fault is caused by excessive movement between plate and paper during impression.

2721 SPH *abb.:* **sheets per hour** The speed of a printing press.

2722 split-duct printing/working A printing technique involving the use of two or more colors on a normal single-color press, achieved by dividing the ink duct into sections for the different inks, and preventing mixing on the forme. Also called **split fountain**.

2723 spot color Any color used for printing that has been "custom mixed" for the job, as opposed to one of the four standard process colors.

2724 start-of-print line The trim line delineated by the trim marks closest to the gripper edge of the printing plate. ➔ *2107 corner marks*

2725 sticking Sheets of printing paper can stick together if they have been guillotined with a blunt knife or stored incorrectly. Sticking after printing is caused by ink remaining wet on the paper, especially hard surface paper.

2726 stopping out/stop out The process of covering with varnish those parts of the etching plate that do not require additional etching by acid. Also called **staging out**.

2727 suction feed A device on a printing press that uses air suction to deliver sheets to the press.

2728 tall copy A book that has been printed with larger head and foot margins than others in the same print run. ➔ *3159 narrow copy*

2729 throughput (**2**) A unit of time measured as the period elapsing between the start and finish of a particular job, expressed in units per hour or per minute, such as impressions or pages.

2730 tile/tiling (**2**) The printing of a document that is larger than the maximum-size paper the printer can accommodate. The document is printed on several pieces of paper, to be assembled by hand to form a whole image.

2731 title signature An identification, marked with a "B" or "2," on the second sheet of a book indicating that there is a preceding sheet (the "title sheet") that may be unmarked.

2732 tone compression The inevitable consequence of printing an image, resulting in a reduction of the range of tones from light to dark.

2733 top and tails A traditional printer's description of preliminary and subsidiary matter.

2734 track (**3**) The printing line from the front edge of a plate to the back. Items imposed in track will all be subject to the same inking adjustments on press.

2735 transfer paper The substrate that contains an inked impression that will become the printing form for litho printing. ➔ *3013 form (2)*

2736 two-revolution press A cylinder on a printing press that rotates twice for each impression without reinking.

2737 two-up A method of printing two copies of each page on a single sheet. They are eventually trimmed into separate entities after binding. ➔ *3118 four-up*

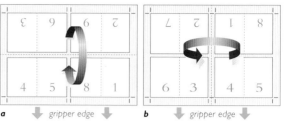

a   ⬇ *gripper edge* ⬇   b   ⬇ *gripper edge* ⬇

*2750 Work and tumble (**a**); 2751 Work and turn (**b**)*

2738 unit (2) A single part of a multicolor printing press that can itself print more than one color.

2739 universal film Color separation film that produces the same results on both litho plates and on gravure cylinders.

2740 vantage A blank page on a printed sheet.

2741 walk off Deterioration of the image on a printing plate during printing.

2742 warehouse work All nonprinting work carried out by a printer, for example, paper- and ink-handling, finishing, and dispatch.

2743 wash-out process Any printing process using photopolymer plates in which the nonimage areas of the plate are washed out after exposure, thus avoiding the need for routing.

2744 washing up Cleaning ink from the printing plate or blanket.

2745 web break The accidental breakage of a web of paper while printing on a high-speed web press. → *2344 web (1)*

2746 web (printing) press A rotary printing press that uses continuous paper from a large roll that is fed through a series of rollers (cylinders) on which the plates are mounted. The impression from the plate is offset onto a blanket before being printed onto the paper. → *2344 web (1); 2962 web offset*

2747 web-fed A press into which paper is fed continuously from a reel, as distinct from feeding individual sheets ("sheet-fed"). Also known as **reel-fed** or **roll-fed**. → *2344 web (1)*

2748 wet pick The deterioration of the surface of coated paper that can occur when it is rerun through an offset press.

2749 wipe A printing fault resulting in a blurred or double image.

2750 work and tumble A printing technique in which pages from both sides of the sheet are printed on one side using a single plate. After printing the first side the sheet is then turned, with the back edge becoming the gripper edge (hence "tumble"), and passed through the press for a second time. The technique produces two copies of each page. → *2751 work and turn; 2752 work and twist; 2718 single printing; 2617 gripper edge*

2751 work and turn A printing technique in which pages from both sides of the sheet are printed on one side using a single plate. After printing the first side the sheet is then turned over and, using the same gripper edge, passed through the press for a second time. The result is two copies of each page. Also called **half sheet work**. → *2750 work and tumble; 2752 work and twist*

2752 work and twist An imposition (layout) technique for printing both sides of the sheet using a single plate. The printing film ("flat") is first exposed on one half of the plate and then rotated ("twisted") through 180° to expose the other half. When printed this produces two copies of each page. → *2751 work and turn;* **2750** *work and tumble*

2753 work off To print a job.

2754 working Any printing job in progress.

2755 zinc plates Metal photoengraving plates used as an alternative to copper or magnesium alloy plates.

2756 additivity failure In printing, the failure of the combined value of each overprinting ink film to achieve the correct ink density, resulting in thinly printed colors.

2757 after-tack An undesirable, sticky property retained by printed ink after it should have dried (without tackiness).

2758 aluminum ink Ink containing particles of aluminum, giving the printed result a silvery property.

2759 aniline An oily liquid — deriving from a nitrobenzene base — that is used in the preparation of dyes and a volatile, quick-drying aniline ink.

2760 Aqua-trol The proprietary name (American Type Founders Company) of a device for removing moisture from the inking system of a lithographic printing press.

2761 backing (away) A printing problem that occurs as a result of an inadequate supply of ink to the fountain roller, resulting in a lighter printed image. → *2930 fountain*

2762 bad color In printing, uneven color caused either by mechanical faults, such as erratic ink distribution, or by operator faults during make-ready. → *2645 make-ready*

2763 Baumé scale A scale used to measure the density of liquids used in printing.

2764 bleed (2) An aberration that occurs when the edge of an area of printed ink spreads into an adjacent area of a different color ink.

2765 body (4) An imprecise term describing the stiffness or softness of printing ink.

2766 bonding strength (1) The ability of a printing ink to resist various faults in printing, such as "picking." → *2672 picking*

2767 breakthrough Penetration of ink through the printed paper.

2768 bronzing (1) A gold or metallic effect produced by dusting a sheet of paper, on which a special ink has been printed, with a metallic powder.

2769 bronzing (2) In four-color process printing, an undesirable "blotching" effect caused by an imbalance of ink constituents. → *2650 mottle/ mottling*

2770 chalking An aberration in printing resulting in loose, dusty ink on the surface of the paper. This is caused by rapid absorption of the ink by the paper, which consequently slows down the drying time.

2771 cissing A printing defect that occurs when wet ink (or varnish) recedes from the paper surface, leaving small uncoated areas.

2775 Color rotation
a *yellow*
b *yellow + magenta*
c *yellow + magenta + cyan*
d *yellow + magenta + cyan + black*

2772 **cold-set ink** A solid ink that, when used on a "hot press" (one that has a heated cylinder), melts into a liquid that then solidifies on contact with the paper.

2773 **color burnout** The undesirable change in the color of printing inks due to chemical reactions, either when the ink is mixed or as it dries after printing.

2774 **color printing** Strictly speaking, multicolor printing in inks other than black. However, the term is used more generally to describe any printing process that uses colored inks — including black — and this encompasses four-color process printing. The major commercial printing processes today are offset lithography (either sheet- or web-fed) and web gravure. Screen printing is also widely used, although generally for specialist work in small runs. Color letterpress printing — the oldest method — has all but died out except for very specialist work. ➔ *2689 printing processes; 2946 offset litho(graphy); 2868 gravure; 3517 four-color process*

2775 **color rotation/sequence** In process color printing, the order in which each of the colors is printed. In four-color process printing, the order is usually yellow first, followed by magenta, cyan, and finally black. This sequence is important since it minimizes the chance of getting undesirable moiré patterns on halftone images, and also because it can affect the efficacy of ink "trapping." ➔ *2061 moiré; 3496 CMYK; 2085 trapping*

2776 **crawling** An imperfection in printing that occurs when thick ink overprints wet ink.

2777 **crocking** The undesirable effect caused when printed ink smudges, or dry ink rubs off.

2778 **crystallization** The process of ink drying too quickly and repelling overprinting inks, causing poor trapping. ➔ *2085 trapping*

2779 **cure** (**2**) The process of drying ink sufficiently to prevent "setoff" (undesirable transfer of ink from the front of one sheet to the back of the next). ➔ *3066 setoff*

2780 **cut** (**4**) To dilute ink, lacquer, or varnish with solvents.

2781 **delamination** (**1**) The separation of the layers in multiple papers and boards. This is sometimes caused during printing by incorrect ink "tack" (stickiness). ➔ *2834 tack*

2782 **diarylide yellow** A pigment used in yellow process inks.

2783 **DIC Color Guide** A proprietary color system of Dainippon Ink and Chemicals used primarily for printing projects in Japan.

2784 **doctor(ing)** To alter the constituents of printing ink to improve the quality of a printed job.

2785 **double tone ink** A printing ink that produces a secondary tone as it dries, creating the illusion of two-color printing in a single pass.

2786 **drawdown** The technique of assessing the color of a printing ink by thinly spreading a small amount on a sample of the paper on which it is finally to be printed.

2787 **drum** (**2**) A roller that distributes ink on a printing press.

2788 **dry trapping** The property of a printed ink, once dry, to accept a wet overprinted ink. ➔ *2085 trapping*

2789 **dry-back** Changes in certain characteristics, such as color or density, of a printing ink after drying.

2790 **dye-based ink** Inks, the colors of which are obtained from aniline dyes, used mainly for flexographic printing and for screen printing onto textiles. In the latter, dye-based inks are sometimes called "dye pastes." → *2759 aniline; 2982 flexography*

2791 **edge acuity** The maintenance of a sharp edge on a printed image. An even ink spread encourages acuity.

2792 **filling in/up** A printing fault in which ink fills the spaces between halftone dots or the counters of type to produce undesirable small areas of solid color.

2793 **flat color** A uniform color of consistent hue. In printing, this usually means an especially mixed color that is printed apart from any other colors. → *2057 mechanical tint; 2046 halftone tint*

2794 **flying** A spray of fine ink droplets generated by the ink rollers on a press running at a high speed. Also called **ink fly**. → *2816 misting*

2795 **fugitive color** An unstable ink color that can change or fade when exposed to certain conditions of light or atmosphere.

2796 **gel** A contraction of "gelation" — the drying of printing ink by evaporation or penetration, for example.

2797 **gloss ink** Printing ink usually consisting of a varnish or synthetic resin base and drying oils. Such ink dries quickly, and does not penetrate far into the paper and is normally used on coated and low-absorbency papers.

2798 **gray balance** The appropriate levels of yellow, magenta, and cyan that produce a neutral gray.

2799 **grayness** A quality of yellow, magenta, and cyan process color inks relating to the degree of contamination. An increase in the grayness value indicates a decrease in purity or saturation.

2800 **heat-set ink** Inks designed to dry quickly to enable faster printing, based on synthetic resins and volatile petroleum oils. Immediately after printing, the web of paper is heated and then cooled to rapidly dry and harden the ink.

2801 **ink** A fluid comprising solvents and oils (called a "medium" or "vehicle") in which a finely ground "pigment" of plant dyes, minerals, or synthetic dyes is suspended to provide color. There are many different types of inks for the various printing processes. → *4138 medium (1)*

2802 **ink abrasion** The abrasive action of certain inks on printing plates, particularly over long print runs.

2803 **ink coverage** The measure of the area that a given amount of printing ink is capable of covering satisfactorily.

2804 **ink drier** A chemical agent that is added to printing inks to assist and speed the drying process.

2805 **ink penetration** The degree to which ink penetrates a substrate, more acute during the moment of impression than after it. Important if smudging or "setoff" is to be avoided. → *3066 setoff*

2806 **ink squash** During printing, the spread of ink beyond the details of an image, caused by excessive ink or pressure. → *2936 ink spread*

2807 ink strength A term describing the degree of color intensity of a printing ink.

2808 ink transfer The critical part of the printing process that determines the thickness of the ink film on the plate or blanket and thus the amount of ink transferred to the paper. → *2834 tack*

2809 ink transparency The degree to which a substrate will show through a printed ink.

2810 job inks Printing inks used for general printing, comprising 75 percent medium and 25 percent pigment.

2811 lampblack A pigment made from carbon used to make black printing ink.

2812 lift An unquantifiable measure of the total amount of ink applied to the surface of paper in multicolor printing.

2813 long ink Printing ink mixed to such a consistency it does not break when drawn out in a thread. The opposite of "short ink." → *2830 short ink*

2814 magnetic ink Ink pigments with a magnetic component, used in magnetic ink character recognition (MICR), such as that used on bank checks. → *0261 magnetic ink character recognition (MICR)*

2815 metallic ink An ink to which a metallic powder such as bronze or aluminum has been added to give the effect of gold, silver, or other precious metals.

2816 misting Mist in a pressroom formed from ink droplets suspended in the air. → *2794 flying*

2817 nonreflective ink A special ink used to print information so it can be easily read by OCR devices. → *1052 OCR*

2818 process ink gamut chart (**PIG**) A chart that compares the colors that can be obtained from a variety of ink and substrate combinations.

2819 quick-set inks A type of printing ink that usually contains thin mineral oil and thick varnish. The oil is rapidly absorbed into the paper, permitting quicker handling than with normal inks, while the varnish sets more slowly, making the surface more receptive to subsequent printings.

2820 red lake C A pigment used in printing ink.

2821 reducer (**I**) A softening agent in printing ink that also reduces its tack. → *2834 tack*

2822 resin An ingredient in ink that helps bind color pigment to the substrate. It also adds gloss and hardness to the printed ink and can provide resistance to chemicals and heat. It is also used to add hardness to the surface of litho plates.

2823 rhodamine A component of magenta process ink, with a blueish pigment, although, theoretically, magenta does not have any blue (cyan) or yellow in it.

2824 rich black A percentage of another color — usually 20 to 40 percent cyan or magenta — which is printed under solid black in color printing to produce a denser black.

2825 roller stripping The failure of ink to adhere to the inking roller.

2836 Three-color black
a 100 percent values of cyan, magenta, and yellow
b 100 percent black

2837 Three-color reproduction
a reproduction using cyan, magenta, and yellow inks only
b with black added

2826 roller train A series of inking rollers through which stiff ink travels until it reaches the correct consistency.

2827 rub-off The occurrence of dry, printed ink transferring from one printed surface to another.

2828 secondary color Color produced by overprinting two primary colors. Also called **overprint color**.

2829 shade Equivalent to hue in the description and manufacture of printing inks.

2830 short ink Printing ink that is heavily viscous and does not flow easily. The opposite of "long ink." → *2813 long ink*

2831 skeleton black A technique involving the use of black to sharpen contrast and enhance detail in four-color reproduction. Also called **half-scale black**. → *2038 full-scale black*

2832 solid An area printed with 100 percent of a color.

2833 strike through (1) A fault caused by the oily medium in printing ink soaking through the paper and causing it to become transparent.

2834 tack The degree of "stickiness" of printing ink, in other words, the degree to which it will divide ("split") between two surfaces so some prints on the substrate (without damaging it) while some remains on the printing surface. → *2781 delamination; 2840 viscosity*

2835 thickening The spreading of ink on a litho plate beyond the image areas. → *2080 spread (2); 2936 ink spread*

2836 three-color black The black that would theoretically result from overprinting solids of cyan, magenta, and yellow. In practice, however, this process often produces a dark brown.

2837 three-color (process) reproduction The now-defunct method of printing using the three process colors — cyan, magenta, and yellow — without black. The four-color process, with black used to add density, is now the norm. → *3517 four-color process*

2838 TOYO colors A system of specifying spot colors, mainly used in Japan. → *3536 PANTONE; 3562 TRUMATCH*

2839 vegetable ink An ecologically sound printing ink made from vegetable oils.

2840 viscosity The degree of resistance of a liquid to flow, expressed in "poises" — the unit of measurement of viscosity. Printing inks used for high-speed rotary presses will have a viscosity in the range of 6 to 12 poises, while a hand letterpress machine might require 500 poises.

2841 watercolor/water-based inks Water-soluble-based, rather than oil-based, inks, sometimes used for printing colors from a rubber surface.

2842 watercolor printing A printing process using water-soluble inks on porous paper that results in the blending of overlapping layers of color.

2843 wet printing process inks Quick-drying inks used in multicolor printing; the last color seals the surface.

2844 wet-on-wet printing Printing subsequent colors on a multicolor press while the previously printed colors are still wet.

2845 **wetting** The process of adding varnish to ink pigments during manufacture, enabling them to be ground more easily. This, in turn, results in improved ink distribution.

2846 **wrinkle** (**2**) Marks occurring during the drying of the ink surface of a printed page, giving an uneven appearance.

2847 **acid** A solution of perchloride of iron used to etch the image cylinders in gravure printing. ➔ *2177 etch; 2896 acid resist*

2848 **angle bar** A metal bar on a web printing press that turns paper between two units of the press. ➔ *2344 web (1)*

2849 **aquatint** An intaglio printing process that builds up even or graded tones using resin and varnish. Although once used as a commercial process, aquatints are now used only for limited-edition fine-art prints. ➔ *2872 intaglio*

2850 **as to press** In gravure-printed magazines, proofs that show the final position of images before printing. ➔ *2868 gravure*

2851 **buffing** The final polishing of a printing plate before it is etched.

2852 **burin** A tool used to engrave wood or metal.

2853 **burning in** In intaglio processes, fusing etching powder to the plate by heating it. ➔ *2872 intaglio*

2854 **burnisher** (**2**) A metal tool used for removing rough spots from printing plates.

2855 **cell** (**1**) In gravure printing, tiny recessed pits in the cylinder or plate that carry the ink. In conventional gravure printing tones are determined by the varying depth of each cell. ➔ *2868 gravure*

2856 **chuck** The core supporting a paper roll in a web-fed printing press. ➔ *2344 web (1)*

2857 **copperplate printing** An "intaglio" printing process used in short-run printing, which produces a very sharp, black image. ➔ *2872 intaglio*

2858 **Dow etch** A proprietary process for etching photoengraved plates.

2859 **dual roll stand** A structure supporting two rolls ("webs") of paper that are simultaneously fed through a press to streamline production. ➔ *2344 web (1)*

2860 **electric etching** An alternative to acid, this method uses electricity to remove the unwanted areas of a copper plate. ➔ *2177 etch*

2861 **electronic engraving machine** A method of making a line and tone printing plate without photographic processing or chemical etching. An electronically controlled stylus cuts or burns away the unwanted surface.

2862 **electroplating** A method of applying a thin metal coating to a different metal surface, for example, a gravure cylinder.

2863 **engraving** (**1**) A block or plate made from wood or metal into which a design or lettering has been cut, engraved, or etched. ➔ *2872 intaglio*

2864 **engraving** (**2**) A print taken from an engraved plate or block. ➔ *2872 intaglio*

2865 **etching** (**2**) A type of fine-art print taken from etched plates. ➔ *2177 etch*

2866 **facet edge** The impression left on a sheet of paper by the edge of a printing plate, such as an engraved plate. Also called a **plate mark**.

2867 **gelatin process** A process of duplication using gelatin to transfer an image in gravure printing.

2868 **gravure** An "intaglio" printing process in which the image areas to be printed are recessed below the nonprinting surface of the printing plate. These recesses (cells) are filled with a liquid ink — the surplus removed from the nonprinting areas by the "doctor blade" — and the paper draws the ink from the cells. ➔ *2872 intaglio*

2869 **gravure screen** A film marked with a grid of parallel horizontal and vertical lines; used for photographically defining the edges of gravure cells.

2870 **halftone gravure** A gravure printing plate in which the cylinder cells vary in surface area as well as in depth — in normal gravure printing only the depths of the cells vary. ➔ *2868 gravure*

2871 **Helio-Klischograph** A system used to engrave gravure printing cylinders, in which an image is electronically scanned and transmitted to a diamond-headed cutting tool that engraves the cells onto the cylinder. ➔ *2868 gravure*

2872 **intaglio** A printing process in which the image to be printed is recessed below the surface of the plate, such as in commercial gravure printing or fine-art etching. ➔ *2868 gravure*

2873 **Klischograph** An electronic photoengraving machine, developed in Germany, that produces plastic or metal plates.

2874 **lands** (**1**) The unetched grid on a gravure plate that forms the edges of the ink-bearing recessed cells. ➔ *2868 gravure*

2875 **line engraving** An intaglio printing process in which the design is cut into the surface of a copper plate — no acid is used. Tonal variations are achieved by cross-hatched lines.

2876 **machine engraving** The process of cutting an image into a gravure printing cylinder with mechanized engraving tools.

2877 **mezzotint** A traditional intaglio engraving process for reproducing tones rather than lines. ➔ *2872 intaglio; 2059 mezzograph*

2878 **offset gravure** A method of gravure printing that uses a rubber-coated blanket to transfer the inked image from plate to paper. ➔ *2868 gravure*

2879 **paster** (**2**) An automatic splicer on a web press.

2880 **photoengraving** The method of engraving or etching printing plates using a photomechanical transfer of the image. ➔ *2675 platemaking*

2881 **photogravure** The photomechanical preparation of plates for use in intaglio printing processes. ➔ *2872 intaglio; 2868 gravure*

2882 **powderless etching** A method of etching metal plates in which an agent in the acid protects the edges of the dots while etching the metal, resulting in a very clean etch. ➔ *2177 etch*

2883 **process block** A plate made by "photoengraving." ➔ *2880 photo-engraving; 2872 intaglio; 2881 photogravure*

2884 **recess printing** An intaglio printing process in which the ink is held in recesses in the plate or cylinder, such as photogravure. ➔ *2872 intaglio; 2881 photogravure*

2885 retroussage A technique used to soften the image and improve the dark tones when printing from an intaglio plate. A fine cheesecloth rag is passed or flicked over the surface, drawing ink from the recesses and onto the surrounding areas.

2886 reversing A term used in photoengraving to describe a change from black to white or from left to right.

2887 rotogravure A rotary press that uses intaglio gravure cylinders to produce an impression, rather than litho plates or cast letterpress stereos. → *2872 intaglio;* *2686 gravure;* *2937 lithography;* *2705 rotary press*

2888 scan plates Any plates made on an electronic engraving machine. → *2863 engraving*

2889 steel engraving A print made from an engraved steel plate. The process was invented in the early 19th century and used initially for making forgery-proof banknotes. Books illustrated with steel engravings were produced until the 1880s. → *2863 engraving (1)*

2890 stipple engraving A technique that combines etching and engraving.

2891 wall The divisions between cells on a gravure plate.

2892 well A single cell on a gravure printing plate.

2893 zinco (2), zincograph An etching using a zinc plate. → *2177 etch;* *2865 etching (2)*

2894 ablation plate Printing plate used in digital offset litho printing. Requiring no chemical processing, ablation plates can be digitally imaged directly onto the printing press using laser. → *2946 offset litho(graphy)*

2895 abrasion resistance The property of a printing plate to resist rubbing without its surface being worn away.

2896 acid resist A protective layer applied to offset litho plates that resists the acid being used to etch the plate, thus limiting the areas being etched. → *2847 acid*

2897 air bar A device on a printing press that prevents a double image from being printed.

2898 albumen plate An obsolescent type of plate used in lithographic printing, in which a photosensitive surface made from albumen is applied to a plate.

2899 anodized plate A standard aluminum litho plate that has been given a fine grain and then electrolytically hardened, making it suitable for a "deep-etch" image that is capable of sustaining print runs of up to 500,000. → *2921 deep-etch;* *2946 offset litho(graphy)*

2900 automatic transfer press A type of web press that allows a change of plates without interrupting the run — while one job is running, another is prepared on a second unit.

2901 auxiliary roll stand A stand for holding an additional roll of paper on a web-fed printing press, which allows continuous printing while the first roll is replaced. → *2344 web;* *2900 automatic transfer press;* *2747 web-fed*

2902 back edge curl/tail-end hook An aberration that occurs at the tail end of a press, either when light papers cling to the blanket cylinder of a sheet-fed litho press, or when too much ink is applied at this edge causing curling. This can result in misregister in later printings. → *2906 blanket cylinder*

2903 bearers The rings on the end of the cylinders of printing presses that determine the plate-to-blanket pressure. ➔ *2906 blanket cylinder*

2904 bimetal(lic) plate A lithographic printing plate made from two different metals, one water-receptive, the other ink-receptive. Such plates allow the printing of long runs on high-speed presses. ➔ *2946 offset litho(graphy)*

2905 blanket (1) In offset litho printing, the rubber-coated sheet that transfers the inked impression from printing plate to paper. In gravure printing, a similar rubber sheet covers the impression cylinder of a printing press. ➔ *2946 offset litho(graphy); 2868 gravure; 2906 blanket cylinder*

2906 blanket cylinder In offset litho printing, the cylinder to which the blanket is attached. The blanket transfers the inked image from plate to paper. ➔ *2905 blanket (1); 2946 offset litho(graphy)*

2907 blanket piling The accumulation of paper fibers and other detritus on the surface of the blanket of an offset printing press, resulting in poor print quality. ➔ *2905 blanket (1); 2277 fluff*

2908 blanket smash Lack of ink on a printed sheet, caused either by insufficient pressure of blanket to paper, or by an area of blanket that is too thin. ➔ *2905 blanket (1)*

2909 blanket-to-blanket press In offset printing, a configuration in which a continuous web of paper is fed between two blanket cylinders, printing both sides at once. Also called a **perfecting press**. ➔ *2905 blanket (1); 2962 web offset; 2906 blanket cylinder*

2910 blinding The poor surface of an apparently sound printing plate, which creates a poorly printed image, or none at all. ➔ *2575 blind image*

2911 catch-up In offset lithography, printing on nonimage areas due to insufficient dampening of the plate. Also called **dry-up**. ➔ *2956 scum; 2946 offset litho(graphy)*

2912 chromolithography Obsolete lithographic printing process in which many colors were printed from separate litho stones.

2913 collotype A "planographic," photomechanical printing process that uses a gelatin-coated plate onto which the image is photographically exposed without using a halftone screen, thus achieving continuous tones. Collotypes are typically used for short-run fine-art edition prints. Also known as **photogelatin printing**. ➔ *2949 planographic*

2914 combination plate A printing plate prepared from a number of separate film negatives or positives, either all at once or individually, requiring several exposures. Also called **photo-composed plate**. ➔ *2951 plate*

2915 converter A type of offset litho printing press that can be converted to print either two colors on one side of a sheet or a single color on both sides in one pass. ➔ *2946 offset litho*

2916 counter-etch The application of acid solution to a litho plate so it becomes receptive to ink. ➔ *2937 lithography*

2917 Cronak process The chemical treatment of zinc plates to improve tonal reproduction.

2918 Dahlgren A proprietary dampening system used in litho printing to reduce levels of moisture. ➔ *2937 lithography*

2919 dampening In litho printing, the necessary process of moistening the nonimage areas of a printing plate to repel ink. ➔ *2937 lithography*

2920 **dampening fountain** A tray on a litho press that holds water for moistening the plate. Also known as **water pan**. → 2937 *lithography;* 2919 *dampening*

2921 **deep-etch(ing)** In lithographic printing, a process that involves etching away the printing areas of the plate so they are slightly recessed below the surface. This technique prolongs the life of the plate and is thus used for printing long runs. Also known as **positive reversal process**. → 2007 *deep-etch halftone*

2922 **deeply-etched halftone** In lithographic printing, the technique of etching a halftone image to extra depth on the plate, but without removing the highlights. This technique is used for holding detail when printing on coarse paper. Not to be confused with "deep-etch halftone." → 2007 *deep-etch halftone*

2923 **desensitize** Chemical treatment of a lithographic plate to make the nonimage areas water-receptive so they repel ink. The chemical solution used is called an "etch." → 2177 *etch*

2924 **development** Removing the unhardened coating from the surface of an exposed lithographic plate.

2925 **direct litho(graphy)** A lithographic printing process in which the printing plate is brought into direct contact with the paper, as distinct from "offset" lithography, in which the printing image is transferred via a "blanket cylinder" to the paper. Also known as **di litho**. → 2946 *offset lithography*

2926 **dressing** Part of the make-ready process whereby the cylinders are packed to change the degree of impression or, by a fractional amount, the "print length" of the final image. → 2645 *make-ready*

2927 **dry litho** A lithographic printing technique in which the nonprinting areas of the plate are etched to leave a relief printing area, thus avoiding the need for water. Dry litho is a variation of the letterset printing technique. → 3016 *letterset*

2928 **ductor roller** A roller on a printing press that carries water or ink from the "fountain" roller to either the "dampening" or the "distributing" roller.

2929 **dusting** In offset printing, a buildup of debris such as paper particles on the nonimage areas of the blanket. Also known as "powdering," although this also describes a printing fault in which the substrate and ink separate after printing. → 3477 *powdering*

2930 **fountain** The reservoir containing either ink or dampening solution on a litho press. → 2920 *dampening fountain;* 2606 *duct*

2931 **french calf** A calfskin material used to cover "nap" (high-quality) rollers on a litho printing machine. → 2940 *nap roller*

2932 **grain** (**3**) The rough property of the surface of some lithographic plates that enables them to hold moisture. → 2937 *lithography*

2933 **graining** The treating of the surface of a lithographic plate to make it more receptive to moisture. Graining is achieved mechanically by various abrasion methods, or by the use of chemicals.

2934 **gum** (**1**) A water-based solution containing gum arabic or cellulose gum, which is used to desensitize the nonimage areas on litho plates to make those areas ink repellent.

2943 Offset (1)
a *plate*
b *blanket*
c *paper*

2935 gum blinding An aberration that occurs in litho printing when ink fails to adhere to an image area. ➔ *2177 etch*

2936 ink spread In offset litho, the increase in the areas of each printed image or text character; caused by the spread of ink during printing as it is transferred from plate to blanket and then to paper. When the size of a halftone dot is affected, it is known as "physical dot gain." ➔ *2670 physical dot gain; 2806 ink squash*

2937 lithography A "planographic" printing process invented in 1798 by Aloys Senefelder, a German, in which an image is produced from a dampened, flat surface, using greasy ink; based on the principle of the mutual repulsion of oil and water.

2938 master plate The plate containing the image in offset litho printing.

2939 metallography A contraction of "metal-lithography," a traditional lithographic printing process in which metal plates are used instead of stone. ➔ *2937 lithography*

2940 nap roller A superior type of lithographic roller with a cover of french calfskin. The nap, or skin, side is outermost and is treated with oil to make it waterproof and supple before being varnished to make it smooth. ➔ *2931 french calf*

2941 near-print Prior to the desktop publishing era, a general term used to describe substitute printing processes, such as typewriter composition and "offset duplicating" (using small offset litho presses). Also called **near letter quality (NLQ)**.

2942 nonimage area The nonprinting area of a litho plate that has been treated to accept water, thus repelling ink.

2943 offset (1) A printing technique in which the ink is transferred from the printing plate to a "blanket" cylinder and then to the paper or material on which it is to be printed. ➔ *2946 offset litho; 2878 offset gravure; 3016 letterset*

2944 offset blanket The rubber-coated blanket used in offset litho printing that transfers the inked image from plate to paper.

2945 offset ink An ink developed for use on offset litho presses. It must not react to the rubber in the blanket; it must have a high concentration of pigment because not all the ink is transferred from blanket to paper; and it must be free from water-soluble particles.

2946 offset litho(graphy) A lithographic printing technique, developed in the United States in the early 1900s, in which the image is printed indirectly by "offsetting" it onto a rubber-covered cylinder, called a "blanket" cylinder, from which the image is printed. It is one of the most widely used commercial printing processes. This book was printed by the offset lithography process. ➔ *2925 direct lithography; 2878 offset gravure*

2947 packing A method involving the placing of material (usually paper or rubber) between the cylinder and the plate/blanket on a printing press. The increased pressure results in a heavier impression being transferred from the plate to the blanket or from the blanket to the paper. ➔ *2645 make-ready*

2948 piling The accumulation of debris on an offset blanket or press rollers, affecting print quality.

2949 planographic (printing) Printing from a flat surface (plane), for example lithography. → *2937 lithography*

2950 plastic plates Plastic printing plates that are hard-wearing and light.

2951 plate (1) A metal, plastic, or paper sheet from which an image is printed. → *3004 curved plate*

2952 precoated plates Litho plates that have received a coating that will not become light-sensitive until they are washed with a sensitizing solution. → *2953 presensitized plates*

2953 pre-sensitized plates Litho plates that have received a light-sensitive coating and are ready for exposure to a positive or negative. → *2952 precoated plates*

2954 printing down The transfer of image from film to plate.

2955 retransfer The process of duplicating the image on one lithographic plate so it can be transferred to another.

2956 scum/scumming A fault occurring in lithographic printing when the ink adheres to the nonimage areas of the plate. → *2911 catch-up*

2957 snowflaking Minute white specks in type and solid ink areas in offset printing.

2958 tinting The effect of ink bleeding into the dampening solution on a litho press, causing unwanted artifacts to appear on the nonimage areas.

2959 ungrained plate A litho plate that is much smoother than normal. It is used to improve the merging of tones, as well as to increase the range of darker tones. A normal litho plate uses the graining to hold water in the nonimage areas, whereas with an ungrained plate other methods are required to achieve this.

2960 wash marks Streaking on a printed image, caused by excessive water on the printing plate.

2961 waterless lithography/printing A lithographic printing process that, rather than using water to repel ink on the nonimage areas of the plate, uses a plate with an ink-repellent rubber layer. → *2937 lithography*

2962 web offset A rotary printing press that uses a continuous reel-fed paper "web" where the impression (image) from the plate is offset onto a blanket (usually rubber) before being printed onto the paper. There are three main systems: "blanket to blanket," in which two plates and two blanket cylinders on each unit print the web; three-cylinder systems, in which plate blanket and impression cylinders print one side of the paper only; and satellite or planetary systems, in which two, three, or four plate and blanket cylinders are arranged around a common impression cylinder, printing one side of the web in as many colors as there are plate cylinders. → *2344 web (1)*; *2746 web (printing) press*

2963 weft (1) The weaker direction of a web offset blanket. → *2905 blanket*

2964 zincography A former name for lithography, now obsolete. → *2937 lithography*; *2689 printing processes*; *2774 color printing*

2965 anilox system The method of inking used in flexographic printing. → *2982 flexography*

2966 archival printing The printing of works for long-lasting storage, using special techniques. → *2461 archival paper*

2967 belt press A printing press that performs the entire manufacturing process of a book, from paper roll to binding. → *3082 binding*

2968 clamshell press A machine with two hinged platens such as are found on diecutting and heat-transfer equipment.

2969 Cromacheck A proprietary off-press proofing system from Du Pont that uses plastic laminates.

2970 curtain coater A machine used for coating flat sheets of paperboard with an even coating of solution such as adhesive.→ *2537 paperboard*

2971 cylinder press A rotary press in which the sheet to be printed is wrapped around a cylinder and brought into contact with the printing surface, which is laid flat. Cylinder presses are mainly used for specialized work, such as diecutting. → *3267 diecutting*

2972 deflection A condition in flexographic printing in which the "fountain" and "anilox" rolls bow slightly. Although this is normal, excessive bending can result in uneven printing. → *2965 anilox system*

2973 demand printing A method of printing in which the copies are produced as and when they are needed. The document is generally stored electronically and produced on an electronic device, such as a laser or ink-jet printer. Demand printing allows frequent modification or updating of documents, and eliminates the need to store bulky quantities of inventory. Also known as **on-demand printing**. → *0258 laser printer; 0257 ink-jet printer*

2974 dielectric printing A nonimpact printing method in which toner is applied to electrically charged paper. Also known as **electrographic printing**. → *2977 electrostatic printing*

2975 dye sub(limation) (printing) A printing process in which vaporized ink dyes are bonded to a substrate by heat, producing near photographic quality proofs. Dye sublimation allows digital printing of large images onto fabric, metal, and other substrates, and is thus particularly suitable for fashion, architectural, and other large-format display items, because size is not a limitation and runs can be as low as a single item. Also known as **dye diffusion**.

2976 electrostatic copying A method of copying an image using an electrically charged, photosensitive drum or plate that temporarily retains the original image before transferring it to paper using an imaging agent ("toner"). → *2977 electrostatic printing*

2977 electrostatic printing A method of "inkless printing" using an electrically charged, photosensitive drum or plate that temporarily retains the original image before transferring it to paper using an imaging agent ("toner"). Typically used for large-format printing.

2978 feint ruling Thin lines that act as a writing guide, typically on the pages of account books and school notebooks, ruled by a special machine.

2979 flatbed (1) A type of printing press on which the paper sheets sit on a horizontal surface; used for proofing.

2980 flatbed cylinder press A type of printing press on which the paper sheets are moved backward and forward beneath the impression cylinder.

2981 flatbed rotary A type of printing press on which the paper is held on a reel ("web"), but receives the impression from a flatbed plate.

2982 flexography/flexo A relief printing process that uses flexible rubber or plastic plates. Used mainly for printing onto various kinds of packaging, and sometimes newspapers, where it may be referred to as "anilox" printing. ➜ *2695 anilox system; 2983 matrix (2)*

2983 matrix The mold used for making the rubber plate in flexographic printing, and also the papier-mâché mold, formed from a page of metal type, used for stereotyping. ➜ *2982 flexography; 3032 stereo(type)*

2984 music printing The printing of musical notation, now done digitally, but traditionally done by engraving directly onto metal plates or by using movable type on previously printed staves.

2985 photopolymer (printing) plates Relief printing plates made with a light-sensitive polymer (plastic) coating; used mainly for flexographic printing.

2986 ruling machine A machine designed specifically for drawing the lines on music and ledger paper.

2987 run-through work The printing of even parallel lines across a sheet using a specialized press. ➜ *2986 ruling machine; 2978 feint ruling*

2988 thermography A printing process that emulates die stamping (but without embossing), in which sheets are printed with a sticky ink or varnish and then dusted with a fine, pigmented powder that forms a raised surface when fused to the paper by heat. ➜ *3009 die stamping*

2989 variable printing Printing in which variable data, such as names and addresses, is inserted during the print run.

2990 xerography A dry copying process in which electrostatically charged powder is bonded to paper.

2991 autoplate machine In rotary printing, a molding cylinder around which "flong" (a papier-mâchélike material) is placed to make the curved "stereos" used for printing. ➜ *3032 stereo(type); 3012 flong*

2992 bed (1) The steel table of a letterpress machine on which the frame containing metal type ("forme") is placed. The expression "put to bed" originally described the secured forme, although it is now generally used in printing to describe plates once they are secured and ready to print.

2993 blanket (2) A rubber sheet used to cover the "flong" when casting a stereotype plate. ➜ *3012 flong; 3032 stereo(type)*

2994 block (1) In traditional letterpress printing, an etched or engraved metal plate after it has been mounted.

2995 block book A book printed from page-size wooden blocks. Originally used before the invention of movable type. ➜ *2996 block printing*

2996 block printing Printing using wooden blocks. The main printing method before the invention of movable type, block printing is still used for specialist work, such as printing wallpapers and fabrics. ➜ *3027 relief printing*

2997 bottoming In relief printing, a fault that occurs when ink is transferred to the nonimage areas of the plate or block, and that is then printed on the sheet. ➜ *3027 relief printing*

2998 bumping up/bump up (1) The preparation of halftone plates for printing, usually on a rotary press, where the original plates are made ready before stereos are cast. ➜ *2645 make-ready; 3032 stereo(type); 2040 halftone (1)*

2999 case (**3**) The base plate, which, when covered with wax, is used in electrotyping for creating the mold. ➔ *3010 electrotype*

3000 chase (**1**) In letterpress printing, a heavy rectangular metal frame into which type and illustration blocks are locked before it is placed on the bed of the press. ➔ *3013 form (2)*

3001 chiaroscuro (pron.: kee"ar"oskooroe); Italian for "clear" (*chiaro*) and "dark/obscure" (*oscuro*), the term describes single-color wood engravings printed using, first, a key block for the darkest tone, followed by a succession of tint blocks to add lighter shades or colors.

3002 cliché Originally a French term, now used elsewhere in Europe, for a stereotype ("stereo") or electrotype ("electro"). ➔ *3032 stereo(type); 3010 electrotype*

3003 crash (**2**) To number a multipart set of forms on carbonless paper by printing, with a letterpress machine, the top sheet of each made-up set so the number appears on the other sheets in the set.

3004 curved plate A plate used on a rotary press that curves around the plate cylinder. ➔ *2951 plate (1); 2705 rotary press*

3005 cut (**1**) A contraction of "woodcut," today used to describe any print made from a relief block, etching, or engraving.

3006 cut (**2**) A metal relief plate from which an image is printed.

3007 die (**1**) An engraved stamp used for impressing an embossed design onto paper. ➔ *3444 embossing*

3008 die press A machine that uses a "die" to cut or emboss a shape into paper or board. ➔ *3007 die (1); 3266 die (2)*

3009 die stamping A printing technique that uses a "die" to emboss a relief image onto a surface. Ink or metallic foil is generally used to add color, but if not the surface is said to be "blind-stamped." Also known as **relief stamping**. ➔ *3007 die (1)*

3010 electro(**type**) A method of making a duplicate of a letterpress plate by pressing a mold into its surface, and then by electrochemical plating, applying a shell of copper to the mold. The mold is then removed and tin plated on the back, before being filled with a backing, such as molten lead or liquid plastic.

3011 electro/electrotype A duplicate relief printing plate made by galvanizing copper onto a forme. ➔ *3032 stereo(type); 3002 cliché; 3013 forme*

3012 flong A papier-mâché-like sheet used for making the molds in which the "stereotypes" used in rotary letterpress printing are cast. ➔ *3032 stereotype*

3013 form (**2**)**/forme** One side of a printed signature, consisting of a number of imposed pages, usually in smaller or greater multiples of eight. The term derives from the "forme" used in letterpress printing, such as type matter and illustration blocks "locked up" in a "chase" ready for printing. ➔ *3337 section (2); 3000 chase (1); 2716 signature (1); 3015 letterpress printing*

3014 foundry proof A letterpress proof pulled prior to sending the forme to the foundry.

3015 letterpress (**printing**) The original relief printing process in which the surface of a raised, or relief, image or piece of type is inked and then pressed onto paper or some other surface.

3016 letterset A contraction of letterpress and offset. A method of offset printing from a relief plate. Also called **indirect letterpress** and **relief offset**. ➜ *2943 offset (1)*

3017 line block A relief printing plate used to reproduce images consisting of lines or solid areas without any tonal graduation.

3018 linocut A crude relief printing block with a linoleum surface into which the design is cut.

3019 mother set The master set of printing plates kept for electrotyping later sets. ➜ *3010 electrotype*

3020 papier-mâché A paper pulp used to create molds for casting stereotypes. ➜ *3012 flong; 3032 stereo(type)*

3021 pierced A block that has been cut away to allow for type to be inserted. ➜ *2200 mortise (1)*

3022 plate-boring machine A machine used to bore out a stereotype plate to reduce it to the required thickness. ➜ *3032 stereo(type)*

3023 platen press A traditional flatbed press that uses a heavy plate ("platen") to press paper to the inked surface to create an impression.

3024 plating The making of a stereotype or electrotype from setup type.

3025 relief block A letterpress line or halftone block.

3026 relief plate A printing plate with a raised printing surface.

3027 relief printing Printing from a raised surface, such as letterpress printing. ➜ *3015 letterpress*

3028 rubber stereo A stereo made in a molding press by pressing a rubber plate against a heated matrix. The rubber is vulcanized by the heat, creating a permanent impression. ➜ *2983 matrix; 3032 stereo(type)*

3029 scorcher A machine used to heat and curve stereo matrices for use on a rotary press. ➜ *3032 stereo(type)*

3030 sgraffito A woodcut printing technique that produces a design in white on a black or red ground.

3031 signature rotary A web-fed rotary letterpress incorporating rubber or plastic plates; used for long print runs.

3032 stereo(type) A duplicate printing plate made by taking an impression of the original in a mold of plaster of Paris or papier-mâché and casting another in lead alloy. ➜ *3010 electrotype; 3002 cliché; 3012 flong*

3033 woodcut A traditional method of printing using images and type carved — out of wood — in relief.

3034 wraparound plates (**2**) Flexible printing plates used on a "wraparound" press (a sheet-fed rotary press).

3035 wraparound press A high-speed, sheet-fed rotary press that uses relief plates. ➜ *3034 wraparound plates (2); 2705 rotary press; 2951 plate*

3036 xylograph A wood engraving.

3037 air pull When ink is flooded across the screen during screen printing without contacting the surface to be printed.

3038 curved screen In screen printing, a curved mesh screen used for printing onto objects with a curved surface. ➜ *3046 screenprinting; 3039 cylindrical printer*

3039 cylindrical printer A screen printing device for printing onto cylindrical objects, such as bottles. ➔ *3046* screenprinting; *3038* curved screen

3040 deep-line cut A method of improving trapping in screenprinting. ➔ *2085* trapping

3041 drying in Loss of detail in a screenprinted image, caused by ink drying and clogging the screen mesh.

3042 mesh The interlaced structure of the threads in screen printing fabric.

3043 mesh marks In screen printing, a crosshatch pattern on the printed surface, left by the mesh of the screen fabric and caused by incorrect ink consistency. Also called **screen marks**. ➔ *3042* mesh

3044 sawtooth An aberration in screen printing in which lines of a design cross the fabric mesh diagonally, giving them a jagged look. ➔ *3046* screenprinting

3045 screen (**3**) The porous silk or synthetic mesh used as an image carrier in the screen-printing process. ➔ *3049* silkscreen; *3046* screen printing

3046 screen printing A printing process in which ink is forced through a porous mesh screen stretched across a frame. The image is formed by means of a hand-cut or photomechanically generated stencil bonded to the screen that blocks the nonimage areas. ➔ *3038* curved screen

3047 selectasine A color printing process that employs a single silkscreen for all colors used.

3048 serigraphy The silkscreen printing process. ➔ *3049* silkscreen printing

3049 silkscreen printing A traditional method of "serigraphic" printing in which ink is forced through a stencil fixed to a screen made of silk. Today, however, the screen is made of synthetic material and the process is generally called "screen printing." ➔ *3046* screen printing

3050 squeegee A blade or paddle device, usually made of rubber or plastic, that forces ink through the open areas of the mesh and stencil in the screen-printing process.

3051 stencil In screen printing, the material used to prevent ink transferring through the screen to the nonimage areas of the paper.

3052 bimetal varnish Varnish added to printing ink to toughen it when dry. Also called **binding varnish**.

3053 blind emboss/stamp An impression made from a relief printing surface, such as with a letterpress block or type, but without applying ink or foil. This produces a bas-relief effect. ➔ *4083* bas relief

3054 BPOP *abb.:* **bulk packed on pallets**. An instruction to the printer to deliver a job on "pallets," wooden trays designed to be used with fork-lift trucks.

3055 chute delivery A method of delivering printed material from a press.

3056 convection drying After printing, drying the ink by circulating warm air around the paper.

3057 driers Various substances, usually metallic salts, added to printing ink to speed up the drying process.

3058 flag (**2**) A tab inserted into a stack or reel of printed paper indicating either a fault that must be examined or a change of edition.

3059 flash drying A method of ink drying on a very high speed web press. The ink contains solvents that are burned off at the very high temperatures involved.

3060 infrared drying The use of infrared radiation to rapidly dry ink, particularly appropriate on a high-speed web press.

3061 interleaved (**2**) Sheets of paper placed between newly printed sheets to prevent ink transfer or set-off. Also called **slip-sheeting**.

3062 microwave drying A method used to dry inks in the drying units of high-speed web presses.

3063 perfect The point at which some or all printed sheets of an edition are ready for binding. ➔ *3323 perfect copy*

3064 run on (**1**) A specified number of sheets printed in addition to the originally specified quantity. ➔ *2661 overs*

3065 second cover An alternative term for the inside front cover of a publication.

3066 setoff The accidental transfer of wet ink on a freshly printed sheet to the back of the next on the delivery pile. ➔ *2779 cure (2)*

3067 setoff reel In reel-fed ("web") printing machines, an extra reel that prevents ink from the printed reel setting off on the packing of the impression cylinder. ➔ *3066 setoff*

3068 slipsheeting Sheets of paper placed between freshly printed pages to prevent setoff. ➔ *3066 setoff*

3069 slit A cut made by a sharp rotary knife on a press, between the impression cylinder and delivery.

3070 spot varnishing Selective application of varnish to a sheet after printing, usually for graphic effect. ➔ *3358 varnish*

3071 spray powder A powderlike substance that can be applied to freshly printed work to prevent ink setoff. Also called **antisetoff spray**. ➔ *3066 setoff*

3072 tip in/on, tipped in/on A page or image inserted separately into a book and secured by pasting one edge.

3073 **adhesive binding** A method of binding that involves gluing the pages or signatures together rather than sewing or stitching them, although some binding methods combine both processes. Also called **perfect binding**. → *3082 binding; 3083 bookbinding; 3101 cut-back binding; 2716 signature (1)*

3074 **adhesive stitch binding** A method of adhesive binding in which signatures are stitched with heat-activated, plastic-coated wire. → *3073 adhesive binding; 3082 binding; 3083 bookbinding; 2716 signature (1)*

3075 **album binding** A volume that is bound along its short side rather than along its long side, as is more common. → *3082 binding; 3083 bookbinding; 3976 oblong*

3076 **annex** A supplement to a publication that is bound into the main body of the publication.

3077 **attaching** A binding method in which a narrow strip of strong paper is used to attach the end leaves of the book block to the boards, as distinct from casing-in. → *3092 casing-in; 3082 binding*

3078 **back** The part of a book formed nearest the edge at which it is bound, and after it is stitched.

3079 **back cornering** The removal of small chips from the four innermost corners of the boards of a book to make them easier to open after they are covered. → *2471 boards*

3080 **back lining** A fabric or paper strip glued to the back of a book to reinforce the binding before casing-in. → *3092 casing-in*

3081 **backed (2)** During the binding process, the term describing a volume after backing, but before casing-in. → *2761 backing; 3092 casing-in; 3082 binding; 3186 rounding and backing*

3082 **binding** The process of joining and securing the assembled leaves of a printed work, such as a book or pamphlet. There are many methods of binding, including mechanical methods, such as plastic comb binding and ring binding, and more conventional methods, such as Smyth-sewn, side-sewn, section-sewn, saddle-sewn, and adhesive binding. → *3083 bookbinding; 3073 adhesive binding; 3202 Smyth sewn/sewing*

3083 **bookbinding** The collecting and fastening together of the printed pages of a work and enclosing them within a cover. The main stages of binding a book are folding the printed sheets of paper, cutting the edges, rounding and backing, lining the backs, making and blocking (stamping) the cases, and, finally, securing the cases to the book block. → *3186 rounding and backing; 3429 blocking; 3082 binding; 3090 case (1); 3242 book block ·*

3084 **bottomband/tailband** A headband placed at the bottom of the spine. → *3129 headband; 3203 spine*

3085 **bound book** Originally used to describe a book with boards attached to the book block, but before it was covered with leather or cloth. Today, the term generally describes any bound or cased book. → *3083 bookbinding; 2471 boards; 3242 book block; 3091 cased/case bound*

3086 **burst binding** A device on a web press that enables glue to penetrate the pages during adhesive binding. → *3073 adhesive binding*

3087 **caoutchouc binding** An early form of adhesive binding in which a pile of single leaves were bonded together by a rubber solution called caoutchouc. → *3073 adhesive binding*

3090 Case (1)

3105 Endpapers

3088 cap (1) A paper covering used to protect a book block during binding. → *3089 capping up; 3082 binding; 3242 book block*

3089 capping up The wrapping of the body of a book with thin paper to protect the edges of the block while adding the covers, head, and tailbands, etc. → *3088 cap (1)*

3090 case (1) The stiff cover of a book, usually made by machine and consisting of two boards, a paper "hollow," and a suitable binding material such as cloth. → *3374 book cloth; 3091 cased/case bound*

3091 cased/case bound Books that have had a case attached to their sewn sections. Also called **hardbound**, **hardbacked**, or **edition bound**. → *3090 case (1)*

3092 casing-in The final stage in the production of cased books, when cases are attached to the sewn and trimmed book blocks. → *3090 case (1); 3091 cased/case bound; 3242 book block*

3093 chamfered edges The beveling of the edges of heavy binding boards so there is a neater turnover of the cover material. → *2467 beveled boards; 3095 cloth boards*

3094 circuit edges A book binding — used typically for limp-backed Bibles and prayer books, in which projecting covers are turned over to protect the edges. → *3235 Yapp binding*

3095 cloth boards A binding in which cloth covers stiff boards, as distinct from limp or flexible covers. → *3082 binding; 2471 boards*

3096 cloth joints A binding in which cloth is used to reinforce the fold of an endpaper. → *3082 binding; 3105 endpaper*

3097 corners (2) Triangular pieces of material or leather that cover the corners of half or three-quarter bound books.

3098 cover Paper, board, cloth, leather, or other material to which the body of a book is secured by glue, thread, or other means. The cover of a machine-bound book is called a case. → *3784 body (2); 3090 case (1)*

3099 covering The process by which a cover is fixed to the spine or by which the endpapers of a book are pasted to the cover. → *3784 body (2); 3105 endpaper; 3092 casing-in*

3100 cropped A book with overtrimmed margins.

3101 cut-back binding An alternative name for adhesive or unsewn binding, so-called because the folded and gathered sheets are trimmed at the back. → *3073 adhesive binding*

3102 drawn on (cover) A paper or board book cover that is glued to the spine of a sewn or adhesive bound book.

3103 easel-binder A display stand with ring binding, for making presentations.

3104 edition binding Sometimes used to describe a "case bound" (hardback) book. Also called **publisher's binding**. → *3091 cased*

3105 endpapers Lining paper at each end of a book. Endpapers are attached to the inner sides of the boards and to the first and last pages of the book block, helping to secure the book to its case. Also called **lining papers**. → *3242 book block*

3106 Etruscan binding A method of decorating calf skin bindings in the style of ancient Etruscan vases. → *3376 calf; 3385 extra calf; 3412 rough calf*

3112 Flat-backed

3120 Full-bound

3107 extension cover A paperback cover that extends beyond the trimmed page size.

3108 extra bound A hand-bound book characterized by lavish tooling and superior finishing details and construction.

3109 false bands A method of simulating a flexibly sewn book by padding out a hollow-backed book with strips of leather or card.

3110 fan binding A superior style of decorative binding made in France and Italy in the latter part of the 17th century. It featured an intricately tooled fan motif with four quarter fans repeated at the corners.

3111 fanfare A style of decorative cover with a design featuring a complex pattern of interlaced ribbons along with foliage and flora bordering a central compartment. The name derives from a book, *Les Fanfares et corveés abbadesques des Roule-Bontemps*, published in the early 17th century.

3112 flat-back(ed) (book) A binding style of either limp or cased books in which the "rounding" is omitted, and the book thus has a square, or flat, spine, as distinct from a case binding that is rounded and backed. Also called **square back**. → *3186 rounding and backing*

3113 flexible binding A method of binding without the use of cover boards, with the back of the endpapers being pasted directly onto the cover, which may be made of leather or some other material.

3114 flexible glue A type of glue that does not dry completely and is used for fixing the book block to the case.

3115 flexicover A durable cover material that strengthens a paperback book. → *3169 paperback*

3116 flush cover/boards A book cover trimmed to the same size as the pages within. Also called **flush work** and, if the covers are "limp" (soft), **limp flush**.

3117 fly leaf The portion of an endpaper that is not stuck down to the case. → *3105 endpaper; 3170 paste-downs*

3118 four-up The printing of four 16-page sections that are gathered, glued, and covered as one unit, after which they are separated. → *2737 two-up*

3119 french joints A method of bookbinding in which the cover boards are inset a little way in from the spine and the covering material pressed into the gap that is left. It is a particularly useful technique when thick cover boards and heavy covering material are used. Also called a **french groove**, **grooved joints**, or **sunk joints**.

3120 full-bound A hardback binding in which the whole case is covered with the same material, such as full leather or full cloth. Also called **whole bound**. → *3180 quarter-bound; 3126 half-bound*

3121 glued back only A book having a paper cover attached by adhesive on the back only, so the sides are left loose.

3122 glued/pasted down to ends A limp cover pasted to the first and last leaves of a book.

3123 gluing up A stage in the bookbinding process in which glue is used to supplement the structural integrity afforded by the sewing process, prior to rounding and backing. → *3171 pasting*

3126 Half-bound

3131 Hinges (**a**)

3129 Head band (**a**)

3134 Hollow back

3124 **grooved boards** Book boards that have grooves in the back edges.

3125 **guards** Narrow strips of paper or linen onto which single plates are pasted before being sewn in with the sections of a book. This process is known as "guarding" or "guarding-in."

3126 **half-bound/binding** A hardback binding in which the back and corners are covered in one material and the remainder of the sides in another. For example, a leather back and corners, with cloth sides. → *3129 three-quarter bound; 3097 corners (2); 3120 full-bound; 3180 quarter-bound*

3127 **half-cloth** A half-bound book with a cloth-covered spine and corners, and paper-covered boards. → *3126 half-bound*

3128 **half-leather** A half-bound book with a leather-covered spine and corners, and paper- or cloth-covered boards. → *3126 half-bound*

3129 **head/tail band** A narrow band of colored silk or cotton cord that is glued to the top (head band) and/or bottom (tailband) of the spine of a cased book, enhancing the strength and appearance of the binding.

3130 **headcap** A small fold of leather at the head and tail of the spine on a hand-bound book. Also called a **french headcap**.

3131 **hinges** The points at which the main body of a book adjoins the covers, forming the channels between the two halves of the endpapers.

3132 **holiday** A traditional term that describes an area of a surface that failed to be pasted in the pasting unit.

3133 **hollow** The strip of brown paper placed in the center of a case to stiffen the spine, which allows the book to be opened easily.

3134 **hollow back** The space at the back of a cased book between the case and the book block. Also called **open back**.

3135 **hooked/hooking** Single leaf illustrations printed on sheets that are slightly wider than the accompanying text pages, thus allowing for an inner fold, or hinge, which fits around the section like a hook. → *3125 guard*

3136 **hot-melt adhesive** An adhesive used in bookbinding.

3137 **imperfection** A book that has been incorrectly bound.

3138 **in boards** A book trimmed after the boards have been attached.

3139 **jacketing machine** A machine that automatically wraps dust jackets around bound books, a practice that, despite the fact that such machines were introduced in the 1950s, is still carried out by hand in many parts of the world where labor is cheap. → *3801 dust jacket*

3140 **joint** The point at which the spine and the boards of a case-bound book are hinged. → *3378 crash (3); 3313 nip (1)*

3141 **laced on** A description of bindings in which the boards are affixed to the book by means of cords onto which the sections have been sewn.

3142 **lacing in** The stage of binding in which the boards are attached to a hand-sewn book before a leather cover is fitted.

3143 **letterpress binding** The bindings of books that are to be read, as distinct from those that are to be written in (stationery binding).

3144 **leveling** A stage in adhesive binding in which a small amount is shaved off the spine, making it flat and square. → *3073 adhesive binding*

3145 library edition/binding Part of a standard edition that is specially bound with strengthened stitching, joints, covers, and so on, to endure continual handling, such as in libraries. In the United States, specifications for library bindings are determined by the American Library Association (ALA).

3146 limp binding A form of binding using a flexible material such as paper, cloth, or leather, with no stiffening, as distinct from case binding. Bibles are often bound in this way, with overhanging, or "Yapp," edges. ➔ *3235 Yapp binding; 3094 circuit edges*

3147 liners Thin, strong paper used to line the boards of a cased book, particularly those bound in leather.

3148 lining/lining up A bookbinding term to describe the strengthening of the back of a book with mull. ➔ *3401 mull*

3149 lip The extended edge of a signature that is gripped during saddle-stitch binding. ➔ *3335 saddle-stitched; signature*

3150 loose-leaf binding A binding method that allows easy insertion or removal of individual leaves of paper, as in 2-, 3-, or 4-ring binders.

3151 machine-binding process The entire automated process, usually in separate units that may or may not be linked together, of bookbinding, comprising: bundling, affixing endpapers, gathering, sewing, nipping, trimming, gluing, rounding and backing, lining, casing-in, and pressing.

3152 machine-sewing A mechanical bookbinding process in which the individual leaves of a folded section are sewn together at the same time as the sections are sewn together.

3153 maquette binding A sample case submitted by the bookbinder for client approval.

3154 mechanical binding A binding method in which individual sheets are held together with a plastic comb, wire, or metal rings. ➔ *3175 plastic comb binding; 3204 spiral binding*

3155 meeting guards V-shaped guards of paper sewn to folds of sections to enable the flatter opening of a book, particularly one with narrow page margins. ➔ *3125 guards*

3156 mitered/miter (1) Said of the corners of a book cover material that have been folded inside to meet at an angle of 45°.

3157 multi-ring binder A mechanical binding method in which the leaves are secured by closely spaced rings. ➔ *3154 mechanical binding*

3158 nailhead A paperback book, so called because its cross-section resembles a nail, thicker at the spine and tapering to the fore-edge.

3159 narrow copy An elongated, tall book. ➔ *2728 tall copy*

3160 nippers Heated clamps that secure the book and case together on a bookbinding line.

3161 nipping The process of clamping book blocks to reduce the swelling caused by sewing when bookbinding. Sometimes called "smashing," although this term is more correctly applied to books printed on soft paper. ➔ *3201 smash*

3162 nipping up A stage in the process of hand binding that gives shape to the bands. ➔ *3129 head/tailband*

3166 Overhang cover

3180 Quarter-bound

3163 notch binding A method of adhesive binding in which small, glue-retaining slits are applied to the spine of a book. → *3073 adhesive binding*

3164 offside The part of the case that is at the end of a book.

3165 one on and two off A method of binding in which a single width of paper is glued to the back of the book, then double folded, and the resulting two layers glued together to add support to the spine. When a double layer of paper is glued to the back it is known as "two on and two off."

3166 overhang cover A book cover that projects past the trimmed edges of the leaves, common with case-bound books.

3167 page flex The amount of stress that a bound book can endure before the pages become loosened.

3168 paper wrappered A paper-covered book. → *3405 paper covers*

3169 paperback A book with a soft outer cover, usually made of thick paper, as distinct from "limp binding," which may be made from other materials. Also called **softback** binding. → *3895 softback edition; 3405 paper covers*

3170 paste-downs The half of an endpaper that is glued to the cover boards, leaving the other half free ("fly leaf"). → *3105 endpaper; 3117 fly leaf; 2471 boards*

3171 pasting In bookbinding, the application of adhesive by hand or machine. → *3123 gluing-up*

3172 pasting down In bookbinding, the affixing of endpapers to the inside boards of a case.

3173 peasant binding A binding of inferior quality used in 17th-century Europe for Bibles made for rural home use.

3174 perf strip A narrow strip of paper bound into a saddle-stitched publication that allows single leaves to be tipped in. → *3072 tip in/on, tipped in/on*

3175 plastic comb/coil binding A method of binding using rings attached to a plastic spine to secure the pages. → *3204 spiral binding*

3176 post binder A method of binding loose leaves (including covers) by individual posts punched through holes.

3177 prebinding A heavy-duty binding used for library editions. It is characterized by extra sewing of the sections, reinforced endpapers, and plastic lamination of the cover.

3178 primary binding The binding used for the first edition of a book.

3179 publisher's binding The standard binding used by a publisher selling to the book trade. Also called **edition binding** or **trade binding**.

3180 quarter-bound/binding A hardback binding in which the back is covered in one material and the sides in another, such as a leather back with cloth sides. Also called **three-part binding**. → *3219 three-quarter bound; 3097 corners (2); 3120 full-bound; 3126 half-bound*

3181 raised bands Ridges on the spine of a book that cover the cords securing the sections.

3182 recessed cords In traditional bookbinding, the use of flax or hemp cords that run along grooves sewn across the gathered sections of a book. This enables the spine to be flat. → *3213 sunken cords*

3186 Rounded and backed

3183 **register ribbon** A ribbon fastened at the back of a book and used as a bookmarker.

3184 **reinforced binding** A heavy-duty binding for public library use.

3185 **reinforced signatures** Additional material used in the fold or around the outer signatures to strengthen them at the point that takes the most strain. ➔ *2716 signature (1)*

3186 **rounding and backing/rounded and backed** The style of binding in which a cased book has a convex back, thus making the fore-edge concave. Backing provides the "joints" (the line along which the spine and the boards of a case-bound book are hinged). ➔ *3112 flat back*

3187 **saddleback book** A book with inset pages secured by stitching with thread through the fold line. ➔ *3848 insert (1)*

3188 **secondary binding** A variant of binding materials that can occur when a single printing of a book is bound in batches over a period of time.

3189 **self ends** When the same paper stock that is used for the text and part of the first and last sections is also used to form the endpapers of a book. Also known as own ends. ➔ *3105 endpapers*

3190 **self wrapper/cover** A cover or wrapper formed of the same paper stock as the text. It is usually printed, as in a pamphlet, for example.

3191 **semiconcealed cover** A piece of material that is slotted, punched, or scored and used in combination with the actual binding device to form the closed backbone of a book or booklet, in the mechanical binding process. ➔ *3154 mechanical binding*

3192 **semi-Yapp** A style of binding midway between limp and Yapp bindings. The protective cover turns over just beyond the book's edges. ➔ *3235 Yapp binding*

3193 **shelf back** The spine of a book.

3194 **shoes** Small, protective corners made of brass or silver, fitted to cover the corners of large hand-bound books.

3195 **shoulder (2)** The edges of the backbone of a book that project slightly from the cover faces.

3196 **side gluing** The securing of the cover on a perfect bound book by means of adhesive on the outside of the outermost signature. ➔ *3073 adhesive binding*

3197 **sides** The front and rear boards of a book.

3198 **siding** The process of fitting and/or gluing the cloth or paper sides of a quarter- or half-bound book to the boards.

3199 **signet** A ribbon bookmark that is stitched into the binding of a book.

3200 **slips** In the binding of a sewn book, the loose ends of the cords that protrude after sewing. The slips are frayed and then attached to the boards. ➔ *3339 sewing; 3211 stitching; 2471 boards*

3201 **smash(ing)** The compression of the pages of a finished book, using heavy pressure to expel all air and fully flatten pages and boards. Sometimes called "nipping," although this term is more correctly applied to books printed on hard paper. ➔ *3161 nipping*

3203 Spine

3204 Spiral binding

3211 Stitch

3215 Tab index

3202 **Smyth sewn/sewing** A sewn binding method in which sections of a book are sewn together to give flexibility; the finished book should lie flat when opened at any given page.

3203 **spine** The part of the outer cover of a book that encloses the back, and usually carries the title, author's name, and so on. → *3082 binding*

3204 **spiral binding** A binding method in which the sections of a book are hole-punched and then held together by a spiral wire coil. Also called **spirex binding**. → *3175 plastic comb binding; 3225 twin-wire binding; 3231 Wire-O binding*

3205 **split boards** Outer cover boards for books, consisting of a thick and a thin board glued together, leaving a split into which endpapers and tapes are inserted. Used for library binding.

3206 **spot glue** Spots of glue used as a temporary fastening to hold gate-folds closed during the binding process, later trimmed off so the gatefold opens when read.

3207 **squares** The portion of the case covers of a book that protrude beyond the edge of the pages when the book is closed, thus protecting the pages themselves.

3208 **start** A binding fault that occurs — particularly in books with many sections — when one section or signature is thrown forward of the others, making it difficult to achieve a strong binding.

3209 **stiff leaves** Endpapers that are glued across the full width of the first and last leaves of a book. → *3105 endpapers*

3210 **stilted covers** A book that has been bound in larger covers than necessary to make it uniform with other, larger books on the shelf.

3211 **stitch/stitching** A binding technique in which all sections of a book are pierced and secured with wire or thread in a single operation. → *3339 sewing; 3152 machine-sewing*

3212 **stub (2)** The narrow margin of a leaf that remains when a canceled page is removed and onto which the correct page is fixed.

3213 **sunken cords** A binding process invented in the 16th century and still used in a modified form for hand-bound books. Cords or leather thongs are laid in grooves made across the assembled sections of the book. After sewing and lacing to the boards the spine of the book is flat. → *3182 recessed cords*

3214 **sunken flexible** A method of sewing the sections of a book in which grooves are made and thin cords inserted that are then completely encircled with the sewing thread.

3215 **tab index** An index guide similar to a "thumb index" except the reference guides, or tabs, project from the pages of the book instead of being cut into them. → *3220 thumb index*

3216 **take down** The process of disassembling a book into its original component parts prior to rebinding it.

3217 **thermoplastic binder** A device used for adhesive binding.

3218 **threadless binding** A binding method in which the leaves of a book are trimmed at the back and glued, but not sewn. Also called **unsewn binding**. → *3073 adhesive binding*

3220 Thumb index

3219 three-quarter bound A method of bookbinding in which cloth- or paper-covered sides are partially overlaid with another material, typically leather, covering the spine and a good part of the sides. → *3126 half-bound; 3180 quarter-bound; 3097 corners (2); 3082 binding; 3083 bookbinding*

3220 thumb index An index guide in a book in which steps are cut down the fore-edges of the page to provide a reference guide to the contents. Also called a **step index**. → *3215 tab index*

3221 ties Tapes or ribbons fixed to the covers of a book that, when tied, stop it from opening.

3222 tight back A rarely used method of bookbinding in which the body of the book (book block) is glued directly to the spine, so no hollow is formed. → *3242 book block*

3223 turned-over cover A binding in which the material used on the case is turned in around the edges so the edges of the boards are not left exposed as they would be if cut flush. Also called **turned-in covers**.

3224 turning-in corners A method of stretching the pasted cover material across the cover boards of a book to enable neatly mitered joints to be made. → *3098 cover*

3225 twin-wire binder A method of bookbinding in which a comb of plastic-covered wire with twin wire loops is used to secure the covers and pages. → *3204 spiral binding; 3231 Wire-O binding*

3226 uncut A book with pages that have not been trimmed.

3227 underbanding The use of false bands on a book cover.

3228 unopened A bound book with untrimmed sections. Pages have to be slit by hand with a paper knife. Also called **untouched edges**.

3229 wallet edged A soft-covered book in which the back cover extends to enclose the fore-edge of the book block, fastening into a slot in the front cover. → *3242 book block*

3230 warping The distortion of hardback book covers due mainly to contraction or expansion of cloth, boards, and endpapers, caused by a variety of reasons such as incorrect grain direction of the paper, changes in humidity during storage or shipping, and inadequate pressing during binding. → *3091 case bound*

3231 Wire-O binding A proprietary method of binding loose-leaf publications with plastic-coated wire → *3225 twin-wire binder; 3204 spiral binding*

3232 witness A book that has had its fore-edge trimmed slightly so some page edges are still rough.

3233 wrapper A paper cover attached to a publication.

3234 wrappering A strengthening process achieved by gluing unstiffened paper to the spine of a book. When large flaps are left at the fore-edge and then folded in, this is known as "wrappered and overlapped."

3235 Yapp binding A bookbinding method in which a limp cover projects over the edges of the book's leaves. The term is derived from the name of the London bookseller William Yapp who, in about 1860, designed the binding so Bibles could be carried in the pocket. → *3094 circuit edges*

3236 zigzag book A book made up of a continuous strip of paper folded in a concertina fold. If secured at the back, only one side of the sheet is

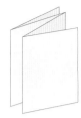

3237 Accordion fold

3240 Binder's creep

3242 Book block

printed. If it is printed on both sides, the book must be left unstitched. ➜ *3237 accordion fold*

3237 accordion/concertina fold A method of folding paper in which parallel folds are made in opposite directions to form pleats. Also called **z-fold** or **fan fold**. ➜ *3282 folding*

3238 advance copies/advances The first delivery of copies of a printed job so the quality of binding can be checked and approved.

3239 bed (**2**) The flat metal surface of a guillotine, on which paper is cut. Also called a **table**. ➜ *3296 guillotine; 1217 table (2)*

3240 binder's creep The displacement of the leaves in the signatures of a book, causing the inner pages of the folded signatures to have a slightly smaller trim size. Creep increases with paper thickness. Also called **thrust**, **shingling**, and **pushout**. ➜ *2716 signature (1)*

3241 bolts The three edges ("head" bolts, "fore-edge" bolts, and "tail" bolts) of a folded sheet that will be trimmed before binding. The remaining folded edge is not called a bolt, but the "back" or "last" fold.

3242 book block A book that has been folded, gathered, and stitched, but not yet cased-in. ➜ *3091 cased/case bound; 3092 casing-in*

3243 book sizes The common sizes used for book production in the United States are as follows:

name	inches	mm
Thirtysixmo (36mo)	4 × 3⅓	102 × 85
Medium Thirtytwomo (Med. 32mo)	4¾ × 3	121 × 76
Medium Twentyfourmo (Med. 24mo)	5½ × 3⅝	140 × 92
Medium Eighteenmo (Med. 18mo)	6⅔ × 4	169 × 102
Medium Sixteenmo (Med. 16mo)	6¾ × 4½	171 × 114
Cap Octavo (Cap 8vo)	7 × 7¼	184 × 178
Duodecimo (12mo)	7½ × 4½	191 × 114
Crown Octavo (Cr. 8vo)	7½ × 5	191 × 127
Post Octavo (Post 8vo)	7½ × 5½	191 × 140
Medium Duodecimo (Med. 12mo)	7⅔ × 5⅛	195 × 130
Demy Octavo (Dy. 8vo)	8 × 5½	203 × 140
Small Quarto (Sm. 4to)	8½ × 7	216 × 178
Broad Quarto (Br. 4to) (varies)	8½ × 7	216 × 178
Medium Octavo Med. (8vo)	9½ × 6	241 × 152
Royal Octavo (Roy. 8vo)	10 × 6½	254 × 165
Super Royal Octavo (S. Roy. 8vo)	10½ × 7	267 × 178
Imperial Quarto (Imp. 4to)	11 × 15	279 × 381
Imperial Octavo (Imp. 8vo)	11½ × 8¼	292 × 210

Until 1969, book sizes in the UK were as follows (the names are still used today):

	inches	mm
Pott Octavo (Pott 8)	6¼ × 4	159 × 102
Foolscap Octavo (F'cap 8)	6¾ × 4¼	171 × 110
Crown Octavo (Cr. 8)	7½ × 5	191 × 127
Large Post Octavo (L. Post 8)	8¼ × 5¼	292 × 133
Demy Octavo (Dy 8)	8¾ × 5	220 × 127
Medium Octavo (Med. 8)	9 × 5¾	229 × 146
Royal Octavo (Roy. 8)	10 × 6¼	254 × 159
Super Royal Octavo (SuR 8)	10 × 6¾	254 × 171
Imperial Octavo (Imp 8)	11 × 7½	279 × 191
Foolscap Quarto (F'cap 4)	8½ × 6¾	216 × 171
Crown Quarto (Cr. 4)	10 × 7½	254 × 191
Large Post Quarto (L. Post 4)	10½ × 8¼	267 × 210
Demy Quarto (Dy 4)	11¼ × 8¾	286 × 220

Medium Quarto (Med. 4) . . . . 11½ × 9. . . . . . . 292 × 229
Royal Quarto (Roy. 4) . . . . 12½ × 10. . . . . . 318 × 254
Foolscap Folio (F'cap fol). . . . . 13½ × 8½ . . . . . 343 × 216

Today, however, UK book sizes are determined by the metric ISO paper sizes, which are used throughout the world, although not widely in the United States. ➔ *2442 paper sizes; 2432 ISO A-series paper sizes*

3244 **broad fold** Paper that has been folded with the direction of grain running along the shorter dimension.

3245 **brochure** A short publication that has its pages stitched together but is otherwise unbound. The term derives from the French *brocher*, meaning to stitch. ➔ *3870 pamphlet*

3246 **buckle folder** A folding machine in which the paper sheet is fed into an adjustable stop that causes the sheet to buckle. Two "nip" rollers then fold the sheet along the buckle. Also called a **plate folder**. ➔ *3282 folding; 3306 knife folder; 3253 combination folder*

3247 **bulk** (**1**) The thickness of the assembled pages of a publication, minus its covers. ➔ *3788 bulking dummy*

3248 **bundling** The tying together of signatures, prior to binding. ➔ *2716 signature (1); 3082 binding*

3249 **center-stitching** A binding that uses thread stitched through the centerfold, similar to wire saddle-stitching. ➔ *3335 saddle-stitch; 3082 binding; 3211 stitching*

3250 **chain stitch** The binding stitch at the head and tail of a section, made before the next section is sewn. ➔ *3337 section*

3251 **closed section/signature** A section or signature in which the bolts have been left uncut. ➔ *3337 section; 2716 signature (1); 3241 bolts*

3252 **collate** The process of sorting printed pages or signatures into their correct order. Also called **conflate**. ➔ *2561 back (step) mark; 2560 back step collation; 2716 signature (1)*

3253 **combination folder** A folding machine that combines both buckle and knife methods of folding. ➔ *3246 buckle folder; 3306 knife folder*

3254 **conjugate leaves** Any two leaves of a publication that consist of one piece of paper, such as the center spread of a signature. ➔ *2716 signature (1); 3940 double (page) spread*

3255 **continuous fold** A paper folding system that converts rolls of paper into "accordion" folds. ➔ *3237 accordion fold*

3256 **converting** The final operation, after printing, that completes the job. This includes finishing processes such as folding, laminating, gluing, diecutting, box manufacture, and so on.

3257 **cover title** The title of a book as stamped or printed on its spine. ➔ *3203 spine*

3258 **creasing** (**1**) An indented line impressed into paper or board that makes it easier to fold — used when making hinges for book covers, for example. ➔ *3131 hinges*

3259 **creep** The displacement of the leaves in each signature of a book due to the effect of folding. Creep increases with paper thickness. Also known as **thrust**, **shingling**, and **pushout**. ➔ *3364 wraparound (2)*

3279 Fold out

3260 cut (**6**) To trim the edges of a book. → *3261 cut edges; 3271 edges*

3261 cut edges All three edges of a book that have been cut so they are all flush. → *3260 cut (6)*

3262 cut flush A book with its cover trimmed to the same size as the pages. Also known as **flush boards** or **trimmed flush**, or, if stiffened, **stiffened and cut flush**.

3263 cut score Partial slitting of paper that acts as an aid in creasing.

3264 cutting and creasing The process — usually carried out on a cylinder press — of cutting special shapes into or out of board, such as in packaging and book covers, and then creasing it in preparation for folding. → *2971 cylinder press; 3267 diecutting*

3265 cutting cylinder A cylinder on a rotary press bearing a knife that cuts the paper web into sheets.

3266 die (**2**) A pattern or design of sharp blades that, when mounted on a press, are used to cut shapes out of paper or board. → *3267 diecutting*

3267 diecutting A process in which paper or board is cut to a particular shape or design using a "die" on a "die press." → *3264 cutting and creasing; 3266 die (2); 3008 die press*

3268 double digest fold A basic fold to make a signature in web printing. → *2716 signature (1); 2746 web printing*

3269 draw (**2**) To gather together all the signatures of a publication prior to binding. → *3283 F & Gs*

3270 drill(ing) Boring holes in paper or binding using a rotating "die." → *3007 die; 3082 binding*

3271 edges The cut edges of a book block.

3272 film lamination/laminating A thin, protective plastic film that is bonded to a printed paper under pressure and heat. Laminates can have a glossy or matte finish.

3273 finishing All operations that take place after printing, such as collating, folding, gathering, trimming, binding, and packing.

3274 flat stitching A method of stitching a flat-backed book from the side, through all the pages. → *3343 side-stitch*

3275 flatbed cutter A device used for trimming the edges of books.

3276 flexible sewing A technique for sewing the sections of a book onto raised bands or cords. The thread is passed around each cord, providing a very strong binding, which, in most cases, can be opened flat.

3277 flocking A method of creating a vaguely 3D texture by blowing fibers over an adhesive ink surface.

3278 fly fold A sheet that has been folded once, making a four-page leaflet.

3279 fold out In a publication, a page that extends when unfolded to a size greater than the page size. The foldout page must be imposed so the fold occurs within the area of the trim size so it is not trimmed off during finishing. Also called a **throw out** (or **thrown out**), and **pull out**. → *3291 gatefold; 3351 thrown clear*

3280 fold to paper Folding paper so all edges — rather than the printed page elements — align. Also called **paper to paper**. → *3281 fold to print*

3281 fold to print Folding paper so printed page elements align, regardless of the alignment of the edges of the paper. Also called **type to type**. → *3280 fold to paper;* **2687** *print to paper*

3282 fold/folding The folding of a single flat sheet to create a desired effect (accordion, french, gatefold, parallel, right-angle, and so on), or the folding of a printed signature/section of a multipage publication prior to gathering, stitching, trimming, and binding.

3283 folded and collated/gathered (**F/C, F & C, F/G, F & G**) Sheets of a publication that, after printing, are folded, collated, and then gathered in preparation for binding.

3284 folder (**2**) A machine that creases and scores printed sheets during finishing. → *3273 finishing*

3285 folder/folding dummy A mock-up showing the sheet folded exactly as it will be in production.

3286 folding plate An oversize book illustration that has been folded to fit within the trim size before being bound in. → *2673 plate (2);* **3291** *gatefold*

3287 folio lap The area of excess paper that is allowed for machine-handling in the bindery. It is eventually trimmed off.

3288 forwarding In case binding, the stages in the bookmaking process after sewing but before the case is covered.

3289 french fold A sheet that has been printed on one side only and then folded twice to form an uncut four-page section.

3290 french sewing/stitch As well as describing the standard method of machine sewing, "french stitch" is also a method of binding a ready-bound item into another publication.

3291 gatefold A sheet folded into three equal segments by first dividing the sheet with two parallel creases and then folding both the outer segments across the middle of the sheet in overlapping layers. Also called a **wallet fold**. → *3279 fold out*

3292 gathering (**1**) Assembling and placing the signatures of a book in the correct order prior to binding. → *3283 folded and gathered;* **2716** *signature (1);* **3082** *binding*

3293 gathering (**2**) An alternative term for a quire or signature. → *3330 quire;* **2716** *signature (1)*

3294 gloss finishing Application of a film, varnish, or lacquer to a printed sheet. Often used for book dust jackets, paperback covers, and so on, to offer protection and also because it can give color a greater "depth," or density. → *3358 varnish;* **3070** *spot varnishing*

3295 glue flap An overlapping flap or other area to which glue is applied to fasten folded containers or cartons.

3296 guillotine A machine in the print finishing line that accurately cuts several sheets of paper at once. These sheets may be either flat, or folded and stitched. Also called a **cutter**.

3297 gusseting Small, unwanted creases at the top of the inner pages of a closed signature. → *2716 signature (1)*

3298 head trim A small amount of paper trimmed off the page above the head margin. → *3962 head margin;* **3356** *trimming*

3299 heat sealing A technique in which two materials, usually plastic, are fused together under heat and pressure.

3300 hinged Separate sheets that have had a narrow fold applied to their inner edges, prior to insertion in a book, so they lie flatter when the book is opened, and turn more easily.

3301 in quires Printed sheets, especially those lying flat, before they are folded and gathered for binding. Also called **in sheets**. → *3330 quire; 3283 folded and collated/gathered*

3302 in-line converting/finishing Any post-print process, such as trimming and folding, that is performed as part of a continuous automated process immediately after printing, common in web printing. → *3315 offline converting; 3256 converting*

3303 insert (**2**) A piece of paper, board, or printed item placed loose between the pages of a book. Also called **loose inserts** or **throw ins**.

3304 jaw folder A folding unit fitted to a web press that cuts and folds signatures. → *2716 signature (1)*

3305 jog(ging) The process of shaking a pile of paper, either by hand or by machine, so the edges of each sheet align before trimming. A "jogger" may be attached to a press or form a separate unit. Also called **knocking up**. → *3356 trimming*

3306 knife folder A folding machine in which a blunt knife forces the sheet of paper between two rollers, folding it in the process. → *3253 combination folder; 3246 buckle folder*

3307 lacquer A solution that provides a glossy finish and a protective coating. → *3294 gloss finishing; 3358 varnish*

3308 lamination/laminate An item composed of two or more layers of material. In print finishing this usually means applying transparent or colored plastic films, with any degree of shininess, to printed matter to protect or enhance it.

3309 letter fold A sheet of paper folded two or more times with the creases running in the same direction.

3310 loop stitching A technique of saddle-stitching in which the wire forms a loop that extends beyond the spine, thus providing an alternative to drilled holes as a means of attaching the publication to a post or ring binder. → *3335 saddle-stitched*

3311 makeup (**2**) A mock-up assembly of all the printed sections of a publication for use as a guide by the bindery.

3312 nib/nibbed A tongue of paper on a folded insert in a book (a map, for example), enabling the insert to open more easily.

3313 nip (**1**) The crease at the joint of a case-bound book. → *3140 joint*

3314 off-cut Trimmed parts of paper, board, and so on that may be used for other jobs.

3315 offline converting/finishing Any post-print process, such as trimming or folding, that is not performed on the same press used for printing the job. → *3302 inline converting; 3256 converting*

3316 orange peel An undesirable effect on laminated surfaces, usually caused by too much setoff spray being used after printing. → *3066 setoff*

3317 oversewing A method of sewing books consisting of separate leaves using a stitch similar to that found on the edge of blankets. Also called **overcasting** or whipstitching. → *3360 whipstitching; 3152 machine-sewing*

3318 oversize (**4**) A size of book or publication that is physically too large for the printing and binding process and thus may involve some handwork.

3319 parallel fold A series of folds aligned in the same direction in a sheet of paper, and usually of equal size.

3320 paste on A method of gluing a printed image into a book by applying paste all over the back of the image. → *3072 tip in*

3321 paster (**1**) The component of a binding line that applies adhesive rather than stitching, in the manufacture of booklets. The term also describes the product of the process.

3322 pebbling A technique of embossing paper after it has been printed to create an undulating effect.

3323 perfect copy A complete set of printed and folded sheets, ready for binding. → *3063 perfect*

3324 pop-ups A folded paper sheet that is diecut and creased to lie flat when closed, but when opened expands into a 3-D model.

3325 pregather The binding of a single section prior to combining it with other sections.

3326 pressing unit A unit of a binding line that presses freshly cased books with heated clamps, avoiding the need to leave them to stand for a time in a "standing press."

3327 print convertors The mechanized functions employed to complete a print job, such as folding, cutting, collating, stitching, and so on.

3328 pull test A method of testing the strength of a perfect bound book by pulling it apart.

3329 quad folder A machine that creases and folds single printed sheets of 64 pages into four 16-page signatures or two 32-page signatures.

3330 quire (**2**) A gathering of four sheets folded once to make eight leaves, or 16 pages. Synonymous with "quaternion." → *3880 quaternion*

3331 quires/quire stock Printed sheets that are folded but not yet bound. Also called **sheet stock**. → *3283 F & Gs*

3332 quirewise A collection of unbound leaves, folded one within another. They are subsequently stitched.

3333 right-angle fold The standard method of folding a printed sheet. It is folded in half and then again at right angles to the first fold. Also known as a **chopper fold**.

3334 saddle-sewn A method of securing multiple pages by stitching them with thread through the fold line while the pages are supported on a saddle-shaped mount. → *3335 saddle-stitched*

3335 saddle-stitched A method of securing pages in pamphlets or brochures by stitching them through the fold line with wire staples while the sheets rest on a saddle-shaped mount. → *3334 saddle-sewn*

3336 score/scoring Marking the line of a crease in paper or card so it can be folded cleanly. Also called **creasing**. → *3282 fold/folding*

3337 section (2) A printed sheet folded to form four or more pages of a book, ready for gathering and sewing. The term is now used synonymously with "signature." ➔ *2716 signature; 3283 folded and gathered; 3292 gathering*

3338 section-sewn book A book in which the gathered sections are sewn together with thread.

3339 sewing The fastening together of sections of a book by means of thread. Can be performed manually or mechanically. ➔ *3211 stitching*

3340 sewn book A book fastened together by the sewing process. ➔ *3339 sewing; 3082 binding*

3341 shining The technique of holding printed sheets up to a light source to make sure they are in register prior to folding.

3342 side-sewing A form of bookbinding in which the whole book is sewn in one single section, instead of in individual sections. Books made in this way usually do not lie flat when open.

3343 side-stitch/stab The process of binding a booklet by stitching the sheets together along the side close to the gutter. If wire is used, this is known as "sidewiring."

3344 slitter A sharp rotary blade that cuts a moving sheet into strips. ➔ *3069 slit*

3345 sophisticated A book in which a page or pages were found to be missing and have been replaced with those from an identical copy or from a carefully printed facsimile, and which can include high-quality photocopied pages.

3346 square folding A folding technique in which printed sheets are folded with the second fold at right angles to the first, the third to the second, and so on.

3347 stabbing (1) Stapling together a booklet or closed section near the back edge.

3348 stabbing (2) Using a sharp tool, such as an awl, to pierce holes in the side of a section prior to stitching.

3349 stapling A binding method that uses one or more pressed wire staples to secure pages.

3350 star signature The inner 16 pages of a 32-page section, identified by the signature letter followed by a star (for example, "AH"). The outer 16 pages are identified by the signature letter alone ("A"). ➔ *3848 insert (1)*

3351 thrown clear A method of adding folded illustrations to a book, usually maps, plans, or equipment diagrams, which, printed alongside a blank page (called a "guard"), open out entirely beyond the page area for ease of reference. ➔ *3279 fold out*

3352 thrown out In a publication, a page that extends when unfolded to a size greater than the page size. ➔ *3279 fold out*

3353 trim To cut printed sheets to the required size.

3354 trimmed edges In traditional bookbinding, the cutting of the leaves at the top edge, but cutting only the larger projecting leaves on the tail and fore-edges, thus giving a rough appearance.

3363 Wraparound

3355 trimmed page size (tps)/trimmed size The size of a printed and bound book, but referring to the page size rather than the size including the binding. → *2573 bleed (1); 2611 full bleed*

3356 trimming The process of cutting the edges of the pages of a publication to remove the folds and produce a regular finish.

3357 two-on binding A method of trimming two books, one on top of the other, at the same time. Also called **two-up binding**.

3358 varnish A liquid that dries with a hard surface and that is generally insoluble in water. It is used in the manufacture of printing inks, in some drying agents, and as a surface protector. → *2361 calendered varnish; 3070 spot varnishing*

3359 varnishing The process of applying a protective covering to a book or periodical. → *3294 gloss finishing*

3360 whipstitching A method of stitching books that consist of single sheets. → *3317 oversewing*

3361 wire stabbing A rudimentary method of side-stitching a book using wire staples. Wire stabbed books cannot be opened flat. → *3335 saddle-stitched; 3211 stitching*

3362 wire stitch(ing) A common method of saddle-stitching with wire, typically used for magazines and brochures. → *3335 saddle-stitched*

3363 wraparound (1) An insert placed around a signature before it is bound. → *3848 insert (1)*

3364 wraparound (2) The increased gutter width required for the outer pages of signatures to make allowance for "creep." → *3240 binder's creep; 3259 creep*

3365 wraparound plates (1) Illustration plates printed separately from the text and bound on the outside of the text signatures. → *3303 insert*

3366 against the grain Folding, marking, or feeding paper at right angles to the direction ("grain") of paper fibers. Also called **cross-grain**. → *2933 graining; 2286 grain direction*

3367 Alaska seal An imitation sealskin binding material made from animal hide, such as cow or sheep.

3368 art canvas A rough-surfaced binding material used for binding cased books. → *3090 case (1); 3091 cased/case bound; 3083 bookbinding*

3369 basil A binding material made from sheepskin and used as a poor-quality substitute for leather. → *3082 binding*

3370 binder's board Board used as a stiffener for binding books, around which cloth or other materials are wrapped. → *2471 boards; 3374 book cloth; 3083 bookbinding*

3371 board covers An inexpensive binding style in which paper-covered boards are used instead of cloth boards. → *2471 boards; 3082 binding*

3372 boarded leather Binding leather that has been dampened and pressed between boards to enhance the natural grain. → *2471 boards*

3373 bocasin A fine-quality buckram. → *3375 buckram*

3374 book cloth A fabric made from dyed, coated calico and used to cover cased books. → *3091 cased/case bound; 3095 cloth boards*

3378 Crash (3)

3375 **buckram** A strong, coarse book cloth made of jute, linen, or cotton that has been glazed and stiffened. → *3374 book cloth; 3373 bocasin*

3376 **calf** Smooth-finished bookbinding material made from calfskin. → *3083 bookbinding; 3082 binding*

3377 **carton** A container, generally designed to be flattened when not in use.

3378 **crash** (**3**) A loose-weave cloth, such as cheesecloth, used for binding case-bound books, or for strengthening their joints. → *3091 case bound; 3140 joint*

3379 **cross-grained morocco** A goatskin binding material embellished with artificially produced diagonal lines. → *3399 morocco*

3380 **deerskin** A bookbinding leather originally used to cover wooden book boards. → *2471 boards*

3381 **doublures** The decorative lining of the inside face of the boards of a hand-bound book.

3382 **drill** A coarse cloth used for binding books.

3383 **elephant hide** A durable bookbinding material made from fabricated parchment. → *3082 binding*

3384 **expandable cloth** A type of flexible cloth used in bookbinding.

3385 **extra calf** An extra bound book with finest calf rather than morocco covering. → *3108 extra bound; 3399 morocco*

3386 **extra cloth** A colored material with a plain finish used for bookbinding. → *3082 binding*

3387 **french morocco** Made from sheepskin grained to resemble genuine morocco, this is used in bookbinding as a cheaper alternative. → *3399 morocco; 3082 binding*

3388 **glazed morocco** A fine goatskin leather used for covering books. Its polished finish is achieved by "calendering" (passing between metal rollers). → *2360 calender*

3389 **grained leather** Fine leather used in bookbinding, that has either had its natural grain or texture enhanced, or has had an artificial grain pressed onto its surface.

3390 **graining boards** Wooden boards or copper plates used to impart various textures to bookbinding leather. Graining boards have a pattern cut into their surface and are pressed onto the leather.

3391 **hard-grain morocco** A fine, supple goatskin leather used for bookbinding. Graining boards are used to give it a deep grain. → *3390 graining boards; 3082 binding*

3392 **holland** A fine-woven cloth, occasionally used for bookbinding purposes. Cloth of this type originated in Holland, hence its name.

3393 **jaconet** A glazed cotton fabric used for lining the spines of books. → *3401 mull*

3394 **kipskin kip** An animal skin sometimes used for bookbinding.

3395 **marbled calf** A traditional method of making a decorative binding material by using dilute acid to stain calfskin, producing a marbled pattern. → *2529 marbling*

3396 maril A bookbinding of marbled, inlaid leather.

3397 membrane A skin parchment.

3398 millboards Strong boards used for the covers of books. Also called **pressboards**. ➔ *3089 cover; 2471 boards; 3370 binder's boards; 3090 case*

3399 morocco Glazed and polished goatskin, used for bookbinding. ➔ *3379 cross-grained morocco*

3400 mottled calf Calfskin that has been given an irregular pattern with colored dyes, used for book covers.

3401 mull A coarse cheesecloth that forms the first lining of a case bound book. Also called **scrim** or **super**.

3402 oasis goat Bookbinding leather obtained from a South African goat. Also used as a trade name for West African tanned morocco skin. ➔ *3399 morocco*

3403 ooze leather Bookbindings made of sheepskin or calfskin with the flesh ("nap") side outermost, giving a suede finish.

3404 paper boards A cased binding of paper rather than cloth.

3405 paper covers A style of binding (without boards) ordinary books sewn in sections, as distinct from mass-produced paperbacks, which are generally adhesive bound. ➔ *3169 paperback; 3073 adhesive binding*

3406 paste-grain A binding material with a polished surface, made from hardened sheepskin coated with paste.

3407 pin seal Young sealskin once used for exotic bindings.

3408 pin seal morocco Goatskin that has been treated to resemble pin seal. ➔ *3407 pin seal*

3409 polished calf High-quality bookbinding material made from calfskin.

3410 publisher's cloth The traditional binding material for edition-bound books. ➔ *3104 edition binding*

3411 roan A cover material made from dyed sheepskin that is sometimes used in bookbinding instead of morocco.

3412 rough calf A traditional calfskin binding with the flesh side outermost. Also known as **reversed calf**.

3413 russia cowhide A traditional, lesser-quality binding material made from cowhide, often impregnated with Russian oil to resemble genuine russia leather. Also called **American russia**. ➔ *3414 russia leather*

3414 russia leather A traditional, high-quality cover material made from calfskin impregnated with aromatic birch tar oil. ➔ *3413 russia cowhide*

3415 sarsanet A type of lining material of stiffened silk.

3416 seal The skin of the Newfoundland seal, used in bookbinding for limp covers. ➔ *3146 limp binding*

3417 show side The best or face side of any material that will ultimately be visible in the finished article. Often used to describe book cloths.

3418 smooth washed Ungrained book cloth, such as cloth that is not mechanically grained.

3419 sprinkled calf Fine calfskin leather used for book covering in approximately the 17th century. A speckled finish was achieved by sprinkling acid onto the leather.

3420 tanned leather The traditional process of converting an animal skin into leather by soaking it in an infusion of the bark of an oak tree, staining it a dark brown. ➔ *3083 bookbinding; 3128 half-leather; 3369 basil*

3421 textile bindings Traditional bookbindings made from fabric such as silk brocade or velvet, which are sometimes embroidered.

3422 watered silk Silk with a wavy pattern, sometimes used for "doublures" (decorative lining inside a hand-bound book).

3423 antique gold edges The finish given to gilt edges that are either left unburnished or are washed over with water after burnishing. ➔ *3456 gilt edges; 3424 art gilt edges*

3424 art gilt edges Gilt-edged books in which the edges have been colored, usually with a tint of the binding, prior to the gold being applied. ➔ *3456 gilt edges; 3423 antique gold edges*

3425 azured tooling The "hatched" effect in hand-tooled bindings, deriving from the heraldic device of using horizontal parallel lines to indicate blue. ➔ *3082 binding*

3426 binder's die/brass A brass block used for blocking, or stamping, the cover of a book. ➔ *3428 block (2)*

3427 blind tooling The process of embossing a design onto a book cover with heated tools, but without foil.

3428 block (2) A metal stamp, usually made of brass, used to impress a design onto a book cover or jacket. Blocks are frequently used with metallic foils ("blocking foils"). The verb "to block" means to emboss a book cover or jacket. ➔ *3426 binder's die; 3429 blocking; 3430 blocking foils; 3486 stamp (2)*

3429 blocking The technique of impressing a design onto book covers or jackets. ➔ *3428 block (2); 3460 gold blocking; 3463 ink blocking*

3430 blocking foils Strictly speaking, a metal beaten to a thin "leaf," which is then applied to a book cover by means of blocking. Today, imitation foils made of plastic and colored with metal powders are used. "Gold blocking" is sometimes erroneously used to describe any blocking finish with a gold metallic foil, but more accurately describes blocking with actual gold metal. The same applies to other precious metals. ➔ *3428 block (2); 3429 blocking*

3431 blocking press A press that uses heated blocks to stamp designs onto book covers. ➔ *3429 blocking*

3432 bosses In traditional bookbinding, the small raised ornaments made of metal and usually fixed at the corners of a book cover to protect against rubbing. ➔ *3083 bookbinding*

3433 brass An engraved plate used by bookbinders to block, or stamp, a design onto a book cover. ➔ *3428 block (2)*

3434 burnished edges The polishing of the colored edges of a book by applying wax and then rubbing with a burnishing tool. ➔ *3577 burnish; 3435 burnisher (1)*

3435 burnisher (1) A hand tool, sometimes made of stone, used for burnishing book edges. ➔ *3577 burnish; 3434 burnished edges*

3436 cameo binding A book cover adorned with a stamped or inset cameo. ➜ *4085 cameo (3)*

3437 chase (**2**) To make a groove or cut a design into a surface, such as a block or book cover. ➜ *3438 chased edges; 3462 holing out; 3476 paring*

3438 chased edges The wavy effect on gilded edges of a book, achieved by using heated tools known as goffering irons. Chased edges are also known as **goffered edges**. ➜ *3456 gilt edges*

3439 colored edges/tops The edges or tops of books that have been colored. Color is usually applied by spray gun to the book blocks prior to binding. After coloring, wax may be applied to give the edges a gloss or, for the most glossy finish, the edges may be rubbed with a burnisher. Also called **stained edges**. ➜ *3434 burnished edges; 3435 burnisher (1); 3242 book block*

3440 cutout (**2**) A display card or book cover into which a pattern or hole has been cut.

3441 deep gold Top-quality gold leaf, used for "tooling" on hand-bound books, unlike the cheaper **pale gold** leaf used for gilding the edges of books. ➜ *3487 tooling*

3442 edge gilding The process of applying a gold edge to a page border. As distinct from "gilt edges," in which the trimmed book edges are covered with gold leaf. ➜ *3454 gild; 3479 red under gilt edges; 3456 gilt edges*

3443 edge staining The application of color to any trimmed edge/edges of a book block. ➜ *3485 sprinkled edges*

3444 emboss(**ing**) Relief printing or stamping in which dies are used to impress a design into the surface of paper, cloth, or leather so the letters or images are raised above the surface. Also known as **waffling**. ➜ *3007 die (1)*

3445 embossed binding A traditional bookbinding of leather or cloth on which an image was impressed using a heated die (and counter die) with the image in relief. Additional gilding and lettering were added later.

3446 embroidered binding An intricate needlework design usually worked in colored silks or gold thread on a canvas, silk, or velvet surface. Popular in the 16th and 17th centuries, books finished with this technique were sometimes adorned with pearls, sequins, and clasps made from precious metal.

3447 entrelac A traditional design used to decorate book covers; it comprises ribbons or interlaced strapwork derived from Islamic arabesques.

3448 fillet Straight lines embossed onto the cover of a book, used as decoration. ➜ *3451 french fillet*

3449 floret A tool used by bookbinders to impress a floral motif.

3450 fore-edge painting The traditional decoration of the edge of a block of pages, visible only when the book is closed. It also describes the painting of the fore-edge of individual pages — only visible when the book is open. Also called **painted edges**. ➜ *3485 sprinkled edges*

3451 french fillet A border comprising three lines, made up from a fine double line and a single line, used on 16th-century French bindings.

3452 full gilt A book with all edges gilded. ➜ *3454 gild*

3453 **giggering** The technique of polishing the interior of a blind impression on a leather binding using a small hand tool. ➜ *3487 tooling*

3454 **gild** The application of gold leaf — or sometimes another metallic leaf — to the trimmed edges of a book. ➜ *3442 edge gilding*

3455 **gilding rolls** Brass rolls, usually with ornamental designs, used for gold tooling. ➜ *3487 tooling*

3456 **gilt edges** Trimmed book edges covered with gold leaf, as distinct from "edge gilding" in which page borders are gilded. ➜ *3442 edge gilding*

3457 **gilt solid** Book edges that have been rounded and then gilded. A process used only for expensive hand-finished bindings. Also known as **gilt after rounding**. ➜ *3454 gild*

3458 **gilt top** (**g.t., g.t.e., t.e.g.**) A book in which only the top is gilded.

3459 **gold** The precious metal traditionally used to decorate bindings and occasionally to illuminate lavish manuscripts. Normally supplied and used in leaf form. ➜ *3461 gold leaf*

3460 **gold blocking** The technique by which a design in gold leaf is stamped into the cover of a book by a heated die under pressure. Also known as **gold tooling**, although this originally referred to the process when it was carried out by hand. ➜ *3463 ink blocking*

3461 **gold leaf** A gold material — to which very small amounts of silver and copper have been added — that is rolled and beaten to an extremely thin foil. The manufacture of gold leaf is a painstaking craft still practiced by hand, although machines capable of producing it have been developed. Gold leaf is the preferred material for the hand decoration of book covers, and so on, but is not used widely for commercial bookbinding even though it is more durable than cheaper synthetic varieties.

3462 **holing out** The punching or drilling of holes through the boards of a hand-bound book.

3463 **ink blocking** A technique in which the title or a design is stamped into the cover of a book with an inked block. ➜ *3429 blocking; 3460 gold blocking; 3487 tooling*

3464 **inlaying** A traditional method of decorating a book cover by insetting pieces of very thin leather or other material of contrasting colors into the surface. Books bound this way are said to be "inlaid bindings." ➜ *3468 mosaic binding; 3471 onlaying*

3465 **laying on** The process of applying gold leaf to a surface.

3466 **medallion** An illustration printed on paper and pasted onto the case of a book. ➜ *3072 tip in/on*

3467 **mordant** (**1**) An adhesive for affixing gold leaf.

3468 **mosaic binding** Book covers decorated with contrasting leather inlays. ➜ *3464 inlaying*

3469 **mosaic gold** Imitation gold made from disulfide of tin and mercury, a cheaper substitute for powdered gold. Also called aurium musicum. ➜ *3472 oriental leaf*

3470 **olivined edges** Green staining applied to the edges of a book.

3471 **onlaying** The traditional method of decorating a calf or morocco bound book cover using additional pieces of very thin leather of contrasting colors glued to the surface. → *3464 inlaying*

3472 **oriental leaf** An alternative to gold foil made from a mixture of brass and bronze. → *3469 mosaic gold*

3473 **pallet** A brass finishing tool used for impressing straight lines or type characters onto the covers or spines of books. → *3448 fillet; 3451 french fillet; 3487 tooling*

3474 **panel back** A hand-bound book with a decorative panel on its spine.

3475 **panel stamp** An engraved block used to create an embossed image on a book cover.

3476 **paring** In traditional bookbinding, the process of thinning the edge of a leather sheet to enable a neater finish when it is folded around the edge of a cover board.

3477 **powdered** The effect of a decorative stippling technique used for traditional book covers.

3478 **printed edges** Printing on the cut edges of a book. → *3485 sprinkled edges; 3271 edges*

3479 **red under gilt edges** Book edges that have been sprayed red and then gilded — used for Bibles, prayer books, and so on. → *3454 gild; 3442 edge gilding; 3271 edges*

3480 **reel gold** A reel of imitation gold blocking foil, usually made from bronze. → *3460 gold blocking*

3481 **roll** (**3**) A tool comprising a brass wheel, sometimes decorated with a repeating pattern, that is used in traditional bookbinding to impress a continuous line on a cover.

3482 **rough gilt** Uncut edges that are gilded before they are sewn. → *3454 gild; 3442 edge gilding*

3483 **run-up spine** A standard decoration on the tooled spine of a book consisting of twin lines running up the spine edges and across the width to form panels.

3484 **skewings** Scraps of waste gold leaf left over from the gold blocking process. → *3460 gold blocking*

3485 **sprinkled edges** A decoration on the cut edges of a book that gives a sprinkled ink effect. Helps to disguise soiling caused by excessive handling and so on. → *3478 printed edges*

3486 **stamp** (**2**)**/stamping** The process of impressing a design into a page or cover by means of a die pressed with considerable force. Various colored foils or gold leaf can be used, or the die may be used without color ("blind" or "blank" stamping). → *3444 emboss*

3487 **tooling** Impressing or laying decorations and lettering onto book covers. → *3441 deep gold*

3488 **top edge gilt** The application of gilding to only the top edge of a book. → *3454 gild*

3489 **zinco** (**1**) A less durable but cheaper alternative to a binder's brass, producing less sharp results.

3496 CMYK
a cyan
b magenta
c yellow
d black

a

b

3499 Color model
a additive
b subtractive

3490 achromatic A color that does not have any no saturation, or "chroma," such as black or white. → *3493 chroma*

3491 additive colors The color model describing the primary colors of transmitted light: red, green, and blue (RGB). Additive colors can be mixed to form all other colors in photographic reproduction and computer display monitors. → *3499 color model; 3555 subtractive colors; 3547 RGB; 3496 CMYK*

3492 calibrate/calibration The process of adjusting a machine or piece of hardware to conform to a known scale or standard so it performs more accurately. In graphic reproduction it is important that the various devices and materials used in the production chain, such as scanners, monitors, imagesetters and printing presses, conform to a consistent set of measures to achieve true fidelity, particularly where color is concerned. Calibration of reproduction and display devices is generally carried out with a "densitometer." → *2008 densitometer*

3493 chroma The intensity, or purity, of a color, thus its degree of saturation. → *3522 hue; 3490 achromatic*

3494 CIE *abb.:* **Commission Internationale de l'Eclairage** An international organization that defined a visual color model that forms the basis for colorimetric measurements of color. → *0735 CIE L*a*b* color space; 3499 color model*

3495 CMY *abb.:* **cyan, magenta, yellow** The primary colors of the "subtractive" color model, created when you subtract red, green, or blue from white light. In other words, if an object reflects green and blue light, but absorbs, or subtracts, red, it will appear to you as cyan. Cyan, magenta, and yellow are the basic printing process colors. → *3496 CMYK; 3547 RGB; 3499 color model; 3555 subtractive colors*

3496 CMYK *abb.:* **cyan, magenta, yellow, and black** (black is represented by the letter "K," for "key" plate). The four printing process colors based on the subtractive color model. In color reproduction, most of the colors are achieved by cyan, magenta, and yellow, the theory being that when all three are combined, they produce black. However, this is rarely achievable and would be undesirable since too much ink would be used, causing problems with drying time. For this reason black is used to add density to darker areas, while to compensate, smaller amounts of the other colors are used (this also has cost benefits because black is cheaper than colored inks). The degree of color that is "removed" is calculated by a technique known as "undercolor removal" (UCR). → *3495 CMY; 3547 RGB; 2087 UCR; 3499 color model*

3497 color (**1**) The visual interpretation of the various wavelengths of reflected or refracted light.

3498 color cast A bias in a color image that can be either intentional or undesirable. If the former, it is usually made at proof correction stage to enhance the color of an image; if the latter, the cast could be due to any number of causes occurring, for example, when the image was photographed, scanned, manipulated on computer, output, proofed, or printed.

3499 color model The method of defining or modifying color. Although there are many proprietary color models, such as PANTONE, FOCOLTONE, TRUMATCH, TOYO, and DIC, the two generic models are those based on the way light is transmitted — the "additive" and "subtractive" color models. The additive color model is used, for example, in

3504 Color wheel

3505 Complementary colors

3506 Contrast
a low contrast
b high contrast

3507 Cool colors

3508 Cyan

computer monitors, which transmit varying proportions of red, green, and blue (RGB) light we interpret as different colors. By combining the varying intensities of RGB light we can simulate the range of colors found in nature and, when 100% values of all three are combined, we perceive white, whereas if there is no light we see nothing or, rather, black. The subtractive color model is based on the absorption (in other words, subtraction) and reflection of light. For example, the printing inks of cyan, magenta, and yellow — if you subtract 100% values of either red, green, or blue from white light, you create cyan, magenta, or yellow. → *3547* RGB; *3495* CMY; *3491* additive colors; *3555* subtractive colors; *3536* PANTONE; *2838* TOYO colors; *3562* TRUMATCH

3500 color picker (2) A book of printed color samples that are carefully defined and graded and from which you can select spot colors. Color pickers generally conform to a color model, such as PANTONE, so you can be confident the color you choose will be faithfully reproduced by the printer, as distinct from a "color chart" that is generally used to select colors made up from process color inks. → *2103* color chart; *3501* color swatch; *3499* color model

3501 color swatch A sample of a specific color, taken either from a color chart, color picker, or some other printed example, and used as a guide either for specification or reproduction of spot colors or process tints. → *2103* color chart; *3500* color picker (2)

3502 color temperature A measure, or composition, of light. This is defined as the temperature — measured in degrees "Kelvin" (a scale based on absolute darkness rising to incandescence) — to which a black object would need to be heated to produce a particular color of light. A tungsten lamp, for example, measures 2,900 Kelvins, whereas the temperature of direct sunlight is about 5,000 Kelvins and is considered the ideal viewing standard in the graphic arts.

3503 color value The tonal value of a color when related to a light-to-dark scale of pure grays. → *3528* lightness

3504 color wheel A circular diagram that represents the complete spectrum of visible colors. → *0742* color picker (1); *3500* color picker (2)

3505 complementary colors Two colors directly opposite each other on a color wheel, which, when combined, form white or black depending on the color model (subtractive or additive). → *3491* additive colors; *3555* subtractive colors; *3499* color model; *3504* color wheel

3506 contrast The degree of difference between adjacent tones in an image (or computer monitor) from the lightest to the darkest. "High contrast" describes an image with light highlights and dark shadows, but with few shades in between, whereas a "low contrast" image is one with even tones and few dark areas or highlights. → *1508* high key; *1518* low key

3507 cool colors A relative (and subjective) term used to describe colors with a blue or green bias. → *3564* warm colors

3508 cyan (c) With magenta and yellow, one of the three subtractive primaries, and one of the three process colors used in four-color printing. Sometimes referred to as **process blue**.

3509 degradé/degradee A graded halftone tint that, by varying the dot size, gradually changes from one edge to the other. → *2040* halftone (1); *4164* vignette; *3519* graduation/gradation/gradient

3509 Degradé

3511 Density
a highlight
b midtones
c shadow

3517 Four-color process
a cyan
b magenta
c yellow
d black
e all four combined

3519 Graduation

3513 Desaturate **a** original image; **b** desaturated color

3510 **dense** An image that is too dark. ➔ *3511 density (2); 3512 density range*

3511 **density** (**2**) The darkness of tone or color in any image. In a transparency this refers to the amount of light that can pass through it, thus determining the darkness of shadows and the saturation of color. A printed highlight cannot be any lighter in color than the color of the paper it is printed on, while the shadows cannot be any darker than the quality and volume of ink that the printing process will allow.

3512 **density range** The maximum range of tones in an image, measured as the difference between the maximum and minimum densities (the darkest and lightest tones). ➔ *3511 density (2)*

3513 **desaturate** To reduce the strength or purity of color in an image, thus making it grayer. ➔ *3548 saturation*

3514 **desaturated color** Color that contains a greater amount of gray in proportion to the hue. ➔ *3513 desaturate; 3548 saturation*

3515 **detail** The degree to which individual features of an image are defined.

3516 **FOCOLTONE** A color-matching system in which all of the colors can be created by printing the specified process color percentages. ➔ *3517 four-color process; 3496 CMYK*

3517 **four-color process** Any printing process that reproduces full-color images that have been separated into the three basic "process" colors — cyan, magenta, and yellow — with the fourth color, black, added for extra density. ➔ *2104 color separation; 2837 three-color process; 3496 CMYK*

3518 **full color** Synonymous with "four color," the term usually used to describe process color reproduction. ➔ *3517 four-color process*

3519 **graduation/gradation/gradient** The smooth transition from one color or tone to another.

3520 **green** One of the three additive primary colors of red, green, and blue. ➔ *3491 additive colors*

3521 **gray** Any neutral tone in the range between black and white, with no added color.

3522 **hue** Pure spectral color that distinguishes a color from others. Red is a different hue from blue and, although light red and dark red may contain

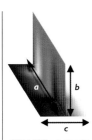

3523 HSL
a hue
b saturation
c lightness/value

3529 Magenta

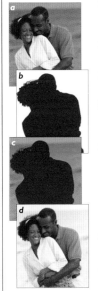

3530 Mask
a original image
b mask
c mask applied,
protecting the
foreground
d result, with a lighter
background

varying amounts of white or black, they may be the same hue. → *3493 chroma; 3548 saturation*

3523 **HSL** *abb.:* **hue, saturation, lightness** A color model based upon the light transmitted in an image or in your monitor, hue being the spectral color (the actual pigment color), saturation being the intensity of the color pigment (without black or white added); and brightness representing the strength of luminance from light to dark (the amount of black or white present). Variously called **HLS** (hue, lightness, saturation), **HSV** (hue, saturation, value), and **HSB** (hue, saturation, brightness). → *3548 saturation; 3522 hue*

3524 **K** (**I**), **k** *abb.:* **key** (plate). The black printing plate in four-color process printing, but now the name is more commonly used as shorthand for the process color black itself. Using the letter "K," rather than the initial "B," avoids confusion with blue, even though the abbreviation for process blue is "C" (cyan).

3525 **Kelvin temperature scale** (**K**) A unit of measurement that describes the color of a light source, based on absolute darkness rising to incandescence. → *3502 color temperature*

3526 **light sensitive** Any material or device that responds either chemically or digitally to light striking it, such as a photographic emulsion or a photosite (the light sensor of a CCD). → *0273 CCD; 1429 emulsion*

3527 **lightfast/colorfast** Ink or other material whose color is not affected by exposure to artificial or natural light, atmosphere, or chemicals.

3528 **lightness** The tonal measure of a color relative to a scale running from black to white. Also called **brightness** or **value**. → *3523 HSL*

3529 **magenta** (**m**) With cyan and yellow, one of the three subtractive primaries, and one of the three process colors used in four-color printing. Sometimes called **process red**.

3530 **mask** (**I**) Any material used to protect — from light, paint, or whatever — all or part of an image or page in photomechanical reproduction, photography, illustration, or layout. Many computer applications provide a masking feature that enables you to apply a mask to all or selected parts of an image. Such masks are stored in an "alpha channel" and simulate the physical material used in platemaking, which is used to shield parts of a plate from light. → *0513 alpha channel*

3531 **metameric** A color that changes hue under different lighting conditions. → *3522 hue*

3532 **midtones/middletones** The range of tonal values in an image anywhere between the darkest and lightest, usually referring to those approximately halfway. → *2060 midtone dot*

3533 **model** Any control specification used to compare the behavior of complex systems — a color model, for example. → *3499 color model*

3534 **mono**(**chrome**)**/monochromatic** (**I**) An image of varying tones reproduced in a single color. → *3535 monotone*

3535 **monotone** Reproduction in a single color, without tonal variation. → *3534 mono(chrome)*

3536 **PANTONE®** The proprietary trademark for Pantone Inc.'s system of color standards, control and quality requirements, in which each color bears a description of its formulation (in percentages) for subsequent

3537 Pastel shades

a

b

3538 Primary colors
a primary colors of printing (cyan, magenta, yellow)
b primary colors of light (red, blue, green)

a   *b*

3548 Saturation
a fully saturated
b desaturated

printing. The PANTONE MATCHING SYSTEM® is used throughout the world so colors specified by any designer can be matched exactly by any printer. → *2838* TOYO colors; *3562* TRUMATCH

3537 **pastel shades** Shades of color that are generally both lighter and less saturated than their equivalent bright hue.

3538 **primary colors** Pure colors from which, theoretically (but not in practice), all other colors can be mixed. In printing they are the "subtractive" pigment primaries: cyan, magenta, and yellow. The primary colors of light, or "additive" primaries, are red, green, and blue. → *3491* additive colors; *3555* subtractive colors

3539 **process white** Opaque, lead-free white paint used for masking and correction of camera-ready artwork.

3540 **purity** The degree of saturation of a color.

3541 **red** One of the three additive primary colors of red, green, and blue. → *3491* additive colors

3542 **reference colors** Colors that are familiar to most people and thus easy to remember, such as sky blue, grass green, and so on.

3543 **reflectance** A value determined by the amount of light reflected from an area of tone compared with the amount of light reflected from a pure white area. → *2284* gloss (1)

3544 **refraction** Light that is bent, typically when passing through one medium to another, such as air to water. → *3545* refractive index

3545 **refractive index** The measurement of the degree to which light is bent by passing through one medium to another, expressed as a ratio of the speed of light between the two. → *3544* refraction

3546 **reverse image** An image that has been reversed, either horizontally or vertically, so what was on the left of the image is now on the right, or what was at the top is now at the bottom, as in a mirror-image. → *4114* flip/flop

3547 **RGB** abb.: **red, green, blue** The primary colors of the "additive" color model, used in video technology (computer monitors, for example) and for graphics, such as for the Web, and multimedia that will not ultimately be printed by the four-color (CMYK) process method. → *3491* additive colors; *3555* subtractive colors

3548 **saturation** The variation in color of the same tonal brightness from none (gray) through pastel shades (low saturation) to pure color with no gray (high saturation, or "fully saturated"). Also called **purity** or **chroma**. → *3523* HSL

3549 **sensitize** To make something, such as a piece of paper, sensitive to something else, such as light. In printing, this includes making the image areas of a printing plate ink-receptive by applying a special coating to an aluminum printing plate.

3550 **sepia** A brown color and also a monochrome print in which the normal shades of gray appear as shades of brown. → *1467* sepia toning

3551 **shadow (area)** The areas of an image that are darkest or densest. → *3511* density (2)

3552 **solarize/solarization** An effect involving the partial reversal of negative to positive tones in an image, achieved originally by overexposing the

3552 Solarize
a original image
b solarize filter applied

3553 Spectrum

3561 Tritone

3564 Warm colors

3567 Yellow

emulsion during photographic processing. Solarization is now more usually achieved digitally. ➔ *1453 posterize*

3553 spectrum The series of colors that results when normal white light is dispersed into its component parts by refraction through a prism.

3554 specular reflectance The reflection (as by a mirror) of light rays at an angle equal to the angle at which it strikes a surface (angle of incidence).

3555 subtractive colors The color model describing the primary colors of reflected light: cyan, magenta, and yellow (CMY). Subtractive colors form the basis for printed process colors. ➔ *3499 color model; 3491 additive colors; 3517 four-color process; 3496 CMYK*

3556 swatch A color sample.

3557 tertiary The resulting color when two secondary colors are mixed.

3558 tint (1) The resulting shade after white is added to a solid color.

3559 tonal value/tone value The relative densities of tones in an image.

3560 trichromatic Comprising three colors.

3561 tritone A halftone image that is printed using three colors. Typically, a black-and-white image is enhanced by the addition of two colors, such as process yellow and magenta that, when added to black, will produce a sepia-colored image.

3562 TRUMATCH colors A system of color matching used for specifying process colors. ➔ *3536 PANTONE; 2838 TOYO colors*

3563 ultraviolet light (UV) Light waves beyond the visible violet part of the spectrum, and, as they can be absorbed by certain photosensitive materials, they are used for platemaking, printing inks, and so on.

3564 warm colors Any color with a hue veering toward red or yellow, as distinct from cool colors, which veer toward blue or green. ➔ *3507 cool colors; 3537 pastel shades*

3565 white light The color of light that results from red, blue, and green being combined in equal proportions. ➔ *3491 additive colors*

3566 Y *abb.:* process yellow, the special shade of yellow that is one of the three process colors used in four-color printing.

3567 yellow (y) With cyan and magenta, one of the three subtractive primaries, and one of the three process colors used in four-color printing. Sometimes called **process yellow**.

3568 © The symbol used to indicate that a work is protected by international copyright laws as defined by the Universal Copyright Convention (UCC). ➔ *3580 copyright*

3569 ® The mark indicating that a name or trademark is registered and cannot be used by any other person or organization, as distinct from "™," which merely identifies a name or trademark that is not registered, but for which registration may have been applied. ➔ *3640 trademark*

3570 absolute value A change in the value of a property that is made in direct relationship to the original value.

3571 acronym A single word made up from several words by using initial letters or syllables of some of the words (although not necessarily all), for example, laser (light amplification by stimulated emission of radiation), and

3576 Bar code

bit (binary digit). Abbreviations, such as ISBN and UCR, which are made up from the initial letters of a collection of words but do not form a word in themselves, are not considered acronyms.

3572 AFK Abbreviation for **away from keyboard.**

3573 analog/analogue Short for "analogous" or "similar to," the use of signals or information processed by a physical variation such as light or voltage, as distinct from digital signals. ➔ *1028 digital*

3574 ANSI *abb.:* **American National Standards Institute** A United States organization devoted to defining standards such as those used for programming languages. ANSI represents the United States at the International Standards Organization (ISO).

3575 audiovisual aids The name given to display equipment, such as projectors and computers, used for teaching and training.

3576 bar code A product identification and coding system in which a number is represented by a pattern of bars of varying thickness, which can be optically scanned to extract information, generally containing details such as country of origin, manufacturer, and product type. There are a number of systems employed for encoding information, the most common being UPC (Universal Product Code) and EAN (European Article Number). Also called **optical bar recognition** (**OBR**), or **optical mark recognition** (**OMR**). ➔ *3624 UPC*

3577 burnish Generally, to polish surface by rubbing. In prepress, printing, and finishing, this can mean a number of operations, such as increasing the dot size of a relief plate by rubbing it, reducing the cell size of a gravure plate, or brightening book edges. ➔ *2868 gravure; 3434 burnished edges*

3578 c.i.f. *abb.:* **cost, insurance, and freight** A shorthand for indicating that a price quoted for a job includes delivery to a location specified by the customer. ➔ *3597 f.o.b.*

3579 concatenate To string together two or more units of information. For example, "Quick" and "Time" becomes "QuickTime" when concatenated, or a split file becomes one.

3580 copyright The right of a person who creates an original work to protect that work by controlling how and where it may be reproduced. This does not necessarily mean that ownership of the work itself automatically signifies ownership of copyright (or vice versa) — ownership of copyright is only transferred if the creator of the work assigns it in writing. While certain aspects of copyright are broadly controlled by international agreement, as defined by the Universal Copyright Convention (UCC), there are, however, some differences from country to country, particularly when it comes to the period, or "term," for which a work is protected (in most countries this is 50 years after its creator's death). In the United States, the Pan American Agreement decrees that ownership of an "intellectual property" (the legal description of copyright ownership) be established by registration, whereas in the United Kingdom it exists automatically by virtue of the creation of the work. There is often confusion between copyright in a work and the "right" to publish it — ownership of the right to publish a work in one country may not extend to other countries, nor does it necessarily signify ownership of copyright. Equally, ownership of copyright may be shared — the author of a book, for example, may own copyright in the text, whereas copyright in the design may be owned by its designer or publisher. ➔ *3581 copyright notice/line; 3611 licence; 3582 copyright-free*

3581 **copyright notice/line** The indication of ownership of copyright in a work ("form of notice"), particularly one that is reproduced, as required by the Universal Copyright Convention. This states that all the first and subsequent editions of a work bear the word "Copyright" or the symbol "©" (most publishers include both), the year of publication (or first publication if it is a straight reprint), and the name of the owner of the copyright in the work. Thus a notice would appear: "Copyright © 2001 A. N. Author." ➔ *3580 copyright*

3582 **copyright-free** A misnomer used to describe ready-made resources, such as clip art. In fact, resources described as such are rarely, if ever, "copyright-free" — it is generally only the licence to use the material that is granted by purchase. The correct description would normally be "royalty-free" — that is, material which you can use — under licence — that is free from payment of additional fees or royalties. ➔ *3580 copyright; 0535 clip art; 0588 image resource*

3583 **cutting edge** At the forefront; pioneering; innovative. Also referred to as **state of the art**.

3584 **deadline** The final date by which a job or process must be completed.

3585 **dedicated** Any system, software, or piece of equipment designed to execute a specific task and not otherwise adaptable. Also known as a **proprietary system**.

3586 **delivery** The process of handing over any part of a process or job to another, or to the method of final output.

3587 **DIN** *abb.:* **Deutsche Industrie-Norm** A code of standards established in Germany and used widely throughout the world to standardize such things as size, weight, and other properties of particular materials and manufactured items — for example, computer connectors and photographic film speed — so they are universally compatible.

3588 **diorama** A small-scale model of a scene, such as a movie set.

3589 **direct cost** The cost of a project related directly to that job, excluding normal overhead costs of the business (indirect costs). For example, a photograph commissioned for a specific job is a direct cost, whereas the cost of heating your office while you brief the photographer is an overhead cost. ➔ *3624 overhead cost*

3590 **discrete value** A value that is individually distinct and varies only by whole, defined units, as distinct from a value that is infinitely variable ("nondiscrete value").

3591 **down time** A period of time in which a person, machine, or device is idle, for whatever reason. ➔ *3623 open time*

3592 **dpsi/dpi²** *abb.:* **dots per square inch**

3593 **dupe** A duplicate of anything, although generally used to describe a copy of an original transparency.

3594 **duplex** Literally, "two-in-one," such as simultaneous two-way communication over telecommunication lines, a single press with two units, or a single sheet of paper made from two different colored sheets. ➔ *2497 duplex board; 2030 duplex halftone; 1078 half duplex; 2717 simplex*

3595 **ergonomics** A design science that studies the efficiency and comfortable interaction between the human form and its working environment, sometimes referred to as **human engineering**.

3596 expertosis An appropriate term, coined in previous editions of *The Macintosh Bible* (Peachpit Press), that describes the prevalent phenomenon of the inability of some experts to understand the needs and limitations of people who are not themselves expert.

3597 f.o.b. *abb.:* **free on board** A term indicating that the price quoted for a job does not include a delivery charge. → *3578 c.i.f.*

3598 fax An acronym for "facsimile." The electronic transmission of copy from one location to another using regular telephone lines. Fax cards and modems can be connected to your computer to enable you to send and receive faxes direct, without the need for a separate fax machine.

3599 FYI *abb.:* **for your information** A frequently used shorthand, particularly in e-mail correspondence.

3600 generation A single stage of a reproduction process.

3601 hex(adecimal) The use of the number 16 as the basis of a counting system as distinct from decimal (base ten) or binary (base two). The figures are represented by the numbers 1 to 0, followed by A to F. Thus decimal 9 is still hex 9, whereas decimal 10 becomes hex A, decimal 16 becomes hex 10, decimal 26 becomes hex 1A, and so on.

3602 high-profile Any item that stands apart or visibly proud of its surroundings. The opposite of low-profile. → *3612 low-profile*

3603 in-line A system or process in which specific components form part of a continuous sequence, such as the converting units attached to the press in a web printing system, a scanner attached to an imagesetter, or an image that displays among text on a Web page. → *3013 online*

3604 index guide The marked divisions in a filing system, allowing rapid access to sections that are categorized alphabetically or by subject. → *2517 index board*

3605 indicia Literally, "distinguishing marks," as required by the post office for bulk mailings.

3606 intermediate A copy of an original from which other copies can be made. → *1443 interneg*

3607 ISO *abb.:* **International Standards Organization** A Swiss-based body responsible for defining many elements common to design, photography, and publishing, such as paper size, film speed rating, and network protocol ("ISO/OSI" protocol).

3608 kilo A unit of metric measurement representing 1,000 (from the Greek "khilioi" for "thousand"). However, although the term is widely used as a measure of computer data ("kilobyte," for example), computers use a binary system (pairs of numbers) in which each number is doubled: 2; 4; 8; 16; 32; 64; 128; 256; 512; 1,024; etc. Thus "kilo" in a data context does not mean 1,000, but 1,024 (210). → *0418 mega; 3617 mille*

3609 knowledge fade An expression that describes the condition arising from lack of continual familiarity with a process or, more commonly these days, with computer software. In other words, unless you use a particular application frequently your knowledge of it — and thus expertize — will rapidly diminish. The condition is said to be a result of the modern-day phenomenon of "information overload" — although we are provided with, and have the means of accessing, vast amounts of information, there is a limit to what human memory can retain, even if we are required to do so.

3610 lcd (**2**) *abb.:* **lowest common denominator** The most basic level that can be understood by everyone concerned.

3611 licence/licensing The right granted to someone to use something that belongs to someone else. The term describes two opposing views of the same meaning: either the licenser licences the right to use, say, an intellectual asset to a licensee (to collect a fee), or the licensee licences it from a licenser (by paying a fee). ➔ *3580 copyright*

3612 low-profile Any item that is at the same level or that blends in with its surroundings. The opposite of high-profile. ➔ *3602 high-profile*

3613 m (**2**) *abb.:* **mille** The Latin term for one thousand. ➔ *3617 mille*

3614 magnifier/magnifying glass A lens used to inspect the quality of printing proofs, film, photographic transparencies, and so on. Some magnifiers incorporate additional features, such as adjustable focus, built-in measuring scales, and its own light source. Also called **loupe**, **lupe**, or **linen tester** (after the folding device used in the textile industries for counting threads in linen).

3615 metrication The introduction of a decimal system of measurement by certain countries. However, even in some countries that have adopted metrication there are inconsistencies — the UK, for example, still uses the Anglo-American point system for measuring type.

3616 micrometer An instrument for measuring thickness, usually of paper. ➔ *3617 mille*

3617 mille Latin for one thousand. Used in the paper industry to describe the unit of quantity in which sheets of paper are sold. In a modern context the unit can be confusing, because in its abbreviated form ("m") it can easily be mistaken, in some situations, for "mega," which means 1,000,000, or "kilo," which is also 1,000. ➔ *3608 kilo; 0418 mega*

3618 millisecond (**ms**) One thousandth of a second. ➔ *0108 seek time*

3619 mint As new — anything in excellent condition, usually applied to secondhand goods.

3620 modular system Any system, such as a computer system, made up from self-contained, but separate, parts ("modules"), rather than a single item that contains all of the parts. For example, a computer that does not incorporate the monitor in its case.

3621 old-tech A colloquial expression referring to prepress technology that has largely been replaced by new, mostly computer-based technology.

3622 on-demand Anything that is supplied only when it is asked for, rather than "live" (as it happens) or automatically.

3623 open/standing time Spare production time due to a break in the schedule. You should be so lucky. ➔ *3591 down time*

3624 overhead cost The residual costs that are inherent in any project, such as office rental, stationery, staff, entertainment, vehicles, and so on, as compared with the costs specifically attributed to the project itself that would not occur if the project did not proceed (printing the job, for example). ➔ *3589 direct cost*

3625 overhead projector A device for making presentations in which images that have been created or output on transparent cellulose acetate are projected onto a flat surface or screen. ➔ *4168 cel (1)*

3626 **patent** The authority granted by a government agency that protects an invention from being copied.

3627 **phonogram** A symbol, which may or may not correspond to the International Phonetic Alphabet (IPA), devised as the written equivalent of a spoken sound.

3628 **post-production** In the movie and photographic industries, all processes that take place after the camerawork has been completed, such as editing, retouching, special effects, and so on.

3629 **proprietary** A design, product, or format developed, marketed, and owned by a company or person, rather than one defined by a standards organization.

3630 **public domain** (**PD**) A description of "intellectual property" that is free of all copyrights, meaning that it can be used by anyone for any purpose, either because the copyright period has lapsed or because, as is sometimes the case with computer software, its author has declared it so. Not to be confused with "shareware," for which a fee is usually required.

3631 **quality control** A procedure implemented to guarantee all stages of a production process are monitored and, if necessary, improved to ensure an end result that exactly matches the original specification.

3632 **R & D** *abb.:* **research and development**

3633 **rate determining factor** (**RDF**) The rate at which progress is determined, defined as the slowest part of any procedure or process. For example, the rate at which you may be able to complete a design job will depend on how long it takes the slowest contributor (an author or illustrator, for example) to complete their task, in which case they are the rate determining factor. It could even be you.

3634 **registered design** A design officially registered with a patent office to protect it from copyright violations.

3635 **relative humidity** (**RH**) A value determined by the percentage of water vapor in a given environment when compared with the amount that would be present if the atmosphere was fully saturated with water vapor at the same temperature. Relative humidity is an important factor, firstly when printing in countries with humid climates because it can have a dramatic effect on print quality in processes such as lithography (which uses water to repel ink), and also in paper storage because humidity can affect dimensional stability along with other properties.

3636 **reprography** Copying and duplicating printed matter. ➔ *2135 reprographic printing*

3637 **snail mail** The standard postal system, differentiated from fax or e-mail.

3638 **support** After-sales assistance from a product supplier.

3639 **tear sheet** A page removed from a publication and used or filed for future reference.

3640 **trademark** (™) A name or logo identifying a product or service and linking it to its maker or supplier. Trademarks are usually identified by an adjacent "™" or "®," the latter indicating that the mark is registered. ➔ *3569 ®; 3568 ©; 3580 copyright; 3611 licence/licensing*

3641 **unit** (**1**) An expression of measurement without reference to any particular system such as inches.

3642 **Universal Product Code** (**UPC**) A product identification system for applying bar codes to products according to specifications provided by Uniform Code Council Inc. There are several specifications: for example, "UPC-A" (or "UPC 10") and "UPC-E" (or "UPC 6") are used mostly for retail items that will be scanned at point of sale, although variations of UPC-A are used in the publishing industry. "UPC-Shipping" is used mostly on materials such as cardboard where print quality is poor. ➔ *3576 bar code*

3643 **viewing conditions** A standardized method (defined in the United States by ANSI) of maintaining consistent lighting conditions when viewing originals such as transparencies and flat copy, making sure a proof made from those originals can be viewed in similar conditions. This enables a more accurate assessment of the quality of a proof.

3644 **widget** A colloquial term for any unspecified device.

3645 **AAAA** *abb.:* **American Association of Advertising Agencies**

3646 **advert**(**isement**) A public notice announcing goods or services, printed or broadcast in journals, posters, television, radio, the Internet, and so on. ➔ *3659 display advertisement*

3647 **agate line** A fixed measurement of space, used in newspaper and magazine classified advertisements — 14 agate lines are equal to one column inch. ➔ *1649 agate*

3648 **bagged** A publication that is placed in a pack along with another publication or promotional item.

3649 **banner** (**1**) A headline that occupies the full width of a page of a newspaper or magazine.

3650 **below the line** A term used in advertising to describe promotional items that fall outside a specific campaign.

3651 **blurb** A colloquial term, originating in the United States in the early 20th century, for the description of a book and/or its author that is usually printed on the book dust jacket flaps or on promotional literature. ➔ *3672 puff; 3854 jacket flaps*

3652 **bogus** An arcane and redundant procedure describing copy for press advertisements that, having been received by the publisher in plate, block, or film form, is then reset in type, which is immediately discarded without being used.

3653 **circular** Advertising matter printed as a single leaf or folded sheet.

3654 **classified ad**(**vertisement**) Small newspaper or magazine advertisement (thus sometimes called "small ad"), appearing in a "personals column," for example. Generally sold by the line or column inch. As distinct from "display" advertisement. ➔ *3646 advertisement; 3659 display advertisement*

3655 **column inch/centimeter** A measure of space signifying one column wide by one inch (or centimeter) deep, used most often for calculating the cost of display advertising in printed journals. ➔ *3647 agate line; 1649 agate*

3656 **copywriting** The creation of copy specifically for advertising and promotional purposes. ➔ *3646 advertisement; 3659 display advertisement*

3657 crowner A store display item used for publicizing a book or product. Crowners are placed on top of, or next to, the product itself. ➔ *3678 streamer*

3658 direct mail Advertising matter sent directly through the mail to prospective customers.

3659 display advertisement In printed publications, advertising matter positioned in a prominent position on the page and designed to a quality that will attract immediate attention. As distinct from "small," or "classified," advertisements. ➔ *3646 advertisement; 3654 classified ad*

3660 dumpbin A free-standing container used to display goods — particularly paperback books — in a self-service retail outlet. Dumpbins are generally supplied to the outlet by the manufacturer or publisher of the goods. ➔ *3667 header card*

3661 ear The advertising spaces on each side of the front-page title line of a newspaper.

3662 eight sheet A standard poster format — 60 × 80 inches (153 × 203cm).

3663 flier An advertising insert loosely bound into a book.

3664 flyer A cheaply produced printed circular, usually a single sheet, used for promotional purposes.

3665 forty-eight sheet A standard poster size: 120 × 480 inches (305 × 1,220cm).

3666 gutting A colloquial expression describing the practice of extracting key phrases or "soundbites" from reviews of a publication, and subsequently printing them on the cover on further editions of that publication for promotional purposes.

3667 header card An advertising card placed above a "dumpbin," to draw attention to the items placed there. ➔ *3660 dumpbin*

3668 rack-jobbing distribution The term for products that are distributed in small product stands or racks placed in retail situations other than where they may normally be expected (a book in a bookshop for example), intended to attract "impulse buyers." Typical locations include supermarkets and airports, which are described as **impulse outlets**.

3669 next reading/text matter An instruction to place advertisement copy next to editorial copy in a publication.

3670 point of sale Advertising material displayed near the cash register.

3671 promotion The process of advocating a product or service to increase production or sales.

3672 puff A term, originating in the 17th century, but still used today, describing the written hyperbole accompanying a new book. ➔ *3651 blurb*

3673 run-of-paper (**2**) In a publication, those advertisement positions that are sold without the client specifying a particular location, such as the inside front cover, and that may thus appear anywhere in the publication.

3674 sampler (**2**) A demonstration of a product, such as software distributed on disks.

3675 sixteen sheet A standard poster size: 120 × 80 inches (3,050 × 2,030cm).

3681 Tummy band

3686 Glyph

3676 solus position An advertisement positioned on a page on which no others are present.

3677 spinner A revolving display stand in a retail outlet.

3678 streamer A publicity poster (usually a strip of paper) supplied by publishers to booksellers for displaying with copies of a new book. ➜ *3657 crowner*

3679 stuffer A publisher's advertising leaflet that is "stuffed" into envelopes when sending other material through the mail, or inserted into books sold over the counter.

3680 thirty-two sheet A standard poster size, measuring 120 × 60 inches (3,040 × 4,060cm).

3681 tummy band A strip of paper containing a sales message fixed around the middle of a publication. Also called a **belly band**.

3682 AIGA *abb.:* **American Institute of Graphic Arts** Founded in 1914 to uphold the standard of the graphic arts in the United States.

3683 corporate identity All aspects — not necessarily just design, but also the "culture" — that any organization assembles to establish an appropriate, recognizable, and consistent identity throughout all of its communication, promotion, and distribution material, both internally and externally. Also called **house style**. ➜ *3692 image (2)*

3684 desktop publishing (**DTP**) The entire computer-based process of generating text, laying it out on a page with images, and then printing the result — in other words, publishing it. The term was originally coined when the first personal "desktop" computers to use a GUI (the Apple "Lisa," which evolved into the "Macintosh") were introduced, before the potential of desktop computers in the professional design and graphic arts industries was fully realized, and was thus used somewhat derogatorily by professional designers to indicate amateurism. However, the massive advances in the capability of the technology have consigned such views to the wastebasket. Alternatively called **electronic publishing**, although this is also used to describe paper-less DTP such as web publishing. ➜ *0012 desktop computer; 3689 graphic design; 0020 Macintosh*

3685 electronic design Any design activity that takes place with the aid of electronic devices, such as computers. Also known as **e-design**. ➜ *1023 CAD; 3689 graphic design*

3686 glyph Strictly speaking, a sculptured character (from the Greek *gluphō* meaning "to carve"), but commonly used to describe a symbol, normally used on packaging, which is intended to convey a message without the need for text, and is therefore understood by speakers of any language. Examples include a skull and crossbones to indicate danger and a shattered glass for fragile. ➜ *4146 pictogram*

3687 golden section A formula for dividing a line or an area into theoretically harmonious proportions. If a line is divided unequally, the relationship of the whole section to the larger section should be the same as that of the larger section to the smaller.

3688 graphic arts The general term encompassing the entire craft of reproduction by means of any of the many printing processes. As distinct from "graphic design" — providing a graphic solution to a specific problem and the implementation of that solution by whatever means. ➜ *3689 graphic design; 3685 electronic design; 3684 desktop publishing*

3693 Isotype

3696 Logo

3700 Symbol

3689 **graphic design** Strictly speaking — and in its literal sense — graphic design is the arrangement and combination of shapes and forms based on 2D processes, such as typography, photography, illustration, video, motion picture, multimedia, and various print methods, but not necessarily excluding 3D design, because graphic design is utilized in many 3D contexts, such as packaging, product design, exhibitions, and architecture. In its less literal sense, graphic design embodies the profession of visual communication in as much as it forms an integral part of any marketing concept or strategy. Traditionally called **commercial art**, there are many alternative names, such as **graphic arts** (although this implies more technical connotations), **graphic communication**, and so on, but it should not be confused with "desktop publishing." → *3688 graphic arts*

3690 **hologram** An image created by lasers to give an illusion of three dimensions, used commonly in security printing, but also as a novelty. → *1040 laser*

3691 **ideogram** A symbol used to indicate a concept or emotion, such as joy, sadness, warmth, and so on. → *3693 isotype*

3692 **image** (**2**) The overall "look" of an organization or product that affects its character, reputation, and marketing potential. → *3683 corporate identity*

3693 **isotype** A method for graphically presenting statistical information in which pictograms or ideograms are used to convey meaning; a technique pioneered by Otto and Marie Neurath's Isotype Institut.

3694 **job jacket/bag** A folder or large envelope that contains all matter relating to a particular project in progress, including copy, transparencies, art, and specifications.

3695 **letterhead(ing)** Strictly speaking, the heading — name, address, telephone and fax number of a business or individual — on any item of stationery, but sometimes used to describe the item of stationery specifically used for writing letters on.

3696 **logo/logotype** Traditionally, a "logotype" is any group of type characters (other than ligatures), such as company names, cast together on one metal body (also called a "logograph" although this term is also used to define word endings such as "ing" and "ity"). However, the term is now used to describe any design or symbol, such as a pictogram, that forms the centerpiece of a corporation or organization's corporate identity. → *4146 pictogram*

3697 **media** (**1**) A plural term now accepted as a singular to cover any information or communications medium, such as "broadcast media" (television and radio) and "print media" (newspapers, magazines, and so on).

3698 **specimen book** A catalog of a manufacturer's products with actual samples, such as an ink manufacturer's catalog of colors, normally showing basic colors and often including halftones, for example, or a catalog of typefaces, showing fonts, sizes, and so on. → *1814 specimen sheet*

3699 **specimen page** A page or group of pages printed as a sample to show the design, style of setting, fonts, paper quality, and so on.

3700 **symbol** A figure, sign, or letter that represents an object, process, or activity. A computer icon, for example, is a pictorial symbol. → *4146 pictogram; 0964 icon*

3701 **archetype** The correct version of a manuscript or printed work, marked or otherwise, which is used for amending later versions.

3702 author's alteration/correction Alterations made to a text by its author, which deviate from the original copy. These corrections are marked on the author's proof and are distinguished from typesetting errors, especially in cases where additional charges may be made for implementing the corrections. ➔ *3703 author's proof*

3703 author's proof Galley or laser proofs, usually of text, supplied to an author for correction. These proofs will have previously been read by a proofreader who will have marked all typesetting errors. ➔ *3702 author's alteration/correction; 3724 galley proof*

3704 b/f (1) *abb.:* **brought/bring forward** Any matter that has been moved forward from previous pages. ➔ *3769 take over/forward*

3705 bad copy A heavily corrected manuscript, making it difficult to read.

3706 cf *abb.:* **confer** The Latin term for "refer to," or "compare," used to point the reader to a footnote to text.

3707 clean proof A galley or press proof that is free from errors. ➔ *3724 galley proof; 2642 machine proof; 3712 dirty proof*

3708 copy (1) Any manuscript, typescript, transparency, or computer disk that is to be used for reproduction. Also called **original**.

3709 cut (3) An instruction to editors and typesetters to delete copy.

3710 dele The name used to describe the symbol (" ℘," representing the letter "d" for the Latin *deleatur*), indicating matter that is to be deleted.

3711 digraph A pair of letters representing one sound, such as "ph" in photo and "sh" in sheet. ➔ *1587 diphthong*

3712 dirty proof A proof that is heavily corrected. ➔ *3724 galley proof; 2642 machine proof; 3707 clean proof; 3723 foul proof*

3713 draft The initial stage of a manuscript, text, or illustration that will subsequently be refined, rewritten, or edited. A draft design is variously called a "rough," "visual," or "scamp." When a manuscript is eventually ready for typesetting, it is called a "final draft." ➔ *4059 rough*

3714 e.g. *abb.:* **exempli gratia** A Latin term meaning "for example."

3715 edit To commission, manage, sanction, amend, or correct material, whether text or images.

3716 et al *abb.:* **et alii** A Latin phrase meaning "and others."

3717 et seq *abb.:* **et sequens** Latin for "and the following," referring to the following pages.

3718 ex libris A Latin phrase meaning "among the books of," which, printed on a bookplate (a panel pasted into the front of a book) and followed by a person's name, indicates ownership of the book.

3719 explicit Derived from the Latin *explitus ex liber*, meaning "it is unrolled to the end," and referring to an inscription at the end of a manuscript roll — usually a repeat of the title, place, or date of publication. When applied to a book, it is often the printer's name.

3720 fecit Latin for "he has made it," an inscription on an engraving or drawing that is sometimes added to the artist's name.

3721 floruit dates (fl) A term used to indicate an approximation, when exact historical dates are not known.

3722 **follow copy** An instruction to a typesetter to follow the exact spelling and punctuation of a manuscript, even if unorthodox, rather than the defined house style.

3723 **foul proof** A printed proof containing many revisions or corrections. → *3712 dirty proof*

3724 **galley proof** A proof of typeset text before it is integrated into a page design, deriving from the days when metal type was proofed from a long, shallow, three-sided metal tray called a "galley." Also called a **slip proof**, referring to the broad strip of paper on which a galley proof is printed. → *3925 catchline*

3725 **hard copy** A physical copy of something, such as matter prepared for printing and used for revision or checking, or a printout of a computer document. As distinct from a "soft" copy — a digital copy of a document to another place. → *0478 soft copy (1); 0479 soft copy (2); 1813 soft copy (3)*

3726 **holograph** A work written entirely in the author's own handwriting.

3727 **house corrections** Corrections to proofs made by the publisher or printer, as distinct from those made by the author.

3728 **i.e.** *abb.*: **id est** A Latin term meaning "that is."

3729 **ibid** *abb.*: **ibidem** Latin for "in the same place," used in the notes of a publication to mean a repeated reference.

3730 **id** *abb.*: **idem** A Latin term meaning "the same person," used in footnotes and bibliographies, and so on, normally to indicate subsequent references to an author previously mentioned.

3731 **illuminated** (**2**) A colloquial term for the "glosses" (explanations placed between lines) in a translated Greek or Latin text. → *3959 gloss (2)*

3732 **in-plant proofing** Proof corrections — made by a proofreader employed by the printing company — that may not be shown to the client.

3733 **incipit** A Latin term meaning "it begins," followed by the first few words of the text, used to identify (usually very old) manuscripts published without a title page.

3734 **lifted matter** Typeset text taken from one job and used in another.

3735 **literal** An error that may occur at any stage of copy preparation, from author's manuscript to typeset galleys, such as a spelling mistake. As distinct from a "typo," which is an error occurring during typesetting, such as the wrong font. → *1823 typo*

3736 **loc. cit.** *abb.*: **loco citato** A Latin term for "in the place named," and used as a reference in footnotes.

3737 **manuscript** (**MS/MSS**) An original text submitted for publication.

3738 **marked proof** A typeset or printed proof marked for corrections.

3739 **master** An original item from which all copies are made, or upon which any changes are marked or made.

3740 **master proof** The final proof that combines all comments or corrections, including the author's, editor's, and typesetter's. → *3739 master*

3741 **matter** The traditional term for anything that is to be printed, at whatever stage, the term particularly applying to material (a manuscript, for example) that is to be, or has been, typeset. → *3737 manuscript*

3742 mf/mtf *abb.:* **more follows/more to follow** Used when preparing a manuscript for typesetting. The mark "**tk**" (**to come**) is also used.

3743 np *abb.:* **new paragraph** A mark used in editing and proof correction to indicate the creation of a new paragraph.

3744 op. cit. *abb.:* **opere citato** Latin for 'in the work already quoted," used as a footnote reference.

3745 ordinal numbers Numbers that indicate placement — first, second, third, and so on — as opposed to cardinal numbers used for sequential counting — 1, 2, 3... ➔ *3924 cardinal numbers*

3746 page proofs A proof of pages that have been paginated (put into the correct page sequence). Traditionally, this is the secondary stage in proofing — after galley proofs and before machine proofs — although there may be other stages of proofing either before or after page proofs, such as the "blues" used to check imposition. Also called **made-up proofs**. ➔ *3749 proof*

3747 pinxit Latin for "he painted it," often following an artist's name — on colored engravings, for example. Sometimes abbreviated to **pinx**.

3748 plagiarism The abuse of another's original work by copying it and passing it off as one's own.

3749 proof A prototype of a job, taken at various stages from laser printers, imagesetters, inked plates, stones, screens, block, type, or so on, to check the progress and accuracy of the work. Also called a **pull**.

3750 proof correction marks A standard set of signs and symbols commonly understood by all those involved in preparing copy for publication. Text proof correction marks vary from country to country, but color correction signs are more or less internationally recognized. ➔ *3751 proof corrections*

3751 proof corrections The corrections made to a proof, for example, after a text has been typeset or images color-proofed. ➔ *3750 proof correction marks*

3752 proofing The production/correction of a prototype or simulation of a print job prior to its subsequent reproduction in quantity.

3753 proofreader Someone who reads proofs for errors and who marks corrections accordingly. ➔ *3754 proofreader's marks*

3754 proofreader's marks A collection of notations, symbols, and marks used to identify errors on a proof and the necessary action needed to correct them. ➔ *3751 proof corrections; 3753 proofreader*

3755 q.v. *abb.:* **quod vide** A Latin term meaning "which see," used to accompany an item which is cross-referenced to another. The plural form is "qq.v."

3756 QA *abb.:* **query author** A mark used by text editors.

3757 query An annotation by editor, author, proofreader, or typesetter in the margin of a proof or galley, sometimes simply a "?," to draw attention to a potential mistake.

3758 references An indication of additional reading matter that is in some way related to the current text, such as in footnotes, bibliography, or sources, often identified with Latin abbreviations such as ibid., loc. cit., id., etc.

3759 **roman notation** Using roman numerals to record dates, still common practice today. ➔ *3760 roman numerals*

3760 **roman numerals** A system of numerical notation that uses letters rather than numbers: I (one); V (five); X (10); L (50); C (100); D (500); and M (1,000). The letters are used in combinations to represent any number. ➔ *3759 roman notation*

3761 **rush changes** A questionable practice in which additional fees are paid to a supplier for completing a job in less time than would normally be taken. Also referred to as **expediting changes**.

3762 **sc.** *abb.:* **scilicet** The Latin term for "namely."

3763 **screamer** A slang term used by printers or journalists for an exclamation mark.

3764 **see copy** A proof mark signaling an omission that is too large to be inserted on the proof. The omission is indicated on the attached copy for the guidance of the compositor. Also used to indicate to the author that the reader is uncertain about a part of the copy.

3765 **sic** A Latin word meaning "thus." Used in brackets immediately after a quoted passage, which was misused or contained an error of spelling or grammar, to indicate the existence of this error in the original.

3766 **single quotes** Single, as opposed to double, quote marks used in marking quotations in a body of text that are inside quoted matter.

3767 **stet** Derived from the Latin term meaning "let it stand." Used by proofreaders when marking up copy to cancel a previous correction.

3768 **take in** An instruction to include additional copy supplied.

3769 **take over/take forward** An instruction to take over characters, words, or lines to the following line, column, or page. Also referred to as **carrying over**.

3770 **transpose/transposition** To exchange the position of any two items of text, or two images, either by design or because they are in the wrong order. ➔ *4114 flip/flop*

3771 **typescript** A typed manuscript.

3772 **verbatim et literatim** Latin phrase meaning "word for word," describing a literal translation.

3773 **vide** A Latin term meaning "see," used in a text as "vide infra" to indicate matter appearing subsequently ("infra" means below), or as "vide supra" meaning "see above."

3774 **video** (**2**) A Latin term meaning "I see," describing all television-related products. ➔ *3773 vide*

3775 **viz.** *abb.:* **videlicet** A Latin term meaning "namely," used when citing a reference in footnotes.

3776 **wild copy** Typeset words that are separate from the main body of text, such as that used as annotation to an illustration or as part of a chart or diagram.

3777 **ABA** *abb.:* **American Booksellers Association**, which issues an annual Book Buyers Handbook, the standard reference for publishers.

3778 addendum/addenda Material supplementary to the main content of a book, printed separately at the beginning or end of the text. ➜ *3780 appendix; 3806 end matter*

3779 APA *abb.:* **American Publishers' Association**

3780 appendix Matter, usually reference material, printed at the end of a work. ➜ *3778 addendum; 3806 end matter*

3781 automated publication Published work of which a digital copy is kept for automatic updating.

3782 bibliography A list of publications, generally included in the end matter of a book, but alternatively printed on the back ("verso") of the half title or title page ("biblio" page). A bibliography may list other titles by the author, or reference material on a particular subject. ➜ *3806 end matter; 3832 half title (2); 3901 title page*

3783 blad Acronym for "book layout and design," originally, the first 32 pages of a forthcoming book printed as a sample for advance-selling to bookstores. Today the term describes any number or sequence of specimen pages printed as a publicity brochure. ➜ *4023 dummy (2)*

3784 body (2) (book) The main part of a book, excluding end matter, covers, prelims, and so on. ➜ *3874 prelims; 3806 end matter*

3785 book A general term describing a set of paper sheets that have been bound together. Various attempts have been made to define the term: it was once assumed in the UK that a book was any publication costing sixpence or more, while other countries define a book as being a publication with a specified minimum number of pages. A UNESCO conference once defined a book as being "a nonperiodical literary publication containing forty-nine or more pages, excluding the covers." ➜ *3083 bookbinding*

3786 booklet Strictly speaking, a booklet is any publication larger than a pamphlet, but containing no more than 24 pages. However, a booklet now tends to mean any publication of a few pages with less than permanent binding. ➜ *3870 pamphlet; 3082 binding*

3787 bookplates Printed labels, usually pasted on to the inside front cover of a book, decreeing its ownership.

3788 bulking dummy A blank book made with the exact number of pages, the same paper stock, and bound to the same specification as the final published edition. A bulking dummy may be used for various purposes, but most importantly for making marketing proposals, sales presentations, and for calculating the exact dimensions of the jacket. Also called a **thickness copy**. ➜ *4023 dummy (2)*

3789 Cataloging-in-Publication (CIP) A classification used by The Library of Congress (U.S.) and British Library (UK) for cataloging books — every book published is assigned a unique number that is put on the imprint page.

3790 co-edition A work, such as a book or multimedia title, that is to be published in another language or territory, either simultaneously or at a later date.

3791 colophon (1) Traditionally, in manuscript books, a message inscribed at the end of the book, indicating such things as the title, scribe's name, date of completion, dedication, and so on. Nowadays, a colophon may be printed at the beginning or end of a book, giving production information such as the title, printer's name, date of printing, copyright, and so on.

3801 Dust jacket

3792 colophon (**2**) The term describing, erroneously, the publisher's logo or emblem, printed on the spine, cover, or title page of a book. Traditionally, however, a colophon is unique to each title the publisher issues. → *3838 imprint*

3793 composite book A book made up of several different parts, such as the complete works of an individual author or collected works by several authors, bound into a single volume.

3794 contents (**page**) The part of the "prelims" (the front matter of a publication) that lists the content: divisions (chapters), the order in which they appear, and their location (by page number). → *3874 prelims*

3795 corrigendum/corrigenda A leaf that is inserted into a publication after printing to indicate errors that were noticed subsequent to printing. Also called **erratum/errata**. → *3812 erratum*

3796 demographic edition An edition of a journal, such as a newspaper or magazine, that has its content — both editorial and advertising — modified to suit a specific geographic area or consumer group.

3797 desk copy A copy of a book that is given to teachers and lecturers so it may become required reading for students, thus increasing sales. Also known as an **inspection copy**.

3798 device (**2**) A trademark or design printed in a book, identifying the printer or publisher. Also called a **printer's mark**.

3799 diurnal A newspaper or journal that is published daily.

3800 double title page A book in which the title page occupies a double-page spread (strictly speaking a "title page" is a single, right-hand page). → *3901 title page*

3801 dust jacket/wrapper The printed paper cover bearing a design, folded around, but not attached to, a bound book, and in which it is sold. Originally employed to protect the binding, but now used as a marketing aid. Also called **book jacket** and **book wrapper**.

3802 edition The complete number of copies of a publication printed and published at one time, either for the first time ("first edition"), or after some change has been made ("revised edition," "second edition," and so on). → *3853 issue (2)*

3803 elhi books Acronym for elementary and high school books, a term used by the American educational book trade.

3804 emblem book A type of book, revived in the 16th century, that first appeared in the medieval period and comprised a series of moral epigrams or mottos illustrated by woodcuts or engravings.

3805 encyclopedia A reference book, with the entries usually in alphabetical order, that summarizes human knowledge, sometimes of a specific subject. The Roman writer Pliny (A.D. 23–79) compiled one of the earliest examples. → *3830 glossary (1)*

3806 end/back matter The final pages of a book, following the main body, usually containing such things as a glossary and an index. Also known as **postlims**, **endlims**, or subsidiaries. → *3874 prelims; 3896 subsidiaries*

3807 ephemeris (**1**) A diary, calendar, or almanac.

3808 ephemeris (**2**) A popular title for 17th- and 18th-century periodicals.

3809 ephemeris (**3**) A star map and almanac of astronomical information.

3810 epigraph A brief synopsis of content, to be found on the first page of each chapter of a book; or a brief text or quotation found within the prelims of a book.

3811 epitome A condensed version of a text pared down to its essential elements, as in a compendium.

3812 erratum/errata (**slip**) A list in a publication that corrects errors in the text or illustrations. This may be printed in the publication itself or inserted into it as an "errata slip" after the publication is printed. ➔ *3795 corrigendum*

3813 even folios Left-hand pages (verso) that are numbered evenly: 2, 4, 6, 8, 10, and so on.

3814 even pages The left-hand pages in a publication — usually those with even folio numbers.

3815 excerpt An extract of text reproduced from a published work.

3816 expurgated edition A book that has been edited to remove matter that is considered to be offensive.

3817 facsimile edition The republishing of an out-of-print book, where each page is photographically copied from the original, with no new material.

3818 fascicule A single, incomplete edition of a publication issued in installments, such as a "partwork." ➔ *3871 partwork*

3819 first edition The first time a book is printed and published. It can also refer to additional printings from the same plates, so long as no changes have been made.

3820 fly-title A subsidiary title page often separating distinct portions of a book. Also, a seldom-used UK alternative term for a "half title" page. ➔ *3901 title page; 3832 half title (2)*

3821 foliation In book publishing, the rare practice of numbering the leaves rather than each page, so each alternate page is numbered consecutively. From the Latin *foliatus* — "leaved." ➔ *3856 leaf (1)*

3822 folio (**1**) Strictly speaking, the number of a leaf of a book when it is not numbered as two separate pages. However, a folio generally describes the number as printed on each page. ➔ *3821 foliation; 3856 leaf (1)*

3823 folio (**2**) The size of a book that is formed when each sheet containing its pages is folded only once, thus making four pages half the size of the sheet. A folio-size book generally describes any large-format book.

3824 foreword Introductory remarks about a work or its author.

3825 free sheet A newspaper distributed without charge to the reader.

3826 free-standing insert (**FSI**) A self-contained item, usually in multiples of four pages, inserted into a publication such as a newspaper. ➔ *3848 insert (1)*

3827 frontispiece Traditionally, an illustration printed separately and then pasted onto the page opposite the title page of a book. Nowadays, any illustration printed opposite the title page.

3828 full edition A complete, original edition of a work, applied only if an abridged edition has previously been published. ➔ *3802 edition*

3829 getup An American term for the general format of a book, covering such aspects as general design, layout, and printing and binding.

3830 glossary (**1**) An alphabetical listing of unfamiliar terms related to a particular subject — usually technical — with an accompanying explanation. This book is one such example.

3831 half title (**1**) The title of a book as printed on the recto (right-hand page) of the leaf preceding the title page, usually the first page of a book. → *3901 title page; 3881 recto*

3832 half title (**2**) The page on which the half title appears. Sometimes called a **bastard title**. → *3901 title page*

3833 hardcover edition/hardbound edition An edition of a book that is cased in boards, distinguishing it from a paperback edition, in which form it may also exist. → *3091 cased*

3834 holster book A traditional name for a long, narrow notebook, designed to fit in the pocket.

3835 house organ A publication produced to give information about a company, distributed internally to employees, but sometimes to customers.

3836 illustrated A description applied to any printed item, particularly books, in which reproductions of images, whether photographs, paintings, drawings, maps, and so on — in fact, anything that is not text — appear as well as text. Although tables, graphs, and other such data were once represented purely as text and thus not normally considered to be illustrations, even these are now deemed to be illustrations.

3837 imprimatur Latin for "let it be printed," at one time used to show that permission to print a publication had been granted by the appropriate authority.

3838 imprint Either the name of the printer and the place of printing — a legal requirement in many countries if the work is to be published — usually appearing on the back of the title page or on the last page of a book ("printer's imprint"), or the name of the publisher, usually printed on the title page of a book ("publisher's imprint").

3839 imprint page The page of a book usually appearing on the back of the title page (title verso), which carries details of the edition, such as the printer's imprint, copyright owner, ISBN, and catalog number. → *3838 imprint*

3840 in print A publishing trade phrase used to describe a book that is available from the publisher, as opposed to one that is "out of print" and therefore unavailable. → *3868 out of print*

3841 incunabula Books printed before 1500.

3842 index (**2**) The part of a publication that gives an alphabetical listing of selected words mentioned in the publication, with appropriate page numbers. → *3844 indexing*

3843 index letter/number A reference character or number used to connect an illustration to its caption or relevant text.

3844 indexing (**1**) The preparation of an ordered list of words, subjects, categories, and so on that forms an "index," an alphabetical listing of selected words and an indication of where they can be found in the volume, document, or file. → *3842 index (2); 3843 index letter/number*

3854 Jacket flaps

3845 indexing (**2**) Cutting or stepping the edges of pages or fixing reference tabs to mark major divisions within a work, such as the start of a new initial letter in a dictionary or encyclopedia. ➜ *3215 tab index; 3220 thumb index*

3846 inedited (**1**) A work published as it was written, to which no editorial changes have been made.

3847 inedited (**2**) Any unpublished works, in particular those of an author who is dead.

3848 insert (**1**) Part of a publication that is printed separately, perhaps using different colored inks or on different paper, but which is bound into that publication. Also called an **inset**. When printed pages are wrapped around the outside of a publication or section, this is called an "outsert" or "outset." ➜ *3826 free-standing insert; 3187 saddleback book*

3849 ISBN *abb.:* **International Standard Book Number** A unique ten-figure serial number allocated to and appearing on every book published that identifies the language in which it is published, its publisher, its title, and a check control number. ISBNs are often represented as a bar code. ➜ *3851 ISSN*

3850 introduction The opening part of a publication, following the prelims, which includes comments on the purpose, content, and logic of the work, usually, although not necessarily, written by its author. ➜ *3874 prelims*

3851 ISSN *abb.:* **International Standard Serial Number** A unique eight-figure number allocated to and appearing on periodicals that identifies the country of publication and the title. ➜ *3849 ISBN*

3852 issue (**1**) Part of an edition that, although consisting mostly of pages printed with the first printing, may have new front and/or end matter.

3853 issue (**2**) One complete printing of all the copies of a periodical published at one time, as in "July issue."

3854 jacket flaps The extremities of a dust jacket that fold inside the front ("front flap") or back ("back flap") of a book (usually hardback, but occasionally softback).

3855 kicker A newspaper and magazine term for a line of text that appears above or below the title of a feature.

3856 leaf (**1**) Each of the folios of a sheet after it is folded, resulting in a page on each side.

3857 lexicon Originally, a dictionary of languages such as Greek and Hebrew, but now used more for dictionaries on specific subjects, such as *The Designer's Lexicon*.

3858 lhp *abb.:* left-hand page, or "verso." ➜ *3881 recto*

3859 LOC *abb.:* **Library of Congress number** In the context of publishing, a reference number applied to books published in the United States and recorded at the Library of Congress.

3860 limited edition An edition of a publication that is confined to a specified number of copies that are usually numbered and, in some cases, signed by the author.

3861 masthead (**1**) The title of a newspaper or journal as it appears on the front page; also called a **nameplate**. ➜ *3862 masthead (2)*

3862 masthead (2) Details about a publication and its publisher, such as ownership and subscription rates, usually printed on its contents page. Also called a **flag**. ➔ *3861 masthead (1)*

3863 microform publishing The storage of data on microfilm, requiring a viewer or projector to enlarge the data to a readable size. Also called **microfiche**.

3864 monograph A treatise on a single subject.

3865 nom-de-plume A pen name, adopted to hide the real name of an author.

3866 numbered copy An individual book taken from a limited-edition print run in which each copy has received an identifying number, such as 3/200 (the third copy from a run of 200 copies).

3867 omnibus book A single edition comprising a number of books previously published separately.

3868 out of print (**o.p.**) A book that is not in a publisher's current list and is unlikely to be reprinted. ➔ *3840 in print*

3869 page (**2**) One side of a leaf. ➔ *3856 leaf (1)*

3870 pamphlet A short publication, usually on a subject of current interest, presented unbound and uncovered or in a soft cover. ➔ *3786 booklet*

3871 partwork A complete work, such as an encyclopedia, published as smaller individual issues, usually in weekly installments. ➔ *3818 fascicule*

3872 pocket edition A small book, usually no larger than approximately 6¾ × 4¼ inches.

3873 preface An introduction to a book, stating its scope and subject. ➔ *3824 foreword*

3874 prelims/preliminary pages The pages of a book before the main text starts, usually consisting of the half title, title, imprint, preface, and contents pages. Also called **front matter**. ➔ *3806 end matter*

3875 promotion copies Copies of a newly published book presented to commercial buyers, magazine editors, reviewers, and so on.

3876 promotional books/edition An edition of a book that is created, printed, and published specifically for the purpose of being "marked down" (sold at a lower price) after having first been offered for sale at full price, albeit for a very short period. Also called "bargain books," which are not to be confused with "remainders" — books that a publisher failed to sell at normal retail price, thus marked down to clear stocks.

3877 pseudonymous A work published under an assumed name.

3878 publisher The person or organization responsible for the creation (though not always), marketing, sales, and distribution of published works.

3879 pull-out section Pages of a publication that can be detached as one piece.

3880 quarternion The gathering of four sheets that are folded once; found in early printed books.

3881 recto The right-hand page of a book, or the front of a leaf.

3882 reprint A second or subsequent printing of a publication, with no changes other than minor corrections.

3883 returns Publications that are returned to the publisher by the retailer if they remain unsold. Such publications will have been supplied to the retailer on a "sale-or-return" basis.

3884 revised edition The reprinting of a book that is essentially the same as the original, except the content has been amended or updated. Also known as an **enlarged edition** or **new edition**.

3885 roll (**1**) An ancient manuscript usually made from parchment or vellum and kept rolled rather than folded.

3886 rubric In a book printed predominantly in black ink, text printed in red, such as chapter headings or other divisional headings.

3887 school edition An edition of a book, printed from the original plates but generally in a different format and with different binding, and sometimes annotated.

3888 scroll (**1**) A document presented as a roll of parchment or paper, usually handwritten.

3889 separate An article from or a part of a periodical reprinted and issued separately. Sometimes called an **off-print**. → *2653 off-print*

3890 serial (**2**) The publication of a book in serial form, such as in parts that appear at regular intervals.

3891 signature title An abbreviated indication of the author's name and title, printed in the signature line on the first page of each section of a book. Also called a **catch title**.

3892 sixteenmo/16mo A book size generated by folding a sheet with four right-angle folds, forming a page size one-sixteenth of the original sheet, with a thirty-two page section. Also known as **sexto-decimo**.

3893 sixty-fourmo/64mo A book size generated (theoretically) by folding a sheet with six right-angle folds, forming a page size one sixty-fourth of the original sheet. As this is not practically possible, a quarter sheet is folded four times to arrive at this size.

3894 slipcase An open-ended box, often of a decorative design, that holds a book or a set of books with the spine(s) remaining visible.

3895 softback edition A paperback edition; a cheaper alternative to a hardback edition.

3896 subsidiaries Those sections found at the end of a book, including the appendix, glossary, bibliography, and index.

3897 supplement Additional printed material forming part of a related work and issued at the same time, usually with its own title page and cover.

3898 synopsis A concise version of a longer work that conveys only the essential information.

3899 textbook A book about a particular subject, designed for study.

3900 thesaurus From the Greek *thesauros* meaning "treasure," a reference book first published in 1852 and long associated with, and devised by, Peter Mark Roget, which lists words in related groups. In the recent past, a thesaurus has been included in many word-processing applications and typically contains synonyms and antonyms as well as definitions.

3901 title page The page, usually a right-hand page, at the front of a book that gives its title, author's name, publisher, and other relevant information.

3902 title verso (**t/v**) The verso (back) of the title page of a book, usually containing copyright information. ➔ *4004 verso; 3901 title page*

3903 trade books A general term describing adult fiction and nonfiction and children's books, as distinct from educational textbooks, and scientific and technical manuals. ➔ *3904 trade edition*

3904 trade edition An edition of a book — generally a trade book — sold to the book trade at the wholesale price. ➔ *3903 trade books*

3905 twenty-fourmo/24mo A book comprising 48 pages (24 leaves) made by folding a sheet at right angles to each previous fold.

3906 two-fold A publication that is folded twice on the same axis to form six panels, three on each side.

3907 vanity publishing Book publishing enterprises based entirely on authors' willingness (vanity, in most cases) to underwrite all costs. Also called **subsidy publishing**.

3908 volume (**2**) A single book, or parts of a book in which each part is separated by its own title page.

3909 volume rights The right of a publisher to publish a book in any volume form, most commonly paperback and hardback.

3910 voucher body A copy of a publication sent to a contributor, reference source, or advertiser.

3911 absolute page number In a publication or document, the position of a page relative to the first page of the document, regardless of the numbering system used. For example, in a publication where a six-page section of prelims uses, say, roman numerals, or none at all, and page 1 identifies the start of the main text, the absolute page number of the first page of text is seven.

3912 annotation (**1**) An identification number or text label added to an illustration.

3913 annotation (**2**) Notes printed as an explanation in the margin of a text.

3914 back (**edge**) **margin** The margin closest to the spine on a page that forms part of a bound volume. Also called the **inner margin**, **binding margin**, or **gutter margin**. ➔ *3203 spine*

3915 body copy/matter The matter forming the main part of a printed work, including text and images, but excluding page headings and, sometimes, captions. ➔ *3784 body (2)*

3916 bottom out Arranging text on a page so it breaks in an appropriate place at the bottom of the page, to avoid aesthetic anomalies such as single words and short lines. ➔ *1827 bad break; 4005 widow; 3979 orphan*

3917 box feature/story Matter printed separately from the main text (body) of a publication, and marked off by a box rule, border, or tint. Also called a **sidebar**. ➔ *4011 box rule; 4009 border; 3922 callout*

3918 boxhead In tabulated matter, the heading of each column.

3919 break (**1**) An interruption in the flow of text, such as at the end of a line, paragraph, or page. ➔ *1834 break-line;*

3920 breakacross An image or tint that extends across the gutter onto both pages of a double-page spread. Also called **crossover**, or **reader's spread**. ➔ *3940 double (page) spread; 3914 back (edge) margin*

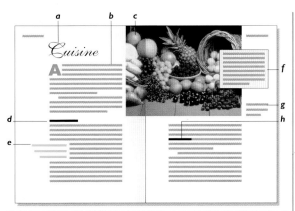

3940 double-(page) spread **a** *3932 chapter heading;* **b** *3933 column (1);*
c *3920 breakacross;* **d** *3935 crosshead;* **e** *3937 cut-in side notes;*
f *3922 callout, box feature;* **g** *3923 caption;* **h** *3936 cut-in head*

3921 byline A label denoting the author of an article. → *3934 credit line*

3922 callout A piece of text separated from the main body of running text,
sometimes emphasized by a box rule, background tint, or other device,
and often associated with an illustration. → *3917 box feature; 4011 box rule*

3923 caption Strictly speaking, a headline printed above an illustration identifying its contents. Nowadays, however, a caption is generally used to mean
any descriptive text that accompanies illustrative matter. A caption may
also be referred to as a **cutline**. → *3972 legend*

3924 cardinal numbers Numbers used in sequential counting, such as 1, 2,
3, and so on, as distinct from "ordinal" numbers, which are used to indicate
placement (first, second, third...).

3925 catchline A temporary heading, used for identification purposes,
printed at the top of a galley proof. → *3724 galley proof*

3926 catchword (1) A word printed (or written, in the case of a manuscript) at the foot of each page that is also the first word of text on the
following page. Originally these served as an aid to compositors, printers,
and binders to make sure pages were set, imposed, and gathered in the
correct order, but latterly their only practical use is as an aid to the reader.

3927 catchword (2) In dictionaries and encyclopedias, the word printed at
the top of each page to indicate the first or last entry on the page. In
cases where only the first three letters of each word is printed, these are
called catch-letters.

3928 center notes Notes set between columns of text.

3929 center-aligned/centered (2) Two or more items — text or pictures
— aligned along their central axes.

3930 change bar When revising a technical publication, the change bar is a
vertical rule beside the text, indicating it differs from the original.

3931 chapter drop The distance beneath a chapter heading at which the
text commences. → *3932 chapter heading*

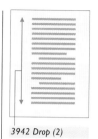

3942 Drop (2)

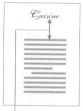

3943 Drop down

3945 Dropped head

3932 chapter heading The display heading at the start of each chapter, traditionally set in a uniform font, size, style, and location (on a right-hand page, for example).

3933 column (**1**) The vertical division of a page to organize text, captions, and illustrations. A column is measured by its width, traditionally in "ems" or "picas," but increasingly in inches or millimeters. → *1686 em; 1706 pica; 4035 grid (1)*

3934 credit/courtesy line A line of text accompanying an illustration or photograph identifying its creator or owner, and/or the organization that supplied it. → *3921 by-line*

3935 crosshead A subsection or paragraph heading, distinguished by font, weight, or size, that sits on a line of its own and usually marks a subdivision of a chapter, as distinct from a "cut-in head," which is set within the text. Also known as a **center head**. → *3936 cut-in head; 3996 subhead*

3936 cut-in head A paragraph or section heading, distinguished by font, weight, or size, that is set within the text. As distinct from a "crosshead," which sits on a line of its own. → *3935 crosshead; 3996 subhead*

3937 cut-in side notes Notes to a text that are indented into the main body of the text. Also called **incut notes**. → *3975 marginal notes*

3938 dateline In newspapers and periodicals, a line of type placed above an item giving the date and place of its creation.

3939 directional In a caption to an image, the words such as "above" and "below," which direct the reader to the relevant picture.

3940 double-(page) spread Generally used to describe any two facing pages of a document or publication. Strictly speaking, however, a double-page spread (or **truck** or **double truck**) occurs when matter crosses the gutter to occupy the two center pages of a section. Otherwise it should be more accurately described as a false double. → *2586 center spread*

3941 drop (**1**) A space, or margin, usually at the top of a page or column, before the printed image starts. A "chapter drop," for example, indicates the place on a page where text starts at the beginning of a chapter. → *3943 drop down*

3942 drop (**2**) The maximum number of text lines, or the maximum depth of an image, in a column, permitted by the page grid.

3943 drop down The point at which text matter starts under a chapter heading. Also called **chapter drop**. → *3941 drop (1)*

3944 drop folios Page numbers positioned at the foot of each page, usually referred to simply as folios. → *3822 folio (1)*

3945 dropped head A chapter title that is set lower than the top of a full page of text.

3946 eighteenmo/18mo A traditional 36-page section comprising 18 folded pages. Also called **octodecimo**.

3947 extracts Quotations found within a text, from another work, and that are usually indented or set in a smaller font, or both.

3948 feet/foot margin The white space at the bottom of a page, between the main body and page trim. → *3958 fore-edge margin; 3960 gutter margin*

3949 figure (**2**) The traditional description of an illustration on a page of text. ➔ *2673 plate (2)*

3950 figure number The reference number identifying an illustration. ➔ *3949 figure (2)*

3951 finished page area The area on a computer layout or printed sheet that will form the page after the sheet is trimmed. Once printed, the finished page area is delineated by corner marks ("trim" or "crop" marks). ➔ *3355 trimmed page size*

3952 fold marks Lines, usually dashed, indicating where a finished document should be folded.

3953 foot The margin at the bottom of a page or the bottom edge of a book.

3954 footer (**2**) A running headline that appears at the bottom of a page, also called a **running foot**. ➔ *3966 headline (1)*

3955 footline The last line of text to appear on a page, often containing the folio.

3956 footnotes Explanatory notes printed at the foot of a page or at the end of a book.

3957 fore-edge The outer edge or margin of a book opposite to, and parallel with, the back, spine, or binding edge.

3958 fore-edge margin The outer margin of a page in a book or publication, sometimes called the **outside margin**.

3959 gloss (**2**) An occasional word or words of explanation in the text ("interlinear matter") or margin of a text. ➔ *3731 illuminated (2)*

3960 gutter Strictly speaking, the spaces on a sheet of paper imposed for printing that, when cut, will form the fore-edges of the pages, plus trim. More commonly, however, the term describes the margin ("back margin") down the center of a double-page spread, or the vertical space between adjacent columns on a page. ➔ *3961 gutter bleed; 3914 back margin*

3961 gutter bleed An image allowed to extend into the fold of a publication, or to extend unbroken across the central margins of a double-page spread. ➔ *3960 gutter*

3962 head margin The space between the first line of text matter and the top of the trimmed page.

3963 headpiece The traditional term for a decorative device or motif, printed in the space above the beginning of a chapter.

3964 heading (**1**) The title at the beginning of a chapter or subdivision of text. A heading that appears in the body of the text is called a crosshead. ➔ *3935 crosshead*

3965 headless paragraph A paragraph set apart from other text, but without a separate heading.

3966 headline (**1**) A line of type at the top of a page, specifying the title of the book, a chapter contained within it, the subject of the page, or the page number. The convention is for the book title to be printed on left-hand (verso) pages with chapter titles on right-hand (recto) pages. Also called a **page head**. If headlines are repeated throughout a book or chapter they are referred to as **running headlines**, **running heads**, **running**

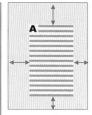

3974 Margin

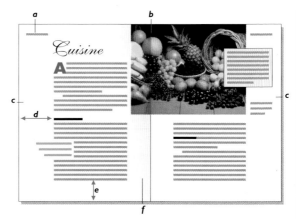

a **3966** *headline, running head;* **b** *3961 gutter bleed;* **c** *3957 fore-edge (1);*
d **3958** *fore-edge margin;* **e** *3953 foot margin;* **f** *3960 gutter, gutter margin*

titles, or **topical heads**. Headlines and running heads placed at the bottom of pages are called "footers" or "running feet."

3967 headline (**2**) The title of the lead story in a newspaper or magazine.

3968 image area (**1**) The area within which a particular image or group of images is to fit, sometimes including text.

3969 jump To continue a text or story on a succeeding page of a publication. ➔ *3970 jump line*

3970 jump line A reference indicating that the text or story is continued elsewhere in the publication, for example: "continued on page X." ➔ *3969 jump; 3994 slug (2)*

3971 key letters/numbers Letters or numbers added to an illustration so specific elements can be linked to a description in a caption.

3972 legend The text printed below an illustration or map, describing the subject or the symbols used. More commonly called a caption, albeit inaccurately. ➔ *3923 caption*

3973 long page A page on which the type area has been extended by one or two lines to avoid an inconvenient break.

3974 margin(s) The blank area of a page that surrounds the text or image area. ➔ *3958 fore-edge margin; 3953 foot margin; 3960 gutter margin*

3975 marginal notes Text printed in the margin of a main text column, adjacent to the passage to which it refers. ➔ *3937 cut-in side notes*

3976 oblong A book of "landscape" format, meaning it is wider than it is tall.

3977 opening Any pair of facing pages — they may or may not form a double-page spread.

3978 orientation The print direction of a page, or the format of an image (portrait or landscape).

3979 orphan A short line — strictly speaking, the first line of a paragraph that falls at the bottom of a column of text, but more generally used to mean a loose word. Also known as **club line**. ➔ *4005 widow*

3979 Orphan

3980 p/pp *abb.:* **page/pages**

3981 page break In continuous text, the place at which text is broken to be taken on to the following page.

3982 pagination Strictly speaking, the numbering of book pages, but also commonly used to describe the makeup of material into pages.

3983 pull quote A sentence or phrase copied from the body of a text and set, within the text, in a larger size or in some other distinctive manner.

3984 quotations Passages in a published work that repeat verbatim the words spoken or text written by another, distinguished usually from the narrative by quotation marks. ➔ *1611 inverted comma; 3766 single quotes*

3985 reflow The automatic repositioning of continuous text as a result of editing.

3986 removes Text set at the foot of a page in a smaller type size, used typically for notes or references.

3987 run-in head/heading A heading starting on the same line as the text, as distinct from a heading placed above the text.

3988 short page A page with less text printed on it than the standard length on other pages. Often employed at the beginning and end of chapters in a book, for example.

3989 shoulder heads Headings that mark the second division of text (after main headings) within a chapter.

3990 shoulder notes Marginal notes situated at the top outer corners of a page.

3991 side notes Notes placed outside the normal type area of a page, usually in the fore-edge margin or occasionally in the gutter.

3992 side heads The headings that mark the third division of text within a chapter, subsidiary to shoulder-heads. ➔ *3989 shoulder-heads*

3993 sinkage The amount of space between the top of the page text column and the first line of text in a new chapter.

3994 slug (**2**) In newspapers, a single line that indicates the story is continued on another page, similar to a "jump line." ➔ *3970 jump line*

3995 strap A subheading that appears above the headline in a magazine or newspaper article to identify the subject matter, page, or section.

3996 subhead/subheading A secondary heading after a headline or chapter heading, usually rendered in less prominent type. ➔ *3935 crosshead*

3997 subtitle A phrase that follows the title offering a brief explanation of the subject matter.

3998 tabloid A page that is half the size of a "broadsheet" or "broadside." ➔ *2580 broadside*

3999 tail The bottom edge of a book, or the margin at the foot of a page.

4000 tailpiece A design, or graphic, at the end of a section, chapter, or book.

4001 text (**2**) Typeset matter forming the main body of a publication.

4002 thumb edge The outside edge of a book, farthest from the spine.

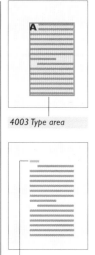

4003 Type area

4005 Widow

4003 type area The area of a page in which the main body of text falls, thus creating margins. Also called a type page.

4004 verso From the Latin *verso*, meaning "turned," the left-hand page of a book or, more precisely, the other side of a "recto" (right-hand page). ➔ *3881 recto*

4005 widow (**line**) A very short line at the end of a paragraph, falling at the top of a column of text. ➔ *3979 orphan*

4006 alignment The placement of type or images so they line up according to an invisible line, either horizontally or vertically. Unjustified text, for example, is generally aligned left, right, or centered. Also called **lining up** or **line up**. ➔ *1835 bumped out (1)*

4007 alley The spaces, or "gutters," between columns in tabular matter. ➔ *3914 back (edge) margin*

4008 blueline (**2**) Nonreproducible blue guidelines printed on paper and used as a grid to assist in laying out long documents such as books. ➔ *4035 grid (1)*

4009 border A decorative design or rule surrounding matter on a page. Sometimes called a **frame**.

4010 box (**1**) A printed item surrounded or defined by a rule, border, or background tint. ➔ *4011 box rule; 3917 box feature*

4011 box rule A rectangular box defined on all four sides by a rule. ➔ *4010 box (1); 3917 box feature*

4012 bump up (**2**) Colloquialism for enlarging an item, particularly with reference to type ("bump up that headline," for example).

4013 camera-ready copy/art (**CRC**) Material, such as artwork, prepared and ready for photographic conversion to film in preparation for printing. Also called a **mechanical**, **composite art**, or **paste-up**. ➔ *4055 paste-up*

4014 column/column-face rule A rule, usually light-faced (thin), used to separate vertical columns on a page. ➔ *3933, 1843 column (1, 2)*

4015 commercial art A general term used to describe any art prepared for commercial reproduction, thus distinguishing it from fine art. This activity is today more widely described as "graphic design." ➔ *4079 artwork; 3689 graphic design*

4016 comping The process of preparing a "comprehensive" (comp), or layout, and also of indicating areas of type in a comp. In the latter, text was traditionally indicated by pairs of ruled lines, but since layouts are now more frequently prepared on computer, text is indicated by "greeked" (grayed-out) type or by "dummy" text (often called "Latin"), a meaningless language used to simulate real text. ➔ *4018 comprehensive; 4034 greek*

4017 composite art(**work**) A rarely used term for camera-ready art that combines several different elements, such as text and illustrations. Commonly used terms include "mechanical," "paste-up," or "CRC" (camera-ready copy). ➔ *4013 camera-ready copy*

4018 comprehensive A preliminary rendition of a design, simulating the printed item, but to show intent rather than final detail. A typical comp will consist of illustrations, photographs, and typeset text — not necessarily

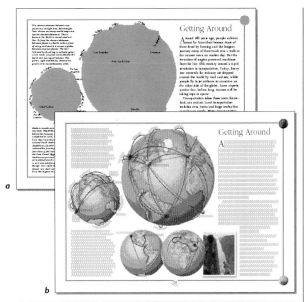

*4034 Greeking **a** pictures greeked; **b** text greeked*

those that will actually be used, but that are close enough to convey the concept. Also variously called a **mockup**, **presentation visual**, **finished rough**, or **dummy**. → *4023 dummy (2); 4016 comping*

4019 **computer graphics** Strictly speaking, any graphic item generated on or output by a computer, such as page layouts, typography, illustrations, and so on. However, the term is sometimes more specifically used to refer to a particular genre of computer-generated imagery, such as that which looks as though it were generated by computer.

4020 **dissonance** The spatial tension between elements in a typographic design.

4021 **dogleg** Colloquial term for a leader line that changes direction toward its point of reference. → *4043 leader line*

4022 **double rule** The term used to distinguish two lines of different thickness (in traditional typesetting, made from brass) from two lines of the same thickness called a parallel rule. → *4054 parallel rule*

4023 **dummy** (**2**) A mock-up of a design, such as a pack or illustrated book, showing the position of headings, text, captions, illustrations, and other details. → *3788 bulking dummy; 4018 comprehensive*

4024 **fine rule** A rule, traditionally of hairline thickness. In graphics applications this can mean a rule of any thickness between 0.20 to 0.50 points, but which is generally defined as 0.25 points. → *4036 hairline rule*

4025 **finished art(work)** Any illustrative matter prepared specifically for reproduction. Artwork that includes or consists entirely of text is usually described as "camera-ready art" or "mechanicals." → *4013 camera-ready art*

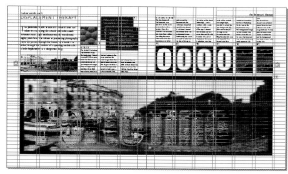

4035 **Grid** *showing a double-page spread layout designed on a grid*

4026 first-generation copy A duplicate of an item, such as a photograph, made directly from the original, as distinct from a copy made from another copy of the original. → *3593 dupe*

4027 flat plan A diagrammatic thumbnail scheme of the pages of a publication, used to determine the distribution of color, chapter arrangement, and so on, usually before any design takes place. Also called a **flow chart**.

4028 flimsy A thin, translucent paper used for layouts. → *4042 layout*

4029 focal point The part of a design with the most impact, therefore the first point of contact.

4030 FPO *abb.:* **for position only** A term used to indicate that items positioned on a layout are of inappropriate quality for reproduction and are displayed only as a guide for positioning in lieu of the properly prepared version. → *0744 composite color file*

4031 format (**4**) The size or orientation of a book or page, or, in photography, the size of film. → *4040 landscape format; 4056 portrait format*

4032 french curves A template, usually made of plastic, used as a guide for drawing smooth, curved lines.

4033 french rule An ornamental rule with a diamond shape at its center.

4034 greek, greeking An indication — in a layout — of type or pictures by substituting fake text, rules, or a gray tint for the actual letters or images. This is common practice when preparing rough visuals or scamps. Some computer applications provide greeking as a feature to speed up the process of screen redraw or proofing. → *4018 comprehensive*

4035 grid (**1**) A structure used for designing publications with multiple pages, such as books and magazines, to aid consistency throughout the publication. The grid usually shows such things as column widths, picture areas, and trim sizes.

4036 hairline rule Traditionally, the thinnest line that it is possible to print. In applications that provide it as a size option for rules, it is usually 0.25 point wide. → *4060 rule*

4037 image (**1**) In graphics, the description of any picture created by any method and used for any purpose. In reproduction an image is printed in one pass through a press, whether it be a single picture or a complete

4050 Optical alignment

0.25pt
0.3pt
0.5pt
1pt
1.5pt
2pt
3pt
4pt
5pt
6pt

4045 Line weight; 4060 Rule

imposed group of pages (in this context individual pictures are called "subjects"). ➜ **4063** *subject;* **2624** *image area (2)*

4038 jim-dash A short rule that divides items in a newspaper, also called **dinky dash**.

4039 keyline (**2**) A line drawing indicating the size and position of an illustration in a layout.

4040 landscape format An image or page format in which the width is greater than the height. Also called **horizontal format**. ➜ **4056** *portrait format*

4041 lateral reverse The transposing of an image from left to right, as in a mirror reflection. ➜ **0655** *reflection tool*

4042 layout A drawing that gives the general appearance of a design, indicating, for example, the position of text and illustrations. The term is also used in the context of preparing a design for reproduction, where it is called a "tissue" or "overlay," the terms deriving from the transparent paper often used for drawing layouts. ➜ **4068** *tissue*

4043 leader line/leader rule A line linking elements of an image to annotation or a caption. ➜ **4021** *dogleg;* **4044** *leader*

4044 leader(s) A row of dots, dashes, or other characters, used to guide the eye across a space to other relevant matter. In some applications, leaders can be specified as a "fill" between tab stops in text. ➜ **4043** *leader line*

4045 line weight The thickness of a line or rule.

4046 markup (**1**) A set of instructions and specifications for any material prepared for typesetting, reproduction or printing. ➜ **4061** *spec*

4047 meteorological symbols A collection of internationally agreed symbols for recording weather. Since that agreement took place in 1935, however, the rapid expansion of graphic design as a profession has meant such symbols have largely been replaced by altogether more appropriate and pleasing graphics, particularly in weather forecasting.

4048 mounting and flapping A method of presenting artwork in which the work is mounted on board and protected by a hinged sheet of cellulose acetate or paper.

4049 open (**2**) The appearance of a design in which the text and pictorial elements are not crammed together.

4050 optical alignment Curved or pointed characters or shapes that project beyond the margin when aligned, giving the overall appearance of being in a straight line.

4051 optical center A point within a scene, usually slightly higher than the actual geometric center, at which the main subject appears to be centrally placed.

4052 Oxford corners A box rule where the lines project beyond the frame corners.

4053 Oxford rule The combination of a thick and a thin rule.

4054 parallel rule The term used to distinguish a rule comprising two lines of the same thickness (made from brass in traditional typesetting) from one comprising two lines of different thickness called a double rule. ➜ **4022** *double rule*

4053 Oxford rule

4054 Parallel rule

4058 Reverse out

4062 Split rule

4064 Swelled rule

4055 paste-up/pasteup The layout of a design, including all elements such as text and illustrations. A paste-up will either be "rough" for layout and markup purposes or "camera-ready" (also known as mechanical), which will be used to make film for reproduction. ➔ *4013 camera-ready copy/art*

4056 portrait, upright format An image or page in a vertical format. ➔ *4040 landscape format*

4057 reading gravity The propensity for most people to begin reading from the upper left to the lower right of a page.

4058 reverse out/reverse type To reverse the tones of an image or type so it appears white (or another color) in a black or colored background. Also called **dropout (D.O.)**, **save out** or **knockout (K.O.)**. ➔ *1848 dropped-out type; 2051 knockout*

4059 rough A preliminary drawing showing a proposed design. Also called a **scamp**, or **visual**. ➔ *4042 layout; 4068 tissue*

4060 rule A printed line. The term derives from the Latin *regula*, meaning "straight stick," and was used to describe the metal strips of type height, in various widths, lengths, and styles, which were used by traditional typesetters for printing lines.

4061 spec(ification) A detailed description of the components of a job, product, or activity, detailing final requirements, preferred methods by which these are achieved, and so on.

4062 split dash/rule A decorative rule, split at its center with a star or similar ornament, and tapering off at the ends.

4063 subject The general term used to denote any single image that is originated or reproduced.

4064 swelled dash/rule Ornamental rules for dividing up text, particularly on a title page. Originating in 18th-century typography, the swelled rule is characterized by a thickening in the center of the rule. Also called a **french dash**.

4065 thumbnail (1) A miniature rough layout of a design or publication, showing a possible treatment or the order of chapters, for example.

4066 tight A general design term describing a design, or text, that is very closely packed and with little blank space.

4067 tint sheet A preprinted sheet of halftone tints, patterns, and other designs that are cut and pasted onto camera-ready artwork. ➔ *4075 Zip-a-tone; 2057 mechanical tint*

4068 tissue Transparent paper that overlays a design and contains instructions for reproduction. Also called an **overlay**. ➔ *4042 layout*

4069 vertical alignment The placement of items such as images or lines of text in relation to the top and bottom of a page, column, or box. ➔ *4006 alignment*

4070 vertical centering The equidistant positioning of text ("vertical justification") or any other item from the top and bottom of a page, column, or box. ➔ *4069 vertical alignment; 1874 justification*

4071 vertical page A page in which the the copy is right-reading when the page is held in a vertical position. ➔ *4056 portrait*

4081 Axis

4083 Bas-relief

4084 Pie chart

4072 visualize/visualizer A term that describes a person who simulates the imagery used for advertisements or cover designs, typically using felt markers to render the image. Such skills are becoming increasingly rare.

4073 white out (**I**) Typeset text that is reversed out of an image or background. ➔ *4058 reverse out; 2051 knockout*

4074 working white (**space**) (**ww/wws**) The areas of white space in a design or layout that do not contain text or images, but which form an integral part of the design.

4075 Zip-a-tone/Zipatone A patented collection of mechanical tint sheets, printed on cellophane.

4076 airbrush/airbrushing A tool, invented in the United States about 1900, used in illustration and photographic retouching, in which a fine spray of paint or ink is propelled by compressed air. ➔ *0512 airbrush tool*

4077 angle of view (**I**) The angle between opposite faces of a viewing pyramid (the structure created by drawing two lines from the center of a view to its edges). The more extreme the perspective, the greater the angle.

4078 animation The process of creating a moving image by rapidly moving from one still image to the next. Traditionally, this was achieved through a laborious process of drawing or painting each "frame" (a single step in the animation, taking up to 30 to fill each second) manually onto cellulose acetate sheets ("cels" or "cells"). However, animations are now more commonly created with specialist software, which renders sequences in a variety of formats, typically QuickTime, AVI, and animated GIFs. ➔ *0789 frame (3); 4168 cel (1); 0806 QuickTime; 0909 AVI; 1232 animated GIF.*

4079 art(**work**) Any matter prepared for reproduction, but generally used to mean illustrations and photographs, thus distinguishing them from text.

4080 aspect ratio The ratio of the width of an image to its height, expressed as x:y. For example, the aspect ratio of an image measuring 200 × 100 pixels is 2:1.

4081 axis (plural: axes;) An imaginary line that defines the center of the 3D universe. In turn, the x, y, and z axes (width, height, and depth, respectively) define each of the three dimensions of an object. The axis along which an object rotates is the axis of rotation.

4082 background (**2**) The area of an image upon which the principal subject, or foreground, sits.

4083 bas-relief An image that is embossed and stands out in shallow relief from a flat background, designed to give the illusion of greater depth.

4084 pie chart An illustration that shows the divisions of a whole quantity as segments of a circle or ellipse.

4085 cameo (**3**) A small relief design, either stamped out of any suitable material or simulated by a computer program. Cameos were originally made from a hard stone such as onyx, and set on to a background of a different color.

4086 caricature The depiction — as a photograph, model, or drawing — of a person or object with exaggerated key features or characteristics. Generally executed for comic or satirical purposes.

4087 cartouche A decorative device, usually in the form of a scroll with rolled-up ends, which is used to enclose a title or illustration.

4092 Corner radius

4095 Crosshatch

4099 Cutout

4088 cause-and-effect diagram A pictorial representation of the analysis of a process, identifying the cause of a problem or the solution to it, and the effect it may have on the process. Also called a **fishbone diagram**.

4089 cel (2) In conventional hand-drawn animation, the individual animated stages of a sequence, drawn on transparent acetate sheets, which are overlaid onto a static background. Each cel forms a "frame" in the animation. → *0789 frame (3); 4078 animation; 4168 cel (1)*

4090 clipping Limiting an image or piece of art to within the bounds of a particular area. → *0347 clipping path*

4091 controlling dimension One of the dimensions — either height or width — of an image, which is used as the basis for its enlargement or reduction in size.

4092 corner radius In a round-cornered rectangle, the dimension of the radius of the curve.

4093 cosmetics Sometimes used to describe the overall appearance of an image, such as color, contrast, sharpness, and so on.

4094 crop To trim or mask an image so it fits a given area, or to discard unwanted portions of an image.

4095 crosshatch A line drawing style in which tonal variations are achieved by groups of parallel fine lines, each group being drawn at a different angle.

4096 cross section An illustration of an object that shows it as if sliced through with a knife, thus exposing interior detail or workings. → *4098 cut-away*

4097 crow quill A very fine ink pen, deriving from the days when scribes used the cut quill of a crow to write with.

4098 cut-away An illustration of an object in which part of its outer "shell" has been removed to show the inner workings or detail. → *4096 cross section; 4118 ghosting (2); 4110 exploded view*

4099 cutout (I) A halftone image in which the background has been removed to provide a freeform image. Also known as an **outline halftone** or **silhouette halftone**. → *2040 halftone (1)*

4100 cylindrical (map) projection A map projection in which all lines of longitude ("meridians") run parallel with each other and at right angles to the lines of latitude ("parallels"). Cylindrical projections are highly distorted at the Polar extremities but, when wrapped around a sphere, appear normal and are thus ideal for use with 3D applications. Cylindrical projections are widely used for navigation purposes and thus for navigational graphics. "Gall" and "Mercator" are typical cylindrical projections, named after the men who devised them.

4101 definition The overall quality — or clarity — of an image, determined by the combined subjective effect of graininess (or resolution in a digital image) and sharpness. → *0773 resolution*

4102 degrade/degradation A decrease in quality, usually by physical erosion — a printing plate during a long print run, for example.

4103 delineate To emphasize outlines in line drawings or artwork by making them heavier.

4104 dimensions In describing the size of 3D objects, the standard dimensions are length, width, and height.

4103 Delineate

4106 Drop shadow

4111 Feather

4105 **dot and tickle** A colloquial expression for an illustration technique in which an image is composed out of small, stippled dots using a fine pen.

4106 **drop shadow** A shadow projected onto the surface behind an image or character, designed to lift the image or character off the surface.

4107 **elevation** The drawn vertical projection of an object, typically front, side, or end.

4108 **ellipse** An oval shape that corresponds to the oblique view of a circular plane.

4109 **enlargement** A reproduction that is greater than 100% of its original size. → *2042 halftone blowup; 4112 final size*

4110 **exploded view** An illustration of an object displaying its component parts separately — as though it were exploded — but arranged in such a way as to indicate their relationships within the whole object when assembled. → *4118 ghosting (2)*

4111 **feather(ing)** The gradual fading away of the edge of an image or part of an image to blend with the background. Feathering tools are a feature of image-editing and painting applications. → *4164 vignette*

4112 **final size** The size at which an image or piece of artwork will be printed. → *4109 enlargement*

4113 **flat** (**2**) Said of any image — original or printed — that lacks sufficient color or contrast, for whatever reason.

4114 **flip/flop** The mirror-image reversal of an item from left to right (horizontal flip) or top to bottom (vertical flip). Also called **reverse image**.

4115 **flow chart** (**1**) A diagrammatic representation of a process.

4116 **foreground** The area or objects between the point of view and the main subject. → *0956 foreground application*

4117 **ghosting** (**1**) To decrease the tonal values in the background of an image so the main subject stands out more clearly. Also known as **fade-back**. → *4164 vignette*

4118 **ghosting** (**2**) An illustration technique in which the outer layers of an object are faded to reveal its inner parts, which would not normally be visible. The technique is used particularly in technical illustration, to show parts of an engine covered by its casing, for example. → *4096 cross section; 4098 cut-away; 4110 exploded view*

4119 **gouache** A watercolor paint in which the pigments are bound with gum arabic and made opaque by the addition of substances such as white lead, bone ash, or chalk.

4120 **graphic** (**2**) A general term describing any illustration or drawn design.

4121 **graticule** A grid system of lines used to provide reference points on an image, particularly the lines of latitude ("parallels") and longitude ("meridians") on a map.

4122 **grotesque** (**1**) An ornate graphic decoration involving combinations of somewhat surreal human, animal, and plant images. Sometimes called a **bestiary**.

4123 **gum** (**2**) A general term describing any organic, resinous binding agent incorporated into inks, varnishes, etc., or used as a binding medium (usually gum arabic) for water-based paints such as gouache.

4096 Cross section

4098 Cut-away

4110 Exploded view

4118 Ghosting (2)

4124 **half-up** A specification for artwork to be prepared at one-and-a-half times the size that it will be reproduced. Artwork that is prepared half-up will need to be reduced by one-third (66.6 percent of its original size) to print as intended. Also called **one-and-a-half-up**. ➔ *4162 twice up; 4112 final size; 4109 enlargement*

4125 **heraldic colors** A standard system of representing the basic colors of heraldry by means of monochrome shading, hatching, and so on. Used when color printing is impractical or unwarranted.

4126 **highlight** (**1**) The lightest tone of an image, the opposite of shadow.

4127 **illuminate, illuminated** (**1**) A term describing the technique of embellishing letters, pages, manuscripts, and so on, by using gold, silver, and colors; common in medieval times.

4128 **illustration** (**1**) Any drawing, painting, diagram, photograph, or other image reproduced in a publication to explain or supplement the text.

4129 **illustration** (**2**) A term sometimes used specifically to distinguish a drawn image from a photograph.

4130 **image library** A source of original transparencies and pictures that can be used for virtually any purpose after payment of a fee, which usually varies according to usage — a picture used in an advertisement will invariably cost a great deal more than if the same picture were to be used inside a school textbook. Many libraries specialize in various subjects, such as garden plants, wildlife, or fine art (in the latter, be aware that, while the library may own the copyright in the photograph of a painting, the ownership of copyright in the painting itself may belong elsewhere). ➔ *0588 image resource; 3580 copyright*

4131 **imbrication** A patterned design featuring overlapping leaves or scales arranged in the manner of roof tiles (from the Latin *imbricare*, meaning "cover with rain tiles").

4132 **in pro(portion)** Two or more subjects for reproduction that are to be enlarged or reduced in proportion to each other, or an illustration whose dimensions are to be enlarged or reduced in proportion to each other.

4133 **india ink/indian ink** A deep black ink used by artists, illustrators, and draftsmen; commonly used to prepare artwork for reproduction.

4134 **inked art** Camera-ready art that is prepared firstly in pencil and then completed in ink.

4135 **lapis lazuli** A mineral used to make ultramarine color pigment.

4136 **line board** Smoothly finished boards with low absorbency, suitable for line artwork drawn with india ink.

4137 **mapping resource** A "kit" of files that you buy and from which you can generate cartographic maps, such as "Mountain High Maps." ➔ *4148 relief map; 0368 DEM*

4138 **medium** (**1**) A substance, such as linseed oil or gum arabic, into which pigment is mixed to create printing ink or artist's paint. Also called a **vehicle**. ➔ *2801 ink*

4139 **montage** An assembly of several images, forming a single original. A montage of photographs is called a "photomontage."

4140 **motif** A decorative design or pattern.

4142 Orthographic

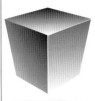

4145 Perspective

4141 **murex** A purple dye, variously known as Tyrian, Royal, and Phoenician purple, obtained from the shellfish murex.

4142 **orthographic** (**projection**) (**I**) An illustration technique in which there is no perspective (or the perspective is infinite), thus giving parallel projection lines.

4143 **oversize** (**I**) Artwork drawn to a larger size than that intended for reproduction.

4144 **parallax** The apparent movement of two objects relative to each other when viewed from different positions.

4145 **perspective** A technique of rendering 3D objects on a 2D plane, duplicating the "real world" view by giving the same impression of the object's relative position and size when viewed from a particular point — the shorter the distance, the wider the perspective; the greater the distance, the narrower the perspective.

4146 **pictogram/pictograph** A simplified, pictorial symbol distilled to its salient features to represent an object or concept. → *3700 symbol; 3686 glyph; 3693 isotype*

4147 **pigment** Ground particles of color dissolved in a suitable medium to form ink or paint.

4148 **relief map** A cartographic map in which elevation is rendered to simulate three dimensions. → *0368 DEM; 4137 mapping resource*

4149 **reproduction size** An instruction to reduce or enlarge an original when it is reproduced, expressed as a ratio (such as 2:1, which is half size), as an absolute size (such as 210mm), or as a percentage of the linear dimensions (such as 75%).

4150 **rest in pro**(**portion**) An instruction to enlarge or reduce other dimensions of an image or artwork in proportion to the one given.

4151 **retouching** Altering an image, artwork, or film to make modifications or remove imperfections. Digital images are usually retouched electronically using appropriate software. → *1471 spotting*

4152 **same size** (**S/S**) An instruction that original artwork/illustrations should be reproduced without enlargement or reduction. → *4158 sizing (2); 4162 twice up; 4112 final size; 4109 enlargement*

4153 **scale drawing** A drawing such as a map or plan that represents the subject matter in proportion to its actual size and to a specified scale. For example, an object drawn to a scale of 1:10 means that one unit of measurement on the drawing is equivalent to 10 of the same units on the object at full size — so one inch on the drawing equals 10 inches at full size. → *4162 twice up; 4112 final size; 4109 enlargement*

4154 **scale/scaling** The process of working out the the degree of enlargement or reduction required to bring an image to its correct reproduction size. → *4158 sizing (2); 4162 twice up; 4112 final size; 4109 enlargement*

4155 **scatter diagram** A graph used to analyze the cause-and-effect relationship between two variables where two sets of data are plotted on x and y axes, the result being a scattering of unconnected dots.

4156 **scraperboard** A board coated with ink (white on black or black on white), at one time used widely in commercial work by artists preparing illustrations for line reproduction, mostly as press advertisements.

4164 Vignette

4157 scratch pad Any space set aside for experimenting with ideas, techniques, and so on. → *0106 scratch (space); 0506 virtual; 0071 virtual memory*

4158 sizing (**2**) The process of defining the dimensions of enlargement or reduction of a photographic image for reproduction. → *4154 scale*

4159 tempera A type of paint in which the pigment is bound by egg yolk rather than by gum or oil.

4160 template (**1**) A shape used as a drawing aid.

4161 trend chart A method of recording and evaluating the performance of a process, such as a press or printing plant. Also called a **run chart**.

4162 twice up Artwork prepared at twice the size at which it will be reproduced. Artwork that is drawn twice up will need to be reduced by one-half, to fifty percent, to print at its intended size. → *4124 half-up*

4163 viewpoint The direction from which a subject is viewed to provide the best analytical or aesthetic study.

4164 vignette Strictly speaking, any image without a defined border, but also used to describe a halftone image in which the tones gradually fade out into the background. → *4111 feathering.*

4165 wash drawing A brush-sketch using pale color mixes.

4166 x, y coordinates The point at which data is located on two-dimensional axes: horizontal (x) and vertical (y) — for example, on a graph, monitor, or bitmap. Three-dimensional coordinates are known as "x, y, z coordinates" (or axes).

4167 blister card/pack Packaging or displays in which the contents are mounted on card and protected by a transparent plastic bubble.

4168 cel (**1**) *abb.:* **cellulose acetate** A synthetic translucent material that may be clear or colored, and with a shiny or matte surface. Cels are used in the preparation of artwork ("mechanicals") as well as in photography for adding colored light effects.

4169 dry mounting To mount items such as photographs onto board using heat-sensitive adhesive tissue.

4170 dry transfer lettering Lettering and other designs that are transferred to artwork by releasing them from the back of a plastic sheet by rubbing the front of the sheet. Also called **rub-ons**, **rub-downs**, and **rub-offs**.

4171 film (**1**) The term used to describe many synthetic materials, transparent or otherwise, but most often cellulose acetate. → *4168 cel (1)*

4172 frisket Paper or transparent material used as a stencil by airbrush artists to mask an area of an image.

4173 greeking sheet A self-adhesive sheet of fake text, used in layouts to create a facsimile of body copy. → *4034 greek*

4174 masking (**2**) A protective layer of film or paper ("frisket") applied to an illustration to protect an area while other parts are painted or airbrushed. → *4172 frisket*

4175 matte/matt A flat, slightly dull surface.

4176 opacity (**1**) The quality of being nontransparent — high opacity means low transparency — particularly with reference to the quality of paper used for printing that reduces "see-through." → *2297 look-through*

4177 **opaque** The opposite of transparent. Any material that does not allow light to shine through. → *2208 photo-opaque; 3539 process. white; 4179 translucent*

4178 **shrink wrap**(**ping**) A packing technique involving the wrapping of products such as books or pamphlets in a plastic film, followed by an application of heat, causing the film to shrink to form a tight and neat package.

4179 **translucent** A material, with a property anywhere between transparent and opaque, that partially obscures the image beyond — frosted glass, for example.

Books

Apple CD-ROM Handbook Apple Computer, Inc. *Addison-Wesley*

CD-I Design Handbook Philips IMS *Addison-Wesley*

Complete Color Glossary Miles Southworth, Thad McIlroy, Donna Southworth *The Color Resource*

Editing for Print Geoffrey Rogers *Writer's Digest*

Electronic Imaging for Photographers Adrian Davies, Phil Hennessy *Focal Press*

Encyclopedia of the Book Geoffrey Ashall Glaister *Oak Knoll Press; The British Library*

Encyclopedia of Practical Photography Michael Freeman *Macdonald*

Glossary of Graphic Communications Pamela Groff *Prentice Hall PTR*

Graphic Designer's Handbook Alastair Campbell *Running Press*

Guide to Color Management and Prepress *Quark Inc*

HTML Visual Quick Reference Dean Scharf *Que Corporation*

Internet for Dummies Dan Parks Sydow *IDG Books*

MacDesigner's Handbook Alastair Campbell *Running Press*

Macintosh Bible Jeremy Judson (ed) *Peachpit Press*

Macintosh Dictionary Andy Baird *Addison-Wesley*

Manual of Typography Ruari McLean *Thames and Hudson*

More HTML for Dummies Ed Tittel, Stephen N. James *IDG Books*

New Print Production Handbook David Bann *Page One*

Print Publishing Guide *Adobe Systems, Inc.*

Production for Graphic Designers Alan Pipes *Laurence King*

Production for the Graphic Designer James Craig *Watson-Guptill*

Twentieth-Century Type Lewis Blackwell *Laurence King*

Typography Friedrich Friedl, Nicolas Ott, Bernard Stein *Könemann*

www.type Roger Pring *Weidenfeld & Nicolson*

35mm Handbook Michael Freeman *New Burlington Books*

Web sites

Acronyms *Computer Knowledge*
www.cknow.com/ckinfo/acronyms/cacaacronyms.htm

AIGA *American Institute of Graphic arts*
www.aiga.org

Alphabytes *Rob Leuschke*
www.alphabytes.com/index.html

Codec Central *Terran Interactive*
www.terran-int.com/CodecCentral/index.html

GATF *Graphic Arts Technical Foundation*
www.gatf.org

Glossary of Internet Terms *Matisse Enzer*
www.matisse.net/files/glossary.html

Typography links *Microsoft*
www.microsoft.com/typography/links/default.asp